URBAN BIOSPHERE AND SOCIETY

Partnership of Cities

ANNALS OF THE NEW YORK ACADEMY OF SCIENCES

Volume 1023

URBAN BIOSPHERE AND SOCIETY

Partnership of Cities

Edited by Christine Alfsen-Norodom, Benjamin D. Lane, and Melody Corry

The New York Academy of Sciences
New York, New York
2004

♾ The paper used in this publication meets the minimum requirements of the American National Standard for Information Sciences—Permanence of Paper for Printed Library Materials, ANSI Z39.48-1984.

Library of Congress Cataloging-in-Publication Data

Urban biosphere and society : partnership of cities / edited by Christine Alfsen-Norodom, Benjamin D. Lane, and Melody Corry.
p. cm. — (Annals of the New York Academy of Sciences ; v. 1023)
Includes bibliographical references and index.
ISBN 1-57331-553-2 (cloth : alk. paper) — ISBN 1-57331-554-0 (pbk. : alk. paper) 1. Urban ecology—Case studies—Congresses. 2. Urban policy—Case studies—Congresses. 3. Environmental policy—Case studies—Congresses. 4. Biosphere reserves—Case studies—Congresses. I. Alfsen-Norodom, Christine. II. Lane, Benjamin D. III. Corry, Melody. IV. Series.
HT241.U69 2004
307.76—dc22

2004012853

GYAT/PCP

Printed in the United States of America

ISBN 1-57331-553-2 (cloth)

ISBN 1-57331-554-0 (paper)

ISSN 0077-8923

ANNALS OF THE NEW YORK ACADEMY OF SCIENCES

Volume 1023
June 2004

URBAN BIOSPHERE AND SOCIETY

Partnership of Cities

Editors
CHRISTINE ALFSEN-NORODOM, BENJAMIN D. LANE,
AND MELODY CORRY

This volume is the result of a conference entitled **Urban Biosphere and Society: Partnership of Cities** held by the New York Academy of Sciences and the Columbia University/ UNESCO Joint Program on Biosphere and Society (CUBES) on October 29 and 30, 2003 in New York, New York.

CONTENTS

Sponsors:

- **THE EARTH INSTITUTE AT COLUMBIA UNIVERSITY**
- **UNITED NATIONS EDUCATIONAL, SCIENTIFIC, AND CULTURAL ORGANIZATION (UNESCO)**

Urban Biosphere and Society: Partnership of Cities

Introduction

CHRISTINE ALFSEN-NORODOM

Columbia University/UNESCO Joint Program on Biosphere and Society, Columbia University Earth Institute, Columbia University, New York, New York 10027, USA

ABSTRACT: This paper reports on issues of conservation, equitable use of resources, and the improvement of quality of life for all persons living in densely populated cites. Case studies are presented that examine UNESCO's concept of biosphere reserve, demonstrating the elasticity and usefulness of the concept as a way to promote global sustainability and governance on local, regional and global levels.

KEYWORDS: urban sustainability; biosphere reserve concept; city planning; environmental conservation

By 2007, an estimated one-half of the world's population will live in urban areas, compared with approximately one-third in 1972. And urban populations are predicted to continue to grow at a rate of 2% per year until 2015, according to the United Nations Population Division.[1] Questions of urban environmental governance therefore are going to be increasingly relevant when setting national—and global—policies for environmental, social, and economic sustainability. There is a pressing need for these deliberations to be informed by the best available knowledge, in the form of both cutting edge research and scientifically validated local expertise.

The **Urban Biosphere and Society: Partnership of Cities** conference, held at the New York Academy of Sciences in New York City on October 29–30, 2004, provided a unique forum for scientists dealing with global issues of sustainability to meet with local specialists from some of the world's most important cities who are confronted with the challenges of balancing environmental conservation with economic and social development. Using the UNESCO biosphere reserve concept, which promotes solutions to reconcile the conservation of biodiversity with its sustainable use, the conference

Address for correspondence: Christine Alfsen-Norodom, Columbia University/UNESCO Joint Program on Biosphere and Society, Columbia University Earth Institute, 405 Low Library, 535 West 116th Street, New York, NY 10027. Voice: 212-854-9449; fax: 212-854-6309.
ca320@columbia.edu

Ann. N.Y. Acad. Sci. 1023: 1–9 (2004).
doi: 10.1196/annals.1319.001

tapped into local knowledge to develop a global approach to urban sustainability.

The conference built on case studies conducted in 11 cities around the world, presented by researchers, policy specialists, and stakeholders. Several of the case studies focus on cities that are actively considering becoming UNESCO biosphere reserves. Others considered specific aspects of urban sustainability, ranging from health issues (e.g., respiratory ailments resulting from pollution) to mechanisms for improving public participation in urban environmental decision making.

The overarching goal of the conference was to inform international deliberations on urban sustainability with the best available knowledge, in the form of both cutting-edge research and scientifically validated local expertise.

The conference was organized by the Columbia University/UNESCO Joint Program on Biosphere and Society (CUBES), hosted by the New York Academy of Sciences and cosponsored by the Man and the Biosphere Program of UNESCO and the UN Human Settlements Program (Habitat).

The conference was very well attended both in its geographic representation and the diversity of backgrounds, disciplines, and mandates of the participants. In addition to the 11 city case studies including Cape Town, Chicago, Dar es Salaam, Kristianstad, Montevideo, Rome, São Paulo, Seoul, Stockholm, Mexico City, and New York, 10 other cities were represented including Beijing, Buenos Aires, Cleveland, Dakar, Delhi, Detroit, Frankfurt, Istanbul, New Orleans, and Tucson (Arizona). On the opening day of the conference, Ellis Rubinstein, CEO of the New York Academy of Sciences, welcomed the participants, and Christopher Ward, Commissioner, New York City Department of Environment, delivered a keynote address including a message from Mayor Bloomberg.

Most of the 113 participants were scientists engaged in research on a variety of urban issues ranging from urban ecology and architecture and urban planning to urban health and urban agriculture. The following U.S. universities were represented: Columbia University (20 participants), New York University, City University of New York, Massachusetts Institutes of Technology, the Parsons School of Design, Cornell University, Hunter College, Rutgers, University of Medicine and Dentistry in New Jersey, University of Massachusetts, Harvard University, Tulane University, University of Florida, University of North Texas, and Yale University. Prestigious institutions and nongovernment organizations (NGOs) such as the New York Botanical Garden, the Brooklyn Botanic Garden, the Chicago Field Museum, and the American Museum of Natural History were also represented.

The conference was structured with the site-based policy expertise of city case studies serving as a foundation for explorations of globally relevant problems of urban sustainability, as well as for the development of strategies for addressing these. In doing so, the conference produced three distinct but closely interrelated outcomes.

First, the conference brought about a deeper understanding of urban sustainability in terms of not only urban ecologies and the impacts of urban areas on global environmental systems, but also and equally important in terms of the well-being, health, security, and enfranchisement of urban people. In doing so, it laid out the groundwork for further research into problems and policy options at the local and global level.

Second, because the UNESCO biosphere reserve concept served as a unifying theme for wide-ranging conference discussions, significant progress was made in identifying potential benefits that could be reaped through application of the concept to urban areas. At the same time, important limitations of the biosphere reserve concept as currently articulated by UNESCO were brought to light, together with important proposals for strengthening its relevance to urban issues and global sustainability.

Finally, throughout the process of case study development, conference planning, and execution, the importance of knowledge networks for supporting global sustainability through coordinated urban initiatives was demonstrated. The networks that were expanded and established through the conference form the basis for an intensified phase of cross-disciplinary research, multi-institutional collaboration and exchange, and for the development and implementation of globally relevant local solutions.

THE CUBES METHODOLOGY

CUBES, the Columbia University–UNESCO Joint Program on Biosphere and Society, since its inception has developed an approach in which humans not only are considered part of nature but also are key to maintaining functioning ecosystems.

The mandate of the program is derived from a declaration adopted by the participants of the UNESCO/Columbia University International Conference on Biodiversity and Society, held in the City of New York in May 2001, who issued a declaration "calling upon our colleagues in government and civil society to embrace flexible, multifaceted and democratic visions of biodiversity conservation and sustainable development tailored to the social cultural and environmental particularities of each location."[2]

At that conference, a session was devoted specifically to urban biodiversity, in which Dr. Cynthia Rosenzweig (NASA Goddard Institute for Space Studies) and Dr. William D. Solecki (Montclair State University) presented a case study entitled "Biodiversity and the City: A Case Study of the New York Metropolitan region," proposing the establishment of New York City as a UNESCO biosphere reserve as a way of "reconciling the city's built environment with its long estranged natural home."

After the conference, the New York Urban Biosphere Group (NYUBG) was created as a working group of CUBES. Its membership consists of individual researchers, United Nations specialists, and scientists from Columbia University's CIESIN, the NASA/Goddard Institute for Space Studies at Columbia, the New York Botanical Garden, Brooklyn Botanic Garden, Montclair State University, and the City University of New York. The UBG was established to further develop a conceptual framework for the application of the biosphere reserve concept to specific urban areas. The aim of the exercise is not to conserve ecosystems in the traditional sense but to recognize and support sustainable urban interactions. The biosphere reserve process has the potential to provide urban stakeholders with a toolbox for conflict mediation, education, and outreach, as well as biodiversity conservation and long-term data observatory for ecological trends. A biosphere reserve is, in other words, "a laboratory for sustainability."

Since October 2001, the Urban Biosphere Group has been meeting monthly to develop an integrated research agenda with practical applications, examining the interactions of cultural and ecological diversity in the New York Metropolitan Area from perspectives such as food consumption, marketing and production, native vegetation and exotic species, impacts of climate change, and land-use and the built environment.

International links have been established with Cape Town in South Africa, where a CUBES Urban Biosphere Group was formed that included scientists and policy makers from the National Botanical Institute, the Western Cape Nature Conservation Board, and the City of Cape Town.

The present conference and book—*Urban Biosphere and Society: Partnership of Cities*—represents the culmination of this 2 years' work of the UBG in New York and Cape Town.

What is given preeminence here is the *process* and not the end result of becoming a biosphere reserve. The process involves the awareness of a problem's going beyond a discipline or the mandate of a local government; mobilization of human resources to deal with the problem; the formation of an interdisciplinary group; the production of case studies as a tool for sharing information and giving visibility to a cause; the involvement of all stakeholders; the scientific culture of investigation; the legitimacy given by government; and the need to address people's economic and social well-being and the connection to the environment.

Chicago Wilderness, launched in 1996 by a coalition of 34 diverse and determined organizations, illustrates the considerable strength derived from forming a coalition of stakeholders of scientists, government officials, local decision makers, and NGOs around a clearly stated goal of conserving globally outstanding natural communities that survive in a metropolis and reconnecting a landless urban population with the pulse of nature. The project is remarkable not only for the restoration work conducted in the remnants of the prairie around Chicago but also because of its efforts to involve underprivileged children in their education campaigns.

The Cape Town case study is remarkable not only because of the explicit link established between the alleviation of poverty and social inclusion and environmental conservation, but also by the strong mandate and support given by the local and the regional government, thus ensuring that outcomes of its work will have a direct impact on policies.

The Seoul study, with its proposal to establish green rooftops as biosphere reserves, is the ultimate example of human ingenuity striving to access nature and its benefits even under severe space constraints and intense population pressures.

Dar es Salaam provided an example in which a rigid master plan that lacked local ownership resulted in severe deterioration of environmental conditions and a proliferation of unplanned settlements. A turnaround occurred when city officials armed with strong political will, community participation, and technical expertise provided by UN-Habitat succeeded in restoring favorable conditions for sustainable development in this coastal city.

In addition to the site-specific case studies demonstrating in practice how environment links up with all other concerns in a city, the conference featured working group sessions intended to examine in depth the linkages and their implications for policy making. Scientists, planners and architects, local public officials, journalists, members of the UN and NGOs, and elected representatives made up the various groups, thus rendering their deliberations rich and meaningful.

The Human Health and the Urban Environment working group explored the connections between public health, health services, and sustainable urban development. It also discussed the links between poverty and socially disadvantaged communities in urban areas and access to health services and environmental services with health implications such as clean air, clean water, waste disposal, and healthy foods.

All panelists pointed to the need to consider the health dimension of urban poverty when making urban policy. Communities concerned must be involved from the planning stage, and linkages between their health and the quality of their environment must be better understood and translated into local policies. Most pointed to the need for more information and statistics on the linkages between environmental hazards such as polluted air to diseases such as asthma and tuberculosis. The specificity of the urban environment and its negative and positive impacts on public health also need to be better researched.

The working group on conservation and urban resilience sought to examine the mechanisms through which ecological biodiversity, cultural diversity, and the built landscape both separately and interactively create the conditions for environmental changes, within the city and its ecological footprint. There are several dimensions and several degrees to resilience, as exemplified by Rome, New Orleans, and Cape Town. In New Orleans, because of the unique environmental challenges posed by the city's geographical location at and below sea level, sustainability challenges are better phrased in terms of survivability. In Cape Town, extreme wealth and extreme poverty cohabitate, and the challenge is to use environmental programs to design socially inclusive policies while preserving the unique natural assets of the Cape Floral Kingdom. New York faces the interesting challenge of having to recognize the resilience and adaptiveness of urban flora and fauna, while acknowledging the useful role and functions of nonnative species. Working group members recommended that city planners should abandon their fixation, based on a Romantic-era perception of nature, that nonnative species be eradicated, and instead focus more on the systems, functions, and services provided in urban areas by vegetation—native and nonnative.

The working group on Planning and Building for Sustainability focused on means to reconnect people to their built environment, foster a sense of place, and build smart buildings. Green Rooftops in Seoul and New York City were discussed in this context, together with the energy-efficient buildings in Frankfurt, a project initiated by a public–private partnership between the city of Frankfurt and Siemens. The discussions showed that support for green, smart, or energy-efficient building is gaining momentum as citizens and decision makers become more aware of the environmental degradation caused by present development patterns, which have led to sprawl, heat islands, and sick buildings. To accomplish private and public support for these efforts, not only are education and information necessary, but also a strategy needs to be devised to reach stakeholders at all levels. The urban biosphere concept has sought to be a possible framework for such an action. The issue of resilience could also be seen though the prism of natural hazards mitigation. This type of resilience must be integrated in the urban planning process because it has an impact on transport and buildings. Communities must also be prepared for postdisaster response, which has been shown to considerably reduce the impact on humans of such disasters. To achieve this, more research needs to be conducted on the relationship between quality of life, economic growth, and the interaction with the environment.

The working group dealing with Governance for Urban Sustainability worked on the premise that a diversity of situation calls for a diversity of solutions and strategies. The issue of scale and overlapping jurisdiction was at the core of the group's discussions. A major obstacle to establishing an urban biosphere reserve is that of crossing artificial and natural boundaries. Often the best intended efforts to create regional agencies can lead to negative results because of lack of accountability to their constituencies and the danger of being co-opted by vested interests. Mixed local jurisdiction over urban and rural land has also failed because of intense land pressures in fast urbanizing areas. The group concluded that the biosphere reserve concept could serve as a useful tool in bringing all stakeholders to the table to resolve some of the conflicts between conservation and development in urban settings.

The Working Group on Environmental Education used as a guiding document the UNESCO Tbilisi Declaration on Environmental Education issued at a UNESCO/UNEP conference held at Tbilisi, USSR, on October 14–26, 1977. The group recognized that in building a successful environmental education program, awareness building and information dissemination are insufficient: Values and ethics are an indispensable component as well, which may sometimes be seen as advocacy rather than education, thus making it difficult to integrate such a program into the school curriculum. Nonetheless, the group recommended that emphasis be placed on experience *in situ*, building a sense of place among youth, giving opportunities for positive action and change, especially for those who have little or no access to education in general. The group also recommended that policy makers be included in environmental education and awareness programs and that networks such as the one being created at the conference be strengthened to foster connectivity among cities and among the disciplines concerned with urban sustainability.

The group charged with discussing Poverty and Urban Environment remarked that poverty was a sustainable downward spiral in that it leads to further deterioration in the quality of life of those affected by virtue of increased exposure to environmental hazards and deteriorating health conditions. Often, too, poorer communities live on environmental resources used by wealthier communities, but without benefiting from them: The examples of Cape Town, where townships are situated on a very rich and biodiverse ecosystem; the Bronx, where polluting waste disposal plants are located; and the São Paolo green belt, where ecotourism resources are provided to outsiders, all illustrate this situation. The group saw improved communication and a better understanding of the process as key to breaking the cycle of poverty and exclusion. It also advocated making the voices of the poor better heard at meetings discussing and deciding their fate.

THE POTENTIAL AND LIMITS OF THE URBAN BIOSPHERE RESERVE CONCEPT

The World Network of Biosphere Reserves has been in existence for almost 30 years and now comprises more than 400 reserves in 91 countries. UNESCO, through the biosphere reserve concept, has been pioneering the idea of combining areas of wise management of biological resources with minimally managed areas targeted for conservation.

This Urban Biosphere and Society conference has provided an opportunity to reexamine the limits and possibilities of the biosphere reserve concept outside its legal framework. In doing so, it demonstrated the robustness of the concept, not only for physical delimitation, but also for its usefulness to local citizens aspiring to contribute to good environmental governance. The concept's elasticity and its very broad application throughout the network certainly contribute to this usefulness. This flexibility is also rooted in the basic structure of the biosphere reserve, namely, in the absence of boundaries to the transition zone, the idea of the buffer zone as an area for sustainable use and/or to provide corridors between protected areas.

The pressures and the interest for having urban areas as potential biosphere reserves come from different directions. First, the biosphere reserve concept as elaborated in the Seville Strategy is one of the very few conservation concepts that recognize the value of urban systems. Second, there is a growing awareness among people concerned with conserving nature and keeping open lands that the solution lies in well-managed large, dense cities rather than in sprawl. Finally, the biosphere reserve concept in its absence of rigidity enables a discussion recognizing the values of biological and human diversity in ensuring urban sustainability.

The biosphere reserve concept proved to be a rich theme for unifying conference discussions through its functions of conservation, development, and research, as well as its spatial applications (core, buffer, and transition zones). The direct applicability of the concept to pressing urban issues such as poverty, health, pollution, waste management, and social inclusion became apparent both in the case studies and in the working groups. It was clear that the connectivity of the concept was a particularly attractive feature. By attempting to capture both natural diversity and cultural diversity, ensuring protection of the most vulnerable spots and promoting sustainable uses, the biosphere reserve concept proved an effective tool for planners and scientists alike.

Spatially mapping and zoning, which is at the heart of the biosphere reserve concept, proved very adaptable to various regional planning strategies that several cities are now developing to address long-term sustainability in terms of access to natural resources, energy, water, food, etc. The concept also proved an excellent tool to bring people to the table for conflict mitigation and for pooling communities together around the multiplicity of goals implied by the sustainability concept.

It also became apparent that to be immediately applicable in an urban context, the concept itself would have to evolve. A major objection lies with the use of the word "reserve" applied to cities. The functions included in the concept also would have to evolve to be more representative of sustainable principles.

In particular, it was proposed that:

- The conservation function, which traditionally covers protection of biodiversity against human intervention, should be expanded to cover urban natural and cultural diversity such as community gardens, urban agriculture, and the relationship between immigration and the introduction of exotics in urban ecosystems.

- The development function should be made more inclusive to introduce the idea of equity of access to urban environmental goods and services such as clean air, clean water, safe environment, and green spaces and environmental education.
- The logistics function, which covers education and research, should look into education as a tool for self-reliance and empowerment. Outreach should include an examination of the ecological footprint of urban lifestyles and consumption patterns, and it should also contribute to making urban dwellers responsible stewards of the planet.

It was proposed that expanding these functions and thinking "outside the box" would make the biosphere reserve concept directly applicable to the goals of global programs such as the Millennium Ecosystem Assessment and the Millennium Development Goals.

This conference fostered important discussion across sectors and disciplines on urban sustainability issues, demonstrated the considerable elasticity and applicability of the biosphere reserve concept, and sparked awareness that such tools may be used at all levels, from neighborhoods to municipalities to international organizations, as a way to promote global sustainability and environmental governance. This discussion will continue within the context of CUBES and the UNESCO Man and the Biosphere Program. In addition, CUBES will continue to explore connections between the environment and the other pillars of sustainable development, including the social economic, health, and cultural diversity components. To support the continuation of this process, CUBES will strengthen and expand its network through collaboration with academic institutions and stakeholders in selected cities, including, among others, Cape Town, Chicago, New Orleans, New York, Frankfurt-am-Main, Istanbul, Montevideo, Dar es Salaam, Phnom Penh, and Seoul.

REFERENCES

1. United Nations Population Division. World Urbanization Prospects. 2001 revision.
2. Alfsen-Norodom, C. & B.D. Lane. 2002. Global knowledge networking site-specific strategies. Environmental Science & Policy **5:** 3–8.

Toward Urban Biosphere Reserves

PETER DOGSÉ

Man and the Biosphere (MAB) Programme, Division of Ecological Sciences, UNESCO, Paris 15, France

ABSTRACT: The objective of this article is to outline the evolution in applying the biosphere reserve concept to urban areas and to present some of the potential benefits and possible difficulties in the design and management of urban biosphere reserves.

KEYWORDS: biosphere reserves; UNESCO Man and the Biosphere Programme (MAB); Seville strategy; Statutory Framework of the World Network of Biosphere Reserves; urban biosphere reserves

INTRODUCTION: THE BIOSPHERE RESERVE CONCEPT

Biosphere reserves are "special places for people and nature" designated through the UNESCO Man and the Biosphere Programme (MAB) to fulfill three complementary and mutually supportive functions:

- A conservation function—to contribute to the conservation of landscapes, ecosystems, species, and genetic variation.
- A development function—to foster economic and human development which is socioculturally and ecologically sustainable.
- A logistic function—to provide support for research, monitoring, education, and information exchange related to local, national, and global issues of conservation and development.

These functions are associated through a zonation system (see FIG. 1), consisting of a core area which is aimed at biodiversity and landscape conservation and where only limited human activities take place, such as research and monitoring (there may be several patchy core areas in a single biosphere reserve). Sustainable economic activities that are compatible with the conservation of the core zone are encouraged in the surrounding zone that

Address for correspondence: Peter Dogsé, Man and the Biosphere (MAB) Programme, Division of Ecological Sciences, UNESCO, 1, rue Miollis, 75732 Paris cedex 15, France. Voice: +33-1-45-68-40-98; fax: +33-1-45-68-58-04.
p.dogse@unesco.org

Ann. N.Y. Acad. Sci. 1023: 10–48 (2004). © 2004 New York Academy of Sciences.
doi: 10.1196/annals.1319.002

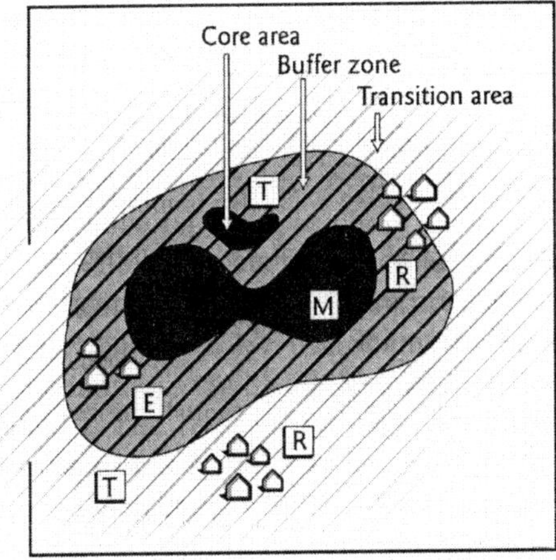

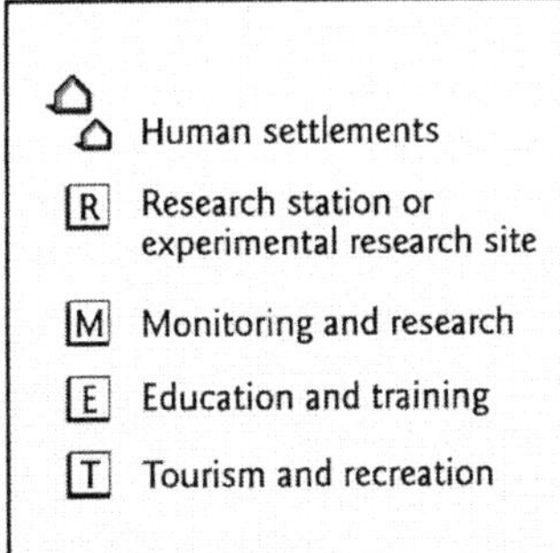

FIGURE 1. Biosphere reserves are based on a zonation system with core, buffer, and transition areas.

functionally acts as a buffer for the core. An outer transition area links with the surrounding region and is typically host to relatively heavier development activities, such industry, agriculture, fisheries, and more densely populated human settlements.

The actual zonation pattern of a biosphere reserve is highly flexible and reflects environmental, socioeconomic, and administrative realities. Usually, it is far more complex than the generic model as can be seen in the highly urbanized Lanzarote Biosphere Reserve in Spain (FIG. 2) and the transboundary East Carpathians Biosphere Reserve of Poland, Slovakia, and Ukraine (FIG. 3).

The biosphere reserve concept dates back to an intergovernmental conference UNESCO organized in 1968 called the "Biosphere Conference." This event recommended the establishment of a network of terrestrial and coastal areas representative of the planet's main ecosystems in which genetic resources would be protected, and where ecosystem research, monitoring and training could be conducted in an intergovernmental program also outlined by the conference participants. Subsequently, UNESCO launched the Man and the Biosphere Programme in 1970, one objective of which was the establishment of a coordinated world network of new protected areas, to be designated as "biosphere reserves."

The World Network of Biosphere Reserves (WNBR) developed rapidly (see FIG. 4) and as of July 2003 consists of 440 sites in 97 countries (for a complete list and site descriptions, see <http://www.unesco.org/mab/wnbr.htm>). The UNESCO General Conference formalized the WNBR in 1995, by adopting the "statutory framework" of the WNBR that outlines the functions of biosphere reserves, qualification criteria, designation, and periodic review procedures (see Annex I).[1]

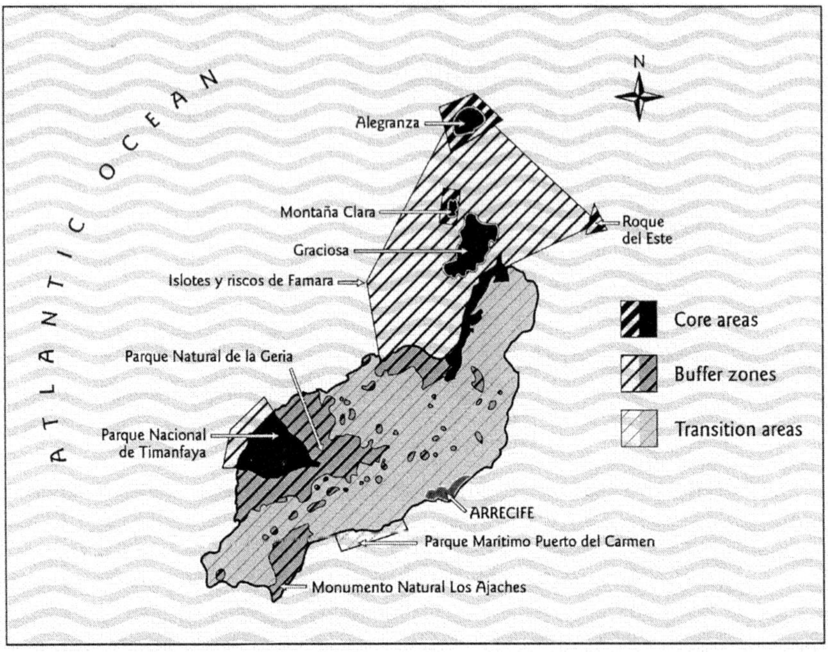

FIGURE 2. Zonation map of the Lanzarote Biosphere Reserve (Spain).

At the same time, the General Conference approved the "Seville Strategy for Biosphere Reserves" that guides activities of the WNBR toward several and objectives (see Annex II),[1] notably to use biosphere reserves:

- To conserve natural and cultural diversity.
- As models of land management and of approaches to sustainable development.
- For research, monitoring, education, and training.

ESTABLISHMENT AND MANAGEMENT OF BIOSPHERE RESERVES

Biosphere reserve nominations are prepared by National MAB Committees with the involvement of relevant key public and private stakeholders. The UNESCO Advisory Committee for Biosphere Reserves assesses nominations and forwards its recommendations to the International Co-ordinating Council of the MAB Programme (MAB-ICC). The MAB-ICC makes decisions on nominations for designation, and the Director-General of UNESCO notifies

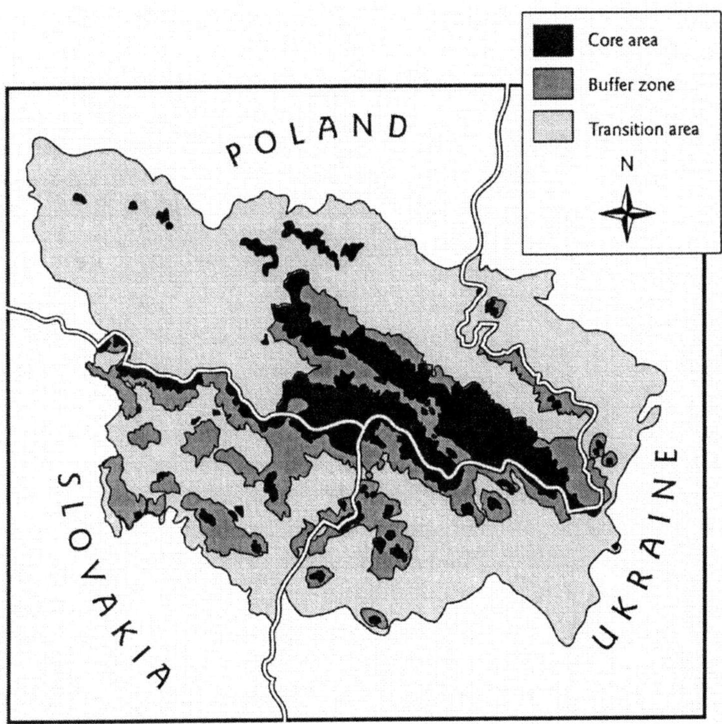

FIGURE 3. The transboundary East Carpathians Biosphere Reserve.

the country concerned of the decision. The institutional arrangements for managing approved biosphere reserves vary from site to site, but they often include the establishment of a management board with the participation of public authorities, local communities, nongovernmental organizations (NGOs), academia, and private interests served by an appointed biosphere reserve coordinator, or manager. It is important to stress here that although biosphere reserves are internationally recognized through UNESCO, they remain under sovereign jurisdiction of the countries where they are located.

BIOSPHERE RESERVES AND URBAN AREAS

Although several of the existing 440 biosphere reserves include cities and towns, or are adjacent to major urban areas (see TABLE 1), it is only in the last few years that UNESCO member states have started to consider seriously nominating more clearly urban-oriented biosphere reserves. This being said, some cities, notably Rome, have explored the biosphere reserve concept for

TABLE 1. Examples of existing biosphere reserves close to major urban areas

Name of biosphere reserve	Country	City
Mornington Peninsula	Australia	Melbourne
Mata Atlantica with the Sao Paulo City Green Belt	Brazil	Sao Paulo & Rio de Janeiro
Cerrado	Brazil	Brasilia
Cordillera Volcanica Central	Costa Rica	San José
Pays de Fontainebleau	France	Paris
Argan	Morocco	Agadir
Cape West Coast	South Africa	Cape Town
Alto Manzanares	Spain	Madrid
Golden Gate	U.S.A.	San Francisco
Can Gio Mangrove	Viet Nam	Ho Chi Minh City

several years.[2] The main reasons why countries are looking at the biosphere reserve concept is of course the strong urbanization trends worldwide and the increasingly critical role that cities and urban areas play in the sustainable development debate.

The prospect that major cities, such as Rome, one day could be subject for biosphere reserve nominations have proved to be a somewhat controversial issue within the MAB Programme, because some think that the inclusion of large cities, or parts thereof, in biosphere reserves would create confusion as to the nature and meaning of biosphere reserves. Primarily to advance the discussion on this issue, the MAB-ICC recommended therefore the establishment of the MAB Ad Hoc Working Group to Explore the Application of the Biosphere Reserve Concept to Urban Areas and their Hinterlands (the MAB Urban Group), which met for the first time in November 2000 charged with the following objectives:

- To identify contributions that the biosphere reserve concept have made or could make in urban planning and management, including in the context of the Convention on Biological Diversity with its focus on the ecosystem approach.
- To examine if there is, or should be, a place for urban areas and cities in the World Network of Biosphere Reserves (beyond as transition areas).
- To explore alternative ways and means of recognizing selected cities, or parts thereof, as sites that exemplify the biosphere reserve model.
- To stimulate a discussion within MAB and with relevant partner institutions and organizations, on the development of an agenda for possible future MAB activities in this area.

MAB, through the CUBES partnership, is also collaborating with Columbia University on several case studies in the field, such as in Cape Town, South Africa, on the application of the biosphere reserve concept to urban areas.

One specific question the MAB Group has examined is the issue of the eligibility of urban biosphere reserves in the context of the Statutory Framework and the Seville Strategy for the World Network of Biosphere Reserves. The preliminary considerations of the MAB Urban Group on this question is that urban biosphere reserves would seem to be compatible with the Statutory Framework and, if not called for, at least not ruled out in the Seville Strategy.[3] These considerations are outlined below in some detail.

URBAN BIOSPHERE RESERVES IN THE CONTEXT OF THE STATUTORY FRAMEWORK AND THE SEVILLE STRATEGY FOR THE WORLD NETWORK OF BIOSPHERE RESERVES

Before assessing whether urban biosphere reserves are compatible with the Statutory Framework, the MAB Urban Group determined that it would be necessary to establish a working definition of the notion of an urban biosphere reserve. Recalling that a typical definition of an urban area is "a geographical area constituting a city or town," a simplistic proposal then would be to say that an urban biosphere reserve is a biosphere reserve constituting a city or town. However, in the discussions now going on in several cities around the world, the idea seems never to have been to restrict an urban biosphere reserve to only the urban areas (i.e., the cities or towns), but to take a regional perspective integrating urban areas and their hinterlands. Furthermore, the mere existence of a city or a town in a biosphere reserve would not be sufficient to call it an urban biosphere reserve. The issue then is that of defining the relative importance of the urban elements in the biosphere reserve.

The "relative importance" possibly could be assessed as a function of several measurable factors in the biosphere reserve, for example, percentage of urban land cover, rate of urbanization and urban sprawl, distance to major urban areas, percentage of people living in urban areas compared with the countryside, impacts of urban areas, and the urban population on the biosphere reserves). The underlying key objectives for which the biosphere reserve was established, for example, conservation of urban biodiversity, promoting sustainable urban development and reduced urban footprints, city networking, etc., also could be defining characteristics of an urban biosphere reserve.

A possible working definition of an urban biosphere reserve based on the above considerations therefore could be as follows:

> Urban biosphere reserve: a biosphere reserve characterized by important urban areas within or adjacent to its boundaries where the natural, socioeconomic,

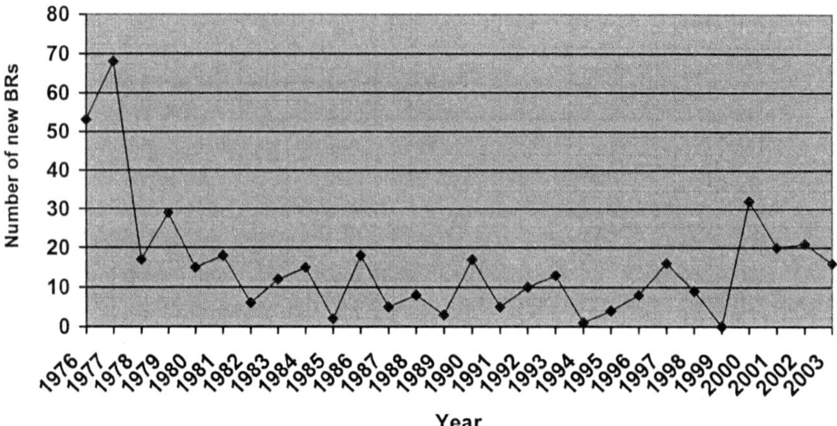

FIGURE 4. New biosphere reserves 1976–2003.

and cultural environments are shaped by urban influences and pressures, and set up and managed to mitigate these pressures for improved urban and regional sustainability.

Depending on their zonation pattern, four different categories of urban biosphere reserves could be envisioned, here called "urban green belt biosphere reserves," "urban green corridor biosphere reserves," "urban green area cluster biosphere reserves," and "urban region biosphere reserves" (see FIG. 5).

Combinations of these categories are of course possible, or even likely. The distribution of the three different biosphere reserve zones (i.e., core, buffer, and transition areas) adds to the large number of possible combinations.

The Statutory Framework of the World Network of Biosphere Reserves (the "Framework") includes an introduction and ten articles. It is the document that guides the Advisory Committee on Biosphere Reserves and the MAB Council and its Bureau when considering biosphere reserve nominations.

So, let us now address the question of whether urban biosphere reserves as defined and categorized above are compatible with the relevant paragraphs of the Framework. Note, however, that the purpose here is not to derive at a formal position on either the definition of, or the different possible categories of urban biosphere reserves, the purpose is primarily to assess whether there are any apparent contradictions between the notion of urban biosphere reserves and the Framework.

It is stated in the Framework's introduction that "Within UNESCO's Man and the Biosphere (MAB) Programme, biosphere reserves are established to promote and demonstrate a balanced relationship between humans and the biosphere." Urban areas and regions will more often than not exemplify such a relationship. On the other hand, urban biosphere reserves could be impor-

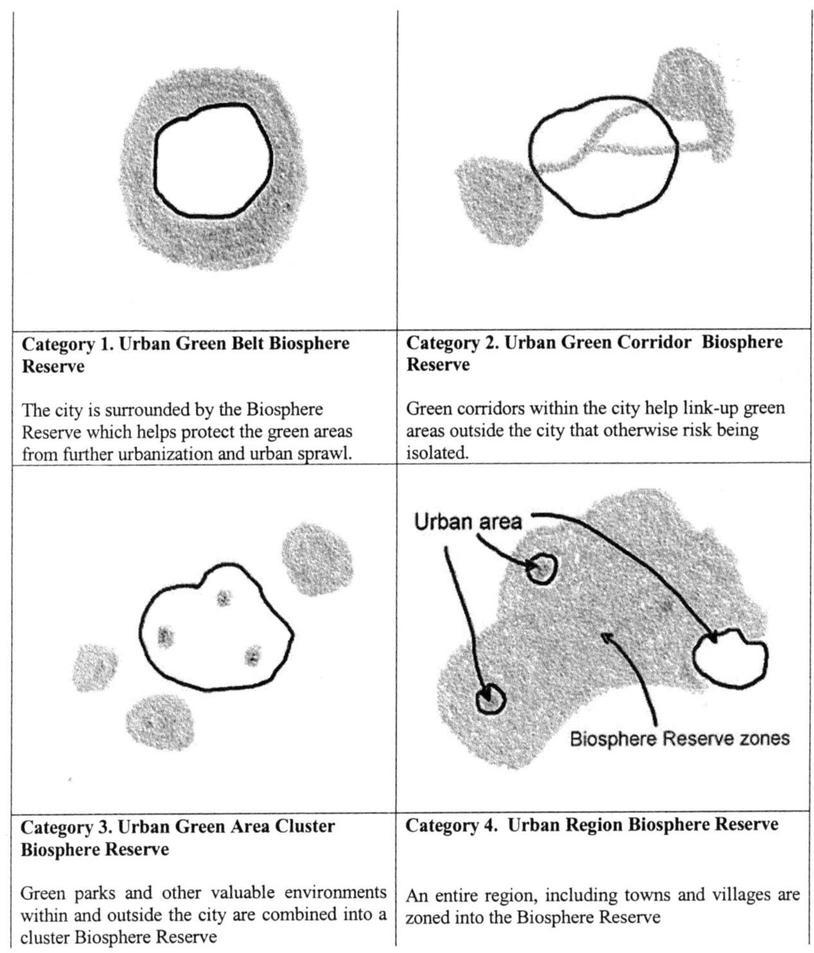

Category 1. Urban Green Belt Biosphere Reserve
The city is surrounded by the Biosphere Reserve which helps protect the green areas from further urbanization and urban sprawl.
Category 2. Urban Green Corridor Biosphere Reserve
Green corridors within the city help link-up green areas outside the city that otherwise risk being isolated.
Urban area
Biosphere Reserve zones
Category 3. Urban Green Area Cluster Biosphere Reserve
Green parks and other valuable environments within and outside the city are combined into a cluster Biosphere Reserve
Category 4. Urban Region Biosphere Reserve
An entire region, including towns and villages are zoned into the Biosphere Reserve

FIGURE 5. Possible categories of urban biosphere reserves.

tant to promote them. Also, urban biosphere reserves could demonstrate examples of a balanced relationship between humans and the biosphere reserves in certain sectors, although it may not contribute to the full range of human–biosphere interactions. The introduction ends with the proposal that "States are encouraged to elaborate and implement national criteria for biosphere reserves which take into account the special conditions of the state concerned." States interested in elaborating criteria for urban biosphere reserves therefore would seem to be encouraged to do so.

Article 1 of the Framework defines biosphere reserves as "areas of terrestrial and coastal/marine ecosystems or a combination thereof, which are internationally recognized within the framework of UNESCO's program on

Man and the Biosphere (MAB), in accordance with the present Statutory Framework." It could be recalled that MAB was one of the pioneers behind the notion of urban ecosystems,[4] and urban biosphere reserves will typically consist of a rich mosaic of terrestrial and coastal ecosystems. The definition, however, is a very general one more aiming at ensuring that sites labeled as biosphere reserves are those that are recognized by MAB as such rather than to define their features in detail.

In Article 3 the Framework sets out the three major functions of biosphere reserves: "In combining the three functions below, biosphere reserves should strive to be sites of excellence to explore and demonstrate approaches to conservation and sustainable development on a regional scale:

(a) conservation—contribute to the conservation of landscapes, ecosystems, species, and genetic variation;
(b) development—foster economic and human development which is socioculturally and ecologically sustainable;
(c) logistic support—support for demonstration projects, environmental education and training, research and monitoring related to local, regional, national, and global issues of conservation and sustainable development."

The first general remark that could be made here is that it actually would be quite difficult to perceive how biosphere reserves that do not include urban areas possibly could demonstrate approaches to conservation and sustainable development on a regional scale. Regions without urban areas, or perhaps without people, would not be good examples of a "balanced relationship between humans and the biosphere" (Introduction). If it is agreed that sustainable development cannot be achieved without sustainable urban development, again, it will be difficult to rule out urban biosphere reserves.

Urban biosphere reserves could certainly contribute to the conservation of landscapes and biodiversity of high importance for a large number of people, locally, regionally, and globally (through reduced urban footprints). They also would form important platforms for fostering development along more sustainable lines. Urban areas are typically cast in the light of their negative impacts; however, it should, of course, not be forgotten that cities and towns are critical in terms of also providing several benefits, such as income and job opportunities, markets, health and educational facilities without which several biosphere reserves, and society at large, actually would not be fully functional or sustainable. Finally, urban biosphere reserves could provide logistic support for education, public awareness, and research on critical issues linked to conservation and sustainable urban development.

It is useful to recognize here that an urban biosphere reserve (or any biosphere reserve for that matter) never would be synonymous with the city, town, or region where it is situated; it would merely be one additional institutional structure among a myriad of human institutions (albeit an important one!). Therefore, an urban biosphere reserve could not and should not be held "accountable" for all facets of human–environment interactions within its boundaries. Being associated with an unsustainable urban area therefore should not automatically be seen to imply that the biosphere reserve does not, or could not, fulfill its functions.

The Framework's Article 4 sets out the general criteria for an area to be qualified for designation as a biosphere reserve. The 7 criteria are as follows:

(1) *It should encompass a mosaic of ecological systems representative of major biogeographic regions, including a gradation of human interventions.* Needless to say, perhaps more than any other reserves, urban biosphere reserves will contain a broad gradient of human interventions and a rich mosaic of ecological systems.

(2) *It should be of significance for biological diversity conservation. Urban areas include important, sometimes unique biodiversity.* In addition, biodiversity in urban areas tends to be essential for the welfare of its inhabitants (food, climate regulation, water catchments, recreation, etc.).

(3) *It should provide an opportunity to explore and demonstrate approaches to sustainable development on a regional scale.* More than perhaps any other types of reserves, urban biosphere reserves would be important tools to address sustainable development on a regional scale by integrating urban areas that often are at the center of the sustainability debate.

(4) *It should have an appropriate size to serve the three functions of biosphere reserves, as set out in Article 3.* There are no restrictions as such as to have big an urban biosphere reserve could be. An appropriate size therefore usually could be envisaged involving urban areas and their hinterlands.

(5) *It should include these functions, through appropriate zonation, recognizing: (a) A legally constituted core area or areas devoted to long-term protection, according to the conservation objectives of the biosphere reserve, and of sufficient size to meet these objectives.* As already discussed, an urban biosphere reserve could be set up in several ways. An urban green corridor biosphere reserve (category 2), for example, could include core areas within the urban area (e.g., park areas, rivers, and lakes). These areas can be the subject to legal protection and of a sufficient size to ensure that the conservation objectives are met. *(b) Buffer zone or zones clearly identified and surrounding or contiguous to the core area or areas, where only activities compatible with the conservation objectives can take place.* Buffer zones may require some innovative thinking in the urban context. For example, residential areas could provide buffer zone protection for rivers and lakes within the city provided they are equipped

with sound wastewater facilities. Furthermore, polluting industrial activities not compatible with the conservation objectives could be avoided in such areas (perhaps to the benefit of human health as well). *(c) An outer transition area where sustainable resource management practices are promoted and developed.* There are no limitations to the possibilities an urban biosphere reserve could provide in terms of promoting and developing sustainable resources management practices in sectors such as agriculture, forestry, recreation, water, energy, transport, housing, and waste management. Of minor importance here is perhaps that the transition areas may not always be the outer areas in an urban biosphere reserve, rather they could find themselves surrounded by buffer zones and core areas.

(6) *Organizational arrangements should be provided for the involvement and participation of a suitable range of inter alia public authorities, local communities, and private interests in the design and performing the functions of a biosphere reserve.* Key public and private stakeholders are concentrated to the urban areas, and this should facilitate their involvement and participation in the design and operations of an urban biosphere reserve. Although the politics of establishing and managing an urban biosphere reserve could be expected to be complex, the benefits of such a process could be substantial in terms of bringing stakeholders aboard on a cooperation platform for regional sustainability that typically will not have existed before.

(7) *In addition, provisions should be made for: (a) mechanisms to manage human use and activities in the buffer zone or zones.* Urban areas often have already established mechanisms in place to oversee and manage economic and other human activities. *(b) A management policy or plan for the area as a biosphere reserve.* An increasing number of cities around the world have developed local Agenda 21 initiatives and have well-established (more or less well implemented) plans and policies covering most facets of urban life. These can in many instances form an effective basis for an urban biosphere reserve policy which in addition, however, also would have to extend to the hinterlands. The fact that an urban biosphere reserve would seek to bridge the often conflicting interests between cities and their hinterlands is what makes it so attractive and potentially powerful. *(c) A designated authority or mechanism to implement this policy or plan.* This is of course a key point for any successful biosphere reserve. It will, however, in many instances be a tough challenge for an urban biosphere reserve to muster the power and authority to ensure the implementation of a comprehensive and ambitious policy or plan that would touch on fundamental urban management issues. There are no fixed prescriptions for how a Biosphere as an institution can or should be set up to ensure implementation. Legislation,

political, public, and financial support are all important ingredients for success. Increasingly, the true strength of biosphere reserves might lie in their ability to produce sustainable economic benefits spurred by a shared vision among key stakeholders of the region as a space for sustainable development cooperation. *(d) Programs for research, monitoring, education, and training.* Easy access to universities, research facilities, schools, and education centers will help ensure that urban biosphere reserves can establish strong programs for research, monitoring, education and training. Urban biosphere reserves also could help promote the establishment of new and innovative training centers for education for sustainable development at different levels.

The above discussion is but a short, partly theoretical analysis of the extent to which urban biosphere reserves are or would be compatible with the Framework. The MAB Urban Group's conclusion is, however, that urban biosphere reserves are compatible with the Framework.

It is one thing to suggest that urban biosphere reserve would be compatible with the Statutory Framework, but are they a welcome contribution to the World Network? One authority on the issue of Biosphere Reserves for the 21st century is the Seville Strategy (the "Strategy"). Drawn up by 400 experts from 102 countries and 15 international and regional organizations in Seville in March 1995, the Strategy seeks to identify "the specific role of biosphere reserves in developing a new vision of the relationship between conservation and development" together with a series if recommendations for developing effective biosphere reserves and for setting out the conditions for the appropriate functioning of the World Network of Biosphere Reserves.

Well, does the Strategy talk about urban biosphere reserves? Not really, but it gets fairly close. Ten key directions were identified by the Seville Conference that formed the foundations for the Strategy. The second key direction is that biosphere reserves should be developed "that include a wide variety of environmental, biological, economic, and cultural situations, going from largely undisturbed regions and spreading towards cities." Exactly where this spread should be interrupted on its way toward the urban areas, if at all, is not specified leaving the question somewhat open.

In relation to the coverage of the World Network, it is however recommended (under Goal I) to "... establish, strengthen or extend biosphere reserves as necessary, giving special attention to fragmented habitats, threatened ecosystems, and fragile and vulnerable environments, both natural and cultural." For many, this would seem to be an implicit call for urban biosphere reserves.

Concerning the transition areas, the Strategy documents explain that it "may contain a variety of agricultural activities, settlements, and other uses and in which local communities, management agencies, scientists, NGOs, cultural groups, economic interests, and other stakeholders work together to manage and sustainably develop the area's resources." This also could be interpreted as a support for urban biosphere reserves (as far as the transition areas are concerned).

It is recommended under the Strategy's Goal II (utilize biosphere reserves as models of land management and of approaches to sustainable development) to "establish, strengthen or extend biosphere reserves to include areas … where there are critical interactions between people and their environment (e.g., periurban areas, degraded rural areas, coastal areas, freshwater environments, and wetlands)." Periurban areas are mentioned as examples here, but the text again stops short of mentioning cities.

Although the Strategy includes many recommendations, it modestly acknowledges that it is deliberately focused on a "few priorities." This is one possible explanation of why the document is not more explicit on urban issues. Also, the focus on urban areas, urbanization, and urban sprawl has become sharper since 1995. The Strategy therefore might have been more sensitive to the urban agenda had it been drafted today.

Another possible explanation is of course that urban biosphere reserves were not seen as such a good idea, perhaps based on the concern that they somehow would stretch the biosphere reserve concept beyond recognition. If so, comfort could be drawn from the Strategy document that underscores that "In fact, one of the greatest strengths of the biosphere reserve concept has been the flexibility and creativity with which it has been realized in various situations."

A parallel possibly could be drawn here to the UNESCO World Heritage Convention, which successfully manages to cover such different entities as cultural and natural properties, recently extended to also cover cultural landscapes. This without eroding either the rationale for or the usefulness of the Convention to its member states. For the Convention, the connecting theme is that of conserving universal cultural values. For biosphere reserves, the connecting theme is contained in their three functions, that is, conservation, development, and logistics with sustainable development as an overarching theme. The MAB Urban Group argues that it would seem only timely that if member states proposed Urban Biosphere Reserves, they would be a welcome addition to the World Network.

The MAB Urban Group also has invited comments on its position, and its views were discussed in some depth at the Bureau of the MAB-ICC at its meeting on July 10, 2003. The MAB Bureau did not, however, reach a consensus on the issue.[5] Some bureau members felt that there should not be any division of biosphere reserves into different categories, such as urban biosphere reserves, and that urban issues best would be addressed through other potential MAB activities rather than through the application of the biosphere reserve concept. One bureau member stressed the difficulty in terms of zoning urban biosphere reserves because of the ecological footprints of urban areas:

> Now, since Seville, it seems for the French MAB National Committee that the biosphere reserves present themselves, first, as laboratories for sustainable development, and that conservation itself is entailed in the sustainability context, and at that moment, it seems intolerable to us to see that biosphere reserve status is given to national parks where people are excluded, and we know such examples, or to see biosphere reserve status given to cities which ecological footprints are not taken into consideration in the definition of the criteria for according their status. In fact, the city of today are completely independent, or most of the mega cities are completely independent from the ecosystems in their immediate surroundings, but they pump and drain the entire planet. The problem therefore is how to define a city as corresponding to a model for sustainable development and at what scale? For the French MAB National Committee, the local scale is totally secondary in according the (biosphere reserve) status. We need evaluation criteria for the sustainability of the urban system at the planetary scale. And at that moment we will have criteria to say that this city could get biosphere reserve status and that one could not.

For the bureau chair, excluding cities from biosphere reserves would be to exclude the real centers of control concerning sustainability:

> When one talks about biodiversity, when one talks about nature in the biosphere reserves, we are thinking in terms of natural equilibrium. That is what is the issue. Equilibrium in nature. It is not the morphology of nature, it is nature in equilibrium. And at that moment, we are searching for the factors that affects the equilibriums in nature. In the environment at large. And if one argues from that point of view, the city becomes essential. The city becomes a command centre. It is not only essential, it becomes an extremely important centre of command. And from this point of view, not only because the decisions are taken in the city, of course, decisions are most often taken in the cities, and the decisions are taken by the urban population, but that is another debate. The most important is that the city, its consumption, its urban morphology, its activities, command the equilibriums in nature. Around the city, and more and more by remote controls. Around the city, and well beyond the city. Even globally. Globally in the sense that it affects the entire globe. And this becomes absolutely fundamental. And at that moment, if one does not consider cities in the biosphere reserves, as command centres in the biosphere reserves, we will get misled. We would ignore essential problems. We are trying to find, we are trying to find the fundamental controls of the equilibrium in nature, in nature, while most often they are elsewhere. They are found around people. And people are increasingly, even in our countries (in the South), mainly in cities.

The MAB secretary advocated a pragmatic, case by case approach:

> On the question of urban biosphere reserves or not, we could argue in space in an "n" universe if it would work or not, and we would all hold our different views on that. I think I hold still firmly to the view that we should do for that what we do for all biosphere reserves. If somebody wishes to nominate, then we look at the nomination and we measure it in the normal way we would measure any biosphere reserve, and if somehow it passes the test, it passes the test, si non c'est non (if not it is no). And that I think would be the way to handle

> that. I don't think it is healthy to rule in or rule out whether we should have urban areas because there may well be some urban areas that could work. Many we think won't. So, I think we, we just set that aside and see what comes.

In the discussion, the MAB Bureau still felt that it would be necessary to seek to develop some criteria for assessing urban biosphere reserve nominations and charged the MAB Urban Group with this purpose. In his concluding remarks, the MAB Chair summed up the discussion as follows:

> You recall that sustainable development is not a science, not knowledge; sustainable development is a *necessity.* The departure point is based solely on need. We have found that the systems in place are insufficient ... [and] we have recognized that they are not sustainable and the concept of sustainable development was invented because there was an urgent need for it. Now, we agree that the city and the relationships between the city and biosphere reserves is an urgent [issue]... it is just that we do not know how to do it. Luckily, there is a ... group [the MAB Urban Group] that is working on it; it was the reason why it was founded. This group has presented an excellent introduction...that shows that the work is progressing, ... but, the Bureau, the [biosphere reserve] Advisory Committee say it is urgent, it is burning. Applications [for urban biosphere reserves]...have already arrived, so we need criteria for envisioning, and to find norms for whether or not to accept them....That is where we are now. [Working with cities]...is a necessity; it is...urgent.... To admit them [the cities] constitutes progress for the biosphere reserve concept. Now, how to do it, the methodological approach, that is our job...[and it is] absolutely necessary to work on it.

This work is now under way by the MAB Urban Group, which in addition also is seeking to identify some of the expected benefits of such biosphere reserves. Again, this is very much work under progress, but let us mention here some of the tentative conclusions.

First, in view of the fact that urban areas are key players in the quest for sustainability, refusing biosphere reserve proposals simply because they include urban areas would seem counterproductive. Actually, among the expected benefits of urban biosphere reserves is the fact that the application of the Biosphere Reserve concept should help cities and their hinterlands to be better placed to respond to political, economic, and social pressures reducing their sustainability prospects. Second, urban biosphere reserve can provide an important, largely politically neutral platform for discussing and negotiating agreements among cities and their surrounding regions toward a shared vision of sustainability.

Another benefit of urban biosphere reserves is the opportunity for city networking and international recognition. Although urban biosphere reserves could be cast in very different geographical, economic, and cultural contexts, they would have a common interest to seek concrete solutions to reconcile the conservation of the environment with economic development for the benefit of their inhabitants and those of the surrounding regions. In the case of the mega cities, improved sustainability would produce global benefits, especially if efforts are in place to reduce and mitigate the mega cities' ecological footprints.

It is expected that the "Partnership of Cities on Biosphere and Society" conference at the New York Academy of Sciences, October 29–30, 2003, organized by the Columbia University–UNESCO Joint Program on Biosphere and Society (CUBES) in cosponsorship with the New York Academy of Sciences, UN-Habitat, and the MAB Urban Group will provide further evidence of such benefits. This important conference also will likely serve as an important milestone in the quest to identify criteria for assessing urban biosphere reserves.

CONCLUSIONS

The biosphere reserve concept is an evolving one, and spurred by the ongoing urbanization trends around the world, several cities are becoming interested in the application of the biosphere reserves concept as a tool for urban management toward sustainability. UNESCO, through the MAB Urban Group and the CUBES partnership, is examining the possible benefits of endorsing urban biosphere reserves under the Statutory Framework of the World Network of Biosphere Reserves. The position of the MAB Urban Group is that such additions to the World Network should be welcomed. However, the issue of the urban biosphere reserve has proved to be somewhat controversial within the international MAB Programme, and only time will tell whether cities such as Paris, Rome, and New York will one day like to join and be accepted to the network.

REFERENCES

1. UNESCO. 1996. Biosphere Reserves: The Seville Strategy and the Statutory Framework of the World Network. UNESCO. Paris.
2. BONNES, M. 2000. The "Ecosystem Approach" to Urban Settlements: 20 Years of the MAB-Rome Project. Paper presented at the First Meeting of the MAB Urban Group, UNESCO Paris, November 9, 2000.
3. MAB URBAN GROUP. 2003. Urban Biosphere Reserves in the Context of the Statutory Framework and the Seville Strategy for the World Network of Biosphere Reserves. Draft June 2003. UNESCO. Paris.
4. CELECIA, J. 2000. UNESCO's MAB Programme and Urban Ecosystem Research: A Brief Overview of the Evolution and Challenges of a Three-Decade International Experience. Paper presented at the first meeting of the MAB Urban Group, November 9, 2000. UNESCO. Paris.
5. UNESCO. 2003. Biosphere Reserve Nominations and Urban Areas. Report of the MAB Bureau Discussion July 10, 2003. UNESCO. Paris.

ANNEX I: THE STATUTORY FRAMEWORK OF THE WORLD NETWORK OF BIOSPHERE RESERVES

Introduction

Within UNESCO's Man and the Biosphere (MAB) Programme, biosphere reserves are established to promote and demonstrate a balanced relationship between humans and the biosphere. Biosphere reserves are designated by the International Coordinating Council of the MAB Programme, at the request of the state concerned. Biosphere reserves, each of which remains under the sole sovereignty of the state where it is situated and thereby submitted to state legislation only, form a world network in which participation by the states is voluntary.

The present Statutory Framework of the World Network of Biosphere Reserves has been formulated with the objectives of enhancing the effectiveness of individual biosphere reserves and strengthening common understanding, communication, and cooperation at regional and international levels.

This Statutory Framework is intended to contribute to the widespread recognition of biosphere reserves and to encourage and promote good working examples. The de-listing procedure foreseen should be considered as an exception to this basically positive approach and should be applied only after careful examination, paying due respect to the cultural and socio-economic situation of the country, and after consulting the government concerned.

The text provides for the designation, support, and promotion of biosphere reserves, while taking account of the diversity of national and local situations. States are encouraged to elaborate and implement national criteria for biosphere reserves which take into account the special conditions of the state concerned.

Article 1: Definition

Biosphere reserves are areas of terrestrial and coastal/marine ecosystems or a combination thereof which are internationally recognized within the framework of UNESCO's program on Man and the Biosphere (MAB), in accordance with the present Statutory Framework.

Article 2: World Network of Biosphere Reserves

(1) Biosphere reserves form a worldwide network, known as the World Network of Biosphere Reserves, hereafter called the Network.

(2) The Network constitutes a tool for the conservation of biological diversity and the sustainable use of its components, thus contributing to the objectives of the Convention on Biological Diversity and other pertinent conventions and instruments.

(3) Individual biosphere reserves remain under the sovereign jurisdiction of the states where they are situated. Under the present Statutory Framework, states take the measures that they deem necessary according to their national legislation.

Article 3: Functions

In combining the three functions below, biosphere reserves should strive to be sites of excellence to explore and demonstrate approaches to conservation and sustainable development on a regional scale:

(i) Conservation—contribute to the conservation of landscapes, ecosystems, species, and genetic variation.

(ii) Development—foster economic and human development which is socioculturally and ecologically sustainable.

(iii) Logistic support—support for demonstration projects, environmental education and training, research and monitoring related to local, regional, national, and global issues of conservation and sustainable development.

Article 4: Criteria

General criteria for an area to be qualified for designation as a biosphere reserve follow:

(1) It should encompass a mosaic of ecological systems representative of major biogeographic regions, including a gradation of human interventions.

(2) It should be of significance for biological diversity conservation.

(3) It should provide an opportunity to explore and demonstrate approaches to sustainable development on a regional scale.

(4) It should have an appropriate size to serve the three functions of biosphere reserves, as set out in Article 3.

(5) It should include these functions, through appropriate zonation, recognizing: *(a)* a legally constituted core area or areas devoted to long-term protection, according to the conservation objectives of the biosphere reserve, and of sufficient size to meet these objectives; (*b*) a buffer zone or zones clearly identified and surrounding or contiguous to the core area or areas, where only activities compatible with the conservation objectives can take place; (*c*) an outer transition

area where sustainable resource management practices are promoted and developed

(6) Organizational arrangements should be provided for the involvement and participation of a suitable range of inter alia public authorities, local communities, and private interests in the design and carrying out the functions of a biosphere reserve.

(7) In addition, provisions should be made for: (*a*) mechanisms to manage human use and activities in the buffer zone or zones; (*b*) a management policy or plan for the area as a biosphere reserve; (*c*) a designated authority or mechanism to implement this policy or plan; (*d*) programs for research, monitoring, education, and training.

Article 5: Designation Procedure

(1) Biosphere reserves are designated for inclusion in the Network by the International Coordinating Council (ICC) of the MAB Programme in accordance with the following procedure. (*a*) States, through National MAB Committees where appropriate, forward nominations with supporting documentation to the secretariat after having reviewed potential sites, taking into account the criteria as defined in Article 4. (*b*) The secretariat verifies the content and supporting documentation; in the case of incomplete nomination, the secretariat requests the missing information from the nominating state. (*c*) Nominations will be considered by the Advisory Committee for Biosphere Reserves for recommendation to ICC. (*d*) ICC of the MAB Programme takes a decision on nominations for designation. The Director-General of UNESCO notifies the state concerned of the decision of ICC.

(2) States are encouraged to examine and improve the adequacy of any existing biosphere reserve, and to propose extension as appropriate, to enable it to function fully within the Network. Proposals for extension follow the same procedure as described above for new designations.

(3) Biosphere reserves which have been designated before the adoption of the present Statutory Framework are considered to be already part of the Network. The provisions of the Statutory Framework therefore apply to them.

Article 6: Publicity

(1) The designation of an area as a biosphere reserve should be given appropriate publicity by the state and authorities concerned, including commemorative plaques and dissemination of information material.

(2) Biosphere reserves within the Network, as well as the objectives, should be given appropriate and continuing promotion.

Article 7: Participation in the Network

(1) States participate in or facilitate cooperative activities of the Network, including scientific research and monitoring, at the global, regional, and subregional levels.
(2) The appropriate authorities should make available the results of research, associated publications and other data, taking into account intellectual property rights, to ensure the proper functioning of the Network and maximize the benefits from information exchanges.
(3) States and appropriate authorities should promote environmental education and training, as well as the development of human resources, in cooperation with other biosphere reserves in the Network.

Article 8: Regional and Thematic Subnetworks

States should encourage the constitution and cooperative operation of regional and/or thematic subnetworks of biosphere reserves, and promote development of information exchanges, including electronic information, within the framework of these subnetworks.

Article 9: Periodic Review

(1) The status of each biosphere reserve should be subject to a periodic review every ten years, based on a report prepared by the concerned authority, on the basis of the criteria of Article 4, and forwarded to the secretariat by the State concerned.
(2) The report will be considered by the Advisory Committee for Biosphere Reserves for recommendation to ICC.
(3) ICC will examine the periodic reports from states concerned.
(4) If ICC considers that the status or management of the biosphere reserve is satisfactory or has improved since designation or the last review; this will be formally recognized by ICC.
(5) If ICC considers that the biosphere reserve no longer satisfies the criteria contained in Article 4, it may recommend that the state concerned take measures to ensure conformity with the provisions of Article 4, taking into account the cultural and socioeconomic context of the state concerned. ICC indicates to the secretariat actions that it should take to assist the state concerned in the implementation of such measures.

(6) Should ICC find that the biosphere reserve in question still does not satisfy the criteria contained in Article 4, within a reasonable period, the area will no longer be referred to as a biosphere reserve which is part of the Network.
(7) The Director-General of UNESCO notifies the state concerned of the decision of ICC.
(8) Should a state wish to remove a biosphere reserve under its jurisdiction from the Network, it notifies the secretariat. This notification shall be transmitted to ICC for information. The area then will no longer be referred to as a biosphere reserve which is part of the Network.

Article 10: Secretariat

(1) UNESCO shall act as the secretariat of the Network and be responsible for its functioning and promotion. The secretariat shall facilitate communication and interaction among individual biosphere reserves and among experts. UNESCO shall also develop and maintain a worldwide accessible information system on biosphere reserves, to be linked to other relevant initiatives.
(2) To reinforce individual biosphere reserves and the functioning of the Network and subnetworks, UNESCO shall seek financial support from bilateral and multilateral sources.
(3) The list of biosphere reserves forming part of the Network, their objectives, and descriptive details, shall be as described.

ANNEX II: THE SEVILLE STRATEGY FOR BIOSPHERE RESERVES

Biosphere Reserves: The First Twenty Years

Biosphere reserves are designed to deal with one of the most important questions the world faces today: How can we reconcile conservation of biodiversity and biological resources with their sustainable use? An effective biosphere reserve involves natural and social scientists; conservation and development groups; management authorities and local communities, all working together on this complex issue.

The concept of biosphere reserves was initiated by a Task Force of UNESCO's Man and the Biosphere (MAB) Programme in 1974. The biosphere reserve network was launched in 1976 and, as of March 1995, had grown to include 324 reserves in 82 countries. The network is a key component in MAB's objective for achieving a sustainable balance between the sometimes conflicting goals of conserving biological diversity, promoting economic development and maintaining associated cultural values. Biosphere reserves are sites where this objective is tested, refined, demonstrated, and implemented.

In 1983, UNESCO and the United Nations Environment Programme (UNEP) jointly convened the First International Biosphere Reserve Congress in Minsk (Belarus), in cooperation with the Food and Agriculture Organization of the United Nations (FAO) and the World Conservation Union (IUCN). The Congress's activities gave rise in 1984 to an "Action Plan for Biosphere Reserves" which was formally endorsed by the UNESCO General Conference and by the Governing Council of UNEP. Although much of this Action Plan remains valid today, the context in which biosphere reserves operate has changed considerably, as was shown by the United Nations Conference on Environment and Development (UNCED) process and, in particular, the Convention on Biological Diversity. The Convention was signed at the Earth Summit in Rio de Janeiro in June 1992, was entered into force in December 1993, and has now been ratified by more than 100 countries. The major objectives of the convention are: conservation of biological diversity; sustainable use of its components; and fair and equitable sharing of benefits arising from the utilization of genetic resources. Biosphere reserves promote this integrated approach and thus are well placed to contribute to the implementation of the convention.

In the decade since the Minsk Congress, thinking about protected areas as a whole and about the biosphere reserves has been developing along parallel lines. Most importantly, the link between conservation of biodiversity and the development needs of local communities, a central component of the biosphere reserve approach, is now recognized as a key feature of the successful management of most national parks, nature reserves, and other protected areas. At the Fourth World Congress on National Parks and Protected Areas, held in Caracas, Venezuela, in February 1992, the world's protected-area planners and managers adopted many of the ideas (community involvement, the links between conservation and development, the importance of international collaboration) that are essential aspects of biosphere reserves. The Congress also approved a resolution in support of biosphere reserves.

There also have been important innovations in the management of biosphere reserves themselves. New methodologies for involving stakeholders in decision-making processes and resolving conflicts have been developed, and increased attention has been given to the need to use regional approaches. New kinds of biosphere reserves, such as cluster and transboundary reserves, have been devised, and many biosphere reserves have evolved considerably, from a primary focus on conservation to a greater integration of conservation and development through increasing cooperation among stakeholders. New international networks, fuelled by technological advances, including more powerful computers and the Internet, have greatly facilitated communication and cooperation between biosphere reserves in different countries.

In this context, the Executive Board of UNESCO decided in 1991 to establish an Advisory Committee for Biosphere Reserves. This Advisory Committee considered that it was time to evaluate the effectiveness of the 1984 Action Plan, to analyze its implementation and to develop a strategy for biosphere reserves as we move into the 21st century.

To this end, and in accordance with Resolution 27/C/2.3 of the General Conference, UNESCO organized the International Conference on Biosphere Reserves at the invitation of the Spanish authorities in Seville (Spain) on March 20–25, 1995. This conference was attended by some 400 experts from 102 countries and 15 international and regional organizations.

The conference was organized to enable an evaluation of the experience in implementing the 1984 Action Plan, a reflection on the role for biosphere reserves in the context of the 21st century (which created the vision statement) and the elaboration of a draft Statutory Framework for the World Network. The Conference drew up the Seville Strategy, which is presented below. The International Coordinating Council of the Man and the Biosphere (MAB) Programme, meeting for its 13th session (June 12–16, 1995) gave its strong support to the Seville Strategy.

The Biosphere Reserve Concept

Biosphere reserves are "areas of terrestrial and coastal/marine ecosystems or a combination thereof, which are internationally recognized within the framework of UNESCO's Programme on Man and the Biosphere (MAB)" (Statutory Framework of the World Network of Biosphere Reserves). Reserves are nominated by national governments; each reserve must meet a minimal set of criteria and adhere to a minimal set of conditions before being admitted to the Network. Each biosphere reserve is intended to fulfill three complementary functions: a conservation function, to preserve genetic resources, species, ecosystems, and landscapes; a development function, to foster sustainable economic and human development, and a logistic support function, to support demonstration projects, environmental education and training, and research and monitoring related to local, national and global issues of conservation and sustainable development.

Physically, each biosphere reserve should contain three elements: one or more core areas, which are securely protected sites for conserving biological diversity, monitoring minimally disturbed ecosystems, and undertaking non-destructive research and other low-impact uses (such as education); a clearly identified buffer zone, which usually surrounds or adjoins the core areas, and is used for cooperative activities compatible with sound ecological practices, including environmental education, recreation, ecotourism, and applied and basic research; and a flexible transition area, or area of cooperation, which may contain a variety of agricultural activities, settlements and other uses and in which local communities, management agencies, scientists, NGOs, cultural groups, economic interests, and other stakeholders work together to manage and sustainably develop the area's resources. Although originally envisioned as a series of concentric rings, the three zones have been implemented in many different ways to meet local needs and conditions. In fact, one of the greatest strengths of the biosphere reserve concept has been the flexibility and creativity with which it has been realized in various situations.

Some countries have enacted legislation specifically to establish biosphere reserves. In many others, the core areas and buffer zones are designated (in whole or in part) as protected areas under national law. Several biosphere reserves simultaneously encompass areas protected under other systems (such as national parks or nature reserves) and other internationally recognized sites (such as World Heritage or Ramsar sites).

Ownership arrangements may vary too. The core areas of biosphere reserves are mostly public land but can also be privately owned or belong to NGOs. In many cases, the buffer zone is in private or community ownership, and this is generally the case for the transition area. The Seville Strategy for Biosphere Reserves reflects this wide range of circumstances.

The Vision from Seville for the 21st Century

What future does the world face as we move toward the 21st century? Current trends in population growth and distribution, increasing demands for energy and natural resources, globalization of the economy and the effects of trade patterns on rural areas, the erosion of cultural distinctiveness, centralization and difficulty of access to relevant information, and uneven spread of technological innovations all paint a sobering picture of environment and development prospects in the near future.

The UNCED process laid out the alternative of working toward sustainable development, incorporating care of the environment and greater social equity, including respect for rural communities and their accumulated wisdom. Agenda 21, the Conventions on Biological Diversity, Climate Change and Desertification, and other multilateral agreements, show the way forward at the international level.

But the global community also needs working examples that encapsulate the ideas of UNCED for promoting both conservation and sustainable development. These examples can only work if they express all the social, cultural, spiritual, and economic needs of society and are also based on sound science.

Biosphere reserves offer such examples. Rather than forming islands in a world increasingly affected by severe human impacts, they can become theaters for reconciling people and nature; they can bring knowledge of the past to the needs of the future; and they can demonstrate how to overcome the problems of the sectoral nature of our institutions. In short, biosphere reserves are much more than just protected areas.

Thus, biosphere reserves are poised to take on a new role. Not only will they be a means for the people who live and work within and around them to attain a balanced relationship with the natural world, but they will also contribute to the needs of society as a whole, by showing a way to a more sustainable future. This is at the heart of our vision for biosphere reserves in the 21st century.

The International Conference on Biosphere Reserves, organized by UNESCO, in Seville (Spain), on March 20–25, 1995, adopted a two-pronged approach:

- To examine past experience in implementing the innovative concept of the biosphere reserve.
- To look to the future to identify what emphases should now be given to their three functions of conservation, development, and logistical support.

The Seville Conference concluded that despite the problems and limitations encountered with the establishment of biosphere reserves, the program as a whole had been innovative and had had much success. In particular, the three basic functions would be as valid as ever in the coming years. In the implementation of these functions and in the light of the analysis undertaken, the following ten key directions were identified by the Conference and are the foundations of the new Seville Strategy.

(1) Strengthen the contribution which biosphere reserves make to the implementation of international agreements promoting conservation and sustainable development, especially to the Convention on Biological Diversity and other agreements, such as those on climate change, desertification, and forests.

(2) Develop biosphere reserves that include a wide variety of environmental, biological, economic, and cultural situations, going from largely undisturbed regions and spreading toward cities. There is a particular potential, and need, to apply the biosphere reserve concept in the coastal and marine environment.

(3) Strengthen the emerging regional, interregional, and thematic networks of biosphere reserves as components within the World Network of Biosphere Reserves.

(4) Reinforce scientific research, monitoring, training, and education in biosphere reserves, because conservation and rational use of resources in these areas require a sound base in the natural and social sciences as well as the humanities. This need is particularly acute in countries where biosphere reserves lack human and financial resources and should receive priority attention.

(5) Ensure that all zones of biosphere reserves contribute appropriately to conservation, sustainable development, and scientific understanding.
(6) Extend the transition area to embrace large areas suitable for approaches, such as ecosystem management, and use biosphere reserves to explore and demonstrate approaches to sustainable development at the regional scale. For this, more attention should be given to the transition area.
(7) Reflect more fully the human dimensions of biosphere reserves. Connections should be made between cultural and biological diversity. Traditional knowledge and genetic resources should be conserved, and their role in sustainable development should be recognized and encouraged.
(8) Promote the management of each biosphere reserve essentially as a "pact" between the local community and society as a whole. Management should be open, evolving, and adaptive. Such an approach will help ensure that biosphere reserves, and their local communities, are better placed to respond to external political, economic, and social pressures.
(9) Bring together all interested groups and sectors in a partnership approach to biosphere reserves both at site and network levels. Information should flow freely among all concerned.
(10) Invest in the future. Biosphere reserves should be used to further our understanding of humanity's relationship with the natural world, through programs of public awareness, information, and formal and informal education, based on a long-term, intergenerational perspective.

In sum, biosphere reserves should preserve and generate natural and cultural values, through management that is scientifically correct, culturally creative, and operationally sustainable. The World Network of Biosphere Reserves, as implemented through the Seville Strategy, thus is an integrating tool which can help to create greater solidarity among peoples and nations of the world.

The Strategy

The following Strategy provides recommendations for developing effective biosphere reserves and for setting out the conditions for the appropriate functioning of the World Network of Biosphere Reserves. It does not repeat the general principles of the Convention on Biological Diversity nor Agenda 21 but instead identifies the specific role of biosphere reserves in developing a new vision of the relationship between conservation and development. Thus, the document is deliberately focused on a few priorities.

TABLE 2. Implementation indicators and their cross-references

Implementation indicators	Cross-reference
International level	
Biosphere reserves included in implementation of the Convention on Biological Diversity	I.1.1
Improved biogeographical system developed	I.1.2
New transboundary reserves developed	I.2.1; IV.2.6
Guidelines developed and published	II.1.1; IV.1.4; IV.1.5
Networkwide research programs implemented	III.1.1
Biosphere reserves incorporated into international research programs	III.1.2
Regional and interregional research programs developed	III.1.3
Interdisciplinary research tools developed	III.1.4
Clearinghouse for research tools and methodologies developed	III.1.5
Interactions developed with other research and education networks	III.1.6
Biosphere reserves incorporated into international monitoring programs	III.2.1
Standardized protocols and methodologies adopted for data and for data exchange	III.2.2; IV.2.10
Mechanism developed for exchanging experiences and information between biosphere reserves	III.3.1
Biosphere reserve communication system implemented	III.3.2; IV.2.4; IV.2.7
International training opportunities and programs developed	III.4.1
Regional training centers identified and developed	III.4.2
Demonstration biosphere reserves identified and publicized	IV.1.1
Guidance provided on elaboration and review of strategies and national action plans for biosphere reserves	IV.1.2
Mechanisms developed for information exchange among biosphere reserve managers	IV.1.3
Statutory Framework of the World Network of Biosphere Reserves is implemented at the international and national levels	IV.2.1; IV.2.2
Advisory Committee for Biosphere Reserves is functional and effective	IV.2.3
Regional or thematic networks developed or strengthened	IV.2.4
Interactions developed between biosphere reserves, and similar managed areas and organizations	IV.2.5
Mechanisms developed to foster twinning between biosphere reserves	IV.2.6
Information and promotional materials developed for the Biosphere Reserve Network	IV.2.7
Strategies developed for including biosphere reserves in bilateral and multilateral aid projects	IV.2.8
Strategies developed for mobilizing funds from businesses, NGOs, and foundations	IV.2.9
Data standards and methodologies applied across the World Network	IV.2.10

TABLE 2. (*continued*) Implementation indicators and their cross-references

Implementation indicators	Cross-reference
Mechanisms developed for monitoring and assessing the implementation of the Seville Strategy at the national level	IV.2.11
National level	
Biogeographical analysis prepared	I.1.3
Analysis of need for new or extended biosphere reserves is completed	I.1.4; II.1.3
Biosphere reserves included in national strategies and other responses to the Convention on Biological Diversity and other conventions	I.2.2; I.1.3
Links developed between biosphere reserves	I.2.4
In situ conservation plans for genetic resources in biosphere reserves	I.2.5
Biosphere reserves incorporated into sustainable development plans	II.1.2
Biosphere reserves developed or strengthened to include traditional lifestyles and in areas of critical people-environment interactions	II.1.3
Conservation and sustainable use activities identified and promoted	II.1.4
Effective management plans or policies in place at all biosphere reserves	II.2.1; IV.1.6
Mechanisms developed for identifying incompatibilities between conservation and sustainable-use functions, and to ensure an appropriate balance between these functions	II.2.2
Biosphere reserves included in regional development and land-use planning projects	II.3.1
Land-use sectors near biosphere reserves are encouraged to adopt sustainable practices	II.3.2; IV.1.7
Biosphere reserves are integrated into national and regional research programs, which are linked to conservation and development policies	III.1.7
Biosphere reserves are integrated into national monitoring programs and are linked to similar monitoring sites and networks	III.2.3
Principles of conservation and sustainable use, as practiced in biosphere reserves, integrated into school programs	III.3.3
Biosphere reserves participate in international education networks and programs	III.3.4
Model training programs for biosphere reserve managers are developed	III.4.3
Mechanisms developed to review national strategies and action plans for biosphere reserves	IV.1.8
Mechanisms developed for information exchange among reserve managers	IV.1.9
Statutory Framework of the World Network of Biosphere Reserves are implemented at the national level	IV.2.12; IV.2.14
National level mechanism developed to advise and coordinate biosphere reserves	IV.2.13
Interactions developed between biosphere reserves and similar managed areas and organizations with congruent goals	IV.2.15
Mechanisms developed to foster twinning between biosphere reserves	IV.2.16
Information and promotional materials developed for biosphere reserves	IV.2.17

TABLE 2. (*continued*) Implementation indicators and their cross-references

Implementation indicators	Cross-reference
Strategies developed for including biosphere reserves in bilateral and multilateral aid projects	IV.2.18
Strategies developed for mobilizing funds from businesses, NGOs, and foundations	IV.2.19
Mechanisms developed for monitoring and assessing the implementation of the Seville Strategy	IV.2.20
Individual reserve level	
Survey made of stakeholders' interests	II.1.5
Factors leading to environmental degradation and unsustainable use are identified	II.1.6
Survey made of the natural products and services of the biosphere reserve	II.1.7
Incentives identified for sustainable use by local populations	II.1.8
Plan prepared for equitable sharing of benefits	II.1.9
Mechanisms developed to manage, coordinate, and integrate the biosphere reserve's programs and activities	II.2.3; IV.1.10; IV.1.12
Local consultative framework implemented	II.2.4
Regional demonstration sites developed	II.3.3
Coordinated research and monitoring plan implemented	III.1.8; III.2.4
Functional data management system implemented	III.1.9; III.2.7
Biosphere reserve is used for developing and testing of monitoring methods	III.2.5
Biosphere reserve is used for developing indicators of sustainability relevant to local populations	III.2.5; II.2.6
Local stakeholders are included in education, training, research, and monitoring programs	III.3.5; III.4.5
Information for visitors to the biosphere reserve developed	III.3.6
Ecology field center developed at the biosphere reserve	III.3.7
Biosphere reserve is used for on-site training activities	III.4.4
A local educational and training program is in place	III.4.6
Different zones of biosphere reserves identified and mapped	IV.1.10.
Buffer and transition zones replanned to promote sustainable development and preserve the core area	IV.1.12
Local community involved in planning and managing the biosphere reserve	IV.1.14
Private sector initiatives to establish and maintain environmentally and socially sustainable activities are encouraged	IV.1.15
Information and promotional materials developed for individual biosphere reserves	IV.2.21
Strategies developed for mobilizing funds from businesses, NGOs, and foundations	IV.2.22
Mechanisms developed for monitoring and assessing the implementation of the Seville Strategy at individual level	IV.2.23

The Strategy suggests the level (international, national, individual biosphere reserve) at which each recommendation will be most effective. However, given the large variety of different national and local management situations, these recommended levels of actions should be seen merely as guidelines and adapted to fit the situation at hand. Especially note that the "national" level should be interpreted to include other governmental levels higher than the individual reserve (e.g., provincial, state, county, etc.). In some countries, national or local NGOs also may be appropriate substitutes for this level. Similarly, the "international" level often includes regional and interregional activities.

The Strategy also includes recommended implementation indicators, that is, a checklist of actions that will enable all involved to follow and evaluate the implementation of the Strategy. Criteria used in developing the indicators were availability (Can the information be gathered relatively easily?), simplicity (Are the data unambiguous?), and usefulness (Will the information be useful to reserve managers, national committees, and/or the Network at large?). One role of the implementation indicators is to assemble a database of successful implementation mechanisms and to exchange this information among all members of the Network (see TABLE 2).

Goal I: Use Biosphere Reserves to Conserve Natural and Cultural Diversity

Objective I.1: Improve the Coverage of Natural and Cultural Biodiversity by Means of the World Network of Biosphere Reserves

Recommended at the international level:

(1) Promote biosphere reserves as a means of implementing the goals of the Convention on Biological Diversity.

(2) Promote a comprehensive approach to biogeographical classification that takes into account such ideas as vulnerability analysis, to develop a system encompassing socioecological factors.

Recommended at the national level:

(3) Prepare a biogeographical analysis of the country as a basis, *inter alia*, for assessing coverage of the World Biosphere Reserve Network.

(4) In light of the analysis, and taking into account existing protected areas, establish, strengthen or extend biosphere reserves as necessary, giving special attention to fragmented habitats, threatened ecosystems, and fragile and vulnerable environments, both natural and cultural.

Objective I.2: Integrate Biosphere Reserves into Conservation Planning

Recommended at the international level:

(1) Encourage the establishment of transboundary biosphere reserves as a means of dealing with the conservation of organisms, ecosystems, and genetic resources that cross national boundaries.

Recommended at the national level:

(2) Integrate biosphere reserves in strategies for biodiversity conservation and sustainable use, in plans for protected areas, and in the national biodiversity strategies and action plans provided for in Article 6 of the Convention on Biological Diversity.
(3) When applicable, include projects to strengthen and develop biosphere reserves in programs to be initiated and funded under the Convention on Biological Diversity, and other multilateral conventions.
(4) Link biosphere reserves with each other and with other protected areas, through green corridors and in other ways that enhance biodiversity conservation, and ensure that these links are maintained.
(5) Use biosphere reserves for *in situ* conservation of genetic resources, including wild relatives of cultivated and domesticated species, and consider using the reserves as rehabilitation/reintroduction sites, and link them as appropriate with *ex situ* conservation and use programs.

Goal II: Utilize Biosphere Reserves as Models of Land Management and of Approaches to Sustainable Development

Objective II.1: Secure the Support and Involvement of Local People

Recommended at the international level:

(1) Prepare guidelines for key aspects of biosphere reserve management, including the resolution of conflicts, provision of local benefits, and involvement of stakeholders in decision making and in responsibility for management.

Recommended at the national level:

(2) Incorporate biosphere reserves into plans for implementing the sustainable-use goals of Agenda 21 and the Convention on Biological Diversity.
(3) Establish, strengthen, or extend biosphere reserves to include areas where traditional lifestyles and indigenous uses of biodiversity are practiced (including sacred sites) and/or where there are critical interactions between people and their environment (e.g., periurban

areas, degraded rural areas, coastal areas, freshwater environments, and wetlands).

(4) Identify and promote the establishment of activities compatible with the goals of conservation, through the transfer of appropriate technologies which include traditional knowledge, and which promote sustainable development in the buffer and transition zones.

Recommended at the individual reserve level:

(5) Survey the interests of the various stakeholders and fully involve them in planning and decision making regarding the management and use of the reserve.

(6) Identify and address factors that lead to environmental degradation and unsustainable use of biological resources.

(7) Evaluate the natural products and services of the reserve and use these evaluations to promote environmentally sound and economically sustainable income opportunities for local people.

(8) Develop incentives for the conservation and sustainable use of natural resources and develop alternative means of livelihood for local populations, when existing activities are limited or prohibited within the biosphere reserve.

(9) Ensure that the benefits derived from the use of natural resources are equitably shared with the stakeholders, by such means as sharing the entrance fees, sale of natural products or handicrafts, use of local construction techniques and labor, and development of sustainable activities (e.g., agriculture, forestry, etc.).

Objective II.2: Ensure Better Harmonization and Interaction among the Different Biosphere Reserve Zones

Recommended at the national level:

(1) Ensure that each biosphere reserve has an effective management policy or plan and an appropriate authority or mechanism to implement it.

(2) Develop means of identifying incompatibilities between the conservation and sustainable-use functions of biosphere reserves and take measures to ensure that an appropriate balance between the functions is maintained.

Recommended at the individual reserve level:

(3) Develop and establish institutional mechanisms to manage, coordinate, and integrate the biosphere reserve's programs and activities.

(4) Establish a local consultative framework in which the reserve's economic and social stakeholders are represented, including the full range of interests (e.g., agriculture, forestry, hunting and extracting, water and energy supply, fisheries, tourism, recreation, research).

Objective II.3: Integrate Biosphere Reserves into Regional Planning

Recommended at the national level:

(1) Include biosphere reserves in regional development policies and in regional land-use planning projects.
(2) Encourage the major land-use sectors near each biosphere reserve to adopt practices favoring sustainable land-use.

Recommended at the individual reserve level:

(3) Organize forums and set up demonstration sites for the examination of socioeconomic and environmental problems of the region, and for the sustainable utilization of biological resources important to the region.

Goal III: Use Biosphere Reserves for Research, Monitoring, Education, and Training

Objective III.1: Improve Knowledge of the Interactions between Humans and the BIOSPHERE

Recommended at the international level:

(1) Use the World Biosphere Reserve Network to conduct comparative environmental and socioeconomic research, including long-term research that will require decades to complete.
(2) Use the World Biosphere Reserve Network for international research programs that deal with topics such as biological diversity, desertification, water cycles, ethnobiology, and global change.
(3) Use the World Biosphere Reserve Network for cooperative research programs at the regional and interregional levels, such as those existing for the Southern Hemisphere, East Asia, and Latin America.
(4) Encourage the development of innovative, interdisciplinary research tools for biosphere reserves, including flexible modeling systems for integrating social, economic, and ecological data.
(5) Develop a clearinghouse for research tools and methodologies in biosphere reserves.
(6) Encourage interactions between the World Biosphere Reserve Network and other research and education networks. Facilitate the use of biosphere reserves for collaborative research projects of consortia of universities and other institutions of higher learning and research, in the private as well as public sector, and at nongovernmental, as well as governmental levels.

Recommended at the national level:

(7) Integrate biosphere reserves with national and regional scientific research programs, and link these research activities to national and regional policies on conservation and sustainable development.

Recommended at the individual reserve level:

(8) Use biosphere reserves for basic and applied research, particularly projects with a focus on local issues, interdisciplinary projects incorporating both the natural and the social sciences, and projects involving the rehabilitation of degraded ecosystems, the conservation of soils and water and the sustainable use of natural resources.
(9) Develop a functional system of data management for the rational use of research and monitoring results in the management of the biosphere reserve.

Objective III.2: Improve Monitoring Activities

Recommended at the international level:

(1) Use the World Biosphere Reserve Network, at the international, regional, national, and local levels, as priority long-term monitoring sites for international programs, focused on topics such as terrestrial and marine observing systems, global change, biodiversity, and forest health.
(2) Encourage the adoption of standardized protocols for meta data concerning the description of flora and fauna, to facilitate the interchange, accessibility, and utilization of scientific information generated in biosphere reserves.

Recommended at the national level:

(3) Encourage the participation of biosphere reserves in national programs of ecological and environmental monitoring and development of linkages between biosphere reserves and other monitoring sites and networks.

Recommended at the individual reserve level:

(4) Use the reserve for making inventories of fauna and flora, collecting ecological and socioeconomic data, making meteorological and hydrological observations, studying the effects of pollution, etc., for scientific purposes and as the basis for sound site management.
(5) Use the reserve as an experimental area for the development and testing of methods and approaches for the evaluation and monitoring of biodiversity, sustainability, and quality of life of its inhabitants.

(6) Use the reserve for developing indicators of sustainability (in ecological, economic, social, and institutional terms) for the different productive activities conducted within the buffer zones and transition areas.
(7) Develop a functional system of data management for rational use of research and monitoring results in the management of the biosphere reserve.

Objective III.3: Improve Education, Public Awareness, and Involvement

Recommended at the international level:

(1) Facilitate the exchange of experience and information between biosphere reserves, with a view to strengthening the involvement of volunteers and local people in biosphere reserve activities.
(2) Promote the development of communication systems for diffusing information on biosphere reserves and on experiences at the field level.

Recommended at the national level:

(3) Include information on conservation and sustainable use, as practiced in biosphere reserves, in school programs and teaching manuals, and in media efforts.
(4) Encourage participation of biosphere reserves in international networks and programs, to promote cross-cutting linkages in education and public awareness.

Recommended at the individual reserve level:

(5) Encourage involvement of local communities, school children, and other stakeholders in education and training programs and in research and monitoring activities within biosphere reserves.
(6) Produce visitors' information about the reserve, its importance for conservation and the sustainable use of biodiversity, its sociocultural aspects, and its recreational and educational programs and resources.
(7) Promote the development of ecology field educational centers, within individual reserves, as facilities for contributing to the education of school children and other groups.

Objective III.4: Improve Training for Specialists and Managers

Recommended at the international level:

(1) Utilize the World Network of Biosphere Reserves to support and encourage international training opportunities and programs.

(2) Identify representative biosphere reserves to serve as regional training centers.

Recommended at the national level:

(3) Define the training needed by biosphere reserve managers in the 21st century and develop model training programs on such topics as how to design and implement inventory and monitoring programs in biosphere reserves, how to analyze and study sociocultural conditions, how to solve conflicts, and how to manage resources cooperatively in an ecosystem or landscape context.

Recommended at the individual reserve level:

(4) Use the reserve for onsite training and for national, regional, and local seminars.
(5) Encourage appropriate training and employment of local people and other stakeholders to enable their full participation in inventory, monitoring, and research in programs in biosphere reserves.
(6) Encourage training programs for local communities and other local agents (such as decision makers, local leaders, and agents working in production, technology transfer, and community development programs) to enable their full participation in the planning, management, and monitoring processes of biosphere reserves.

Goal IV: Implement the Biosphere Reserve Concept

Objective IV.1: Integrate the Functions of Biosphere Reserves

Recommended at the international level:

(1) Identify and publicize demonstration (model or illustrative examples of) biosphere reserves, whose experiences will be beneficial to others at the national, regional, and international levels.
(2) Give guidance/advice on the elaboration and periodic review of strategies and national action plans for biosphere reserves.
(3) Organize forums and other information exchange mechanisms for biosphere reserve managers.
(4) Prepare and disseminate information on how to develop management plans or policies for biosphere reserves.
(5) Prepare guidance on management issues at biosphere reserve sites, including, *inter alia*, methods to ensure local participation, case studies of various management options, and techniques of conflict resolution.

Recommended at the national level:

(6) Ensure that each biosphere reserve has an effective management policy or plan and an appropriate authority or mechanism to implement it.
(7) Encourage private sector initiatives to establish and maintain environmentally and socially sustainable activities in appropriate zones of biosphere reserves and in surrounding areas, to stimulate community development.
(8) Develop and periodically review strategies and national action plans for biosphere reserves; these strategies should strive for complementarity and added value of biosphere reserves, for other national instruments for conservation.
(9) Organize forums and other information exchange mechanisms for biosphere reserve managers.

Recommended at the individual reserve level:

(10) Identify and map the different zones of biosphere reserves and define their respective status.
(11) Prepare, implement, and monitor an overall management plan, or policy, that includes all of the zones of biosphere reserves.
(12) Where necessary, to preserve the core area, replan the buffer and transition zones, according to sustainable development criteria.
(13) Define and establish institutional mechanisms to manage, coordinate and integrate the reserve's programs and activities.
(14) Ensure that the local community participate in the planning and management of biosphere reserve.
(15) Encourage private sector initiatives to establish and maintain environmentally and socially sustainable activities in the reserve and surrounding areas.

Objective IV.2: Strengthen the World Network of Biosphere Reserves

Recommended at the international level:

(1) Facilitate provision of adequate resources for implementation of the Statutory Framework of the World Network of Biosphere Reserves.
(2) Facilitate the periodic review, by each country of its biosphere reserves, as required in the Statutory Framework of the World Network of Biosphere Reserves, and assist countries in taking measures to make their biosphere reserves functional.
(3) Support the functioning of the Advisory Committee for Biosphere Reserves and fully consider and utilize its recommendations and guidance.

(4) Lead the development of communication among biosphere reserves, taking into account their communication and technical capabilities, and strengthen existing and planned regional or thematic networks.
(5) Develop creative connections and partnerships with other networks of similar managed areas, and with international governmental and NGOs with goals congruent with those of biosphere reserves.
(6) Promote and facilitate twinning between biosphere reserve sites and foster transboundary reserves.
(7) Give biosphere reserves more visibility by disseminating information materials, developing communication policies, and highlighting their roles as members of the World Network of Biosphere Reserves.
(8) Wherever possible, advocate the inclusion of biosphere reserves in projects financed by bilateral and multilateral aid organizations.
(9) Mobilize private funds, from businesses, NGOs, and foundations for the benefit of biosphere reserves.
(10) Develop standards and methodologies for collecting and exchanging various types of data and assist their application across the Network of Biosphere Reserves.
(11) Monitor, assess, and follow up on the implementation of the Seville Strategy, utilizing the implementation indicators and analyze the factors that aid in attainment of the indicators, as well as those that hinder such attainment.

Recommended at the national level:

(12) Facilitate provision of adequate resources for implementation of the Statutory Framework of the World Network of Biosphere Reserves.
(13) Develop a national-level mechanism to advise and coordinate the biosphere reserves and fully consider and utilize its recommendations and guidance.
(14) Prepare an evaluation of the status and operations of each of the country's biosphere reserves, as required in the Statutory Framework, and provide appropriate resources to address any deficiencies.
(15) Develop creative connections and partnerships with other networks of similar managed areas, and with international governmental and NGOs, with goals congruent with those of the biosphere reserves.
(16) Seek opportunities for twinning between biosphere reserves and establish transboundary biosphere reserves, where appropriate.
(17) Give biosphere reserves more visibility by disseminating information materials, developing communication policies, and highlighting their roles as members of the Network.
(18) Include biosphere reserves in proposals for financing from international and bilateral funding mechanisms, including the Global Environment Facility.

(19) Mobilize private funds, from businesses, NGOs, and foundations for the benefit of biosphere reserves.
(20) Monitor, assess, and follow up on the implementation of the Seville Strategy, utilizing the implementation indicators and analyze the factors that aid in attainment of the indicators, as well as those that hinder such attainment.

Recommended at the individual reserve level:

(21) Give biosphere reserves more visibility by disseminating information materials, developing communication policies, and highlighting their roles as members of the Network.
(22) Mobilize private funds, from businesses, NGOs, and foundations for the benefit of biosphere reserves.
(23) Monitor, assess, and follow up on the implementation of the Seville Strategy, utilizing the implementation indicators and analyze the factors that aid in attainment of the indicators, as well as those that hinder such attainment.

Regreening the Metropolis: Pathways to More Ecological Cities

Keynote Address

RUTHERFORD H. PLATT

Department of Geosciences, University of Massachusetts, Amherst, Massachusetts 01003, USA

ABSTRACT: **Eighty percent of the American population now lives in metropolitan regions whose geographic extent continues to expand even as many core cities and inner-tier suburbs lose middle-class populations, jobs, and tax base. Urban sprawl and the socioeconomic polarizing of metropolitan America have been fostered by public policies including (1) federal subsidies for new infrastructure on the urban fringe; (2) tax policies that favor home ownership over rental properties; (3) local zoning codes; and (4) federal and state neglect of older urban neighborhoods. In the face of diminished access to "nature" outside of metropolitan areas, locally based efforts to protect and restore greenspaces within urban areas seek to make older communities more habitable and more "ecological." Some pathways to more ecological cities include the following: (1) the notion of *rus in urbe* ("the country in the city"); (2) the "usable outdoors"; (3) garden cities and eco-villages; (4) green buildings and green roofs; (5) urban biodiversity; (6) ecological services; and (7) space, nature, and place.**

KEYWORDS: **urban ecology; city nature; urban biodiversity; spirit of place**

INTRODUCTION

One century ago, in 1900, the urban population of the world amounted to only approximately 160 million people—one-tenth of the world's present population. Now the world is crossing the 50% urban–rural threshold with some 3.2 billion people inhabiting urban areas, a 20-fold increase since 1900. The United Nations Development Programme (UNDP) estimates that the world's urban population will swell by another 2 billion people by 2030, equal to the entire human population attained by 1930 (Rees 2003, p. 116)[1] (TABLE 1).

Address for correspondence: Rutherford H. Platt, Professor of Geography and Director of the Ecological Cities Project <www.ecologicalcities.org> University of Massachusetts, Amherst, MA 01003. Voice: 413-577-6060.
ecologicalcities@cas.umass.org

**Ann. N.Y. Acad. Sci. 1023: 49–61 (2004). © 2004 New York Academy of Sciences.
doi: 10.1196/annals.1319.020**

TABLE 1. World population growth and urbanization 1850–2030

Year	World population	Urban population	% Urban
1850	1 billion		
1900	1.6 billion	160 million	10%
1930	2 billion	400 million	20%
1960	3 billion	1 billion	30%
1975	4 billion	1.6 billion	40%
1987	5 billion	2.1 billion	43%
2000	6.1 billion	2.9 billion	47%
2030 est.	8.1 billion est.	4.9 billion est.	60%

SOURCE: Wright[22] (p. 472).

TABLE 2. Metropolitan America: 1950 and 2000

	1950	2000
U.S. population	152 million	281 million
No. of metro areas	169	>331
Metro population	84 million (55% of U.S.)	229 million (80% of U.S.)
Central city population	49 million (32% of U.S.)	85 million (30% of U.S.)
Suburban population	35 million (23% of U.S.)	141 million (50% of U.S.)
Metro % of U.S. land area (48 states)	9%	16%

NOTE: Adapted from Wright[22] (p. 242).

The most dramatic percentage increases in urban population are occurring in Asia, which is growing from 37% to 53% urban between 2000 and 2030 and in Africa from 38% to 55% urban (TABLE 1).[2] As cities worldwide struggle to provide housing, jobs, schools, and habitable environments for their swelling populations, attention inevitably turns to the veterans in this endeavor—the large postindustrial cities of Europe and North America.

Since 1950, the United States has nearly doubled in population. Metropolitan areas designated by the Bureau of the Census have increased from 169 to over 330 in number. Four-fifths of Americans now live in metropolitan areas as compared with 55% in 1950. The land area occupied by those metro areas has approximately doubled (TABLE 2).

In 1960, central cities, suburbs, and nonmetro areas each represented approximately one-third of the nation's population. Since then, suburbanites have quadrupled in number and now make up slightly more than one-half of the entire American population, which gives them consequent political and economic clout.

The rate of land urbanization has far exceeded the rate of population growth for all regions of the United States.[3] Contrary to conventional wisdom, however, the disparity between these rates is greater for the older urban regions of the Northeast and Midwest than for the newer cities of the South and West—the latter are expanding more compactly and sprawling less than the former!

As the metropolitan fringe sprawls ever further into the rural hinterland, core cities generally have declined in population and economic health while outlying fringe communities and "edge cities" have reaped the benefits of jobs and taxes from new growth.

In the absence of sound land-use planning, new development often ignores natural hazards. Property owners assert the "constitutional right" to build wherever they want, while also demanding governmental investment in flood control projects and disaster assistance to protect them from the effects of natural disasters.

Metropolitan America has become ever more polarized between relatively affluent suburban areas and declining older central cities. Most older American cities are geographically "inelastic," in the phrase of David Rusk,[4] and unable to benefit from the new residential and commercial development occurring beyond their city limits. They have lost middle class populations, jobs, and taxes, while accommodating a disproportionate share of the nation's poor, nonwhites, and elderly. As Myron Orfield[5] has observed, the residents of central cities through their federal and state taxes have contributed part of the cost of public infrastructure in urban fringe localities even as they struggle to maintain their own deteriorating schools, water and sewer services, parks, and other facilities.

Urban sprawl and the socioeconomic polarizing of American metropolitan areas result in part from public policies that favor new low-density growth on "greenfield" sites on the urban fringe over redevelopment of older communities. These policies include (1) federal and state funding for highways and other public infrastructure in newly developing areas; (2) federal and state tax policies that favor home ownership over rental properties; (3) local zoning codes that favor low-density, costly homes on large lots and taxable commercial development; and (4) neglect of older central city neighborhoods.

The low-density sprawl promoted by such policies has yielded many negative "externalities" and costs to society, including but not limited to the following:

(1) Lack of affordable housing (rental and low-cost ownership) and consequent rising numbers of homeless individuals and family groups.
(2) Increasing traffic congestion and energy waste. Since 1970, the population has grown by 40% while the number of vehicles has doubled. In Atlanta, the average commuter spent 25 hours a year stuck in traffic in 1992 and 72 hours in 2000.[6]
(3) Increasing air and noise pollution from heavy vehicles, leading to rising rates of childhood asthma and reduced property values in

neighborhoods adjoining freeways, as well as an increase in "urban heat islands."

(4) Degradation of urban watersheds, groundwater, and estuaries as well as contamination of local streams and coastal waters from septic runoff, construction site runoff, phosphorus from landscape fertilizers, combined sewer overflows, etc.

(5) Rising urban flood and earthquake losses due to encroachment on floodplains and increased flood levels and "flashiness" in local streams due to sewers and expansion of impervious surfaces in metropolitan watersheds.

(6) Loss of productive agricultural land.

(7) Loss of natural habitat, biodiversity, and contact with nature.

This presentation is largely concerned with the last of these factors, namely, the loss of "nature" and natural processes due to urbanization. No one has stated this concern more eloquently than the distinguished urban historian Lewis Mumford:

> The blind forces of urbanization, flowing along the lines of least resistance, show no aptitude for creating an urban and industrial pattern that will be self-sustaining, and self-renewing. [The modern city tends] to loosen the bonds that connect [its] inhabitants with nature and to transform, eliminate, or replace its earth-bound aspects, covering the natural site with an artificial environment that enhances the dominance of man and encourages an illusion of complete independence from nature.[7]

However, even the mighty Mumford may be faulted for perpetuating a false dichotomy, namely, between the human environment and "Nature." City and Nature have too long been viewed as mutually exclusive. The urban ecologist William E. Rees[8] refers to this as "humanity–nature apartheid" (p. 118).

In the 1950s, the conventional wisdom—for the affluent at least—was that cities are where people are, and the country is where you go on weekends and vacations to find Nature in some place bucolic or maritime. But today, even for those who can afford it, the time and cost of escaping the metropolis has grown with the spread of the metropolis itself and the growing numbers of vehicles trying to leave it. (SUVs are cleverly named to imply a "virtual outdoors"—Explorers, Expeditions, Sierras, Navigators, and Outbacks. You're not stuck in traffic on the Beltway: you're really climbing Denali!). Meanwhile, those who cannot afford to sit in traffic in their SUV—the poor, the elderly, the infirm—are sentenced to live out their lives in the metropolitan environment, come what may.

"Nature" today is presented in TV documentaries and school videos to be found mostly in the Galapagos, the Great Barrier Reef, the vanishing rainforest, and Antarctica. Most ecologists have reinforced the idea that nature is to be found only in such exotic locations, accessible only to scientists and the rich and leisured. For instance, a National Academy of Sciences volume

Biodiversity, edited by E. O. Wilson and published in 1988, devoted only 1 of 57 chapters (8 pages out of 520) to "Biodiversity in Urban Areas."[9]

A contrarian view is slowly gaining momentum, however: that "urban ecology" is not an oxymoron and "city" and "nature" are not necessarily opposites. This is reflected in a statement by landscape architect, Ann Whiston Spirn (1985):

> The city, suburbs, and the countryside must be viewed as a single, evolving system within nature, as must every individual park and building within that larger whole ... Nature in the city must be cultivated, like a garden, rather than ignored or subdued.[10]

Mumford is thus "Spirned" and the false dichotomy of city and nature is refuted. This suggests that cities and metropolitan areas, now too large to conveniently escape, must themselves be viewed as incorporating both *built* and *unbuilt* environments. Whatever roles nature plays out there in "the country" must be reestablished in "the city" because there is nowhere else to turn. And into the bargain, the urban environment will prove to be more habitable, more sustainable, more "ecological." This is the vision of "the ecological city."

ROOTS AND BRANCHES OF "ECOLOGICAL CITIES"

The term "ecological cities" is used informally in this paper—with a small *e*. As a nonecologist, I will not attempt to dazzle you with discussion of *autotrophic* versus *heterotrophic* organisms. Nor does time allow me to follow all the diverse pathways leading to ecological cities such as transportation, waste management, water resources, and alternative energy. Instead, I want to concentrate on the forms and functions of *urban open space* (green and otherwise). The following are some of the "roots and branches" of this neighborhood of "ecological cities":

- the notion of *rus in urbe*: "the country in the city"
- The city's "usable outdoors"
- Garden cities and eco-villages
- Green buildings and roofs
- Urban biodiversity
- Urban ecological services
- Urban watershed management
- Space, nature, and place

Rus in Urbe: "Country in the City"

In response to rampant industrial squalor in the first half of the 19th century, the concept of incorporating oases of "created countryside" into large cities was developed by Andrew Jackson Downing, Frederick Law Olmsted, and other visionaries. The archetypal expression of urban "designed nature" in the United States was the 1858 *Greensward Plan* for Central Park by Olmsted and Calvert Vaux.[11] Their plan artfully blended terrain, tree canopy, meadows, and water features to produce pleasing and functional outdoor settings. Essential to the experience was the location and design of walks, equestrian and carriage routes, fountains, and statuary, all deliberately scattered about to create the impression of informality and "naturalness." Central Park and its progeny—including Prospect Park in Brooklyn, Franklin in Boston, Fairmont in Philadelphia, and Golden Gate in San Francisco—did not preserve or restore nature: they *created* it. Other than immovable rock outcrops, nothing in Central Park is original. Yet today nature thrives in these and other designed parks in the form of an overarching tree canopy, abundant bird life, turtles, fish, and small mammals, all sharing with people the garden that 19th century landscape architects created and 20th century park managers revived and enhanced.

The City's "Usable Outdoors"

Another root of the ecological city lies in the long tradition of providing opportunities for urban residents to simply get outdoors. The Olmsted parks offered a range of character-building activities such as strolling, riding, and skating. For those preferring less virtuous and more exciting outdoor pastimes, there were "pleasure gardens" modeled on London's Vauxhall Gardens and Copenhagen's Tivoli. These were privately owned leisure facilities offering popular music, cafes, amusement park rides, fireworks, and other delights in a crowded, festive environment. The presence of nature was reflected mainly in flower gardens and a few shade trees, but at least they gave the urban public a reason to be "outdoors."

In the early 20th century, pleasure gardens metamorphosed into "amusement parks," often constructed by local commuter railroads to generate customers on weekends and holidays. Those, in turn, evolved into the theme parks pioneered by the Walt Disney organization and today represented by such mega-complexes as Six Flags and Epcot.

A recent study by the Trust for Public Land[12] reports that the park systems of the 50 largest cities (excluding their suburbs) amount to more than 600,000 acres and that annual visitors number as high as 25 million for Central Park and 12 million each for Lincoln Park in Chicago and Griffith Park in Los Angeles.

Today, many older city parks are being rediscovered and revisioned in light of 21st century demands and demographics; likewise, many cities, counties, and regional park authorities and environmental organizations are piecing together new kinds of parks and systems of greenspaces under such rubrics as greenways, conservation areas, areas of special significance (ecological, geological, or cultural), environmental education centers, and so on.[12] Particularly important has been the proliferation of rail trails, hiking paths, and other linear greenways that accommodate nonvehicular mobility on foot, bicycle, inline skates, and skis.

Garden Cities and Eco-Villages

The idea of eco-communities in North America may be traced back to the early utopian villages built by such religious groups as the Shakers and the Mormons in the 19th century. Another root was the "Garden City" concept proposed by the British progressive writer Ebenezer Howard at the turn of the century. Howard's garden city model sought to merge "city" and "countryside" to obtain the benefits and avoid the shortcomings of each.[13] Such communities were to be interlaced with individual gardens planted by local residents and surrounded by a "greenbelt" of working farmland. Howard's concept underlay the British New Towns and Greenbelt programs after World War II, albeit at a vastly larger scale.

Since the 1960s, thousands of *eco-villages* around the world have been established, such as Ecolonia in the Netherlands. Eco-villages take many forms and reflect diverse philosophies. They generally use sustainable practices in land-use, building design and construction, food production, energy use, water and sanitation, and protection of nature. Many also involve social interaction among residents, progressive education, health care, and spiritual growth.[14]

Gaviotas, Colombia is a renowned eco-community begun in 1971 by Paolo Lugari and publicized by the American Journalist Alan Weisman[15] in his book *Gaviotas: A Village to Reinvent the World.* The founders and citizens of Gaviotas have developed and applied new technologies such as light-air windmills, solar collectors that work in the rain, hydroponic methods for food and medicinal crop production, and ultraefficient pumps to tap deep groundwater aquifers. They also have made pioneering agricultural advances such as proving that the Caribbean Pine would thrive as a cash crop in the Colombian savanna.

Curitiba, Brazil is a much larger scale Latin American success story. Under Mayor Jaime Lerner, beginning in 1972, the city of 2.5 million overhauled its public transit and park system. According to environmental writer Bill McKibben (1999):

> Though its doubled in population in the last twenty years, it has managed to nonetheless increase its green space to the point where UNESCO says it has more per capita parkland than any city on earth. And it's a city whose residents use 25% less fossil fuel than other Brazilians … mostly because it has the best bus system on earth.[16]

In the United States, there are many co-housing ventures and a few experimental urban eco-villages. Ecocity Cleveland is sponsoring an innercity rehab project using energy efficiency, recycled materials, and offering space for gardening. A comparable project is in place in Los Angeles.

Green Buildings and Roofs

The Chicago City Hall is covered by a 20,000 square foot expanse of soil in which some 100 varieties of plants including shrubs, vines, and two trees are currently growing. The project was inspired by a visit by Chicago's mayor, Richard M. Daley, to Hamburg, Germany, where green roofs have become widespread over the past 25 years. The Chicago project is being monitored in comparison with surrounding large buildings to evaluate how the roof garden affects microclimate. Other benefits attributed to green roofs include energy efficiency, storage of storm water, aesthetic views from nearby taller buildings, and use as miniparks. Green roofs, if properly designed, should be durable and relatively self-sustaining. Except ın arid climates, irrigation is probably not required, and the diversity of plant species should gradually adapt to local conditions.

The Chicago project is the most conspicuous of hundreds of green roofs in place or under construction in the United States, which, in turn, are a part of a subset of thousands of *green buildings* being built or retrofitted (U.S. Green Building Council <www.usgbc.org>). Public buildings, especially schools, are candidates for green design, including the use of passive solar heating, large windows, green plants outside and within the structure, and water conservation. From the Pittsburgh Convention Center to the new public library building in Leverett, Massachusetts, energy-efficient and "green" designs are being increasingly used in public buildings. Incorporating such practices in private residential construction, however, is impeded by the conservatism of building codes, builders, and consumers.

Urban Biodiversity

Another Chicago innovation is the remarkable oxymoron *Chicago Wilderness*, also known as the Chicago Biodiversity Council. Chicago Wilderness is an alliance of more than 160 public and private organizations whose goal is to promote understanding and protection of biodiversity in the Greater Chicago Region. Office space and staff resources are provided by three Chicago area organizations: the Field Museum of Natural History, the Brookfield Zoo, and The Nature Conservancy. A comparable network for the New York metropolitan region is currently under discussion. Participants in those discussions include representatives from the New York Museum of Natural History, the New York and the Brooklyn Botanical Gardens, the Metropolitan Conservation Alliance, New York University, and the organizers of this conference.

In urban settings, the influence of biodiversity can be subtle but profound. Michael Klemens, director of the New York Metropolitan Conservation Alliance, puts it this way:

> Biodiversity is inextricably part of our sense of place, the very fabric of our comfort and our "being" at a particular locus. The natural world provides the texture and variety that define where we live, work and play. So defined, biodiversity is the tapestry of colors on a wooded hillside in October, the interplay between water and reeds, the chirping of crickets on a summer's night, the ebb and flow of natural systems evolving over time. And it is that natural template, the very foundation upon which our society is built, that I define as biodiversity, or more simply stated, nature.[17]

Urban Ecological Services

Nature does provide many utilitarian benefits which are threatened by urbanization. The impact of human activities on the natural world has been a scientific concern dating back to George Perkins Marsh's 1862 treatise: *Man and Nature*.[18] But cities continued to be viewed as ecologically barren until the 1980s, when Ann Whiston Spirn and others called for efforts to "cultivate" nature in urban design and redevelopment. Since then, a growing number of urban ecologists have begun to identify ecological services bestowed free of charge to human society. According to Gretchen Daily (pp. 3–4),[19] these include the following:

- Purification of air and water
- Mitigation of floods and drought
- Detoxification and decomposition of wastes
- Generation and renewal of soil and soil fertility
- Pollination of crops and natural vegetation
- Control of potential agricultural pests
- Dispersal of seeds
- Maintenance of biodiversity
- Protection from solar UV rays
- Partial stabilization of climate, including extreme temperature and wind

- Support of diverse human cultures
- Aesthetic and intellectual stimulation

Loss or degradation of ecological services often requires costly technical substitutes such as flood control projects, water treatment plants, air conditioning, and sun block. Of primary importance to urban regions are those natural functions affecting streamflow and water quality, protection and recharge of groundwater, moderation of urban "heat islands," protection of local and regional biodiversity, and aesthetic variety.

The National Science Foundation Urban Long Term Ecological Research Programs presently under way in Phoenix <http://caplter.asu.edu> and Baltimore <www.lternet.edu/sites/bes> are studying the interaction of human and natural systems and impacts on ecological services in those regions.

American Forests, a nongovernmental organization based in Washington, D.C. <www.americanforests.org>, is measuring change in the urban tree canopy for selected metropolitan areas and estimating the effects of such changes on ecological services provided by urban forest cover.

A joint project of Rutgers and the Brooklyn Botanic Garden is testing ways to establish ecological communities on closed landfills <www.i-cure.org>.

Urban Watershed Management

As urban development encroaches on local streams, watersheds, wetlands, and estuaries, numerous initiatives in the United States are trying to protect and restore urban aquatic resources. The Ecological Cities Project, under a grant from the National Science Foundation, is conducting research on comparative experience and approaches in managing small urban watersheds to restore ecological services, to provide recreation opportunities, and to promote community spirit in shared projects.

The Charles River Watershed in the Boston metro area is one of the leading examples of regional cooperation at the local watershed scale to retain wetlands, to improve stream quality, and to reduce flooding through sensible land-use planning <www.crwa.org>.

The City of New York is engaged in an ambitious watershed management program to protect the purity of its drinking water sources in the Catskill Mountains northwest of the city. This represents a bold attempt to retain the watershed's ability to provide healthy water and avoid having to build a costly filtration plant to replace this ecological service.[20]

Space, Nature, and Place

Finally, the concept of "ecological cities" reflects the importance of open spaces and ecological character in defining local and regional "sense of place." For example, certain parks and public spaces serve as icons for their cities. The Boston Common and Public Garden *are* Boston, at least in the minds of visitors. Jackson Square *is* New Orleans, the Mall *is* Washington, D.C., and Trafalgar Square *is* London. Such iconic urban spaces are not treasured for their naturalness, but rather for their centrality in the history and culture of the city, and even the nation, that they represent.

Similarly, the "sense of place" of certain regions and cities is often closely related to signature biotic species and ecosystems, such as the redwood for the Bay Area, the saguaro cactus in Tucson, the Douglas fir in the Pacific Northwest, the palmetto in South Florida, and the lowly scrub pine on Cape Cod.

Loss of signature trees or groves to disease or development may devalue real estate, impair sense of place, and cause emotional distress. Conversely, the protection of a special tree or stand of timber strengthens the communal sense of place, as with the battle to save "old growth forest" in Oregon and California or a local preservation campaign to save an ancient butternut tree in Poughkeepsie, New York (Harvey Flad, personal communication, November 18, 2002).

A related concept is *bioregionalism*, the defining of particular regions (urban or rural) in terms of distinctive ecological, economic, and cultural characteristics.[21] The Connecticut River Valley in Massachusetts, known locally as the Pioneer Valley, is a good example.

Characterizing a "bioregion" is as much an artistic and literary exercise as a scientific task. The Hudson River School artists, most notably Thomas Cole and Frederick Church, indelibly identified that valley—its ecology, economy, and culture—as a bioregion in the national consciousness. The Cape Cod National Seashore resulted from political action in the 1960s motivated by the writings of Henry David Thoreau and Henry Beston and the paintings of Edward Hopper, among others. Creation of the Indiana Dunes National Lakeshore in the 1960s was motivated by the poet Carl Sandburg, landscape architect Jens Jensen, and economist-turned-Senator Paul Douglas. Each of those three bioregions—the Hudson Valley, Cape Cod, and the Indiana Dunes—is currently being engulfed by the expansion of metropolitan New York, Boston, and Chicago, respectively. However, their distinctive natural and cultural qualities are at least partially retained through ecological preservation and restoration.

CONCLUSIONS

The unrelenting sprawl of metropolitan areas thus has a "green lining." As nature outside the metropolis recedes, nature within the urban fabric is gaining new attention. Older cities are rediscovering and reusing their parks, forest preserves, canals, and abandoned rail lines. New York's Central Park,

Washington's regional parks, Boston's "Emerald Necklace," and Chicago's lakefront parks—each a legacy of early crusades for nature within cities—now swarm with suburbanites coming *into* the city to find greenspace.

The Ecological Cities Project, based at the University of Massachusetts, Amherst <www.ecologicalcities.org>, views these disparate strands as part of an ecological tapestry of de-centralized, community-based strategies to protect and restore the unbuilt spaces within urban regions. These initiatives are conducted by informal coalitions that potentially involve all sectors of society and sometimes help to bridge the socioeconomic divides of the contemporary metropolis. They also can be an excuse for a good day's work in the outdoors!

Even as battles continue over the fate of natural areas beyond the receding urban fringe, remnants of regional ecology in our urban backyards—old growth trees, wildflower meadows, bogs, streams, prairies, dunes, deserts—are beginning to be appreciated and nurtured. The city itself is beginning to be recognized as the ultimate nature refuge.

REFERENCES

1. REES, W.E. 2003. Understanding urban ecosystems: an ecological economics perspective. *In* Understanding Urban Ecosystems: A New Frontier for Science and Education. Springer-Verlag. New York.
2. SHEEHAN, M. 2001. City Limits: Putting the Brakes on Sprawl. Worldwatch Paper No. 56. Worldwatch Institute. Washington, D.C.
3. FULTON, W., R. PENDALL, M. NGUYEN & A. HARRISON. 2001. Who Sprawls Most? How Growth Patterns Differ Across the United States. (Survey Series Monograph) The Brookings Institution. Washington, D.C.
4. RUSK, D. 1999. Inside Game, Outside Game: Winning Strategies for Saving Urban America. Brookings Institution Press. Washington, D.C.
5. ORFIELD, M. 1997. Metropolitics: A Regional Agenda for Community and Stability (rev. ed.) Brookings Institution Press. Washington. Lincoln Institute of Land Policy. Cambridge.
6. SEABROOK, J. 2002. The slow lane. The New Yorker (Sept. 2): 120–127.
7. MUMFORD, L. 1956. The natural history of urbanization. *In* Man's Role in Changing the Face of the Earth. University of Chicago Press. Chicago.
8. REES, W.E. 2003. Understanding urban ecosystems: an ecological economics Perspective. *In* Understanding Urban Ecosystems: A New Frontier for Science and Education. Springer-Verlag. New York.
9. WILSON, E.O. 1988. Biodiversity. National Academy Press. Washington, D.C.
10. SPIRN, A.W. 1989. The Granite Garden: Urban Nature and Human Design. Basic Books. New York.
11. PLATT, R.H., R.A. ROWNTREE & P.C. MUICK, EDS. 1994. The Ecological City: Preserving and Restoring Urban Biodiversity. University of Massachusetts Press. Amherst, MA.
12. HARNIK, P. 2004. The Excellent Park System: What Makes It Great, and How to Get There. *In* The Humane Metropolis: People and Nature in the 21st Century City. University of Massachusetts Press. Amherst, MA.

13. Howard, E. 1902/1965. Garden Cities of To-Morrow. MIT Press. Cambridge.
14. Beatley, 2000. Green Urbanism: Learning from European Cities. Island Press. Washington, D.C.
15. Weisman, A. 1998. Gaviotas: A Village to Reinvent the World. Chelsea Green Publishers. White River Junction, VT.
16. McKibben, B. 1999. Livable Cities: Creating a Sustainable Urban Environment. Transcript of radio interview <www.alternativeradio.com/>.
17. Klemens, M. 2003. Balancing Biodiversity and Land Use Planning. Op-Ed column in Westchester Gannett Newspapers. (August 26), p. 10.
18. Marsh, G.P. 1862/1965. Man and Nature or, Physical Geography as Modified by Human Action. Belknap Press of Harvard University Press. Cambridge.
19. Daily, G.C., Ed. 1997. Nature's Services: Societal Dependence on Natural Ecosystems. Island Press. Washington, D.C.
20. Platt, R.H., P.K. Barten & M.J. Pfeffer. 2000. A full, clean glass: managing New York City's watersheds. Environment **42:** 8–19.
21. Foster C.H.W. 2002. Reviving Environmental Regionalism Land Lines (Newsletter of the Lincoln Institute of Land Policy), pp. 7–10. The Institute. Cambridge.
22. Wright, J.W., Ed. 2003. The New York Times Almanac 2003. Penguin Reference. New York.

Sustainable Cities Programme:

A Joint UN-HABITAT–UNEP Facility on the Urban Environment with Participation of the Dutch Government

Presented by AXUMITE GEBRE-EGZIABHER

UN-HABITAT, New York, New York 10017, USA

ABSTRACT: The fundamental objective of the Sustainable Cities Programme is to promote environmentally sustainable local development to more fully realize the vital contributions that urban areas make to over-all social and economic development by: (1) enhancing efficiency in the use of local environmental resources, reducing environmental risks, and strengthening application of environmental conventions and agreements with growing regard to the Climate Change Protocol; (2) reducing poverty by promoting more equitable access to resources and environmental services; (3) mobilizing and strengthening local capacities to plan, co-ordinate, and manage sustainable local development in partnership; and (4) combining the complementary strengths of UN-HABITAT, UNEP, and other partners in support of Agenda 21, and the Habitat Agenda sustainable development commitments including improved local environmental governance.

KEYWORDS: Sustainable Cities Programme (SCP); UN-HABITAT; UNEP; environmental planning and management (EPM); stakeholder participation; city consultation; urban governance; environment; local development; capacity building; institutionalization; sustainable urbanization

INTRODUCTION

Background

Cities worldwide are faced with the challenge of achieving sustainable development in the overall context of poverty reduction and good urban

Addresses for correspondence: Mr. Ole Lyse, Coordinator, Susatinable Cities Programme, UN-HABITAT, P.O. Box 30030, Nairobi, Kenya. Voice: 254-20-623715.
scp@unhabitat.org

Dr. Axumite Gebre-Egziabher, Director, UN–HABITAT, New York Office, 2 United Nations Plaza, Room DC2-950, 9th floor, New York, NY 10017. Voice: 212-963-4200.
habitatny@un.org

Ann. N.Y. Acad. Sci. 1023: 62–79 (2004).
doi: 10.1196/annals.1319.016

FIGURE 1. Cities participating in the Sustainable Cities Programme.

governance. The Sustainable Cities Programme (SCP), a joint initiative of UN-HABITAT and UNEP, provides a well-proven model process to help cities respond to this challenge. Progressively developed through the experiences gained in more than 40 demonstration cities during the last 10 years, the SCP focuses on strengthening local capacities for environmental planning and management (EPM). It directly helps local authorities and their partners to achieve a well-managed urban environment as part of a sustainable urban development process founded on broad-based stakeholder participation which includes and empowers all city dwellers.[a] The SCP process is also guided by the principle that the environment is not an end in itself, not something to be merely "protected" from development; instead, the environment is viewed as a resource to be carefully managed on a sustainable basis for the betterment of humankind's living environment. (For a fuller description of the SCP operational process, and of the EPM approach used by the SCP, see CONCEPT AND PROCESS: THE EPM APPROACH AND THE SCP PROCESSES and FIG. 1.)

As a joint UN-HABITAT/UNEP capacity-building and institutional-strengthening facility, the SCP promotes and supports good environmental governance at all levels in all regions of the world:

- Locally, by supporting partners in more than 40 cities in 26 countries to apply a proven four-stage cross-sectoral and participatory EPM process

[a]The SCP is implemented through a series of linked operational activities which demonstrate in practice new ways of managing urban and environmental development and thus progressively develop local capabilities; the EPM approach is a logical framework, systematized through the experience of the SCP, which underlies the whole process (see also THE EPM APPROACH AND THE SCP PROCESSES and FIG. 1).

(FIG. 1). This process has increasingly placed environmental concerns at the very forefront of decision making in the context of sustainable urban development through improved partner understanding of the complexities of development–environment interactions. The SCP/EPM process provides a particularly appropriate framework for implementing informal sector development strategies and improving basic urban services delivery mechanisms to help alleviate poverty, with most cities targeting support to marginalized groups and women.

- Nationally, by supporting national partners (currently in 9 countries) to replicate local-level best practices onto a national scale and to integrate lessons of experience into national policy and legal frameworks.
- Regionally, by facilitating city-to-city exchanges and technical cooperation among developing countries through partner networks and regional conferences.
- Globally, by combining the complementary strengths of the two agencies at both local and global levels in applying specialized expertise and synthesizing experiences for awareness building, policy formulation, and national replication; acting as secretariat and organizer to the global SCP/LA21 Environment Meeting, the Programme also supports the regional dissemination of knowledge and global normative debate.

In a global perspective, the Programme applies Agenda 21 principles to support implementation of the Habitat Agenda while building local capacities to help apply UNEP's environmental agreements and global topics at the local and national levels, activities that have been strengthened after the integration of UN-HABITAT's Localising Agenda 21 Programme into the Sustainable Cities Programme.

Urban Development, the Environment, and Poverty Reduction: Global Mandate of the SCP

The 21st century is undoubtedly the "city millennium": half of the world's six billion people live in cities today, and it is expected that two billion more people will be added to the cities of the developing world over the next 25 years. This urbanization process, though stimulated by and necessary for economic development, also has resulted in a massive increase in "urbanization of poverty," which already numbers at least one billion persons.[b]

It is, however, well recognized that cities make a vital contribution to national (and global) social and economic development: (1) they are essential

[b]The United Nations Millennium Declaration, 17th Session, New York, September 20–22, 2000.

engines of economic and social advancement; (2) they absorb two-thirds or more of the population growth in developing countries; (3) they offer economies of scale in the provision of jobs, housing, and services and generate the majority of the Gross National Product (even in countries where most people are engaged in agriculture). However, if not properly managed, urbanization can bring serious environmental and social problems, particularly for the poor. Environmental degradation can also prevent the city's positive contributions from being realized, thus threatening the sustainability of development achievements.

Thus, it will be increasingly necessary to find better ways of balancing the needs and pressures of urban growth and change with the opportunities and constraints of the local environmental resource base. At the same time, as the poor, marginalized groups, and especially women and children, are disproportionately affected by environmental degradation, greater efforts are necessary to promote more equitable access to urban and environmental services, along with more engagement and inclusiveness in urban governance, as well as enhanced employment opportunities. In many countries infrastructure provision has undergone sector reforms leading to public–private partnerships, which has attracted urgently required capital and management for improvements and expansions. The challenge for municipal authorities in this case is to put in place effective regulatory mechanisms and measures to oversee the efficient and equitable provision of increasingly privatized services, especially to balance the need for full cost recovery and the requirement to provide subsidies to the urban poor to not to further marginalize already disadvantaged groups.

Cities, Environmental Concerns, and Current United Nations Support

It is in the area of urban environment that the mandates of UN-HABITAT and UNEP coincide, and in which their scientific, technical, and financial resources are uniquely complementary. The extensive operational experience of UN-HABITAT in project-level local development and its accumulated expertise in practical urban management appropriately combine with the scientific and technical strengths of UNEP with its data banks, international networks, global accords, and expertise in all aspects of the environment. As a result, the SCP became a *joint* UN-HABITAT/UNEP capacity-building and institutional strengthening facility in January 1996.

Another major complement is between UN-HABITAT's and UNEP's current global campaigns for developing urban governance and secure tenure norms and commitments on environmental agreements and global topics, which both seek to encourage local responses and applications, and also their reflection in more sustainable development approaches in national policies. To promote this, there is a need to establish mechanisms and capacities at the local level to support a two-way interaction including both priority issues, means and opportunities, and on adaptation and application.

In 2000 and 2001, respectively, the United Nations Millennium Declaration[c] and the Declaration on Cities and Other Human Settlements in the New Millennium[d] further reinforced the international community's commitment for sustainable urban development and poverty reduction:

(1) Reaffirming support for Agenda 21 and the Kyoto Protocol, while resolving to stop the unsustainable exploitation of water resources by developing water management strategies at the regional, national, and local levels which promote equitable access and adequate supplies; and

(2) Resolving to halve, by 2015, the proportion of people without sustainable access to safe drinking water; and by 2020 to have achieved a significant improvement in the lives of at least 100 million slum dwellers:

- Reconfirming that success depends on the promotion of good (environmental) governance through strong public, private, and popular sector partnerships.
- Recognizing the need for integrated and participatory approaches to urban environmental planning and management and committing to intensifying efforts for improving sustainable environmental planning and management practices and to integrate the local Agenda 21 process in the Global Plan of Action for the implementation of the Habitat Agenda.
- Facilitating the provision of basic infrastructure and urban services, including adequate sanitation, waste management, and sustainable transport.

Other Global Mandates

The basic concept and thrust of the SCP reflects the United Nations mandate on sustainable development, responding to the 1992 Earth Summit which specifically cited the SCP and recommended that its role be strengthened as an interagency vehicle for implementing Agenda 21 at the city level. The creation of the SCP as a joint facility of UN-HABITAT and UNEP responded to repeated calls of the Commission on Human Settlements[e] and the Governing Council of UNEP for more effective collaboration between the two Nairobi-based agencies, and specifically to Resolution CHS 15/8 and

[c]The United Nations Millennium Declaration, 17th Session, New York, September 20–22, 2000.

[d]Declaration on Cities and Other Human Settlements in the New Millennium, Special Session of the General Assembly (Istanbul +5), New York, June 6–8, 2001.

[e]The Commission on Human Settlements was transformed into the Governing Council of UN-HABITAT by the General Assembly as of 01 January 2002.

Decision GC 18/15 on UN-HABITAT/UNEP cooperation in the urban environment, as emphasized through resolution CHS 17/22 of the 1999 Commission on Human Settlements meeting. The thrust of the SCP represents an operational response to the theme of the 1996 City Summit: "sustainable human settlements in an urbanizing world," with the SCP to various degrees supporting the six key commitments of the Habitat Agenda: environmental management, social development and poverty eradication, economic development, shelter, governance, and international cooperation.

The SCP provides core environmental governance inputs to UN-HABITAT's Global Urban Governance Campaign for poverty alleviation, often in support of and complementary to respective national Poverty Reduction Strategy Papers and policies. By strengthening program support at the regional and national levels, the new phase two ensured that the SCP partners will play an increasingly important role in achieving the Millennium Development Goals for poverty reduction, particularly contributing to the target of improving the lives of 100 million slum dwellers by 2020.

UN-HABITAT's normative and operational responsibilities are also well reflected in the Type 2 outcomes of the 2002 concluded World Summit on Sustainable Development (WSSD), specifically in its partnership implementation commitments. The Coalition for Sustainable Urbanisation, which had its origins in the first World Urban Forum (WUF) held in Nairobi the same year, was formally announced in a WSSD plenary session and launched by UN-Habitat together with some 40 Habitat Agenda partners. The coalition is a coherent cluster of 11 mutually supportive initiatives linked by the common conceptual framework of "sustainable urbanization." Three of them are partnerships spearhcaded by the SCP through its new phase two support: Demonstrating Local Environmental Planning and Management, National Capacities for Up-scaling Local Agenda 21 Demonstrations, and Local Capacities for Global Agendas. In addition to UN-HABITAT and the Netherlands Government, main supporting partners for these partnerships include UNEP, UNDP, ILO, WACLAC, IULA, and the governments of Japan and Belgium.

CONCEPT AND PROCESS

The EPM Approach and the SCP Processes

The urban EPM approach recognizes that sustainable development depends on the management of the city's environmental resource base including the impact of development on these resources (in terms of depletion and of contributing to hazards, risks, and potential disasters). It is crucial to sustainable urban development that all decision makers have a clear understanding and

TABLE 1. Ways that EPM principles are achieved through the corresponding SCP process

EPM concept and approach	SCP operational process/stages
Improve environmental information and technical expertise	Identify stakeholders, especially those directly affected and those with interest, information, and expertise; clarify issues; produce city environmental profile
Improve decision-making and policy/strategy formulation	Hold city consultation; review issues and policy options, build consensus; set priorities; involve stakeholders; undertake issue consultations
Improve local actors policy implementation capacities	Issue-specific working groups and technical support; project development; application of available instruments; mobilization of resources; implementing urban services and demonstration projects; replication of EPM activities
Strengthen institutional arrangements and local EPM capacities	Strengthen systemwide and cross-sectoral capacities for EPM; make broad-based participatory approaches routine; clarify and strengthen city development planning and coordination functions
Improve local actors ability for managing the process of change	Inter-Agency cooperation and coordination at city level; networking, regional and global exchange

acceptance of this two-way relationship between environment and development. In short, the challenge is to make use of environmental resources in a sustainable way for the sake of firmly based and lasting development, in turn contributing to improving living conditions particularly for the urban poor. Urban environmental problems are complex, multidimensional, cross-sectoral, interactive, and dynamic, as well as often poorly understood, and with environmental opportunities and constraints not always accepted by local decision makers.

TABLE 1 indicates how EPM principles are achieved through the corresponding SCP process. Through replication, scaling-up, and development of administrative and policy changes, the approach and elements of EPM as operationalized through SCP initiatives, become widely understood, accepted, and routinely applied to decision making in urban management. Consistent internalization and mainstreaming of the EPM process activities within the existing institutional framework enables SCP processes to become rooted through practical demonstration on real issues, and thus over time become widely accepted new practice. This leads to the consolidation of participatory and inclusive approaches, better governance, and the strengthening of system-wide capacities, and the improvement of cross-sectoral and interagency coordination.

Although each city initiative develops independently in response to local needs, all demonstrations are designed to generate certain outputs such as:

- Development planning information—an environmental profile and a GIS-based environmental management information system.
- A strategic development planning framework for the municipality.
- Priority investment packages and technical assistance projects.
- Capacity development programs.
- Stakeholder-based review mechanisms for evaluating the impact of interventions, documenting learning experiences, and sharing lessons learned.

Typical development issues dealt with at the municipal level include water resource and water supply management, environmental health risks, and solid and liquid waste management/on-site sanitation, air pollution and urban transport, drainage and flooding, industrial risks, informal sector activities, and land-use management in the context of open space/urban agriculture, tourism and coastal area resource management, and mining.

GOALS

Development Objective and Target Groups

The fundamental objective of the SCP is to promote environmentally sustainable local development and more fully realize the vital (and growing) contributions that human settlements make to overall social and economic development by:

- Enhancing efficiency in the use of local environmental resources, reducing environmental risks, and strengthening application of environmental conventions and agreements for instance with regard to the climate change protocol.
- Reducing poverty by promoting more equitable access to environmental resources and services; and by supporting sustainable local economic development, in support of and complementary to national policies such as Poverty Reduction Strategy Papers.
- Mobilizing and strengthening local capacities to plan, coordinate, and manage sustainable local development in partnership with public, private, and community sectors.
- Combining the complementary strengths of UN-HABITAT, UNEP, and other partners in supporting implementation of the sustainable development commitments of Agenda 21 and the Habitat Agenda, including improved local environmental governance.

The overall purpose of this program is to enable municipal authorities to better address high-priority local environmental issues and to better achieve sustainable urbanization by providing them and their partners with an improved EPM capacity and policy application processes. The broader purpose is to reduce poverty by more efficiently and equitably managing the use of environmental resources and the control of hazards and by promoting employment through improved environmental services delivery.

The phase two envisaged major results at municipal level are strategic development planning frameworks, including sector investment strategies for improved basic urban services, based on replication of local environmental improvement initiatives. Municipal EPM capacity-building activities targeting the full range of local actors will enable them to produce such frameworks through a broad-based participatory process ensuring common development visions and commitment for implementation, including an agreed upon replication mechanism.

Target Groups

Local communities in participating cities are the program's ultimate target group. They are the hundreds of millions of persons living in the cities and towns of developing countries, many of whom belong to marginalized low-income groups in crowded and poorly or nonserviced townships and periurban areas. The urban poor typically make up 25 to 60% of the population in the citities in most developing countries, and they suffer more from environmental degradation than any other group. They will benefit through slum upgrading initiatives including improved environmental and public health conditions, improved basic urban services, generation of employment, and more equitable socioeconomic development in the places where they live and work.

All citizens of participating cities, as individuals and households, as local private sector businesses, and in their social and economic groupings, will also benefit from the participatory decision-making process which, when institutionalized, enhances their influence and leads to more responsive and transparent urban governance on priorities for sustainable development.

Municipal authorities and their partners in the public, private, and community sectors in developing countries are the program's immediate target group. Through the Programme, they will increase their capacities and know-how for urban environmental planning and management including strategies to leverage resources at the local, national, and subregional level and support through international networking linkages and the UN system.

Local, national, and subregional anchoring institutions for research, capacity-building, and expertise are particularly benefiting from the thrust of the new phase of SCP, building on and expanding cooperation with learning

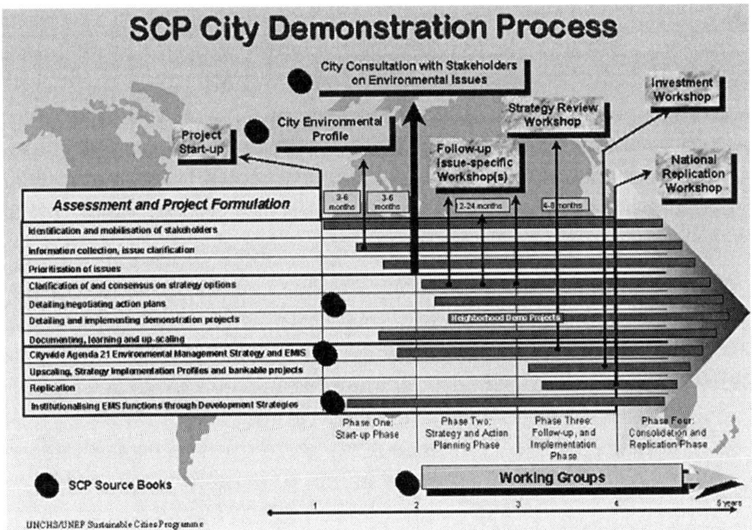

FIGURE 2. The SCP City demonstration process.

institutions in the area of EPM and urban development planning; the program will also link them with new international partner institutions (IHS, IRC, IHE in the Netherlands) to add further specialized expertise. This will enable local institutions to better meet the growing demand for local-level capacity development in both urban environmental planning and management and in basic urban service delivery. They will benefit as well from the mutual learning synergies and networks at global SCP meetings and related urban fora.

The Present Situation: Summary of Achievements

Since its launch in 1991, the SCP has grown from a modest UN-HABITAT initiative to a global multiagency program leveraging in the range of $25 million USD at different levels. It has built partnerships at the local level with national and city governments, UNDP, the World Bank, ILO and bilaterals; and at the global level the SCP has been supported by UN-HABITAT, UNEP, Denmark, the Netherlands, Japan, Italy, France, and the United Kingdom. The program's well-established and flexible institutional framework at the local level also has facilitated operational collaboration with several other major international programs, including ICLEI, MELISSA, WHO Healthy Cities, ILO-ASIST, UNDP-LIFE and UNDP-PPPUE, UNEP-APELL, UNEP-IETC/CP, and GRID-Arendal.

Part of this collaborative reality derives from SCP's global mandate to promote, support, and strengthen urban environmental governance at the local, national, regional, and global levels:

Locally, the SCP brings together all the key stakeholders in a commitment to (1) clarify and identify key environment issues of mutual concern; (2) agree upon joint strategies and action plans; (3) implement these through public/private and popular sector demonstration project partnerships and, by synthesizing lessons of experience to (4) develop citywide Agenda 21 with supporting investment programs and technical cooperation packages addressing the special needs of the poor (FIG. 2).

Nationally, SCP activities are conducted through local-authority support units including national governments, their public, private, and popular sector partners (including local associations of local government and local training support institutions), supported by local and international technical advisors to integrate lessons of experience from local-level demonstrations into national environmental and poverty-alleviation policies and legal frameworks. By these means the widespread replication of best practices can be promoted in secondary cities nationally.

Subregionally, SCP activities are based on city and national level SCP experiences, which aim to (1) facilitate the systematic collection, assessment, sharing, and dissemination of information; (2) share operational lessons of experience in local environmental management and promote capacity development of scientific and technical resources with urban institutions; and (3) create joint EPM training, synthesizing lessons learned into curricula development, expertise and support functions, and networking for sustained EPM technical support to the local and national levels.

Globally, SCP activities promote and catalyze capacities at all levels for local, national, and regional activities in local environmental management, responding to the needs and building on the lessons of local demonstrations. It is here that the complementary strengths of UN-HABITAT and UNEP are applied through their specialized expertise, the packaging of pragmatic solutions through training materials, and the synthesis of experiences for awareness building, upscaling, national and regional replication, and normative debate.

The first phase of the SCP, particularly supported by the Netherlands and UNEP since 1995, recognized the need to leverage SCP's special local-global-local linkages by synthesizing local EPM knowledge and experiences to make global strategies more responsive to local needs and conversely to help implement environmental topics of global concerns at the local level. It furthermore strengthened SCP global level capacity to document, analyze, systematize, and widely disseminate the lessons of experience from the local level through national replications and regional/global conferences. The principal achievements are:

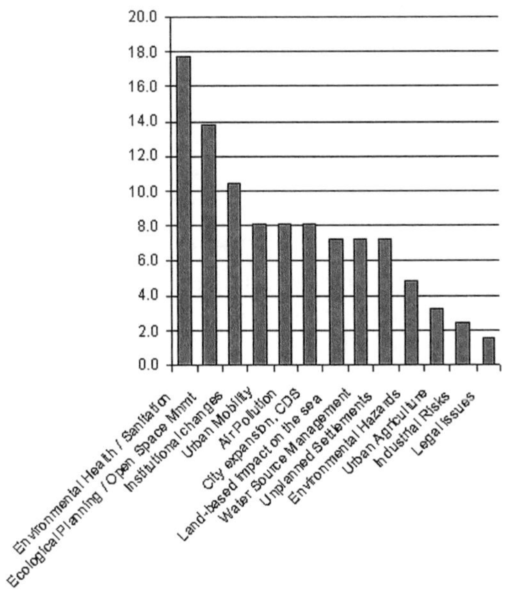

FIGURE 3. SCP/LA21 partner cities: priority issues (in %).

- Development of a systematic documentation process at the local level based upon stakeholder monitoring and local self-evaluation systems, to record and consolidate EPM process experiences and synthesize the lessons learned from SCP demonstrations in ~25 partner cities (FIG. 3). Full documentation was completed in 12 cities: Dar-es-Salaam (Tanzania), Ismailia (Egypt), Lusaka (Zambia), Ibadan (Nigeria), Accra (Ghana), Dakar (Senegal), Shenyang and Wuhan (China), Lipa, Tagbilaran, and Cagayan de Oro (Philippines), and Chennai (India). This formed the basis for production of five SCP process sourcebooks: (1) Environmental Profile; (2) Organizing, Conducting and Reporting a City Consultation; (3) Establishing and Supporting Working Groups; (4) Strategies and Action Planning; and (5) Institutionalizing the EPM Process. These materials have been further developed into an EPM training module to be used as a basis for the future development of urban planning and management curricula in the subregional and national EPM capacity-building institutions. At the same time, four EPM topic-specific handbooks and toolkits were developed: (1) Environmental Management Information Systems, (2) Air Quality Management, (3) Gender Responsive EPM, and (4) Measuring Progress—an Indicators Tool. These were based on local experience and discussed and validated at global and regional conferences and workshops and now form part of the proposed support services to be provided by subregional and national EPM capacity-building institutions.

- Application of the handbooks and toolkits to strengthen EPM process implementation, reduce dependence on direct SCP technical support at the local level, and "leverage" widened impact through their application by "local authority support units" when implementing national replication strategies.
- The use of catalytic funds to establish both the SCP Global Meeting Network of cities and national partners, as well as the Urban Environment Forum (UEF), which increased from 40 cities and 20 program partners in 1996 to 100+ cities and 50+ programs/agencies in its last meeting in 2000 (now incorporated in WUF). Meetings of these fora, as well as intervening subregional thematic meetings, were used to systematically capture local lessons of experience in EPM, using the SCP/EPM process as a common analytical framework. UEF meetings were especially useful to continue the dialogue on "the urban environmental governance agenda" and global environmental topics, exploring new opportunities for further program and agency collaboration.
- The development of a knowledge management and outreach information service in support of the above global, regional, and national networks through establishment of two major local-level networks: SCP partners (with 30+ cities regularly interacting) and the UEF (with 100+ cities and 50+ program and agency partners).
- The SCP and partners Web sites developed and regularly updated, supported by the SCP Newsletter, Summary Publications, SCP Working Papers, 4 SCP/UEF meetings reports, 16 city posters, 9 videos, and 3 major exhibitions per year; all backed by an information response service.

International agency support therefore was critical in strengthening SCP's local-global-local linkages in several different ways: (1) facilitating the production and dissemination of practical handbooks, toolkits, and training materials to strengthen application of the EPM process at the local level and replicate best practices nationally; (2) establishing nuclei of regional and national networks for the further upscaled dissemination of EPM experiences; and (3) consolidating SCP's knowledge management and information exchange, including contributions to UN-HABITAT's normative functions under its Global Urban Governance Campaign. In short, the phase one funding support, especially from the Netherlands, Denmark, and Japan, allowed the SCP to further increase its level of support to cities, further consolidating SCP's position as one of the major United Nations programs to build urban environmental governance capacities, and established solid foundations for formulating phase two.

Lessons Learned: Challenges and Emerging Opportunities to Be Addressed

The SCP applies a pragmatic learning-by-doing approach, constantly refining and further developing its EPM process framework and toolkits in response to local partner applications and emerging needs. An integral part of this approach has been the synthesis of a succession of built-in and independent project evaluations over the past 5 to 6 years, to take stock of experiences and learn from positive results, difficulties and constraints, to better respond to challenges and opportunities. The key observations of these evaluations in terms of challenges can be summarized as follows:

Demo Project Upscaling, Investment Packaging, and Policy Application

The growing number of national replications are testimony to the applicability of the SCP/EPM approach in different local and national contexts, a point emphasized as well by independent evaluations. However, those same evaluations have also emphasized the need to:

- Consolidate the demo project approach.
- Deepen its impact by targeting disadvantaged people through pro-poor and gender-responsive action plans, directly linking these to, and contributing to, local, national, and internationally supported poverty alleviation strategies.
- Design the demo project approach as the first step in a deliberate upscaling process which will facilitate and support the development of citywide investment packages in partnership with private investors and development banks (national, regional, and international).
- Strengthen the local–national connections so that properly documented lessons of experience more systematically influence national environmental and poverty reduction policy dialogues and legislative reforms, including adaptation of relevant international environmental conventions and agreements.

Meeting the Growing Demand, Sustaining and Institutionalizing the EPM Service

Meanwhile, the global SCP core team has reached the limit of its capacity to provide direct local technical assistance in response to the constant increase of city and national requests for support. There is an urgent need therefore to build the institutional framework for sustained EPM support at all levels, strengthening mutually reinforcing capacity-building infrastructure from the global level through regional "anchor" and national capacity-building institutions to the local action level to:

- Consolidate and sustain SCP direct support activities;
- More efficiently respond to new requests;
- Maximize application of the SCP handbooks, toolkits, and training materials;
- Strengthen local and national EPM capacity-building, advocacy, and implementation processes that better target the urban poor and marginalized groups;
- Better coordinate regional EPM networking and capacity-building support;
- Collaborate to promote the implementation of environmental conventions and agreements at the regional level; and
- Improve documentation of local experiences, feeding lessons into national policies as well as global normative processes.

Consolidating and Institutionalizing SCP's Normative Functions

The first phase was instrumental in expanding the application of EPM principles through a documentation and wider dissemination of EPM and SCP tools and national replications. It initiated regional and national networks and developed the foundations for consistent knowledge management and information exchange functions. Building on this work, opportunities exist in phase two to:

- Leverage application of local EPM experiences through new sourcebooks, handbooks, and toolkits, especially those that strengthen implementation, synthesize lessons, and provide guidelines from issue-specific strategies which have a pro-poor focus, as well as new generic tools in support of implementing UNEP's emerging urban environmental strategy;
- Support UNEP in the development (and subsequent implementation) of its new urban environment policy, including continued support at the local level to achieve national compliance with environmental agreements and global topics, especially the involvement of the megacities in the climate debate;
- Consolidate awareness building and dissemination processes at all levels;
- Strengthen networking modalities and advocacy mechanisms for EPM policy and normative debate, fully utilizing UN-HABITAT/UNEP synergies;
- Institutionalize SCP's global activities under UN-HABITAT's Global Urban Governance Campaign;

- Help wider dissemination and application of the publication "Tools to Support Participatory Urban Decision Making," which is a toolkit building on a multitude of program and city experiences.

Expected End of Program Results

- The regional anchoring and national capacity-building institutional framework for sustained EPM support to cities will be established and operational, involving at least 10 institutions globally. These supporting partners will be regularly delivering direct local technical support, monitoring progress, documenting experiences, synthesizing lessons, customizing and developing new management tools, and disseminating EPM experiences through strengthened networks. In addition, selected subregional and national capacity development "centers of excellence" will have integrated the EPM process, and lessons and experiences into their EPM curricula.
- National replications of local demonstration initiatives will be under way as a routine in 12 countries, built into the regional and national level support functions anchored upon local-authority support units including a partnership of national ministry(ies), local government associations, the national capacity-building institution, and the local demonstration initiative. Lessons learned will have been integrated into national policy and legislative frameworks and increasingly will be strengthening national monitoring systems for compliance with signed global conventions and agreements.
- In addition to replications, 20 new main cities will be benefiting from implementing the EPM process as a routine, supported by their national partners.
- The SCP process will have been further strengthened from more operational lessons and field applications, particularly the implementation of action plans through (pro-poor) demonstration projects addressing especially basic urban environmental services and sustainable urban mobility.
- Concurrently, the management tools developed under the first phase will have been customized as part of key national replication strategies and will be systematically and routinely used by the national capacity-building partners to strengthen all aspects of EPM process implementation.
- At least three new management tools will have been produced and will be used routinely in new cities to strengthen implementation mechanisms and disseminate common strategies in basic environmental service delivery and sustainable urban mobility and EPM poverty-alleviation strategies.

- Demonstration projects will have become the nucleus of an upscaling process into citywide investment packages, mobilizing local, national, and international resources through routine linkages to local, national, and international social development and poverty-reduction strategies, including partnerships with regional development banks.
- The knowledge management framework established under the first phase will have been strengthened and be operating as a routine, feeding documented experiences into the normative operations of both UN-HABITAT and UNEP, especially the proposed Declaration of Norms under UN-HABITAT's Global Campaign for Urban Governance, while also supporting UNEP's Division of Environmental Conventions in building global understanding of the role of cities in their implementation, and the Division of Policy Development and Law in its urban environment policy.
- Existing partnerships will have been strengthened, with new ones created at both the global and regional levels (especially when developing the new sourcebooks).
- The SCP/LA21 global core team will be routinely supporting the Global Urban Governance Campaign of UN-HABITAT's Urban Development Branch, in the Global Division.

THE ROLE OF THE SCP IN INTERNATIONAL COOPERATION

Collaboration and coordination with other international efforts in the area of local environmental management/urban development has from the outset in 1991/92 been a clear strategy of the SCP. The envisaged strong international partner focus on environmental governance programs is a natural continuation which is responding well to international priorities and trends.

In the effort to improve their local environments, local authorities and their partners are supported by a wide range of international programs, implemented by United Nations agencies, other multilateral development organizations, bilateral agencies, and international nongovernmental organizations. Coming from different institutional and political backgrounds, these various programs naturally have different resources, scope of work, and orientation. Some programs work only in specific geographical areas, others worldwide; some focus on particular issues, others on special sectors; some are concerned with technology, others with planning, technical cooperation, information exchange, or research.

Overall, special efforts are in hand to continue to strengthen collaboration between the SCP and the Urban Management Programme (UMP), with the former mainstreaming its lessons of experience through UMP anchor institution support to cities that request environmental governance inputs, and with agreements in principle that (wherever possible) SCP channels its capacity-building and institutional-strengthening inputs to the same anchoring and national capacity-building institutions, aiming to maximize leverage, impact, and long-term sustainability. Wherever possible, SCP will combine with UMP regional anchoring and national capacity-building institutions (examples include All India Institute of Local Self-Government, Sri Lanka Institute of Local Government, Sevanatha [Sri Lanka] and the Thailand Environment Institute, IAGU [Senegal] and also CEDARE in Egypt).

The SCP is further developing close joint efforts with the Cities Alliance, for example, partnering with the World Bank and Canada in support of the League of Cities' City Development Strategy (CDS) activities in the Philippines, where the three (SCP-supported) Local-Environmental Planning and Management Project demonstration cities have teamed with the seven CDS pilot cities to upscale and replicate their experiences to 30 other cities throughout the country, with a special emphasis on developing urban poverty reduction strategies. In Africa, SCP support and experiences also provide the foundations for UN-HABITAT's Regional Office for Africa and Arab States' support together with the World Bank, to partners implementing the Cities Alliance/CDS in Madagascar, Egypt, and Nigeria.

The UNESCO Biosphere Reserve Concept as a Tool for Urban Sustainability

The CUBES Cape Town Case Study

R. STANVLIET,[a] J. JACKSON,[b] G. DAVIS,[c] C. DE SWARDT,[d] J. MOKHOELE,[e] Q. THOM,[f] AND B. D. LANE[g]

[a]*CUBES Cape Town, Western Cape Nature Conservation Board, Stellenbosch 7599, South Africa*

[b]*City of Cape Town Environmental Management, Vlaeberg 8018, South Africa*

[c]*National Botanical Institute Urban Conservation Unit, Claremont 7735, South Africa*

[d]*University of the Western Cape, School of Government, Bellville 7535, South Africa*

[e]*City of Cape Town Health Department, Bellville 7535, South Africa*

[f]*Table Mountain National Park, Constantia 7848, South Africa*

[g]*CUBES, Columbia University Earth Institute, New York, New York 10027, USA*

ABSTRACT: The Cape Town Case Study (CTCS) was a multi-institutional collaborative project initiated by CUBES, a knowledge networking initiative of UNESCO's Ecological Sciences Division and the Earth Institute at Columbia University. Cape Town was selected as a CUBES site on the basis of its high biological and cultural significance, together with its demonstrated leadership in promoting urban sustainability. The CTCS was conducted by the Cape Town Urban Biosphere Group, a cross-disciplinary group of specialists drawn from national, provincial, municipal, and civil society institutions, mandated to examine the potential value of the UNESCO Biosphere Reserve concept as a tool for environmental management, social inclusion, and poverty alleviation in Cape Town. This article provides a contextualization of the CTCS and its collaborative process. It also reviews the biosphere reserve concept relative to urban sustainability objectives and proposes a more functional application of that concept in an urban context. A detailed analysis of key initiatives at the interface of conservation and poverty alleviation is provided in table format. Drawing on an examination of successful sustainability initiatives in Cape Town, specific recommendations are made for future application of the biosphere reserve concept in an urban context,

Address for correspondence: R. Stanvliet, CUBES Cape Town, Western Cape Nature Conservation Board, Private Bag X5014, Stellenbosch 7599, South Africa. Voice: +27-21-866-8020; fax: +27-21-866-1523.

stanr@cncjnk.wcape.gov.za

Ann. N.Y. Acad. Sci. 1023: 80–104 (2004).
doi: 10.1196/annals.1319.003

as well as a model by which urban areas might affiliate with the UNESCO World Network of Biosphere Reserves, and criteria for such affiliation.

KEYWORDS: **Cape Town Case Study (CTCS); biosphere reserve**

INTRODUCTION

Cape Town, the capital city of the Western Cape Province, one of the nine provinces of South Africa, is situated in the south westernmost corner of the African continent (FIG. 1). The city and surroundings feature spectacular biodiversity that is of high conservation value. Indeed, Cape Town is situated within the Cape Floral Kingdom, the smallest and most diverse of the six floral kingdoms of the world, with the highest known diversity of plant species in the world, namely, 1,300 species per 10,000 m^2. Moreover, Cape Town houses one of the highest presences of threatened and/or endemic taxa, and it is one of the centers of endemism within the Cape Floral Kingdom. In Cape Town, the challenge of urban development and environmental conservation is aggravated by the rapid urban sprawl of extremely impoverished communities, as well as extreme development pressures, with resultant clearance and denudation of large areas of natural vegetation. Because dwindling biodiversity, increasing poverty, and exponential expansion in social problems are among the most serious issues facing Cape Town, it is important that these are managed coherently.

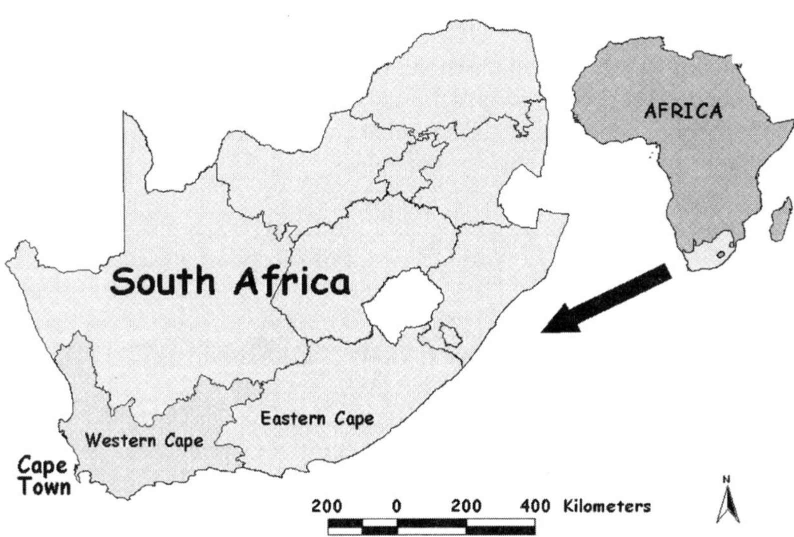

FIGURE 1. Cape Town in the regional setting.

Cape Town is not alone. Around the world, large urban centers are facing coexisting and interrelated pressures of environmental degradation and increasing populations. In response, many cities have designed and implemented policies and programs related to the improvement of environmental management and human development. In working toward urban sustainability, the management authorities of a city can adopt policies developed and supported by a wide range of international programs and organizations, including inter alia Local Agenda 21,[1] the UN Habitat Sustainable Cities Programme,[2] Sustainable Cities Initiative of the Canadian Government,[3] and the WHO Healthy Cities Project.[4]

Another promising framework is offered by the UNESCO Biosphere Reserve concept, which arose in the late 1960s and is regarded by many as one of the most valuable international approaches for promoting sustainable living practices.[5] However, throughout the years, the biosphere reserve concept has been applied mainly to rural areas and in some cases to periurban areas. With the recent formation of the MAB Urban Group by UNESCO in 2000,[6] international discussions have started on the applicability of the concept to the urban interface.

The Cape Town Case Study (CTCS) has evolved as one of several studies coordinated by CUBES, a joint initiative of UNESCO's Ecological Science division and Columbia University's Earth Institute.[7] The purpose of the CTCS was to develop a multi-institutional, interactive process, using an examination of urban applications of the UNESCO Biosphere Reserve concept as a vehicle for a broader consideration of the importance and potential benefits of environmental conservation to impoverished and marginalized communities in greater Cape Town.

This paper contextualizes the CTCS and its collaborative process, reviews the biosphere reserve concept relative to urban sustainability objectives, and provides a rationale for a proposal on a more functional application of the biosphere reserve concept in an urban environment. Drawing on the examination of successful sustainability initiatives in Cape Town, recommendations are made for future application of the biosphere reserve concept in an urban context, as well as a model by which urban areas might affiliate with the UNESCO World Network of Biosphere Reserves.

THE CUBES CAPE TOWN CASE STUDY

Cape Town was selected as a CUBES site on the basis of its high biological diversity and social, economic, and cultural importance, as well as in recognition of its demonstrated leadership in promoting more sustainable practices in the urban context. For the launch of the CUBES Cape Town site, the CTCS was commissioned in early 2003.[8] A distinguishing feature of the CTCS is that its outputs were both a policy research document and long-term collaborative process involving key local institutions, CUBES, and UNESCO's Man and the Biosphere Programme. This provided a context in which to examine and seek potential synergies among existing municipal, provincial, and parastatal programs and initiatives.

This case study was conducted by the Cape Town Urban Biosphere Group (CTUBG), a cross-disciplinary group of specialists drawn from national, provincial, and local (municipal) government, as well as nongovernmental organizations and civil society. The CTUBG includes representatives of the major relevant public sector role players, and alliances were formed as a result of the project among a variety of governmental departments, local authorities, and other institutions. In addition, the work of the CTUBG was endorsed by the Cape Action for People and the Environment (CAPE), a regional strategy for conserving the Cape Floral Kingdom.[9]

The group was mandated by the City of Cape Town, the Provincial Authority of the Western Cape, Western Cape Nature Conservation Board, the National Botanical Institute of South Africa, and Table Mountain National Park, to work in partnership with CUBES in the preparation of a case study on urban sustainability in the Cape Flats,[a] as a contribution to the CUBES/UNESCO/UN-HABITAT/New York Academy of Sciences–sponsored conference Urban Biosphere and Society: Partnership of Cities, held at the New York Academy of Sciences in October 2003. The fact that mandates were sought and received from governmental partners for such a project is significant, because it is governmental institutions that have a legitimate mandate to develop and implement policies, have the greatest long-run stake in their success, and have the most long-term institutional experience. To involve all major public sector role players and initiatives and to create and strengthen alliances, an institutional seminar was held in May 2003. The aim of the seminar was to gather information on the wide variety of public sector urban sustainability initiatives under way in Cape Town, as well as to raise awareness of the biosphere reserve concept and to strengthen linkages for alliances between CUBES, the CTUBG, and other local institutions. The information gathered from the seminar[10] formed a key input into the CTCS document that provided the basis for this article.

The CTCS focused on a specific area in the Cape Flats, including a marine section along the False Bay coastline (FIG. 2). The geographical focus of the case study was selected to include both important local communities and

[a]The *Cape Flats* is the common term for the area to the east of the central business district of Cape Town, adjoining False Bay. It is home to some of the most impoverished and disadvantaged communities in Cape Town, but it also supports some of the most diverse and threatened ecosystems of the world. In an area like the Cape Flats, it is understandable that issues of housing, primary health care, unemployment, crime, and education will receive priority over the environmental concerns lodged to a large extent in communities not subject to those immediate and sometimes life-threatening pressures. Implementation projects that address the relevance of biodiversity conservation to marginalized and disadvantaged communities are therefore important.

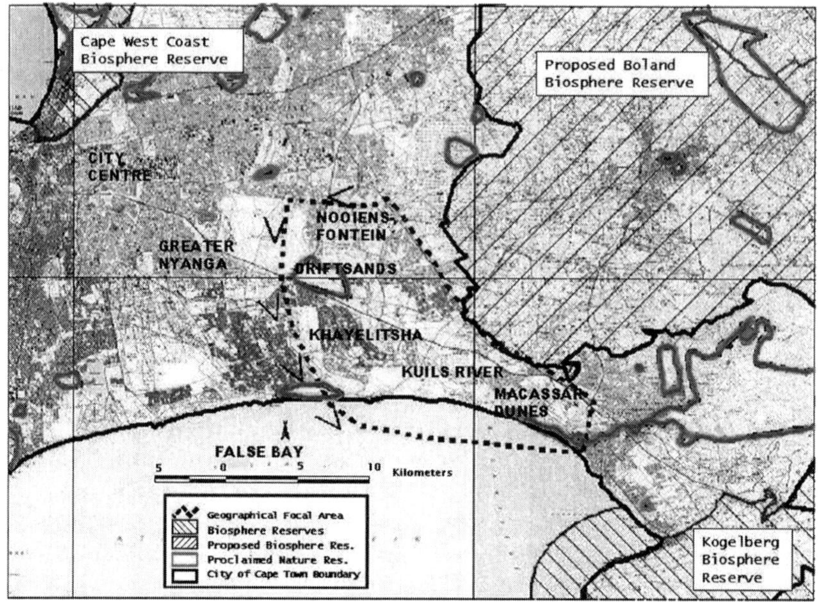

FIGURE 2. Cape Town case study focal area.

conservation corridors, as well as to reflect and support the policy priorities of the bodies represented on the CTUBG. This focal area provided many unique assets and challenges that are briefly described below.

ENVIRONMENTAL CONSERVATION AND POVERTY ALLEVIATION IN CAPE TOWN

Although Cape Town is widely recognized as a hot spot for biological diversity, it is also a city of great cultural diversity, harboring a population of ~3.5 million people with a wide range of ethnic, cultural, and religious backgrounds.[11] Three of South Africa's nine official languages are spoken widely in the city, these being English, Afrikaans, and Xhosa. Cape Town has a strong and relatively varied economy with a monocentric structure, characteristic of South African cities in general. It is, however, also an extremely polarized city, with affluent suburbs and economic centers on the one hand, and overcrowded, impoverished communities in the townships with a very low economic base on the other. As the economic hub of the Western Cape Province, the City of Cape Town thus faces the challenge of promoting development and managing the redistribution of resources to redress current inequities, as well as enormous social and health problems, while concurrently nurturing its unique environment.

The Cape Flats were relatively unpopulated until the 1960s. Since then, two major waves of human settlement have taken place. The first occurred during the 1960s after the apartheid government forcefully resettled people on the Cape Flats, especially those classified as "colored." The second wave started in the 1980s when a then illegal process of migration started en masse from the Eastern Cape African population, caused by extreme poverty in that region. A quarter of a century later, this latter process has resulted in Khayelitsha and Greater Nyanga being home to about three quarters of a million people. Remoteness from places of work, fragmentation of communities, and the trauma of disruption increased the problems of poverty, crime, and indifference to environmental issues. The "townships" of the Cape Flats are recognizable as settlement areas with no more than a tenuous relationship to the remnants of natural vegetation that they engulf. Many of these problems and challenges remain, even 10 years after democracy was attained in South Africa.

Generally, poverty on the Cape Flats is rife. Extensive areas on the Cape Flats are covered with informal housing structures, with ~20% of the population living in these. Many households do not have access to clean running water and good sanitation services. More than 75% of the residents in Khayelitsha and Greater Nyanga live below the poverty line of R352 per adult equivalent per month.[12] The poorest third of the population live on less than R100 per month. Among the adult population in Khayelitsha, a mixture of diseases (39% HIV, TB, and TB/HIV) and assault (29%) are the main causes of death.[12] The HIV/AIDS epidemic is expected to lower the life expectancy of black Cape Town residents living in the poor African townships to 47 years, decreasing it by 17 years by 2010 to 2015.[13]

It thus is clear that environmental conservation in this area has to be closely associated with poverty alleviation,[b] which could be considered to be a far more pressing need. Indeed, for them to be effective and politically sustainable, environmental policies should be focused to yield maximal benefits to the poor, while respecting the constraints implied by environmental conservation.

Several initiatives have been put into place in the past years to address these challenges and to promote sustainable living practices.[16] These present a vision of integrated environmental management that embraces not only diverse natural resource uses such as manufacturing, private fishing, watershed protection, agriculture, and conservation, but also elements from the socioeconomic sphere that are influenced by and in turn influence the natural environment. Thus, a notable aspect of the City of Cape Town's

[b]Poverty is "the state or fact of being in want." The importance of poverty alleviation is seen in the social and environmental costs of its absence. [14] Poverty alleviation thus refers to the situation of having programs in place to eradicate the root causes of poverty such as hunger, illiteracy, inadequate medical and child care, lack of employment, and population pressures. [15]

TABLE 1. Environmental management initiatives informing the Cape Town Case Study (CTCS)[a]

Project site	Description	Lessons for Urban Biosphere Reserve development
A. Large protected areas abutting the Cape Town urban fringe The Biosphere Reserves of Kogelberg and the Cape West Coast, together with the Table Mountain National Park, are large protected areas that share common boundaries with the City of Cape Town. Together with the proposed Boland Biosphere Reserve, these potentially allow the City to be bounded by large conservation areas along a significant proportion of its perimeter. As the policies and management strategies of these protected areas evolve, they could have a profound influence on integrated management of the metropolitan environment, and provide a useful backdrop for exploring and experimenting with the concept of an Urban Biosphere Reserve for Cape Town. (See Figure 3).		
Kogelberg Biosphere Reserve (KBR)[24] **MAP REF 1**	A Biosphere Reserve to the east of Cape Town, designated by UNESCO MAB in December 1998. The KBR is approx 100,000 ha in extent, and includes both terrestrial and marine ecosystems in its biodiversity core. The Kogelberg area, with its very high levels of plant species richness and endemism, is widely regarded as the floristic heart of the globally unique Cape Floral Kingdom.[29]	This is a classic Biosphere Reserve design which protects the biodiversity and habitats of the core area against metropolitan creep from the west, and rural development from the north and east. Its southern coastal boundary is threatened by uncontrolled resort development and poaching of marine resources, especially abalone. The buffer and transition zones are well-designed according to the traditional Biosphere Reserve model, and management of the reserve is co-ordinated by a non-profit, private sector company. This arrangement has created certain expectations from local communities of effective nature conservation linked to economic development, which cannot always be met. Lessons learned to date are: • Administrative and management responsibilities of partner institutes need to be defined according to clear contractual terms of reference • Full-time, dedicated staff, providing a predictable point of presence, is essential for continuity • The management structure needs a secure financial resource-base, and cannot rely on civil society volunteerism • Political buy-in and support at local, regional and national level is important to the success of a Biosphere Reserve

[a]The CTCS is based on experiences gained over a wide range of project- and policy-based work. In this table a selection of activities that have been bearing on exploration of the Biosphere Reserve concept in an urban context are listed. They are grouped in sets ranging from implementation of the classical Biosphere Reserve concept in large areas of biodiversity significance adjacent to the metropolitan fringe (A), to a broad overview of civil society iniatives (D). The set of work included here is only indicative and by no means constitutes a comprehensive listing. The initial case study was restricted to the southeast portion of the Cape Flats, although the analysis presented in this table extend beyond. Map references are to FIGURE 3.

TABLE 1. Environmental management initiatives informing the Cape Town Case Study (CTCS) — *continued*

Project site	Description	Lessons for Urban Biosphere Reserve development
Cape West Coast Biosphere Reserve (CWCBR) [23] **MAP REF 2**	A Biosphere Reserve to the north of Cape Town, designated by UNESCO MAB in November 2000. It occupies an area of 377,000 ha, with two protected core areas that include both terrestrial and marine ecosystems with high biodiversity value. A feature of the Reserve is a Fossil Park [30] which provides access to examples of the biodiversity of the region five million years ago.	This classically designed Biosphere Reserve protects coastal resources that are under threat from tourism and urban expansion driven by the growth of Cape Town northwards. The CWCBR is managed by a non-profit, private sector company with a Board of Directors. It incorporates rural, peri-urban, and even urban areas within its boundaries. Inclusion of urban landscapes, although initially considered of dubious value to municipal stakeholders, provides the opportunity to test some of the assumptions and predictions regarding application of Biosphere Reserve planning in these environments. A strategic plan for the CWCBR is in the process of being drafted, which is likely to include themes, goals, objectives and priority strategies.
Proposed Boland Biosphere Reserve (BBR) [25]MAP REF 3	A proposed Biosphere Reserve included in the integrated development plans for the municipalities of Stellenbosch and the Winelands District. The proposed reserve falls within the jurisdiction of five local authorities and is designed around the wine-growing areas adjacent to the north-east boundary of metropolitan Cape Town. The stated aim is to "establish a system of protected areas regulated and managed to achieve the conservation of the district's biological and landscape diversity".	The design of the proposed BBR falls within the classic concept in that the core area comprises a large nature reserve. The surrounding buffer and transition zones, however, are being considered specifically in the context of wine production, a major agricultural activity in the Western Cape. Implicit in this focussed perspective is the fact that economic and cultural filters are being applied to these zones, a factor that will have bearing on development of activities adjacent to the core area. Wine-route tourism, and possibly even wine production and export, will be linked by way of branding to biodiversity conservation, with possible impacts on commercial perceptions of protected area management and the interlinked nature of natural and agricultural ecosystems.
Table Mountain National Park [31] **MAP REF 4**	A National Park of 22,000 ha, based on the consolidation of all protected natural areas associated with the mountain chain of the Cape Peninsula. It was proclaimed in 1998, and more recently (2004) an extensive marine reserve has been added. The terrestrial biota protected includes over 2,000 indigenous plant species.	Because of its long history abutting human settlement, there exists a steep conservation gradient between protected natural areas and transformed urban environments. This necessitates novel and collaborative people-centred approaches to biodiversity protection, and the value that it presents to human economy and the local way of life. Land consolidation and alien clearing are major focus areas of the current development phase. Many parts of the Park are extremely valuable to the tourism industry. Table Mountain for instance, itself situated within the Park, receives 4.1 million visits per year, and the Cape Point Nature Reserve is on most tour-guides' itineraries.

TABLE 1. Environmental management initiatives informing the Cape Town Case Study (CTCS) — *continued*

Project site	Description	Lessons for Urban Biosphere Reserve development
B. Key Protected Areas significant for biodiversity conservation on the Cape Flats The Cape Flats is the name given to the lowland area east of the Cape Town central business district. It is has a quaternary sand substrate, and in pre-settlement times comprised a mosaic of dunes and wetlands with a distinct subset of the biota of the Cape Floristic Region [29]. Sites with leached neutral to acid sands were settled relatively early in colonial times and exploited for vegetable farming and industrial sand mining. Other sites have since been used for housing, in many instances as the destinations for people removed from more central locations during the apartheid era. Many of these "apartheid townships" are beset by problems of winter flooding. Residual land valuable for biodiversity conservation is now more or less restricted to wetlands and the more mobile coastal dunes, river corridors and the few pockets of land that have enjoyed some form of conservation status.		
Driftsands Nature Reserve [20] (DNR) **MAP REF 5**	A statutory protected area (900 ha) in the process of reclamation from disturbance. This site was placed under jurisdiction of the Western Cape Nature Conservation Board in 1983, and is now part of the *Biodiversity Network* (see *IMEP* below). It is surrounded by very poor communities, who reside in sub-economic and informal settlements. The mission of the DNR is to find a balance between delivery of services to support social upliftment, and conservation of the rare and endangered lowland vegetation it contains.	Small-scale zonation is applied within DNR, with rare vegetation and habitats being demarcated as focus areas for conservation. Servicing of adjacent community needs is planned by including: (1) an initiation village; (2) a cultural emporium to link local craft production with the tourism market; and (3) a youth development programme (see *Cape Flats Nature* below for a parallel model). DNR is an urban nature reserve in the true sense of the word, and could form part of a fragmented core area in a larger Biosphere Reserve framework. Functionally, DNR can play a very important role in linking the needs and lifestyles of people on the Cape Flats to the natural resource bases from which they have been alienated by creating a sense of ownership in the reserve and over its resources.
Rondevlei Nature Reserve [32] (RNR)	A statutory local authority nature reserve (210 ha) on the Cape Flats, established in 1952. This small reserve is especially important for its wetland flora and avifauna, and also provides a managed habitat for the only group of hippopotamus in theWestern Cape. RNR is home to important red data species of plants, birds and amphibians, and is managed by local government as part of its Biodiversity Network (see *IMEP* and the *False Bay Ecology Park* below).	RNR provides an example of challenges and achievements where an important conservation area is highly impacted by urban development: This is a wetland area with direct hydraulic connectivity to a highly polluted system that drains the densely populated south-east quadrant of the Cape Flats. Buffering relies on maintaining the best possible relations with surrounding human communities, rigorous control of alien invasive weeds, and system management to accommodate the effects of attenuated flooding. Buffer and transitional qualities are also provided by well-developed environmental education and general visitor facilities. These serve both the education and tourism sectors. Approx. 6,000-8,000 learners participate annually in the Environmental Education programme. A successful community-based commercial tourism partnership project has been established, with overnight accommodation

TABLE 1. Environmental management initiatives informing the Cape Town Case Study (CTCS) — *continued*

Project site	Description	Lessons for Urban Biosphere Reserve development
		and conference facilities in the reserve. Strong niche market tourism relating to the resources, e.g. birding, is undertaken, which has shown a direct and beneficial relationship between biodiversity conservation and socio-economic opportunities.
Four Pilot Sites (see *Cape Flats Nature* Below)	The four pilot sites described below form part of both *Cape Flats Nature*, and the broader *Biodiversity Network* (see *IMEP* below). They were selected as the strategic entry point for broader urban conservation work on the Cape Flats because of their specific locations, their stages of conservation development, and the communities that they abut.	The focus on these sites allow for close examination and exploration of the dynamic relationships that exist between adjacent communities, local authorities, conservation stakeholders, and potential beneficiaries. The specific lessons for Urban Biosphere Reserve thinking, most still being learned, cover the full transect of core/buffer/transition, and are addressed site by site below.
• *Edith Stephens Wetland Park (ESWP)*	A public sector partnership (City of Cape Town and National Botanical Institute) established in 2000, consolidating a small protected wetland with municipal open space to form a 35 ha conservation park. The Park supports the only known population of *Isoetes capensis.* It is surrounded by poor communities, small industries and market gardening practices.	Clearing of alien vegetation has both restored biodiversity value and made the area safer with respect to crime. Restoration of an old farmhouse provides space for an environmental education centre, and is also the base of operation for *Cape Flats Nature* at a location close to participating communities. Utilisation of the Park, by people from the surrounding communities, as a recreational space is increasing. The social benefits of positive space, and as alternative to other anti-social behaviours (e.g. gangsterism), have been elucidated by some community members.
• *Wolfgat Nature Reserve (WNR)*	A statutory local authority nature reserve (248 ha) proclaimed in 1986. This comprises a section of the False-Bay coast marked by unique calcrete-cemented dune cliffs and adjacent mobile dunes. Respectively they provide habitats for the only breeding colony of Southern Black Backed Gulls on the False Bay Coast, and rare and threatened dune flora.	The scenic beauty of WNR has great tourism potential, but lacks infrastructure. In addition, control has not yet been properly reclaimed from criminal stakeholders. Along its length, the area is contiguous to a number of different communities, all with different political outlooks and a poor history of civic co-operation. Overcoming these obstacles, which several CBOs are dedicated to doing, will promote sustainability through effective conservation governance (core function) and co-operative development of tourism potential (transition function).
• *Maccassar Dunes (MD)*	Coastal dunes with no formal protection status, but an important habitat for several species of threatened flora (several hundred ha in extent). These dunes are under	The lessons to be learned here are similar to those of WNR above, although extreme poverty and the inability of local authorities to fully contain the proliferation of informal dwellings are more serious problems

TABLE 1. Environmental management initiatives informing the Cape Town Case Study (CTCS) — *continued*

Project site	Description	Lessons for Urban Biosphere Reserve development
	threat from sand-mining, invasion by alien shrubs, uncontrolled harvesting of medicinal plants, and land invasion by informal settlements.	than political tension. In this respect, *Cape Flats Nature* is engaged in facilitating dialogue between supportive elements of the local community, settlers, and the local authority. This is seen as a fundamental engagement in transition zone activity.
• *Harmony Flats Nature Reserve (HFNR)*	A statutory local authority nature reserve (approx 8 ha) on the eastern edge of the metropole. It was proclaimed in 1998 to protect the endangered geometric tortoise and a number of threatened geophyte species.	A community much smaller and more homogeneous than those adjacent to WNR and MD (see above) surrounds HFNR. Proactive involvement of interest groups makes environmental education activities and management training (eg for alien vegetation clearing and fire-fighting) a more productive area of endeavour, with more effective buffering of the core conservation area.
C. Initiatives for an integrated approach to Biodiversity Conservation and Environmental Management in Cape Town Programmes and projects considered by the Cape Town Case Study under this heading revolve chiefly around a long-standing and on-going programme of the City of Cape Town local government, and its need to be involved in the management of areas of intrinsic biodiversity and habitat value. The first two entries below describe current status and forward-looking perspectives of this process, while the other two are specific implementations that were influenced by the processes and debate that accompanied policy level developments. Many public and non-governmental agencies have been involved in these initiatives.		
IMEP: City of Cape Town's *Integrated Metropolitan Environmental Policy* [17], and its *Biodiversity Strategy*	*IMEP* is an overarching policy framework for development of environmental management strategies in a range of sectors. A *Biodiversity Strategy* was adopted as an implementation strategy of the policy in October 2003. At the core of this strategy is a *Biodiversity Network*, comprising a set of ecologically representative conservation areas connected through a network of nodes and corridors. See Figure 4.	The *Biodiversity Network*, comprising 261 sites, nodes and corridors, presents an ideal opportunity for exploring the Urban Biosphere Reserve concept in Cape Town. Sites are being prioritised into three categories: 'A' sites for biodiversity protection, 'B' sites managed mainly for biodiversity, but also permitting other activities, and 'C' sites not managed primarily as biodiversity areas but where the primary function supports biodiversity conservation. Functionally, buffering of the sites against damage and degradation will be achieved through environmental education, awareness raising and promotion of biodiversity benefits. Use of the Biodiversity Network for socio-economic benefit and exploration of development opportunities can be regarded as the transitional function.
False Bay Biodiversity and Development	A project in its start-up phase, which aims to implement the southern component of the City's *Biodiversity Network* (see *IMEP*). It will use areas of	The conservation core of this area is the beach and dune environment supporting unique marine and plant biota, and includes WNR and MD described above. On the inland side of this strip are the large, sprawling,

TABLE 1. Environmental management initiatives informing the Cape Town Case Study (CTCS) — *continued*

Project site	Description	Lessons for Urban Biosphere Reserve development
Plan: [19] Implementation of the Southern Component of the *Biodiversity Network*, including the False Bay Ecology Park (FBEP) **MAP REF 6**	biodiversity importance to realise social and economic opportunities provided by their natural assets. It will also provide a corridor link between the Kogelberg Biosphere Reserve, and the southern section of the Table Mountain National Park. The FBEP project, initiated in 2001, will form part of the broader initiative. It comprises two statutory Nature Reserves (see Rondevlei above for one of these), a waste-water treatment plant, a landfill site, and a coastal strip. It is a project that is based on co-operation between different service sectors, and between government and civil society. The area is regarded as the fifth most important wetland bird habitat in southern Africa, amongst other important biodiversity attributes. Conservation, together with realisation of socio-economic opportunities, are at its core.	and mostly very poor communities of Khayelitsha and Mitchell's Plain. A buffer against human abuse is promotion of the area's use by interest groups (bathers, anglers, surfers, hikers), backed by local law enforcement. Special efforts are being made to encourage local leadership in conservation via environmental CBOs (see *Cape Flats Nature* below). The realisation of socio-economic opportunities of conservation, e.g. environmental education, niche market tourism, etc, relates to the buffer and transition area function discussed in the body of the paper. The FBEP illustrates how co-operative relationships between different sectors, including those not traditionally associated with biodiversity conservation, can be established to the benefit of biodiversity conservation and for the realisation of socio-economic opportunities.
Cape Flats Nature (CFN) [33]	A partnership project between the City of Cape Town and other agencies. It focuses on four pilot sites, all within the *Biodiversity Network*, including sites that will fall within the False Bay Biodiversity and Development Plan (see above). Its aim is to empower local community structures to engage pro-actively in conservation action.	CFN focuses on developing the mechanisms of buffering, and has no direct responsibility for the core conservation value of the pilot sites. Its aim is to support local government in developing the resources for that protection function, as well as to build local leadership that will lead to effective conservation action endorsed and supported by communities living adjacent to areas of biodiversity value. Activity outputs include establishment of nature trails, bird-ringing and monitoring workgroups, litter patrols, fire-fighting training, alien vegetation removal, etc.
Public Health Programme [21]: A school and community de-	This initiative addressed the problem of water-borne parasites in informal settlements in the township of Khayelithsa. It was included in the case study as a typical example of the connectivity between	Within the broad construct of an Urban Biosphere Reserve for a large city such as Cape Town, it is useful to consider functional linkages between system processes in core areas, and the ecosystem services required for human survival in areas totally transformed by urban development. An

TABLE 1. Environmental management initiatives informing the Cape Town Case Study (CTCS) — *continued*

Project site	Description	Lessons for Urban Biosphere Reserve development
worming project	environmental degradation and human health. It was driven by the "Khayelitsha Task Team" (KTT), which included representatives from: institutes of tertiary learning; local and provincial government; the Medical Research Council; private sector entrepreneurship, local primary schools, and CBOs. The aim of the project is to link sanitation technologies with improvement action and local awareness.	important element of the "transition zone" function is engendering of social responsibility that will improve as far as possible the environmental sustainability of urban life, and reduce impacts on the underlying natural processes. In this instance, Khayelitsha could be designated as a high maintenance area that requires focused programs on awareness raising of environmental issues and sustainable living practices, designed for people whose extreme poverty has cut them off from a sense of environmental continuity and their ultimate reliance on natural ecosystem functions.
D. Civil society initiatives working at the interface between social development and the protection of biodiversity This is a very broad area of endeavour, and draws heavily on the international trend of local action informed by global experience. In Cape Town, with its very high levels of poverty, and its long history of social exclusion through colonial and apartheid times, human rights agendas have tended to predominate in this sector. However, during the first decade of democracy in South Africa (1994-2004) environmental issues have received more attention: there has been significant global politicisation of green issues; national government has greatly strengthened its environmental portfolio; and South Africa hosted the 2002 World Summit on Sustainable Development. These and other circumstances have greatly raised environmental awareness locally, and civil society groups are increasingly embracing biodiversity conservation as an element of social development. Some of the motivation comes from a growing awareness of the links between the natural environment and socio-economic growth: jobs via tourism; improved ecosystem services and a better quality of life; a vehicle for integrated learning in the formal education sector; and a breadth of recreational opportunities.		
	A wide range of NGOs and CBOs are operational in the Cape Town metropolitan area; addressing environmental issues linked to individual and community well-being (examples [34-37]). Organisations that previously focussed solely on biodiversity protection are increasingly tending towards inclusion of social dimensions. New projects include: environmental education; indigenous knowledge and traditional medicine; food gardens; community-based tourism; developmental outdoor adventure and youth leadership; and many others.	The projects and activities that operate under the civil society umbrella are crucial to the development of the sustainable environmental management model embodied in the concept of the Urban Biosphere Reserve. They provide the mechanisms for defining the processes that can buffer core biodiversity areas from human driven degradation; as well as modify social behaviour patterns in the buffer and transitional shells of Biosphere Reserve thinking.

approach has been the explicit inclusion of considerations such as HIV infection rates, housing shortages, and crime prevention as issues of environmental concern.

The Integrated Metropolitan Environmental Policy (IMEP) of the City of Cape Town is one such overarching initiative that is widely recognized and valued. The sectoral approaches of IMEP include strategies to be developed within 5 years covering the 14 sectors identified, namely: air; water resources; landforms and soils; fauna and flora; cultural heritage; urbanization and housing; infrastructure; transportation; energy; waste; economy; environmental health; environmental education; safety and security; and environmental governance.[17] Three detailed strategies have already been developed, namely the Biodiversity Strategy; the Coastal Zone Management Strategy; and the Environmental Education and Training Strategy. These strategies are aimed at integrating the goals of development, poverty alleviation and conservation, and were adopted as key implementation strategies of IMEP by the City of Cape Town in October 2003 [17]. Other strategies related to energy, open space, litter, noise and air quality are in the process of preparation.

Given the framework of the CTCS and its focal area, IMEP and several other key initiatives were selected to be profiled in detail in the main document of the CTCS.[18] These include the Biodiversity and Development Plan for the False Bay Coast,[19] Driftsands Nature Reserve,[20] the City of Cape Town's Public Health Program,[21] and Cape Flats Nature.[22] TABLE 1 provides a comparison of the initiatives, their approaches to environmental conservation and poverty alleviation, and their relevance to the biosphere reserve concept. Also included is a selection of other relevant activities that have bearing on exploration of the biosphere reserve concept in the Cape Town urban context. The initiatives are grouped in sets ranging from implementation of the classic biosphere reserve concept in large areas of biodiversity significance adjacent to the metropolitan fringe, to a broad overview of civil society initiatives. Each of these demonstrates the interface between environmental management and poverty alleviation, and each is largely compatible with and in the spirit of the biosphere reserve concept. As an ensemble, they provide a snapshot of current public sector programs to promote sustainability in an urban context, as well as a view toward the applicability and value of the biosphere reserve concept in an urban context.

BIOSPHERE RESERVES IN AND AROUND CAPE TOWN

Although the focus of the CTCS was on the City of Cape Town, the city itself is set within a wider context that includes surrounding biosphere reserves (FIG. 3). More specifically, the Cape West Coast Biosphere Reserve incorporates a city section immediately north of Cape Town,[23] the Kogelberg

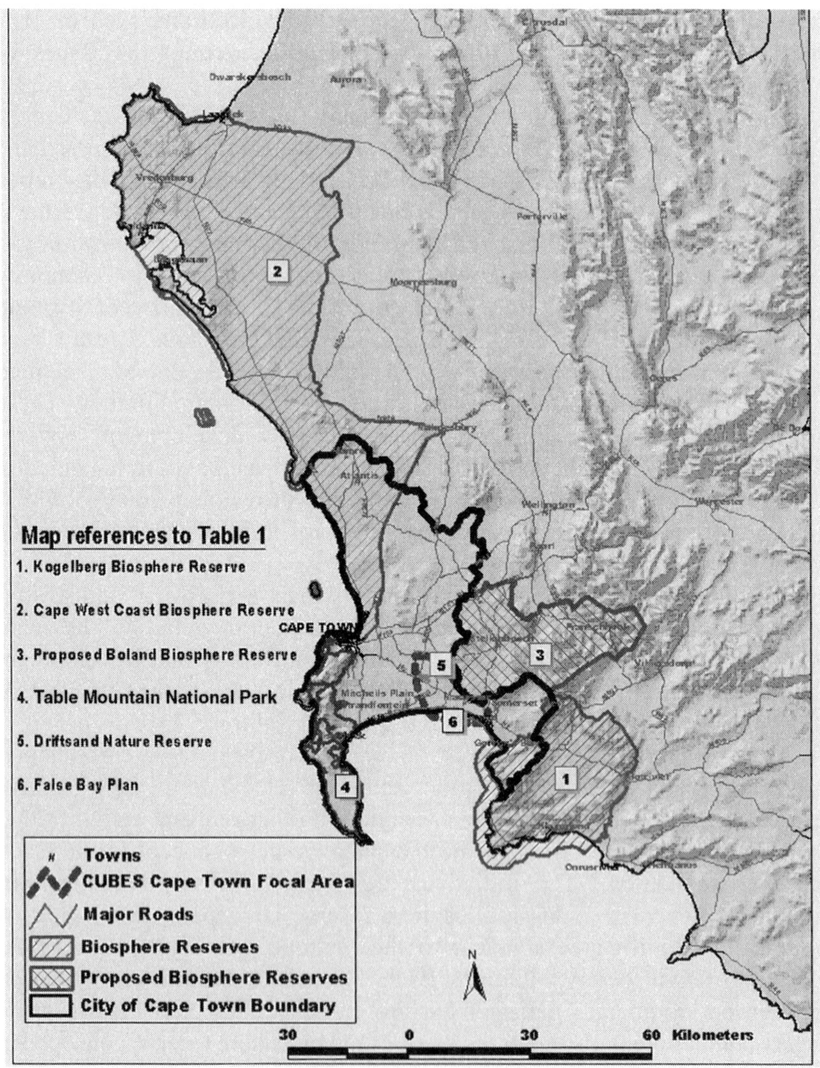

FIGURE 3. Biosphere reserves of the greater Cape Town.

Biosphere Reserve borders the metropolitan area to the east,[24] and the proposed Boland Biosphere Reserve will link to the Kogelberg Biosphere Reserve.[25] These vast areas enrich the city by supporting the most needed natural ecosystems as a basis for sustainable living practices of urban inhabitants.

In 2000, the Provincial Government of the Western Cape adopted "bioregional planning," a planning and management approach generally implemented as a management system by various institutions around the world, as a framework for the region. This bioregional planning framework provides guidelines for all planning documentation in the Western Cape Province.[26] The application of UNESCO's MAB Program is increasingly being considered as an effective tool for the implementation of bioregional planning principles. However, note that the biosphere reserve concept comprises a much wider range of issues than just bioregional planning through inter alia the incorporation of natural, socioeconomic, and cultural aspects.

Of particular relevance to the debate on urban sustainability in the context of the biosphere reserve concept is a prefeasibility study for a Table Mountain Chain Peninsula Biosphere Reserve, which was commissioned by the City of Cape Town in 2000.[27] This study was undertaken to assess the applicability, appropriateness, and desirability of pursuing the establishment of a biosphere reserve on the Table Mountain Chain Cape Peninsula in Cape Town. The key question addressed in the study revolved around whether a biosphere reserve would add value to existing environmental initiatives in the city. The study area focused on the Table Mountain Chain and the immediately adjacent urban areas and did not extend onto the Cape Flats.

In this prefeasibility study, the proposed core and buffer areas were identified as areas currently being managed in terms of the National Parks Act as the Table Mountain National Park. In discussions about the outer boundary of the transition zone and given difficulties highlighted in considering delineation of an outer extent of a possible biosphere reserve within an urban context, a long-term vision of a greater cluster biosphere reserve was proposed, wherein the entire developed metropolitan area of Cape Town could function as a transition zone or zone of cooperation. The focal area of the CTCS is situated within this proposed "transition zone." The study recommended that the city should give priority to implementing current initiatives, especially the Metropolitan Open Space Program on the Cape Flats, and the establishment of a coastal park along False Bay, which could become building blocks of a possible future biosphere reserve. It also recommended that the future option of a biosphere reserve should not be compromised in the adjudication of environmental programs and projects.[27]

APPLICABILITY OF THE BIOSPHERE RESERVE CONCEPT TO THE URBAN SITUATION

In simple terms, the biosphere reserve model works within a conceptual framework that spans a range of land-use types, from pristine wilderness to highly "impacted upon" systems of human habitation.

Note that there can be different levels of applying the biosphere reserve concept (from the regional to the very local: such as bioregional, municipal, ecosystem, community, or habitat level), depending on the scale of implementation. In traditional rural biosphere reserves, the concept has tended to be applied in a strict spatial way. However, we would argue that the spatial organization of biosphere reserves may best be viewed as a mechanism to support their conservation, logistic, and development functions. Thus, if the guiding principles in determining a zonation system should follow from the functions that biosphere reserves are intended to fulfill, then it is reasonable to expect that the implementation of biosphere reserve zonation should be allowed to vary depending on the particularities of different sites.

Similarly, in the urban context at least, even though the biogeographical conditions usually associated with a given zone type may not hold, especially given that the gradient from one end of the zonation spectrum to the other is very steep, "zonation" may be implemented through the development of specific policies and interventions to support the intended functions of that zone. For example, because of a lack of space for adequate spatial buffer zones in an urban context, buffering functions can be implemented that could result in changes to how people perceive the areas where they live and how they react to them. In the same way, transitional functions could include awareness campaigns, indigenous gardening, establishment of food gardens, recycling, and wise water use. All these actions will result in connecting urban dwellers more closely with their natural resource base.

Core Areas

Cape Town's biodiversity network (FIG. 4), based on the acknowledged need to ensure ecological representation and functionality of the vegetation types in the city, can easily be equated to a "core area" of a biosphere reserve. Unlike the conventional core of a biosphere reserve, however, these sites form an archipelago of islands in a sea of urban development, or a fragmented core area representing several threatened habitats unique even within the Cape Floral Kingdom. Within the biodiversity network, there is also a distinction between areas based on levels of protection and conservation, land-use management, and use for other nonbiodiversity purposes.

Buffer Areas

The essence of a buffer is to protect the core. The steep transformational gradient between core biodiversity areas and human habitation in the metropolitan context sets some challenges for urban conservation planners. In rural situations, there is often the opportunity to include intervening spatial areas in a biosphere reserve design that provide the opportunity to buffer the core with conservation-friendly activities in a first layer and then a belt of

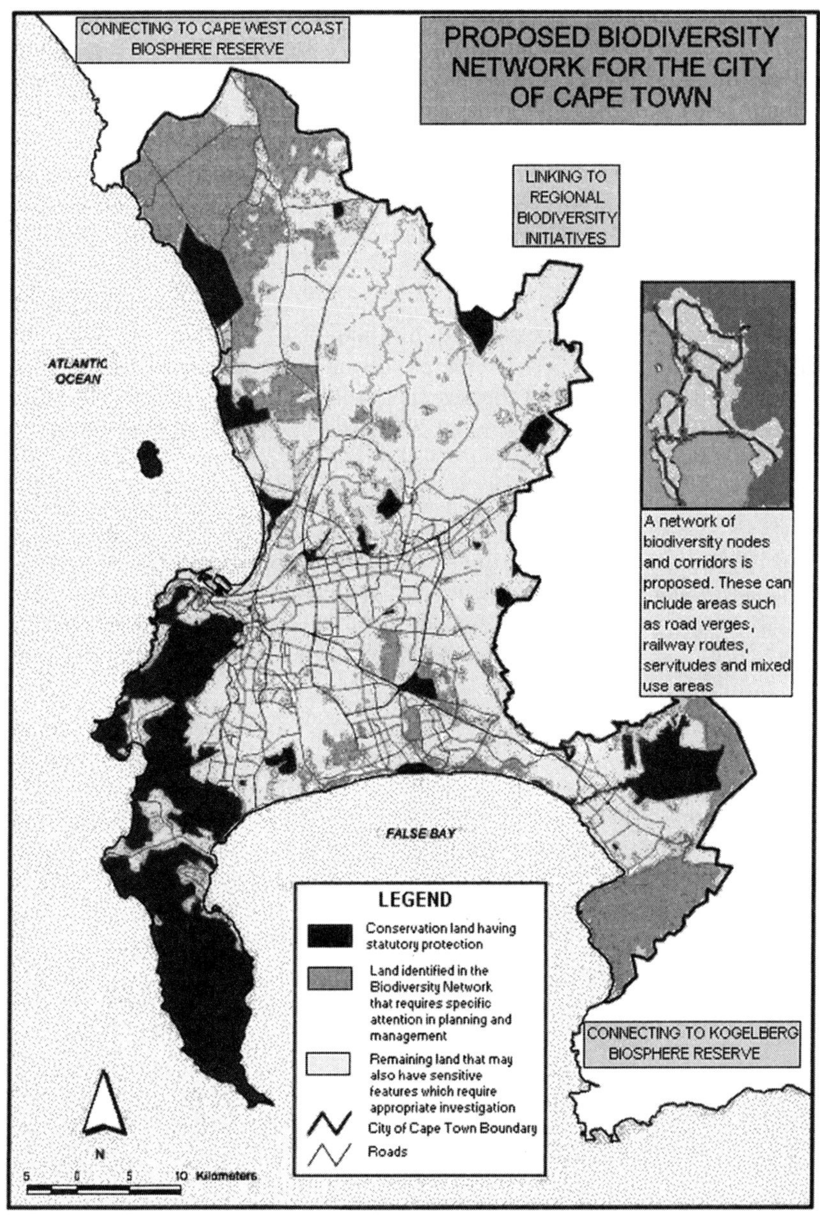

FIGURE 4. Map of the Cape Town Biodiversity Network and Corridors.

transitional activities that will not have outputs sufficient to penetrate the buffer zone to have an impact on the core. In urban nature conservation, there is rarely the luxury of intervening land. There are, however, functional interpretations of buffers and transitions that could help to make the biosphere reserve concept applicable, and in so doing improve global understanding of the hurdles that need to be overcome in the less favorable city environment.

In the focal area of the study, as well as at most other core areas on the Cape Flats, there is usually some significant threat immediately adjacent to the sites of biodiversity value. These threats, which more often than not include invasion by alien vegetation, but also may include uncontrolled foraging by small livestock, require direct control, such as investment in weed removal, the erection of goat-proof fences, or relevant management intervention. Although these physical measures may be thought of as replacing the buffer area that supports benign activity, there is also a set of interventions that serve this purpose as well. Most of the threats to the core relate directly to human activities. Buffering therefore can in many cases be achieved by modification of human behavior. An option is to implement and enforce regulations. Perhaps more important, however, is the investment in forward-looking interventions such as environmental education in both school and adult learners, nature-based activities that accommodate local visitors to core areas to experience nature in a way that does not have an impact on the species and habitats, and campaigns of information transfer that create general awareness of the value of these sites to surrounding communities.

Transition Areas

The transition, instead of being represented by an area of agricultural or settlement practice, may in the urban context be seen as human enterprise that draws from the core area and set of buffer activities in such a way as to feed into local economies. One of the most important products that can emerge from community knowledge about a local pocket of biodiversity is the acceptance of environmental responsibility. Currently, there is a relatively wide-scale awareness of environmental issues, especially in South Africa in the wake of the World Summit on Sustainable Development. Environmental resources are being recognized at all levels of the economy as being able to provide benefit, from the use of special pockets of nature as destinations for niche market tourism, to opportunities for job creation by the clearing of alien invasive vegetation, and the secondary industries that might use the products (e.g., Acacia wood for pizza ovens and rustic furniture making). Job creation is also entering into a more direct relationship with environmental protection on the Cape Flats as part of a wetland restoration program, which the City of Cape Town is able to link to its catchment management system.

Local centers of environmental protection can provide less direct economic spin-offs, such as adding impetus to greening of townships in general. Schools greening projects have been in place for several years, in which agencies such as the National Botanical Institute have engaged with schools to establish gardens inside their grounds while using the opportunity for skills transfer in horticulture and learning of biological and ecological processes linked to learning curricula. These activities have promoted more directly beneficial initiatives such as the establishment of food gardens. More recent developments have been the establishment of gardens for medicinal and other useful plants. In a close parallel to buffering or transition in the classic biosphere reserve, there is now also cautious acceptance of sustainable harvesting outside of core conservation sites of appropriate plant species for traditional medicine and crafts.

Cultural Areas

The added flexibility of a functional approach opens up the possibility of explicitly including cultural diversity and heritage in the implementation of biosphere reserves and their zonation. Thus, in the context of an urban biosphere reserve, it is possible that a cultural dimension could be introduced in a city, resulting in cultural core areas that coincide with areas of high cultural diversity or significance. A cultural core can provide a target area for public and civil society cultural initiatives increasing cross-cultural awareness through programs such as the demonstration of historic and current sociocultural practices, or the development of cultural and educational centers. In addition, biocultural interdependencies may be highlighted and supported through synergies between adjacent or overlapping cultural and biodiversity core areas.

In the Cape Flats, these sorts of synergies are already at work in the Driftsands Nature Reserve, where biodiversity conservation is pursued simultaneously with innovative cultural programs such as the proposed *Driftsands Initiation Village*, a joint venture between the Western Cape Nature Conservation Board, the City of Cape Town, the Provincial Administration of the Western Cape, and traditional leaders.[c] After close consultation with people from surrounding settlements and traditional healers, it was determined that Driftsands provides an ideal place where traditional initiation rituals can be practiced in a safe environment. The Xhosa youth undergo these rituals at a certain age, and it has proved to be very difficult to find suitable open spaces

[c]Initiation: Xhosa boys went and still go through a traditional transition from boyhood to manhood marked by the *abakweta* circumcision ceremony. In the past, every Xhosa youth had to go through this ceremony before he was considered to be a man. It is still a strong tradition in rural areas (where it is a communal matter and a number of boys undergo initiation together) and to a lesser extent in the urban centers. The Driftsands Initiation Village was officially opened by a traditional leader on March 2, 2004.

in urban areas. Through access to a safe environment for cultural practices, the reserve can provide a real support to the culture and identities of surrounding communities, while increasing awareness of the value of natural open spaces.

An urban biosphere reserve therefore could be a means for a city to actively acknowledge, celebrate, and protect its biological *and* human diversity. This is a particularly relevant and attractive option for an urban area such as Cape Town, whose ultimate success will depend on its ability to capitalize on its rich environmental and cultural patrimony as a foundation for ecological, social, economic, and political sustainability.

A MATTER OF TERMINOLOGY

A contentious matter that arose during the CTCS was the use of the term "biosphere reserve" in an urban context. The term "reserve" is inevitably coupled to the historical meaning of an exclusion area. We therefore would propose that different terminology be used in the case of urban areas corresponding to the biosphere reserve framework, such as "MAB city" or a "MAB city network," which could be a parallel network to the World Network of Biosphere Reserves.[d] This change in terminology (and area of application) could result in a new and very valuable dimension that can be linked to the World Network of Biosphere Reserves. To retain a status of excellence and importance, a set of criteria or guidelines also should be developed to inform a procedure of selecting and designating urban areas within a MAB city network. In addition, a monitoring and review process should be implemented to evaluate cities on their performance related to targets set in light of some of the criteria, and especially for achieving tangible benefits as a result of involvement with the program.

We would propose that a MAB city should conform to the following:

(1) It should include a densely populated urban area.
(2) It should include a system of natural or near-natural open spaces that can fulfill the function of a (possibly fragmented) core area for biodiversity conservation.
(3) There should be important cultural areas that will enhance the MAB city, fulfilling the role of cultural core areas in which to demonstrate historic and current sociocultural practices and promote cross-cultural awareness and social inclusion.

[d]The MAB Advisory Committee at their fifth meeting in July 1998 suggested that there might be ways of recognizing cities as models of sustainable development other than by simply associating them with the World Network of Biosphere Reserves.[28]

(4) "Zonation" could be implemented either functionally or spatially. (4.1) A functional implementation could result in specific actions that perform the functions related to traditional spatial zones of a biosphere reserve and could be more appropriate in an urban context. (4.2) A spatial implementation could result in a dual approach: (i) from a biodiversity point of view, with core areas and buffer zones demonstrating the interface between humans and biodiversity, and transition zones that focus on sustainable living practices; and (ii) from a cultural point of view, with cultural core areas to target programs supporting areas of high cultural diversity or significance.

(5) It should establish a cooperative network between all major role players in the urban context.

(6) It should address the levels of environmental, social, and economic responsibility within the urban area.

(7) It should make publicly available a record of the perceived benefits of alignment with the UNESCO MAB Program.

Clearly, careful consideration should precede an application for a MAB city designation. The advantage of being incorporated as part of a MAB city network should add tangible benefits to the region as a whole, and this needs to be demonstrable to the general public. It is also important to carefully consider that there are fundamental differences between a "MAB city" program and other initiatives such as the UN Habitat "Sustainable Cities Program." Differentiating between such concepts would allow for different approaches for urban areas wanting to pursue the sustainability agenda.

CONCLUSIONS

The value of using the biosphere reserve concept in an urban context lies in its ability to inclusively stretch beyond biodiversity by giving equal priority to socioeconomic issues. There are several ways in which the biosphere reserve concept can be implemented as suggested in discussions around the functional implementation of the zonation framework. In addition, the biosphere reserve concept should provide added dimensions to current initiatives.

Membership of a MAB city network, linked to the World Network of Biosphere Reserves, also should enhance the global support network and related resources for cities involved. In the case of Cape Town, there are still many questions and trials that would need to be considered and addressed: for example, what tangible environmental management solutions can the application of the biosphere reserve concept offer in the face of extensive socioeconomic impoverishment? And most important of all, what is the potential functional and tangible impact of the biosphere reserve concept on the everyday lives of the impoverished Cape Flats communities?

During the evaluation phase and the compilation of the background document on the CTCS, it became clear that one of the most important values of applying the biosphere reserve concept to an urban context lies in the process itself. Within the cross-disciplinary team involved in the project, the process thus far has strengthened conceptual bridges between the needs of people and the necessities for sustaining the environment. This is obviously a very small step, but it is also a robust one. And it is through such incremental advances in knowledge sharing, consultation, and collaboration that implementable and effective long-run strategies for sustainability are best developed.

ACKNOWLEDGMENTS

We thank the rest of the CTUBG for support, namely, Keith Wiseman, Trevor Sandwith, Chrizette Kleynhans, Kier Hennessy, Willem Smith, Trevor Farr, Kallie Naude, Chris Hewett, and Pete van Heerden. We also thank Riki de Villiers of the Western Cape Nature Conservation Board for help in preparing the maps.

REFERENCES

1. Environmental Evaluation Unit. University of Cape Town, Local Agenda 21 South Africa < http://www.egs.uct.ac.za/la21/about.html/>.
2. UN-HABITAT, Sustainable Cities Programme. <http://www.unhabitat.org/programmes/sustainablecities/>.
3. Industry Canada, Sustainable Cities Initiative. <http://strategis.ic.gc.ca/epic/internet/inscin-idvd.nsf/vwGeneratedInterE/Home/>.
4. WHO, Healthy Cities and Urban Governance. <http://www.who.dk/eprise/main/WHO/Progs/HCP/Home/>.
5. Batisse, M. 2001. Biosphere reserves: a personal appraisal. *In* Proceedings of Seville + 5 International Meeting of Experts, Proceedings. MAB Report Series No. 69. UNESCO. Paris.
6. UNESCO, MAB Urban Forum. <http://www.unesco.org/mab/urban/urbangroup.htm/>.
7. CUBES, Earth Institute at Columbia University, About CUBES, http://www.earthinstitute.columbia.edu/cubes/.
8. CUBES, Earth Institute at Columbia University. CUBES Cape Town Site <http://www.earthinstitute.columbia.edu/cubes/sites/southafrica.html/>.
9. Cape Action for People and the Environment C.A.P.E. <http://www.cape-action.org.za/.>
10. CUBES Cape Town Urban Biosphere Group. 2003. CUBES Cape Town Institutional Seminar Proceedings. Unpublished report.

11. City of Cape Town, Statistical and General Information for the Cape Metropolitan Area <http://www.capetown.gov.za/home/profile.asp/>.
12. Program for Land and Agrarian Studies (PLAAS). 2002. Household Livelihood Survey report. University of the Western Cape, School of Government. South Africa. Unpublished report.
13. Nattrass, N. 2002. AIDS and Human Security in Southern Africa. CSSR Working Paper No. 18. AIDS and Society Research Unit, Centre for Social Science Research, University of Cape Town. <http://www.uct.ac.za/depts/cssr/pubs.html/>.
14. NepalNet, Poverty and Its Incidence in Nepal <http://www.panasia.org.sg/nepalnet/socio/poverty_nepal.htm/>.
15. Jonfia-Essien, W. & M. Obodai. Impact Assessment of Storage Management in the Poverty Alleviation Programme: A Case Study in Ghana and Lessons for Sub-Saharan Africa. University of Nottingham, School of Biosciences, Nottingham. http://foodafrica.nri.org/security/internetpapers/WilliamJonfia-Essie.doc
16. City of Cape Town, State of the Environment Report <http://www.capetown.gov.za/soe/>.
17. City of Cape Town. 2003. The Environmental Policy of the City of Cape Town. Unpublished report.
18. Stanvliet, R., J. Jackson, G. Davis, *et al.* 2003. Applicability of the Biosphere Reserve Concept to an Urban Context: An Overview Evaluation of the Cape Town Case Study. Unpublished report.
19. City of Cape Town. 2003. Biodiversity and Development Plan for the False Bay Coast. Unpublished report.
20. The Western Cape Nature Conservation Board. 2003. Driftsands Management Plan. Draft unpublished report.
21. The City of Cape Town, Health Department. 2003. Khayelitsha Task Team. Unpublished report.
22. Mkefe, X. & T. Goldman. 2003. Biodiversity for the People: Cape Flats Nature. Veld & Flora, 89.
23. West Coast District Council. 1996. Proposed West Coast Biosphere Reserve. Unpublished report.
24. Cape Nature Conservation. 1998. Motivation for the Establishment of the Kogelberg Biosphere Reserve, Western Cape Province, South Africa. Unpublished report.
25. Stellenbosch Town Council. 2002. Towards the establishment of the Boland Biosphere Reserve. Unpublished report.
26. Department of Planning, Local Government and Housing. 2000. Bioregional planning Framework for the Western Cape Province.
27. Cape Metropolitan Council. 2000. Table Mountain Chain–Peninsula Biosphere Reserve: Pre-feasibility Study. Environmental Management Department. Unpublished report.
28. UNESCO. The Role of MAB with Regard to Urban and Peri-Urban Issues <http://www.unesco.org/mab/urban/Urban.doc/>.
29. Cowling, R.M. & D.M. Richardson. 1995. Fynbos: South Africa's Unique Floral Kingdom. Fernwood Press, Cape Town, South Africa.
30. IZIKO, Museums of Cape Town, West Coast Fossil Park <http://www.museums.org.za/wcfp/>.

31. TABLE MOUNTAIN NATIONAL PARK, Profile/General Information <http://www.cpnp.co.za/>.
32. RONDEVLEI NATURE RESERVE, Rondevlei Nature Reserve <http://www.rondevlei.co.za/>.
33. CAPE FLATS NATURE, About Cape Flats Nature <http://www.capeflats-nature.org/>.
34. YOUNG, T. 2003. How 2 Help. Aardvark Press. Bridgeport, CT.
35. ENVIRONMENTAL JUSTICE NETWORKING FORUM, The Environmental Justice Networking Forum <http://www.botany.uwc.ac.za/inforeep/EJNF.htm/>.
36. WILDLIFE AND ENVIRONMENT SOCIETY OF SOUTH AFRICA, WESSA Western Cape Region <http://www.wcape.school.za/wessa/>.
37. BOTANICAL SOCIETY OF SOUTH AFRICA, About the Botanical Society of South Africa <http://www.botanicalsociety.org.za/>.

Biodiversity, Biosphere Reserves, and the Big Apple

A Study of the New York Metropolitan Region

WILLIAM D. SOLECKI[a] AND CYNTHIA ROSENZWEIG[b]

[a]*City University of New York–Hunter College, New York, New York 10021*

[b]*NASA Goddard Institute for Space Studies, Columbia University, New York, New York*

ABSTRACT: **The objectives of this article were to assess the dimensions of biodiversity–urban society interactions within the New York Metropolitan Region, a 31-county area with a population of 21.5 million, and to explore pathways to reconcile dysfunctional relationships between these two ever-entwined systems. The article builds on the premise that urban biodiversity exists at a crucial nexus of ecological and societal interactions, linking local, regional, and global scales, and that urban ecologies are projected to become even more dynamic in the future, particularly as a result of global climate change. The pathway proposed to reconcile the biodiversity–urban society relationships is the incorporation of biosphere reserve strategies into regional environmental planning efforts focused on the New York/New Jersey Harbor/Estuary specifically and on the greater New York Metropolitan Region in general. The concepts of the "ecological footprint" and vulnerability to global environmental change are used to analyze the current interactions between biodiversity and urban society, and to evaluate the efficacy of adopting biosphere reserve strategies in the region. New York has long been at the forefront of American environmentalism and landscape planning. Coupled with this history is a still small but growing interest in regional environmental planning efforts (e.g., the U.S. EPA Harbor Estuary Program) and green infrastructure (e.g., the 2002 Humane Metropolis Conference organized by the Ecological Cities Project). The research presented here aims to contribute to these nascent activities. As a megacity, New York may serve as a model for other major cities of the world.**

KEYWORDS: **urban biodiversity; biosphere reserve; New York Metropolitan Region; environmental change; ecological footprint**

Address for correspondence: William D. Solecki, Department of Geography, City University of New York–Hunter College, 695 Park Avenue, New York, NY 10021. Voice: 212-772-4536; fax: 212-772-5268.
wsolecki@hunter.cuny.edu

Ann. N.Y. Acad. Sci. 1023: 105–124 (2004). © 2004 New York Academy of Sciences.
doi: 10.1196/annals.1319.004

> On this river there is great traffick in the skins of beavers, otters, foxes, bears, minks, wild cats, and the like. The land is excellent and agreeable, full of noble forest trees and grape vines, and nothing is wanting but the labor and industry of man to render it one of the finest and most fruitful lands in that part of the world … "—Johan de Laet, *Nieuwe Werldt ofte Beschrijvinghe van West-Indien* (New World, or Description of West-India) Leyden, 1625. Observation of New York Harbor

Human impacts on native biodiversity[a] throughout the globe have been profound. Urban biodiversity exists at a crucial nexus of ecological and societal interactions, linking local, regional, and global scales. It is becoming increasingly important to understand the impact of urbanization on the environment and how these kinds of impacts affect regional and global sustainability. Coastal wetlands, for example, in urbanized areas simultaneously provide sites for water runoff filtration, spawning ground for regional fisheries, and stopover points for migrating birds.

Although more traditional notions hold that the environments of cities are static and that once intensive development has taken place (e.g., urbanization), ecological functions and properties disappear, continual change in both the natural and the built environments characterizes even the most urbanized sites.[1–3] Urban ecologies are projected to become even more dynamic in the future, particularly as a result of global climate change. By the end of this century, global climate-related increases in sea level could be up to four times greater than the current rate of increase occurring naturally in the New York City region.[4]

Regional identity and structure underpin analysis of urban biodiversity in any location. As de Laet's description of the Hudson River's natural bounties illustrates, the Hudson River harbor estuary has long been at the core of the New York Metropolitan Region's structure and function (FIG. 1). The latter part of the 19th and early part of the 20th centuries brought accelerated resource demands as the region's population grew and industrialized, associated change in regional identity and structure, and decline of the core role that the harbor traditionally played, both literally and figuratively. Recent shifts in cultural values and redevelopment of coastal zones for financial services and residences have brought renewed interest in the harbor estuary region and calls for increased protection from groups and programs such as the NY/NJ Bay Keeper, Metropolitan Waterfront Alliance, and the Harbor Estuary Program.[5] As old port facilities and industries are replaced with commercial and residential developments, rejuvenated port infrastructure, and recreational sites, attention is again turning to the land–sea interface. As a result of these

[a]A common definition for biodiversity has evolved, although scholars and practitioners often stress varying elements of its definition. "All hereditarily based variation at all levels of organization, from the genes within a single local population or species, to the species composing all or part of a local community, and finally to the communities themselves that compose the living parts of the multifarious ecosystems of the world."[31] (p. 1).

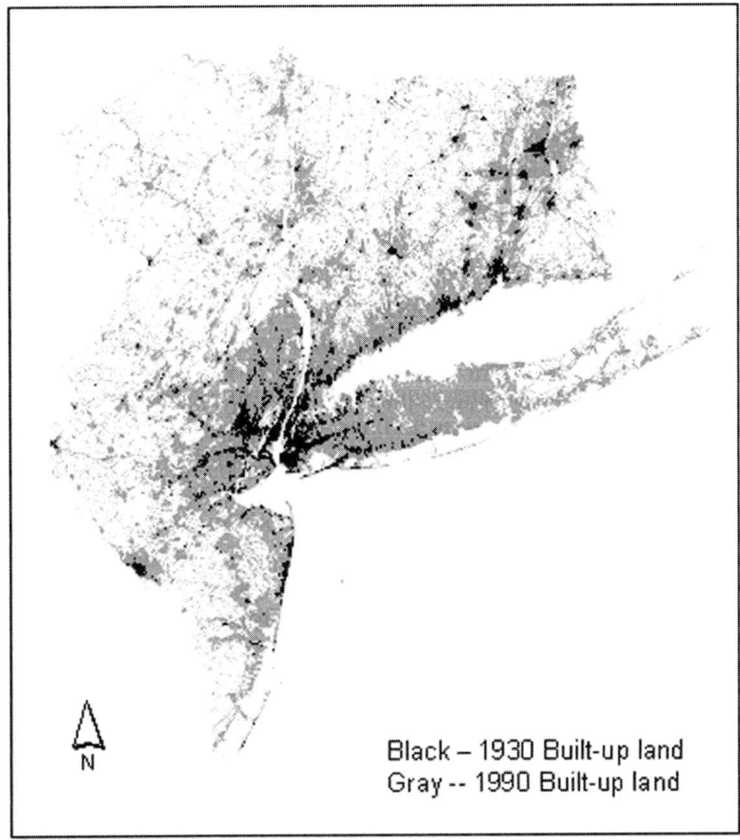

FIGURE 1. Urban and suburban land use in the New York Metropolitan Region–1990. (Source: Authors from USGS Urban Dynamics Program data.)

transformations, the New York Metropolitan Region as a whole, and, more particularly, its core area of the harbor estuary is an ideal place to study the dynamic relationships between urban ecology and culture, to evaluate the functions of biological and social diversity and to create a laboratory for sustainability planning.

The objectives of this article are to assess the dimensions of biodiversity–urban society interactions within the New York Metropolitan Region, a 31-county area with a population of 21.5 million, and to explore pathways to reconcile dysfunctional relationships between these two ever-entwined systems in a global megacity. Situated at the top of the urban hierarchy, megacities are massive in size, typically defined as having more than 10 million residents, and often play critical roles in the global economy.[6] The overall goal of the article is to increase awareness and knowledge leading to better environmental resource management in urban areas. This is especially critical given UN estimates that, by the year 2025, five out of eight billion people will live in urban settlements, particularly in coastal locations.[7]

The pathway proposed to reconcile these relationships is the incorporation of biosphere reserve strategies into a regional environmental planning effort focused on the New York/New Jersey Harbor/Estuary specifically and on the greater New York Metropolitan Region in general. The concepts of the "ecological footprint" and vulnerability to global environmental change are used to analyze the current interactions between biodiversity and urban society and to evaluate the efficacy of adopting biosphere reserve strategies in the region.

As a megacity, New York may serve as a model for other major cities of the world. Although dense human settlements, by definition, put tremendous pressure on resources, individual resource demands in developed-country cities tend to be lower on a per capita basis than in adjoining lower-density suburban and rural areas. In developing countries, the resource demands of urban inhabitants are typically higher than in the surrounding rural areas. As developing countries, such as China, urbanize, it is useful to have models of developed-country cities that have been able to manage their resource demands and impacts on biodiversity in an equitable and sustainable fashion.

By embracing the urban biosphere reserve strategy, the New York Metropolitan Region once again could serve as a testing ground for new initiatives to meet the environmental challenges known collectively under the rubric of "the transition to sustainability."[8] The goal is for New York City and its environs to be known not only as the "Empire City," but also as the "Ecological City," a place where both biological and societal diversities flourish.

THE NEW YORK METROPOLITAN REGION

The generalized effects of cities on the environment are all abundantly and specifically present in the New York Metropolitan Region. The region is one of the most densely settled urban areas in the world, with a total population of roughly 21.5 million persons, of whom 8.0 million live in New York City.[9] Jurisdictionally, there are 31 counties and 1,600 cities, towns, and villages in the three states of New York, New Jersey, and Connecticut, besides the federal government and several regional organizations.[10] The largest financial trading market of the world defines the economic heart of the region.[11] The general economy is mostly based on service industries, which depend on modern, sophisticated means of communication and transportation. The gross regional product (GRP) is estimated at ~US$1 trillion. The region maintains a versatile, high-volume transportation system by air and land (above and belowground roads and rails), as well as on the water. These and other essential infrastructure elements often are used to capacity.

With close to 1,500 miles (2,413.5 kilometers) of coastline, the region's development has been intimately connected to the ocean. Four of the five New York City boroughs are located on islands (Brooklyn, Manhattan, Queens, and Staten Island). Large waterways and water bodies, among them the Newark Bay/Hackensack Meadowlands, Hudson River, East River, Long Island Sound, Peconic Bay, Jamaica Bay, Arthur Kill, and the Raritan River estuary, cut deeply into the land area. The Hudson–Raritan River watershed encompasses about half of the area and includes some of the most densely settled parts of the region. Given its coastal location, much of the land area is at relatively low elevation; ~1% is below 3 meters (~10 ft) in elevation. This 1% encompasses some of the most heavily developed land and regionally important infrastructure, such as lower Manhattan, the three major airports (La Guardia, Kennedy, and Newark), and the Hackensack Meadowlands area. Besides the coastal plain, the Piedmont and Appalachian highlands physiographic regions are present in the west.

Although the region's ecology had been modified to a certain extent by Native Americans before the advent of European settlers, the scale of human modification has greatly increased since the Dutch founded the trading center in the 17th century. Some exurban areas, such as far eastern Long Island, northwestern New Jersey, and parts of Connecticut and New York State more distant from New York City still maintain extensive wildlife habitat. The native ecological function of the more densely settled part of the region is relatively low. However, the few remaining habitat sites there—for example, the Hackensack Meadowlands and the Great Swamp (both in New Jersey) and Jamaica Bay (in New York) and smaller-scale locations, such as in Newark Bay and the Kill Van Kull—provide critical stopping points for migratory bird species. By some estimates, these sites have witnessed significant increases in species-richness in the past several decades as some of the waters have become cleaner.[12]

Critical and vulnerable habitats in the region have been heavily degraded. Most of the region's prehistoric wetlands have been lost, and buffer areas around wetlands or rivers typically no longer exist.[13] In many areas, smaller rivers and streams have been filled, channelized, or placed into culverts. Surface water and groundwater supplies, particularly in the more heavily urbanized areas, have been compromised and typically exceed federal water pollution standards. There are more than 100,000 leaking underground fuel tanks, spill sites, or former industrial sites included on the federal government's register of known or potential toxic sites.[14] Many are located in lowland locations where coastal wetlands were used as landfill sites. There are 131 Superfund hazardous waste sites in the region that are undergoing varying levels of remediation.

TABLE 1. Energy and water consumption in the New York Metropolitan Region and developing countries of similar population

	New York Metro Region	Ghana	Iraq	Malaysia	Peru
Population	21,500,000	19,678,000	22,450,000	21,830,000	25,320,000
Energy consumption (quadrillion Btu)	7.50	0.11	1.09	1.86	0.56
Per capita energy consumption (million Btu)	348.84	5.50	47.40	79.80	21.80
Domestic water consumption (million m^3)[a]	2121.56	105.00	1280.00	1342.00	1260.00
Per capita water consumption (m^3)[a]	265.20	5.34	57.02	61.48	49.76

SOURCES: Energy Information Administration, U.S. Department of Energy, 2002; FAO Aquastat Online Database, 2000.

[a]Values are for New York City (population: 8,008,278).

New York's Ecological Footprint

Urban areas require more resources than their regions can provide and must import food, building materials, and fuel from elsewhere. One way of comparing resource use and land management is by calculating an area's *ecological footprint*, or what can be otherwise designated its *resource-shed*. The ecological footprint is the interactive relationship between an urban area and its hinterland (see Rees,[15] Folke *et al.*,[16] and *Ecological Economics*[17] for more information about the concept and its application). The large, relatively wealthy population of the New York Metropolitan Region consumes more goods and resources than many developing countries (TABLE 1). Estimates of per capita and total use of resources may be calculated for water, food, and energy.

The New York City Water Supply System serves as an excellent example of the character and shape of a local ecological footprint (FIG. 2). The system supplies 1,500 million gallons per day (MGD) to residential, commercial, and industrial users throughout the region and flows from upland reservoirs in the Catskills down through all parts of New York City. Water is collected from upland watersheds, held in storage reservoirs, and sent via a system of tunnels and aqueducts through balancing and distribution reservoirs to distribution mains in the city and other user areas. Water is collected and stored in three upland reservoir systems, the earliest of which began service in 1842. The total area of the watersheds is nearly 2,000 square miles. The most

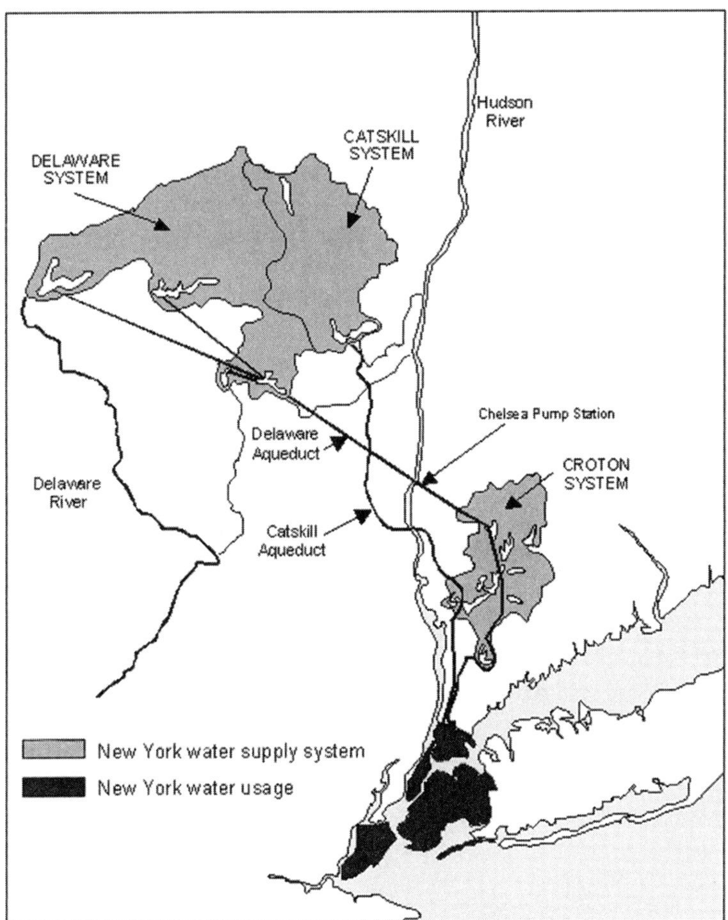

FIGURE 2. The New York City water supply system and water usage area. (Source: Major and Goldberg.[18])

pressing problem facing the system is the potential decline in water quality associated with increased suburbanization and nonpoint pollution around some of the upstate reservoirs. Rising water demand and long-term vulnerability to climate change–induced droughtiness and floods are other problems of increasing concern for decision makers.[18,19]

The New York Metropolitan Region also places demands on locales very distant from its borders and even its watershed. For example, the population's demand for food and energy extends throughout the nation and the globe. Almost all of the region's food must be imported, especially because remaining nearby farmland is continuously converted to suburban land uses. For one aspect of the ecological footprint of the region's food demand, we estimate that the population consumes bread and pasta products from approximately 800,000 hectares of wheat. This is roughly equivalent to the total acreage of wheat grown in the state of Nebraska. The region's annual energy demand is equivalent to approximately 7.7% (7.5 quadrillion Btu) of the nation's total consumption. The region's demand then is comparable to the total of energy consumption of South Korea (7.35 quads) and slightly less than that of Brazil (8.51 quads).[20]

A major by-product of the United States' consumer society is a tremendous amount of waste. For the New York Metropolitan Region, some 2.5 billion gallons of treated effluent are put into the Hudson-Raritan Estuary every year.[21] Some locales in the region are among the most contaminated in the country. There are potentially hazardous levels of organopollutants (PCBs, PAHs), carcinogens, and heavy metals (i.e., cadmium, lead, mercury) floating freely in the water, trapped in sediments, and bioaccumulated in the tissues of marine organisms.

The New York City commercial and municipal sectors generate approximately 45,000 tons of waste per day (TABLE 2). Historically, much of the

TABLE 2. Disposal, recycling, and export of New York City waste

(a) New York City waste disposed and recycled in 2000 (tons/day)	
Waste managed by the NYC Department of Sanitation (municipal waste)	18,327
Disposed	11,926
Recycled[a]	6401
Waste managed by private companies	27,555
Total waste	45,882
(b) Percentage of municipal waste exported	
1997	0.0%
1998	14.9%
1999	24.2%
2000	48.4%
2002 (projected)	100.0%
(c) Municipal waste export locations and disposal methods: July 2001 to January 2002 (tons/day)	
Ohio landfill	1174
Pennsylvania landfill	8074
Hempstead and Peaksfield, NY, incinerated	258
New Jersey 15% landfill, 85% incinerated	1760
Virginia landfill	1631

SOURCE: New York City Independent Budget Office, 2001.
[a]As of 2002, plastic and glass recycling has been discontinued.

waste disposal in the region has taken place locally via either landfill or ocean dumping. Volumes, types of disposed materials, and disposal methods have changed over time. Increasingly, wastes are being exported out of the region, as dumping restrictions are put into place and waste facilities become more difficult to site. In recent decades, dozens of landfills in the region have closed. The famous Fresh Kills landfill on Staten Island, the last operating facility in New York City, closed early in 2001, although it was temporarily reopened to receive debris from the World Trade Center disaster. Today, trainloads of containers filled with residential and commercial waste are shipped hundreds of miles out of the region to states throughout the Middle Atlantic and the Midwest regions, particularly Pennsylvania, Ohio, and Virginia. As of 2002, plastic and glass recycling in New York City was suspended, increasing the amount of disposed and exported waste,[22] although the recycling program has now re-commenced.

Within-Region Resource-Use Differences

Although an ecological footprint may be estimated for the New York Metropolitan Region as a whole, there are significant demographic and spatial variations between urban and suburban residents in the level of per capita demand for resources (e.g., land and energy), other raw materials, waste production. Decentralization of the region and the rapid growth of far-flung suburban and exurban communities has been associated with increased resource demands, especially for transportation and living area (TABLE 3).

As the region grew, more land was converted to urban and suburban uses, including industrial, commercial, and residential areas. More than 30% of the total land area has been converted to such uses. There is currently a greater than 30-fold difference in density measures between the five boroughs of New York City and the other 26 counties in the region (TABLE 3). New York City had a population density in 2000 of 10,238 persons/km^2, whereas the rest of the region has a mean density of just 422 persons/km^2. Suburban counties have a far greater percentage of inhabitants who commute alone, and they use public transportation far less than do New York City dwellers. The result of sprawl has been a significant decrease in vegetative cover as well as fragmentation and destruction of animal habitats.

Suburbanization also brought greater demand for water resources, particularly for water for lawns, gardens, and swimming pools. Although only a relatively low percentage of the region's residents have swimming pools, most suburbanites have lawns and gardens onto which they apply high-quality drinking water to ensure vigorous growth. Overall, water demand among urban residents is much lower. A similar scenario is played out with respect to energy use. Urban areas, because of economies of scale, promote public transportation and walking, whereas suburban areas are built around the use of the automobile.

TABLE 3. Resource-use indicators in New York City and selected surrounding suburban counties

Location	New York City	Suffolk County, NY	Morris County, NJ	Rockland County, NY
Population	8,008,278	1,419,369	470,212	286,753
Persons per km^2	10,238	600.9	387.1	636
Number of commuters	3,192,070	670,406	239,839	132,302
Percentage of people who commute alone	24.9%	78.1%	81.2%	73.7%
Percentage of people who carpool	8.0%	10.1%	8.0%	11.0%
Percentage of people who use public transportation	52.8%	6.8%	4.2%	8.0%
Mean travel time (minutes)	40.0	31.8	29.4	32.6
Median number of rooms in one-family residence	3.8	6.3	6.6	6.3

SOURCE: U.S. Census, 2000.

Global Climate Change

Climate change may be viewed as the ultimate stress on a city where the dense population already puts tremendous demand on land and water resources.[23] Global climate models predict that New York in the 21st century will experience higher temperatures throughout the year and more heat waves in summer, rising seas, shorter recurrence periods for flooding associated with severe storms, and increased frequencies of drought and flooding.[24] These climate shifts, in turn, are likely to inundate coastal wetlands, threaten vital infrastructure and water supplies during extreme weather events, augment summertime energy demand, and directly and indirectly affect public health, all at the same time. Ecological diversity will be affected both directly and indirectly by these changes.

Climate change is already occurring in New York. Over the past century, average regional temperature has increased ~2°F, after the effects of the urban heat island have been removed. Precipitation levels in the region have increased slightly by an average of ~0.1 inch/decade over the same period. Climate change projections for New York City have been derived from extrapolations from the current trends and from global climate models (GCMs). The GCM-projected temperature changes are higher (4–10°F by the 2080s) than those projected by current trends (over 2°F in the 2080s), because the GCM scenarios account for increasing feedback from greenhouse gases that act as forcing mechanisms to warm the Earth's atmosphere (FIG. 3). Precipitation projections for the region do not agree in magnitude or direction, indicating hydrological uncertainty in the future.

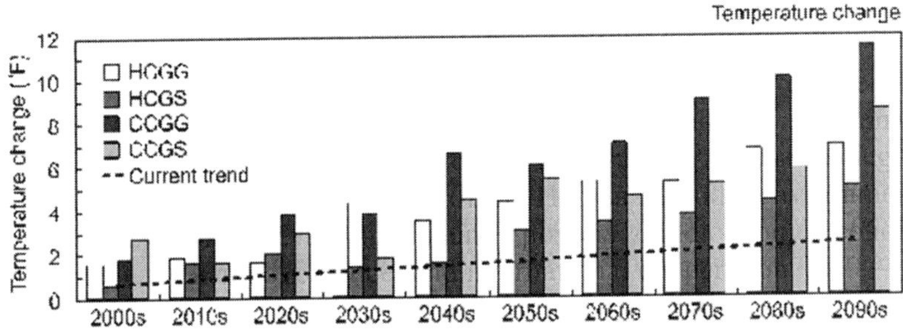

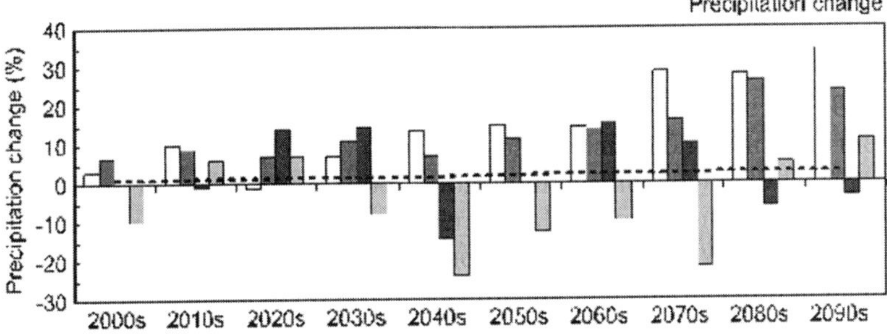

FIGURE 3. Decadal temperature and precipitation changes in the New York Metropolitan Region projected by the Hadley Centre (HC) and Canadian Centre (CC) climate change scenarios with greenhouse gases (GG) and with greenhouse gases and sulfate aerosols (GS), and by continuation of current trends. (Source: Rosenzweig and Solecki.[24])

Sea-level rise associated with global warming is the key vulnerability, resulting in widespread impacts on a region as closely linked to the ocean–land interface as New York. The current rate of sea-level increase is approximately 0.1 in/yr, with some regional variation.[25] Approximately half of this rate is associated with regional land subsidence linked to isostatic rebound of formerly glaciated land to the north; the other half is associated with the observed increase in global mean temperature rise (~1.2°F) over the period from 1900 to 2000.

The key threat of sea-level increase for the coastal city of New York is its effect on flood heights associated with storms. Heightened flood levels associated with future hurricanes and nor'easters (strong winter extratropical cyclonic storms) will cause the most significant damage. Given the projected rates of sea-level increase, Gornitz[26] and Gornitz and Couch[4] have estimated that, under a worst-case scenario, by 2090 a coastal storm event comparable to a 100-year flood could occur every 3–4 years. Much of the region's important infrastructure will be at increased risk to damage resulting from the augmented flood heights (FIG. 4).[26,27] The default public policy of placing

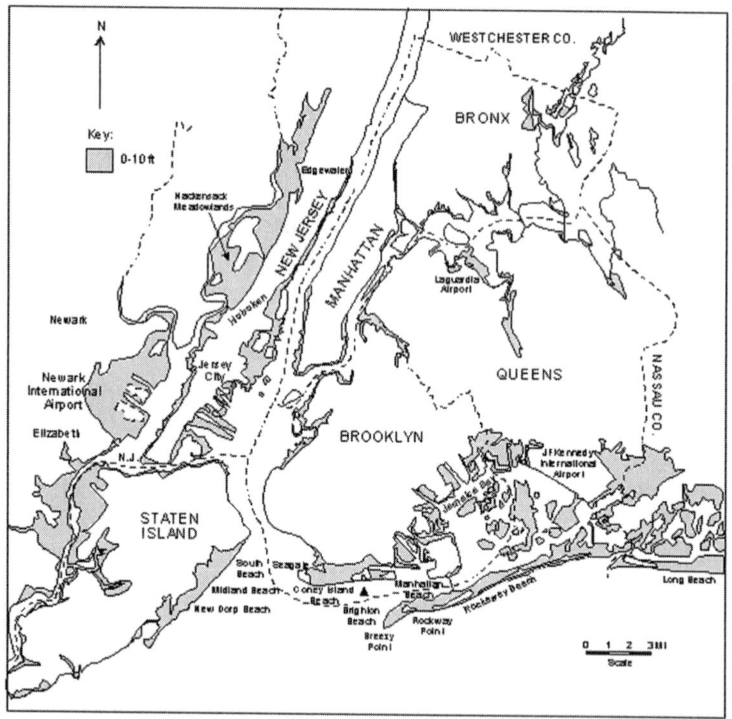

FIGURE 4. Flood risk zone, New York City and neighboring area. (Source: Gornitz.[26]).

necessary yet "locally unwanted land uses" on marginal lands, such as transportation infrastructure across and along the edges of wetlands, bays, and estuaries, has engendered risks of unintended consequences related to global climate change.

A different vulnerability is exhibited by the region's salt-marsh wetlands, important remaining habitat arcas. Under natural conditions, wetlands respond to sea-level increase through accretion and in-migration; however, many of the wetlands in the New York Metropolitan Region can no longer respond in this way because of the reduction of sediment input and loss of upland migration sites resulting from extensive land development in the coastal zone. As the wetlands disappear with increased rise in sea level, their capacity to serve as habitat for local and migratory animals, particularly for waterfowl species, as protection of inland development from storm surges, and as natural filtration water purifiers will be diminished.

Severe wetland loss in the region's remnant coastal marshlands already has been recorded. Recent research indicates that salt-marsh islands in the Jamaica Bay Wildlife Refuge, part of the Gateway National Recreation Area, have decreased approximately 12% in size from 1959 to 1998.[28] Future scenarios illustrate that rate of sea-level increase is likely to continue to exceed the accretion rate of the wetlands by the mid-part of this century, contributing to even more rapid disappearance of the wetlands.

PROPOSING THE NEW YORK BIOSPHERE RESERVE

As illustrated above, the 20th century brought dramatic increases in residents' resource demands in the New York Metropolitan Region and associated burdens on local and global biodiversity. Simultaneous economic and social transformations include increased overall wealth, suburbanization, and drastic shifts in the patterns and landscapes of consumption. Although the region became a site of global power and wealth, many within the region believe that its social, economic, and environmental fabric is threatened (e.g., see discussion in the Regional Plan Association 1996 report, *A Region at Risk*[14]). The dominant ecological and economic trends have made the region more vulnerable to perturbations such as extreme coastal storms, less sustainable as a result of increased per capita resource demands, and less equitable in terms of pollution exposure and quality of life.

To remedy these trends and promote more efficient and effective long-term ecologic and economic patterns of consumption and greater resilience of the region to future perturbations, we propose the development and implementation of a biosphere reserve management strategy. We contend that applying the biosphere reserve concept to the New York Metropolitan Region will result in direct and significant benefits for both the region's ecology and economy. The economic benefits of biosphere reserve planning will flow from the enhanced social importance and amenity values of greater and more nurtured open space and waterfront access, reduction in existing pollution and the costs of its control, and a reversal of the disharmonies and diseconomies of suburban sprawl.

Biosphere Reserves

As defined by the UNESCO Man and the Biosphere Programme, biosphere reserves are designed to serve three primary functions: to protect biodiversity, to encourage long-term observation of ecological trends, and to be laboratories for sustainability study and planning.[29]

A multitude of strategies can be used to achieve these programmatic goals. A common strategy has been the demarcation of *core*, *buffer*, and *transition* management zones. The *core* of the biosphere reserve is defined as the most important with respect to resource protection. These are sites where critical habitats and biodiversity resources are protected. The role of the *buffer* area is to protect the core, and the *transition* area serves as an intermediate zone between the buffer and the surrounding region.

Relatively few of the existing Biosphere Reserves are composed of three concentric rings of management areas. In most cases, the core is not a single site nor is it completely surrounded by a buffer zone. The core areas are often a set of parcels with the most exclusive zoning restrictions.

The UNESCO Man and the Biosphere Programme Biosphere Reserve designation does not come with any mandatory management constraints and is not associated with any loss of sovereignty of the host region or country to the UN or any other international body, counter to concerns occasionally voiced by local residents. The designation of an area as a Biosphere Reserve most often is largely a political act that adds to the legitimacy of environmental protection strategies already existing or proposed.

Zones and Functions

In the case of New York, a biosphere reserve could be constructed in two ways. The overall reserve region is the New York/New Jersey harbor estuary, including the New York Upper and Lower Bays, and adjacent coastal areas (e.g., Hackensack Meadowlands and Jamaica Bay), and the multiple adjoining resource-sheds. In the first approach, the New York/New Jersey harbor estuary area, as the site of the most significant ecological biodiversity in the region, is suggested as the *core* of the reserve (FIG. 5a). In the second approach, there is a distributed core encompassing all open spaces, parks, and wetlands across the New York Metropolitan Region (FIG. 5b). The designation of the latter as core emphasizes the need for rehabilitation, restoration, nurture, and appreciation of all remaining natural areas of the city. These two approaches to the core could be either alternative or simultaneous.

The *buffer* zone would include the watershed areas that surround either or both cores, including the watersheds of the Raritan River and Passaic River

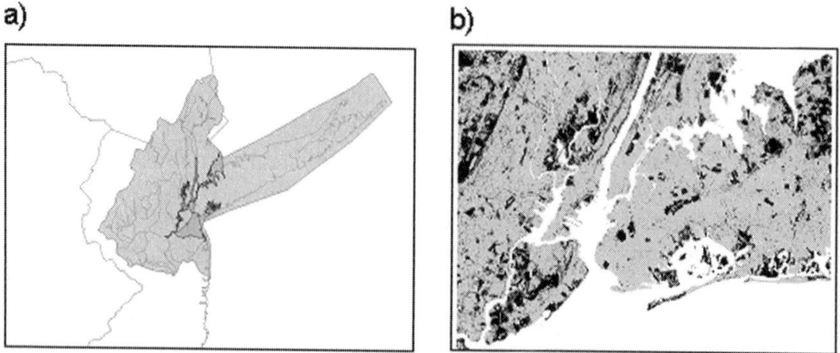

FIGURE 5. Biosphere reserve planning concept for the New York Metropolitan Region. (**a**) Core and buffer areas. (**b**) Parks and open space.

watersheds, the Hudson River watershed, and the highly degraded watershed region represented by southern Westchester County, New York City, and Nassau County on Long Island. These watersheds have the most direct ecological impact on the biodiversity of the core as a result of upstream land-use and habitat changes, water runoff, and the resulting pollution. The *transition* zone in the reserve would be represented by the resource-shed of the city, including all locations throughout the country and the globe that provide resources that serve the core and the buffer and/or receive its wastes. This transition zone is conceptualized as malleable, reflecting the changing spatial patterns of the region's resource demands. The distributed core creates transitions to neighborhoods, their vitalization, and reappreciation and emphasizes connections to social diversity.

This prototype urban biosphere reserve will function similarly to other reserves (i.e., by protecting regional biodiversity, becoming an observatory for long-term monitoring of ecological trends, and providing a laboratory for sustainability planning efforts). However, the role and significance of the core of the New York biosphere reserve represents a significant departure from traditional biosphere reserve planning. Traditionally, the principal objective of protecting the core is to preserve its critical biodiversity resources. Sustainability often is defined for the level of long-term resource protection that can take place. In the case of the New York biosphere reserve, the core is important both for ecological biodiversity and for societal and economic function. In this case, the core's local societal function, for its role as the focus for the region's activity and identity, is more important than its global ecological status. (The harbor estuary core of the New York biosphere reserve, while home to a wide array of species comparable to that of the Chesapeake and Delaware bays, is by no means a global biodiversity hot spot.)

Of heightened importance in the case of New York biosphere reserve is the sustainability function. Through the two different approaches to the core described above, the reserve will serve as an urban laboratory for sustainability experimentation. To augment and sustain the societal function of the core for the region as a whole, its ecological function needs to be sustained as well. And in turn, to sustain the ecological function of the core, the environmental inputs from the buffer areas (e.g., the surrounding watersheds) and other nearby transition-zone population centers (e.g., areas of western New Jersey and Long Island whose pollution inputs have an indirect impact on the core) need to be limited. In contrast, then, to most biosphere reserves where the transition and buffer areas serve the core in a largely unidirectional fashion, the New York biosphere reserve represents a much more interactive relationship among the three zones. In this case, the protection of the core preserves the ecological integrity of the areas and simultaneously enables it to fulfill its critical role as the social center of the region. This condition represents the true interdependence of the three zones that is the essence of the biosphere concept at its most effective.

SOCIAL AND ECONOMIC BENEFITS

In the case of the New York biosphere reserve, the promotion of the ecological function of the region will have at least three key local social and economic benefits: enhanced waterfront development, effective water-resource management (quality and quantity), and improved resilience to climate extremes and change.

Waterfront Development

Biosphere reserve management will help foster continued redevelopment of the waterfront zones, enhancing their economic amenity value. The Hackensack Meadowlands are an excellent example of the amenity value of a healthier ecosystem. In the 1960s, many residential and commercial developers shunned the Meadowlands because of its reputation as a polluted and severely ecologically degraded place. Since the late 1980s, the area has become increasing desirable real estate because of the environmental enhancement activities of the Hackensack Meadowlands Commission (closing of the garbage dumps and partial protection of the remaining wetland and natural areas) and the natural regenerative properties of the ecosystems themselves. Ecological areas, such as remnant wetlands, also can add value to adjacent brownfield sites that are undergoing redevelopment.

Water Resource Management

The biosphere reserve planning strategies applied to the New York Metropolitan Region will promote more efficient and effective water pollution–control activities. To promote the enhancement and protection of the harbor/estuary areas, the biosphere reserve strategies will encourage further controls of point and nonpoint sources of water pollution in upstream watershed areas. Biosphere reserve planning also will further promote strategies to encourage a reduction in suburban sprawl. This will be an integral part of the biosphere strategy because of the connection between sprawl and increased nonpoint source pollution into streams and rivers that eventually would flow into the harbor/estuary.

Although existing federal and state water pollution–control regulations have brought significant improvement to the water quality in the region, the biosphere reserve planning efforts will enable a system-wide review and analysis of synergistic impacts of water pollution on regional ecological conditions. By looking at the system as a whole, it could encourage greater amount of bi-state (between New Jersey and New York) cooperation in managing the harbor/estuary area. Each state has separately developed comprehensive environmental protection programs; however, there is little coordination between the two beyond the limited amount that has been facilitated by the U.S. EPA New York/New Jersey Harbor Estuary Program.

Biosphere reserve planning will promote institutional adaptation and flexibility that allows for more integrated and adaptive decision making regarding current and future environmental management and biodiversity protection concerns. As has been shown in other sectors, when intergovernmental cooperation takes place, the management of resources becomes more effective (i.e., better able to respond to a wider spectrum of environmental concerns) and more efficient (i.e., less costly per unit of pollution reduction).

Climate Extremes and Change

Another economic advantage of biosphere reserve planning is that it will help lessen the vulnerability of the region to climate extremes and change. Vulnerability to flooding events will be lessened through reduction in impervious surfaces, leading to lower and less erosive runoff. Suburbanization causes a dramatic growth in impervious surfaces and inputs of stream sediments, both of which negatively affect the hydrologic regimen for increased flooding potential and to the degradation of downstream aquatic and wetland ecosystems. Impervious surfaces are associated with larger amounts of water being more quickly run off into stream and rivers. The resulting stream sediments are associated with a drastic decline in the stream and river channel depth. Biosphere reserve management can lead to decreases in flood-related property damage and destruction caused by these processes.

Biosphere reserve management also will help to protect coastal development and settlements from climate change–related sea-level increase and extreme event storm surges. The damage potential of an extreme coastal storm (a hurricane or large nor'easter) ranges into the tens of billions of dollars.[27] The promotion of an ecologically healthy core, particularly through the protection and restoration of coastal wetlands, will help promote locally important resilience to storm surges. During storm surges, coastal wetlands can become floodwater catchment areas, thereby protecting the surrounding built environment from inundation. As an example, remaining wetlands in the Hackensack Meadowlands currently serve as floodwater catchment areas for the surrounding urban and suburban lands.

CONCLUSIONS—BARRIERS AND BRIDGES

Regional planning efforts of any type, particularly that exemplified by biosphere reserve planning, have been inherently difficult to achieve in urban areas such as the New York Metropolitan Region. Gunderson *et al.*[30] discuss some of the barriers. Home rule and a splintered political landscape characterize the region with its more than a thousand jurisdictions. In this setting, short-term political concerns tend to dominate, and long-term biodiversity and ecological issues often are not represented as having a wide-reaching societal impact. Policy responses to biodiversity protection also are hampered by the generally reactive nature of management organizations. Institutional action often is directed at immediate and obvious problems; issues that might emerge fully only after several decades are perceived as less pressing.

What is needed to move forward? Several initiatives will help to build the necessary foundation for the biosphere reserve strategy to be followed. These include education and outreach programs, methods for defining and entraining potential biodiversity impacts into planning decisions, and increased interagency communication and cooperation. Several organizations and programs are currently at work and achieving some success. Examples of these include the Regional Plan Association, Port Authority of NY/NJ, Metropolitan Transportation Authority, and federal agencies and programs such as EPA Region II and the New York/New Jersey Harbor Estuary Program.

Application of the biosphere reserve strategies described in this article will enable these and other regional decision makers to better understand the connections between biodiversity and urban societal demands, be more responsive to potential environmental changes on longer time horizons, and be more flexible in the face of increased climatic uncertainty. At the operational level, a New York biosphere reserve will provide an excellent pathway for integration of new environmental management proposals, such as wetland restoration programs and climate change adaptation strategies, into stakeholders' decision-making practices.

ACKNOWLEDGMENTS

We thank Christine Alfsen-Norodom and Benjamin Lane (UNESCO), Roberta Miller (CIESIN/Columbia University), and other members of the Urban Biosphere Group for support and stimulating discussion in developing this case study; and Frank Popper (Rutgers University), Rutherford Platt (University of Massachusetts), and Gregory Remaud (NY/NJ Baykeeper) for comments on the paper. We also thank Noah Edelblum (Columbia University), Mary Wiencke (Barnard College), Carolin Stroehle (Montclair State University), and Lauren Sacks (Columbia University) for work on the case study preparation and for their help in organizing our Case Study Stakeholders Workshop. An earlier version of this article was presented at the Biodiversity and Society Conference held in New York City in May 2001, sponsored by UNESCO and the Columbia Earth Institute. The Climate Impacts Group at NASA/Goddard Institute for Space Studies supported this work.

REFERENCES

1. HAUGHTON, G. & C. HUNTER. 1994. Sustainable Cities. Regional Studies Association. Bristol, PA.
2. PLATT, R. & P.C. MUICK, Eds. 1994. The Ecological City, Preserving and Restoring Urban Biodiversity. University of Massachusetts. Amherst, MA.
3. BENNETT, M. & D.W. TEAGUE, Eds. 1994. The Nature of Cities: Ecocriticism and Urban Environments. The University of Arizona Press. Tucson, AZ.
4. GORNITZ, V. & S. COUCH. 2001. Sea level rise and coastal hazards. *In* Climate Change and a Global City: An Assessment of the Metropolitan East Coast (MEC) Region. C. Rosenzweig, and W. Solecki, Eds. Metro East Coast Sector Report of the U.S. National Assessment of Potential Climate Change Impacts. Columbia Earth Institute. New York.
5. NEW YORK/NEW JERSEY HARBOR ESTUARY PROGRAM HABITAT WORKGROUP AND CITY OF NEW YORK/PARKS & RECREATION. 2001. New York/New Jersey Harbor Estuary Program Habitat Workgroup, April 2001 Status Report. New York.
6. UNITED NATIONS CENTRE FOR HUMAN SETTLEMENTS (HABITAT). 2001. Cities in a Globalizing World, Global Report on Human Settlements 2001. Earthscan. Sterling, VA.
7. UNITED NATIONS POPULATION FUND. 2001. The State of the World Population 2001. United Nations Population Fund. New York.
8. BOARD ON SUSTAINABLE DEVELOPMENT, POLICY DIVISION, NATIONAL RESEARCH COUNCIL. 1999. Our Common Journey, A Transition toward Sustainability. National Academy Press. Washington, DC.
9. U.S. CENSUS BUREAU. 2000. U.S. Census of Population. Washington, DC.
10. ZIMMERMAN, R. & M. CUSKER. 2001. Institutional decision-making in the New York Metropolitan Region. *In* Climate Change and a Global City: The Metropolitan East Coast Regional Assessment. C. Rosenzweig & W.D. Solecki, Eds. New York. Columbia Earth Institute.
11. WARF, B. 2000. New York: The Big Apple in the 1990s. Geoforum **31:** 487–499.
12. WALDMAN, J. 1999. Heartbeats in the Muck: A Dramatic Look at the History, Sea Life, and Environment of New York Harbor. Lyons Press. New York.
13. HARTIG, E.K., V. GORNITZ, A. KOLKER, *et al.* 2002. Anthropogenic and climate-change impacts on salt marshes of Jamaica Bay, New York City. Wetlands **22:** 1.
14. YARO, R. & T. HISS. 1996. A Region at Risk: The Third Regional Plan for the NY/NJ/CT Metropolitan Area. Regional Plan Association. New York.
15. REES, W.E. 1992. Ecological footprint and appropriated carrying capacity: what urban economics leaves out. Environ. Urban. **4:** 121–130.
16. FOLKE, C., A. JANSSON, J. LARSSON & R. COSTANZA. 1997. Ecosystem appropriation by cities. Ambio **26:** 167–172.
17. Ecological Economics. The International Society for Ecological Economics. <http//www.ecologicaleconomics.org>.
18. MAJOR, D. & R. GOLDBERG. 2001. Adapting water supply systems to climate change. *In* Climate Change and a Global City: An Assessment of the Metropolitan East Coast (MEC) Region. C. Rosenzweig, and W. Solecki, Eds. Metro East

Coast Sector Report of the U.S. National Assessment of Potential Climate Change Impacts. Columbia Earth Institute. New York.

19. Frei, A. R.L. Armstrong, M.P. Clarke & M.C. Serreze. 2002. Catskill Mountain water resources: vulnerability, hydroclimatology, and climate-change sensitivity. Ann Assoc. Amer. Geographers **92:** 203–224.
20. U.S. Department of Energy, Energy Information Administration. 2002. <http://www.eia.doe.gov>.
21. HydroQual, Inc. 1991. Assessment of Pollutant Loadings to NY/NJ Harbor. Draft Final Report to EPA Region II, NY/NJ Harbor Estuary Program. HydroQual. Mahwah, NJ.
22. Independent Budget Office of New York City. 2001. Background paper: overview of the waste stream managed by the NYC Department of Sanitation. Independent Budget Office. New York.
23. Aspen Global Change Institute. 2001. Climate Change and Cities. Aspen Global Change Institute. Aspen, CO.
24. Rosenzweig, C. & W.D. Solecki, eds. 2001. Climate Change and A Global City: The Metropolitan East Coast Regional Assessment. New York. Columbia Earth Institute. New York.
25. Gornitz, V. 1995. A comparison of differences between recent and late Holocene sea-level trends from eastern North America and other selected regions. J. Coastal Resources (special issue) **17:** 287–297.
26. Gornitz, V. 1995. Monitoring sea level changes. Climate Change **31:** 515–544.
27. Jacob, K.H., N. Edelblum & J. Arnold. 2001. Infrastructure in the New York metropolitan region. *In* Climate Change and A Global City: The Metropolitan East Coast Regional Assessment. C. Rosenzweig & W.D. Solecki, Eds. Columbia Earth Institute. New York.
28. Hartig, E. 2001. Climate Change Impacts on Tidal Wetlands. *In* Climate Change and a Global City: An Assessment of the Metropolitan East Coast (MEC) Region. C. Rosenzweig & W. Solecki, Eds. Metro East Coast Sector Report of the U.S. National Assessment of Potential Climate Change Impacts.
29. UNESCO. 1996. Biosphere Reserves: The Seville Strategy and the Statutory Framework of the World Network. UNESCO. Paris.
30. Gunderson, L.H., C.S. Holling & S.S. Light, Eds. 1995. Barriers and Bridges to the Renewal of Ecosystems and Institutions. Columbia University Press. New York.
31. Wilson, E.O. 1997. Introduction. *In* Biodiversity II: Understanding and Protecting Our Biological Resources. M.L. Reaka-Kudla, D.E. Wilson & E.O. Wilson, Eds.: 1–6. John Henry Press. Washington, DC.

Managing the Megacity for Global Sustainability

The New York Metropolitan Region as an Urban Biosphere Reserve

CHRISTINE ALFSEN-NORODOM,[a] SUSAN E. BOEHME,[b] STEVEN CLEMANTS,[c] MELODY CORRY,[d] VALERIE IMBRUCE,[e] BENJAMIN D. LANE,[d] ROBERTA BALSTAD MILLER,[f] CHRISTINE PADOCH,[e] MARTA PANERO,[b] CHARLES M. PETERS,[e] CYNTHIA ROSENZWEIG,[g] WILLIAM SOLECKI,[h] AND DANIEL WALSH[a]

[a]*CUBES: Columbia University/UNESCO Joint Program on Biosphere and Society*

[b]*Harbor Project, New York Academy of Sciences, New York, New York*

[c]*Brooklyn Botanic Garden, Brooklyn, New York*

[d]*CUBES: Columbia University/UNESCO Joint Program on Biosphere and Society, New York, New York*

[e]*New York Botanical Garden, New York, New York*

[f]*CIESIN/Columbia University, New York, New York*

[g]*NASA–Goddard Institute for Space Studies, Columbia University, New York, New York*

[h]*Department of Geography, Hunter College of the City University of New York, New York, New York*

ABSTRACT: The UNESCO World Network of Biosphere Reserves (WNBR), while not originally conceived to include urban areas, was intended to include sites representing all significant ecosystems with the goal of support for sustainable development locally and globally. Drawing on the example of the New York Metropolitan Region (NYMR), which has a population of 21.4 million, it is argued here that the eventual inclusion of the largest of the world's cities in WNBR not only is within the logic of the biosphere reserve concept, but would also benefit the network and its goals. The ecological significance of the NYMR, its role as a driver for global environmental change, as well as the efforts under way in the city to improve urban environmental management and governance are all

Address for correspondence: Benjamin D. Lane, Field Coordinator, CUBES, Earth Institute at Columbia University, 2910 Broadway, Hogan Hall B-16, New York, NY 10027. Voice: 212-854-0268; fax: 212-854-6309.
ben2002@columbia.edu

Ann. N.Y. Acad. Sci. 1023: 125–141 (2004). © 2004 New York Academy of Sciences.
doi: 10.1196/annals.1319.005

examined. Potential added value to the WNBR of including megacities such as the NYMR is considered, in particular, regarding the sharing of best practices, lessons learned, and the strengthening of links between megacities and their global natural resource bases.

KEYWORDS: biosphere reserves; world network of biosphere reserves; urban ecosystems; industrial ecology; ecological footprint; urban agriculture; megacities; environmental governance

INTRODUCTION

Since its inception in the 1970s, the UNESCO biosphere reserve concept has developed into a powerful management and governance tool for sustainable development at widely diverse sites around the world. Although first conceived as a means for protecting pristine ecosystems, biosphere reserves have increasingly been established in areas where human activities play more obvious roles in ecosystem functioning. In recent years, the biosphere reserve model has been employed in periurban and urban areas; however, its potential for large cities remains untested.

Rosenzweig and Solecki (2001) first proposed that the New York Metropolitan Region (NYMR) could benefit from becoming a biosphere reserve, arguing that "application of the biosphere reserve strategy [would] enable resource decision makers to better understand the connections between biodiversity and urban societal demands," thereby allowing them to be "more responsive to potential environmental changes on longer time horizons, and flexible in the face of increased uncertainty," and that an NYMR Biosphere Reserve would "provide an excellent pathway for integration of new environmental management proposals, such as climate change adaptation strategies into stakeholders' decision-making practices."[1]

A major theme of the CUBES/UNESCO/UN-Habitat/New York Academy of Sciences conference *Urban Biosphere and Society: Partnership of Cities* was to examine how the biosphere reserve concept could be successfully applied to urban areas such as New York,[2] Seoul,[3] Rome,[4] Stockholm,[5] and Cape Town.[6]

We pose a complementary notion. Whereas others are concerned primarily with the value of the biosphere reserve concept to large cities, we argue that the application of the biosphere reserve concept to large cities is a potentially valuable contribution to global sustainability. In particular, we argue that the eventual inclusion of the largest of the world's cities in the UNESCO World Network of Biosphere Reserves (WNRB) not only is within the logic of the biosphere reserve concept, but would also actively benefit the network and its goals. To illustrate our arguments, we draw on the example of the NYMR, one of the world's largest urban areas and one of its most radically transformed environments.

The World Network of Biosphere Reserves was established in 1975 by UNESCO's Man and the Biosphere Programme (MAB) to promote "a sustainable balance between the sometimes conflicting goals of conserving biological diversity, promoting economic development and maintaining associated cultural values."[7] A defining aspect of biosphere reserves is the emphasis on fulfillment of three distinct functions of sustainability, these being *conservation* ("of landscapes, ecosystems, species and genetic variation"), *development* ("economic and human development which is socioculturally and ecologically sustainable"), and *logistic* ("demonstration projects, environmental education and training, research and monitoring related to local, regional, national and global issues of conservation and sustainable development").[8] Following from these functions are the technical implementation procedures for biosphere reserves, including, notably, the zonation structure of core, buffer, and transition zones that was pioneered by the biosphere reserve concept. The sites selected for biosphere reserve status were by design highly diverse, with the goal of developing a "world representative network for research, monitoring, information exchange, and training."[9] Thus, while the WNBR originally was not conceived to include urban areas, it *was* intended to include sites representing all significant ecosystems with the goal of support for sustainable development locally and globally.

The NYMR is ecologically significant in its own right, as well as in terms of the global impact of consumption and production activities concentrated there. Indeed the NYMR and other megacities should be seen as drivers of global environmental change, for better or for worse. Sustainable management of highly complex and dynamic systems such as the NYMR, including strengthening of linkages with its global natural resource base, is therefore of fundamental importance to global sustainability as well as to the well-being of urban ecosystems.

Our focus is on "megacities," that is, cities with populations over 10 million. Global urbanization is occurring most rapidly in small to medium-sized cities, and it is in these middle cities that we may in the near future expect the most drastic environmental consequences of urbanization. By 2015 it is projected that there will be 61 very large cities, with populations over 5 million. Of these, 20 are already megacities.[10] These have enormous economic, social, and political influence and may be thought of as the world's leading cities. Moreover, megacities represent the extreme end of the continuum from "pristine" areas to built or completely "human generated." If it is reasonable and beneficial to include both ends of the continuum in the WNBR, then it should follow that the same will hold for other types of urban areas and urban/periurban/rural mixes. Thus, in arguing here for the value of including megacities such as the MYMR, we are by extension arguing the benefits of including the entire range of cities.

THE NEW YORK METROPOLITAN REGION AS AN URBAN ECOSYSTEM

Megacities are typically characterized by a history of progressive densification of population and supportive infrastructure, and buildup and succession of industrial land-uses, with development initially superimposed on a natural landscape and displacing existing habitats. This brings with it profound changes in the physical and biotic components of the environment from changes in the climate, soils, hydrology, and biodiversity. Increasing population and urbanization frequently are accompanied by air and water pollution, soil compaction, reduction in soil organisms and calcification of soils, increased loads of heavy metals and organics, and altered temperature and moisture regimes.

The process of urbanization frequently is seen primarily in terms of this superimposition, displacement, and destruction of habitats. However, the process is also one of ecological adaptation and resilience, as well as the development of new and dynamic anthropogenic habitats. Indeed, megacities may be seen as the most drastic examples of the interactions between people and nature. Because of their long history of human habitation and the density and diversity of settlement and land-use, megacities can serve as laboratories for studying such interactions, ranging from species and ecosystem resilience to the relationship between societal and biological diversity. Megacities would also seem to be particularly well suited for inclusion in a network of sites devoted to promoting healthy interactions of humans and biota within the urban environment.

The NYMR provides a dramatic illustration of these interactions. It is one of the most densely settled urban areas in the world, with a total population of some 21.5 million persons, of whom 8.0 million live in New York City.[11] Although the region covers only 33,670 square kilometers, it maintains great demographic diversity. New York has always been defined as a region of immigrants, and in the period from 1950 to 2000, international migration from new areas such as Latin America, Asia, and Africa has further diversified the population. Because of its large population, New York has pioneered in developing new urban infrastructure, including skyscrapers, subways and new forms of transit, and massive apartment complexes. These uses of land require supporting infrastructure for the water, energy, waste disposal, and other services needed by large, densely settled populations.

The prehistoric ecology of the region has been significantly modified. The NYMR is a water-dominated region with a diverse landscape. Large waterways and water bodies, among them the New York Harbor, Hudson River, East River and Long Island Sound, and Jamaica Bay cut deeply into the land area. The three physiographic regions are the coastal plain, the Piedmont, and the Appalachian highlands. Given its coastal location, much of the land area is at relatively low elevation. Human settlement has always played a part in transforming the pre-European ecosystem of the New York Harbor, and successive waves of settlement have each had an impact on the region. Since 1950, suburban settlement has extended the human-dominated landscape to the farther reaches of eastern Long Island, northwestern New Jersey, and parts of Connecticut and New York State more distant from New York City.

From the early days of European settlement, land and open water in the areas surrounding the urban fringe were commonly utilized for disposal of refuse (solid wastes). This process accelerated in the 19th century with the exploitation of submarginal tidal and freshwater wetlands along the waterfront adjacent to the early urban core (southern Manhattan and northwest Brooklyn). These early landfills were commonly used to raise bulkheads and extend the reach of usable land. In conjunction with dredging, these straightened and heightened waterfront areas supported development of the city's port, providing access for shipping commerce and marine transportation.

During the early part of the 20th century, the population increased rapidly and denser settlement expanded outward from the urban core, northward into Bronx, eastward into Queens County and southeast into Brooklyn. The spread of land development was supported by expansion of urban infrastructure, such as the network of paved streets and systems for water supply, sewage control, stormwater conveyance, and solid waste disposal. New York City's five counties are all largely bounded by water, and most of this shoreline originally was occupied by highly productive marsh environments. Filling of these submarginal lands, which were deemed useless by city managers of the period, would provide the base for much of the municipal infrastructure that would support 20th century expansion of the city's population, including airports, highways, bridges, parks, and public beaches. Like wetlands on Manhattan's shoreline, which were largely filled by the end of the 19th century, the waterfront and inland wetlands in the other boroughs of the city were largely eradicated in the early and mid-20th century. This occurred largely through the disposal of refuse as fill material and was justified on a variety of grounds, including protection of public health (e.g., the elimination of breeding grounds for mosquitoes and rats). In addition to providing for municipal infrastructure, these new lands ultimately would expand the city's usable land area by 25% and would greatly increase the city's taxable land area. Although the total population in New York City proper peaked by 1940, redistribution of inhabitants would continue for the remainder of the century, leading to the consumption of almost all nonpark, open land in the city's four inner boroughs.

The dramatic effects of these transformations have not been limited to the topography of the region. New York City has experienced rainfall that has an average pH of 4.4 for the last 30 years; local soils contain levels of heavy metals such as lead, nickel, and copper, which are 5–10 times higher than those in rural areas; and daytime temperatures may be 6–8 degrees above those recorded outside the city. Add to this millions of pedestrians, hikers, shoppers, and delivery people, who compact the soil, inadvertently trample seedlings, disperse seeds, and sometimes forget to dispose of trash properly, and the result is a host of new niches for plants and animals. In effect, the northern hardwood forest has been transformed into vacant lots, backyards, city parks, sidewalks, and urban gardens.

It therefore might come as a shock to visitors or even residents of New York City, but the city is in fact very green: 49,854 acres or 25.7% of the surface of New York City is parkland or open space.[12] It also contains a very diverse flora of 2,330 species. These species represent natives to the region as well as species brought to the city through its ports over the past 400 years.

The vegetation of the city can be classified into three types: residual native vegetation, cultivated areas, and restored vegetation growing where the natural vegetation has been disturbed by humans. The major open space is made up of residual native vegetation found either in parks or peripheral regions of the city. This native vegetation is extremely important for a variety of reasons: it provides ecological services to the city, habitat for native and migrating fauna, a reservoir of native species that can repopulate restored regions, and it creates areas of great enjoyment for the people of the city.

Many of the tree species native to the area have not adapted well to the changed environmental conditions and new habitats. Growth rates and plant vigor in the city have decreased, and several native taxa have become highly susceptible to pathogens and interspecific competition. The hemlocks are being attacked by wooly adelgids; flowering dogwoods and butternut hickory are plagued by canker; the beech trees have beech bark disease; the oaks have oak wilt; and a bacterium carried by leafhoppers is killing the white ash trees. Many of the oaks and hickories in city parks are unable to regenerate themselves because of the intense seed predation from resident squirrel populations.

Nonetheless, these areas still maintain extensive wildlife habitat and ecological function. The ecological function of the more densely settled part of the region is low. Yet the few remaining large-scale (i.e., greater than 500 hectares) habitat sites such as Jamaica Bay provide critical stopping points for migratory bird species.

Research at the Brooklyn Botanic Garden's New York Metropolitan Flora program has found that some native species appear to be more resilient to the effects of urbanization than other species. For instance, virtually all members of the Ericaceae (blueberry family) in the region are showing a decline over the past century. On the other hand, all native maples and most oaks are showing an increase over the same period. And while much of the native habitat has been lost over the past 400 years of settlement of the region, we still find federally threatened and endangered species within the city limits, such as the seabeach amaranth found on city beaches.

With the demise of the native flora, new niches were created for species that could tolerate the new conditions. Although many of these plants would be designated as "exotic," "nonnative," "alien," or "invasive" in the current vernacular, these species have a demonstrated ability to grow and reproduce under acidic rainfall in droughty compacted soils with toxic levels of heavy metals. By some estimates, between 20% and 60% of the animals and plants in the Hudson River system are nonnatives that have systematically replaced many native populations.[13] In the process, nonnative species have filled important ecological niches left open by less resilient natives, thereby contributing to the robustness of the new urban ecosystems. These transformations have an added social dimension, because the variety of introduced species over the past four centuries have reflected the origins and preferences of the various waves of immigration to the city.

Concurrent with the transformation of original ecosystems and displacement of original habitats, the region has seen the development of a multitude of new habitats that are to a large extent anthropogenic. Filling of wetlands created a suite of "second-generation" (filled) land areas that have escaped subsequent redevelopment. Their resilience to development is related mainly to their landfill origin, which rendered them less desirable than other available properties. These filled and altered lands have since had sufficient time to accommodate new habitats, and repopulation with unique flora and fauna has been reported in some areas. This repopulation has been largely unmanaged and has occurred by natural means on properties that otherwise are considered to be vacant and nonfunctional lots. With the few remaining areas of undeveloped land, mostly contained in parks, these lands constitute much of the city's natural habitat. Less visible new habitats include cemeteries, gardens, backyards, balconies, green rooftops, road verges, railway sidings, and vacant lots, as well as subterranean and interior habitats. The variety and success of these habitats is the product of many factors, including planning decisions or lack thereof, public attitudes, the property market and institutional incentives affecting it, as well as the diversity of the people living in the city. Thus, while we may expect a great diversity of habitats in most large cities, the particular mosaic of habitats present is specific to the dynamics of that city's ecological and human history.

The practice of urban agriculture exemplifies many of the social and ecological processes described above, and it presents a context in which urban inhabitants interact directly within their local environment as well as distant, if not nostalgic environments of cultural, historic, or psychological significance through the preferential cultivation of plant species and varieties. In New York City, urban agriculture primarily exists in the form of community gardens. Within the agroecological context of the garden plot, the diverse social makeup of the city comes together with its abiotic and biotic environment. The services that urban agriculture provides to the city are many. They range from social, ecological, and political to economic importance.

Currently, cities across the world have varying dependencies on urban agriculture for food security and local economy. In New York, there was little planning of urban agriculture within the confines of the city limits, most likely because the outlying or peripheral zones of the city are easily accessible and were highly productive agricultural zones. With few exceptions, as the city grew it pushed its agricultural areas further and further away, so that in 2003 the last working family farm within the city limits of Queens County was sold for 4.3 million dollars. The 20,000–square foot property could become 22 three-family homes. Urban agriculture does, however, continue to exist through backyard gardening and cultivation of abandoned lots.

Long a feature of the social, cultural, and ecological vitality of New York City, urban agriculture also has played an important role in the city's political agenda during times of financial crises. During the Great Depression, the city's welfare department along with a federal program sponsored "relief" gardens for the unemployed. The program was canceled in 1937 and lay dormant until World War II, when the city announced that all available public land could be cultivated as Victory Gardens. The post–World War II economic boom quenched the financial need for urban agriculture, and many gardens were abandoned, but with the 1970s came other needs that led to a resurgence in community gardening. The sort of urban agriculture that began in 1973 is now a vital part of urban life, but is of a different character than the agriculture of the past. While economic considerations still play an important role, it is now centered at the interface of social and ecological issues.

The founders of current urban agriculture in the NYMR see themselves as social and political activists. They took the initiative to cultivate and beautify abandoned lots with creativity, astute fundraising skills built on social justice, and political savvy to earn the recognition and support of the New York City government after their project was under way. These "Green Guerillas," as the organization is still called, incited community development through gardening around the City. The Parks Department established the Green Thumb program in 1978 which leases city land for a nominal fee to community gardens and turns gardeners from squatters to people with contractual rights to the land.

By nature, community gardens support ecosystem functions, such as carbon, water, and oxygen cycling, and biodiversity, such as soil microbes and invertebrates, insects, and birds as well as volunteer and cultivated plants species. But as managed agroecosystems, they reflect the cultural preferences and ethnic pride of their gardeners. As products of the interactions between diverse cultures and the built and natural environment, they exemplify the dynamism of urban environments.

The NYMR is anything but pristine, but neither is it simply a "concrete jungle." Although often viewed as a giant agglomeration of degraded natural ecosystems, the NYMR presents an example of a highly dynamic and complex ecological environment that provides an excellent laboratory for studying resilience to environmental change, options for ecosystem conservation and restoration, and the interactions between biological and societal diversity.

One of the primary purposes for establishing the World Network of Biosphere Reserves was to create a global network of representative ecosystems as "living laboratories" for research into ecosystem function, conservation and sustainable development.[9] In order that such a network may achieve its scientific potential, it should therefore cover the entire global range of ecosystems. While there may be ideological justifications for excluding a megacity such as the NYMR from consideration for biosphere reserve designation, the scientific value of such a study site is clear.

NEW YORK AS A DRIVER FOR GLOBAL ENVIRONMENTAL CHANGE

The efficiencies provided by urban density have demonstrated themselves to be a key ingredient of economic growth, ideally bringing with it increased wealth for urbanites and society as a whole, but with this growth comes increased consumption of natural resources. Indeed, urban areas require more resources than their regions can provide and must import food, building materials, and fuel from elsewhere. Because consumption levels tend to increase linearly with wealth, urban areas—particularly those in developed countries—place a disproportionate demand on resources and produce a disproportionate amount of waste and pollution. Wealthier cities also contribute disproportionately to global environmental problems such as emissions of greenhouse gases, creation of tropospheric ozone pollution, acid rain production, release of carcinogens and toxic materials, surface runoff contamination, erosion, and natural resource depletion, all of which affect local and global biodiversity.[14] While waste production, water, and land-use primarily have had regional impacts (although New York City sends much of its waste out of the state for disposal), food, energy, and other natural resource extraction, as well as certain pollutants such as CO_2, have global significance.

One way of comparing resource use and land management is by calculating an area's ecological footprint, or what can be otherwise designated its resource shed. The ecological footprint is the interactive relationship between an urban area and its hinterland (see Rees 1992[15]; Folke *et al.* 1997[16]; and the April 2001 special issue of *Ecological Economics* for more information about the concept and its application). This relationship often is defined as the measure of resources extracted and waste emitted for a given city or urban region. The ecological footprint also can be defined spatially as the area from which a city draws its resources and to which it delivers its wastes, or as the amount of productive land needed to sustain a city's population and its consumption levels.[17]

With a gross regional product of slightly less than one trillion dollars per year,[17] the NYMR's economy is roughly on a par with that of countries such as Canada and Brazil.[18] Not surprisingly, its regional and global environmental impacts are enormous. The NYMR's annual energy demand is the equivalent of approximately one billion barrels of petroleum, half of the total U.S. production.[19] It relies on 5,000 km^2 of watershed and consumes 5,300 million liters of water daily.[1] The city produces some 14,000 tons of garbage[20] and 1.7 billion gallons of treated effluent daily.[21] It must import almost all of its food, and it has been estimated that it consumes approximately 800,000 hectares of wheat annually.[1] The city's wealth enables it to consume large quantities of ecologically inefficient meat products, as well as luxury goods such as coffee, tea, and tobacco, which has a corresponding impact on the warm climate ecosystems from which these goods are imported.

A less dramatic but illustrative example of the global impact of the NYMR's consumption patterns is presented by its enormous and ever-changing market for a large variety of plant species. Some of the diverse plant products consumed in the city are produced locally and regionally; much is imported from around the world. As a populous and ethnically diverse urban area, the city's demands in volume and variety of products affect the state of biological diversity both in surrounding rural areas as well as distant corners of the world. Much of the city's "ecological footprint" is formed by the breadth and weight of this consumer demand.

Demand in urban areas for ethnic or otherwise "exotic" produce is driven in part by immigration and in recent years is facilitated by free-trade agreements. A particularly significant trend is the "tropicalization" of consumer demand in northern, temperate cities such as New York. Tropical peoples move to temperate environments, bringing with them needs and desires from their tropical homes. This type of demand, coupled with the increasing political ease and economic advantage of growing export crops in tropical areas, has contributed to emerging types of export production for northern cities such as New York. Many complexities arise from the increasing demand for agricultural products from biologically rich, but often economically impoverished tropical areas of the world.

Immigrant communities in the NYMR have always contributed to the cultural diversity of the city, perhaps most visibly through the foods they offer urban inhabitants. The culinary diversity of the city is a great source of pride as well as income for the city, but its links to ecosystems abroad are obscure and not well understood. In the past century alone, the agriculture that supports city consumption has drastically changed, as has the city's cultural composition. The wave of immigration around the turn of the 20th century brought people from Ireland, Italy, and Eastern Europe, many of whom settled on regional farmland or had home gardens to cultivate the crops they were accustomed to eating. The availability of land, as well as the climatic adaptability of the "old immigrants" choice crops facilitated integration of new modes of consumption and production into metropolitan area. The second half of the 20th century saw the majority of its immigrants from Asia,

Latin America, and the Caribbean in place of Europeans. Currently Chinese, Indians, Mexicans, and Dominicans are the fastest-growing immigrant groups in the NYMR.

Paralleling the diversification of the city's demographic profile, there has been a substantial increase in the variety of fresh fruits and vegetables sold in city markets. As national and international trends have shown, sale of "exotic" produce is a lucrative and fast-growing segment of the fruit and vegetable trade. Over the past two decades in the City of New York, the number of species of tropical fruits and vegetables sold has increased by approximately 70%, and the number of Asian vegetables by 200%.[22] Analysis of the origin of the production areas shows shifts from countries that have long been providing tropical exports in the Caribbean to new production areas in South and Central America. Exports from Brazil, Argentina, Chile, and Colombia are replacing exports from Ecuador, Puerto Rico, and elsewhere in the West Indies. This shift is representative of the recent trend of diversification of exports from the Caribbean and Latin America. As the demand for a larger diversity of fresh fruit and vegetables as well as counter-seasonal produce has been growing in northern cities, there have been corresponding shifts in production. There has been a decrease in production of traditional exports from the tropics such as sugar, soy beans, and bananas to more profitable nontraditional agricultural exports.

Immigrants from tropical environments have demands that cannot be satisfied locally and create new connections to distant production landscapes. Although tropical fruits have been imprted to the city for at least a century, today the frequency, quantity, and variety of fresh tropical imports are cause for reevaluation of the processes of distribution and consumption of these items. The ease of transportation and communication, reduction of trade barriers, and the psychological importance of traditional food, including their role in maintaining non-American identities, has largely shaped these processes.

Clearly, the global reach of a megacity such as the NYMR gives it disproportionate influence over environmental and social conditions within and outside its boundaries, and the city's resource demands cannot be sustainable over the long term. The net effect of this influence is, however, largely a function of the consumption and production decision made possible by the city's wealth, rather than by its density in and of itself or merely the size of its population. Indeed, the efficiencies of urban density have direct environmental benefits as well. Recycling and composting usually are more cost-effective in higher-density cities, where there is a large surplus of used materials and sufficient industrial and residential need. Energy utilization tends to be more efficient in such cities because of the presence of high-rise buildings and public transportation systems. For example, in the NYMR, public transport use in 2003 was 9.06 million passengers per day,[23] saving millions of automobile miles and associated fuel consumption and CO_2 emissions. The same gains in efficiency that make the accumulation of wealth and higher consumption possible also provide opportunities for social change and awareness building. This may partially explain why per capita expenditures on environmental protection also tend to be higher in urban areas, both in absolute terms and as a percentage of the gross national product.[24]

The NYMR is a driver for environmental change at the local, regional, and global levels. This can be change for the better or for the worse, depending on the consumption decisions made by New Yorkers as well as their degree of social, political, and economic engagement in support of global sustainability. An understanding of the relationships among all of the key factors involved in New York's ecological footprint will, however, require considerably further integrated research. The development and implementation of a research agenda to this end therefore is an important step toward a more sustainable NYMR. It also would be a vital policy-oriented scientific contribution to the World Network of Biosphere Reserves and its goals.

ENVIRONMENTAL MANAGEMENT FOR THE NEW YORK METROPOLITAN REGION

The concentration of population and wealth in a city such as New York makes good urban environmental management an imperative for the health of local, regional, and global ecosystems. This requires policies informed by scientific understanding, political commitment, public awareness, and a governance structure that allows for implementation.

Despite serious failings in all of these regards, the NYMR has some tradition of leadership in urban environmental conservation and management. It has stringent environmental laws that have resulted in improvements in the quality of its air and water since the 1960s, and it increased public parklands by 350,000 acres.[25] Significant research capacities in the city's academic institutions, botanical gardens, and conservation and planning organizations have been mobilized to increase understanding of urban ecosystems and urban sustainability, and far-sighted conservation, management, and planning initiatives have influenced its development.

One of the keys to the development of successful management has been the use of cross-disciplinary approaches integrating appropriate methodologies, policy instruments, and social coordination. This can help optimize interactions among socioeconomic, policy, and natural systems by pointing to opportunities to reduce negative impact on the environment and in some cases enhance quality of life. An example of this systems-view approach to natural and anthropogenic processes may be found in the new field of industrial ecology, which seeks to optimize the use of resources by dematerialization of the economy or material integration between production and postconsumption processes. With its cradle-to-cradle approach, industrial ecology describes the flow of materials from nature through the economy and back to the environment, including pathways through different environmental media. Its analytical tools, such as material flow analysis and life cycle assessments, help find leverage points for intervention. The methodology of industrial ecology has been applied by the New York Academy of Sciences to examine the flows of specific contaminants into the New York/New Jersey Harbor and has been instrumental in identifying best management practices and opportunities for pollution prevention.

In any sociopolitical environment, the availability of good science alone will not ensure good policies. In the NYMR, the linkage between the two is often frustratingly weak, largely because of the dominance of an extremely large and diverse set of stakeholders implicated in any decision. In this situation, scientists become just another group of stakeholders.

Particular difficulties arise because of frequently overlapping and competing jurisdictions and mandates, resulting in the fragmentation of the city into smaller units. In the case of the NYMR, only 8 million of the total population of 21.5 million actually live in the City of New York. The rest live in hundreds of smaller municipalities spread across three states. With more than 2,000 separate jurisdictions within the NYMR, regional coordination is a daunting task.[25] Without coordinated policy and planning, many of the potential social, economic, and environmental advantages of urban density may go unrealized. It therefore is not surprising that some of the most influential and successful environmental management initiatives in the region have focused their efforts on developing regional solutions. An example of this type of initiative is the Port Authority of New York and New Jersey (PANY&NJ). PANY&NJ was established as an autonomous public-sector body to address the complicated transportation issues of a highly populated region situated in an estuary with a major port serving the region. The PANY&NJ defines its mission as "to identify and meet the critical transportation infrastructure needs of the bi-state region's businesses, residents, and visitors … move people and goods within the region, provide access to the rest of the nation and to the world, and strengthen the economic competitiveness of the New York–New Jersey Metropolitan Region."[26]

Organizations that unite the region around specific issues have been successful; however, this type of cooperation for a comprehensive management of this region has not been formally established. The kind of regional overview that would be necessary for integrated and collaborative environmental management of the NYMR not only will require cooperation and participation from a wide range of stakeholders from both states and federal entities, but, to be successful, these participants must have a strong sense of ownership of the process.

Many less formal programs and projects exist working on issues that cross state boundaries and thus include representatives from both states. The success of these efforts can be limited, however, by the same boundary issues they are trying to overcome. It is very difficult to achieve consensus for example, when one entity is being asked to give up more than another for the good of the whole. Attempts to apply approaches using strategies of "decide, announce, defend" are unlikely to be successful when issues are affecting states, cities, and regions in very unique ways. A new paradigm in community outreach,[27] centering on communication follows a strategy of "inform, include, and decide."

The New York Academy of Sciences' Harbor Consortium[a] is an example of the application of this paradigm to a group with very diverse interests and backgrounds. This group has come together to take on issues of contamination in the NY/NJ Harbor, seeking to develop regional pollution prevention strategies. Its success stems from not only the inclusion of participants from all sides of the issues, but, more importantly, the transparency of the entire process in front of this group. This means that all of the participants see the logic and reasoning behind the scientific research being described and the next step of using that knowledge to make policy recommendations. Although many of the participants have points of view that are rooted in their own set of expertise, occupations, and interests, through the process they are better able to see how the person sitting next to them may have a different interest. The Consortium over a period of several years has coalesced into a group that sees itself as a true working group, and its members are willing to give their time and effort to identify pollution prevention strategies that are good for the region as a whole, even when those recommendations could have an impact on their own livelihoods.

Other important examples from the wide array of municipal, regional, national, and civil society initiatives improving the quality of life of citizens, protecting ecosystems, educating and raising awareness, and managing the global impact include Sustainable South Bronx, a civil society initiative focusing on environmental justice in some of the city's most underserved neighborhoods; the Regional Plan Association, a not-for-profit regional planning organization serving New York, New Jersey, and Connecticut; the Clean Ocean and Shore Trust (COAST), addressing coastal and ocean issues; the Brooklyn Botanic Garden/Rutgers University Center for Restoration Ecology; various Riverkeepers groups in the region; City and State environmental programs in the tristate area; the New York City Parks and Recreation Department; and the Gateway National Recreation Area, which protects some of the region's most sensitive wetlands. Although there remains ample room for in-

[a]The Harbor Consortium is composed of scientists, local, state, and federal government, industry and small businesses community and environmental groups, and labor and union representatives. The Consortium is the decision-making body for the project: Industrial Ecology, Pollution Prevention and the New York/New Jersey Harbor; and they participate in and oversee all aspects of the project from the initial research through the pollution prevention and management recommendations

creased cooperation, coordination, and commitment at all levels, these are long-standing and highly visible and successful initiatives that support conservation, development, and logistic functions espoused by the biosphere reserve concept.

THE ADDED VALUE OF MEGACITIES

The New York Metropolitan Region is ecologically significant. It is representative of increasingly important urban ecosystems and as such provides a valuable laboratory for the study of human impact, the resilience of native and ecosystems and species, the emergence of new ecosystems, and the dynamic social and ecological adaptive processes associated with all of these. The global ecological, economic, social, and political reach of a megacity such as the NYMR makes good urban environmental governance a key factor in the sustainability of ecosystems worldwide. Although environmental governance in the NYMR is flawed at best, there are significant public-sector and civil society processes under way to support sustainable development, research, education, policy coordination, and biodiversity conservation. It would be an exaggeration to suggest that the NYMR is in essence already a biosphere reserve, except for a formal zonation structure and designation as such. However, a NYMR Biosphere Reserve in principle could be achieved, and the necessary processes for a successful biosphere reserve are already well established in the city.

By including the NYMR and other cities in the WNBR, important networking opportunities present themselves. Lessons learned and other knowledge can be exchanged, and lost informational linkages between urban areas and their natural resource bases may be reestablished and strengthened through awareness building, education, exchange, and partnerships.

As one of the first megacities, New York City and its metropolitan region have been dealing with the ecological and social implications of extreme urbanization for longer than most cities, and there should be lessons available that would be of value to younger cities. For example, environmental conservation and management may be seen as a relatively low priority for cities in less-developed countries facing severe housing, health, and other poverty related issues. Yet many of the most successful environmental initiatives of the NYMR were developed in the context of interventions to alleviate poverty and improve public health.

Other lessons learned have been through the serious mistakes made over the years, such as the destruction of the region's wetlands, inappropriate infrastructure choices, jurisdictional and fiscal fragmentation, sprawl, and excessive pollution. All of these have imposed high costs on current and future generations, costs that may be avoided by younger cities.

One of the main problems posed by urbanization in general and megacities in particular is the increasing detachment of consumption activities from their natural resource bases; however, this is not limited to cities, but is in fact a feature of globalization in general. Awareness programs, partnership programs within the WNBR, and possible subnetworks of sites can help to strengthen and reestablish these linkages. This is particularly important as large cities become increasingly global in their makeup and their consumption. One could, for example, foresee a subnetwork within the WNBR that would link a conurbation such as the NYMR with biosphere reserves that are directly affected by its economy, consumption, and social and political influence. The establishment of such partnerships indeed could be a part of the establishment process for an urban biosphere reserve. This would provide an added value not only to the city's own environmental programs, but especially to the WNBR.

Given the stated goals of the UNESCO Man and Biosphere Programme (MAB) and the World Network of Biosphere Reserves, as well as the key functions that biosphere reserves are designed to serve, the inclusion of megacities in that network seems appropriate. Indeed, this could greatly benefit the long-term relevance of biosphere reserves. This will, however, depend on the full networking potential of the WNBR's being recognized and supported by the MAB. It will also depend on the MAB's revisiting the biosphere reserve concept, not simply to facilitate the inclusion of megacities and other urban areas, but also more generally, to thereby enable biosphere reserves to meet the needs of the situation in which the world finds itself today.

REFERENCES

1. ROSENZWEIG, C. & W. SOLECKI. 2001. Biodiversity and the City: A Case Study of the New York Metropolitan Region. Presented at the UNESCO/Columbia University International Conference on Biodiversity and Society, New York, 2001.
2. SOLECKI, W. & C. ROSENZWEIG. 2004. Biodiversity, biosphere reserves and the Big Apple: a study of the New York Metropolitan Region. Ann. N.Y. Acad. Sci. **1023:** 105–124.
3. KIM, K.-G. 2004. The application of the biosphere reserve concept to urban areas: the case of green rooftops for the Habitat Network in Seoul. Ann. N.Y. Acad. Sci. **1023:** 187–214.
4. BONNES, M. *et al.* 2004. Inhabitants' environmental perceptions in the City of Rome within the framework for urban biosphere reserves of the UNESCO Programme on Man and Biosphere. Ann. N.Y. Acad. Sci. **1023:** 175–186.
5. ELMQVIST, T. *et al.* 2004. The dynamics of social-ecological systems in urban landscapes: Stockholm and the National Urban Park, Sweden. Ann. N.Y. Acad. Sci. **1023:** 308–322.

6. STANVLIET, R. *et al.* 2004. The UNESCO Biosphere Reserve concept as a tool for urban sustainability: the CUBES Cape Town case study. Ann. N.Y. Acad. Sci. **1023:** 80–104.
7. UNESCO. 1996. The Seville Strategy for Biosphere Reserves. UNESCO, Paris.
8. UNESCO. 1996. Statutory Framework of Biosphere Reserves. UNESCO, Paris.
9. BATISSE, M. 2001. Biosphere Reserves: A Personal Appraisal. In Proceedings of the Seville +5 International Meeting of Experts, Pamplona, October 23–27, 2000. UNESCO, Paris.
10. UNITED NATIONS. 2003. World Urbanization Prospects: the 2003 Revision. United Nations, New York.
11. US CENSUS. 2000. U.S. Census Bureau, Washington, DC.
12. OASIS. 2001. Comparison of Park Space in US Cities. OASIS, New York.
13. MILLS, E.L. *et al.* 1998. Exotic species in the Hudson River Basin: a history of invasions and introductions. Estuaries **19:** 814–823.
14. UNITED NATIONS CENTRE FOR HUMAN SETTLEMENTS. 2001. The State of the World's Cities Report 2001. UNCHR, Nairobi.
15. REES, W.E. 1992. Ecological Footprint and Appropriated Carrying Capacity: What Urban Economics Leaves Out. Environment and Urbanization **4:** 121–130.
16. FOLKE, C., J. LARSSON & J. SWEITZER. 1995. Renewable Resource Appropriation by Cities. Bener Discussion Paper Series No. 61. International Institute of Ecological Economics, Stockholm, Sweden.
17. The U.S. Conference of Mayors Metro Economies Report. July 2003.
18. WORLD RESOURCES INSTITUTE. 2004. Earth Trends Country Profiles.
19. U.S. DEPARTMENT OF ENERGY, 2001.
20. MILLER, G.T. 1996. Living in the environment: principles, connections and solutions. Wadsworth . New York.
21. NEW YORK CITY DEPARTMENT OF ENVIRONMENTAL PROTECTION. 2003. 2002 New York Harbor Water Quality Report.
22. USDA MARKETING SERVICE, FRESH FRUIT AND VEGETABLE DIVISION. New York City Terminal Market Fresh Fruit and Vegetable Arrivals. 1998.
23. Travel Patterns in the New York Metropolitan Area: 2nd Quarter 2003, New York Metropolitan Travel Council, 2003.
24. PORACSKY, J. & M. HOUCK. 1994. The Metropolitan Portland Urban Natural Resources Program. *In* R.H. Platt, R.A. Rowntree & P.C. Muick, Eds. The Ecological City: Preserving and Restoring Urban Biodiversity. University of Massachusetts Press.
25. A Region at Risk: A Summary of the Third Regional Plan for the New York–New Jersey–Connecticut Metropolitan Area. Regional Plan Association, New York, 1996.
26. Mission statement of the Port Authority of NY and NJ.
27. SADIK-KAHN, J. From Parsons Brinckerhoff, Company 39; Regional Plan Association Meeting April 2003.

Improving Air Quality in Megacities

Mexico City Case Study

LUISA T. MOLINA AND MARIO J. MOLINA

Massachusetts Institute of Technology, Cambridge, Massachusetts, USA

ABSTRACT: The development and effective implementation of solutions to the air pollution problems in the Mexico City Metropolitan Area is essential to guarantee the health and welfare of its inhabitants. To achieve this, it is essential to have the active and informed participation of the civil society, the academic community, the private sector, and the government, because dealing with pollution requires the use of different strategies in multiple fields of action. The Mexico City case study brings together health, transportation, administration, and many other interdisciplinary approaches to understanding and defeating air pollution. Although focused on the Mexico City area, the work conducted under this case study has significance for developing nations generally. Although policies to reduce air pollution should be based on the best available scientific knowledge, political will and capacity must transform this knowledge into action. This case study has developed a series of recommendations emphasizing the interaction between different disciplines that have provided the foundation for the 10-year air quality management program prepared by the Mexican Metropolitan Environmental Commission.

KEYWORDS: Mexican Metropolitan Environmental Commission; megacities; developing nations

One of the great challenges facing society in the 21st century is to find practical ways to bring the benefits of economic growth to developing countries without damaging the environment. Mexico City, São Paulo, and Beijing all experience similar and serious environmental problems, including severe air and water pollution. As many cities in developing countries swell with people and automobiles, the number of cities with poor environmental quality continues to grow. There is an urgent need to address the interrelated issues and common obstacles experienced by these urban areas around the world and to understand more completely the connections between air pollution, human health, and climate change.

Address for correspondence: Luisa T. Molina, Massachusetts Institute of Technology, Cambridge, MA 02139. Voice: 617-253-1603; fax: 617-258-6525.
ltmolina@mit.edu

Ann. N.Y. Acad. Sci. 1023: 142–158 (2004). © 2004 New York Academy of Sciences.
doi: 10.1196/annals.1319.006

Air pollution problems of megacities differ greatly and are influenced by several factors, including topography, demography, meteorology, mobility and transportation patterns, fuel quality and usage, and the level and rate of industrialization and socioeconomic development. These problems are of growing importance because the projected growth in the urban population worldwide increases the number of people exposed to air pollution. According to a 1992 report published by UNEP/WHO,[1] there were only three cities with populations over 10 million in 1950; this number doubled in 1980 and doubled again in 1990. They evaluated the air quality in 20 megacities and found that air pollution was widespread: each had at least one major pollutant that exceeds WHO health guidelines, 15 had at least two and 7 had three or more pollutants that exceeded the guidelines. A high level of suspended particulate matter was the most prevalent form of pollution, followed by sulfur dioxide and ozone. Sources of pollutants include emissions from the combustion of fossil fuels in motor vehicles and for industrial processes, energy production, domestic cooking and heating, and high dust levels due to local construction, unpaved roads, and long-range transport from surrounding barren landscapes.

Although many of the impacts of high air pollution levels often are centered in the urban areas, the impacts of urban activities are not confined within the city boundaries. The regional and global dispersion of pollutants generated locally has been well established in the case of acid deposition, climate change, and stratospheric ozone depletion. Concerns for tropospheric ozone and particulate matter have heightened recently because long-range transport of these pollutants could influence air quality in regions far from their sources and because they also contribute to climate change.[2] Furthermore, land-use and land cover are changing rapidly over all the urban centers of the world. Increasing human population growth and human demands on ecosystems are changing the landscape, resulting in important atmospheric consequences.

Thus, rapid population growth, uncontrolled urban expansion, unsustained economic growth, increased energy consumption, and increased motorization all translate into serious air pollution problems in cities throughout the world. A persistent and pervasive threat to health, air pollution does more than choke lungs, impair visibility, and damage the ecosystems; it also poses a tremendous economic and social cost to society. Policy initiatives to address these problems effectively are urgently needed.

MEXICO CITY AIR QUALITY PROGRAM

Over the past 3 years, a team of Mexican, U.S., and other international scientists and engineers, economists, and political and social scientists has undertaken an integrated assessment of air quality in the Mexico City Metro-

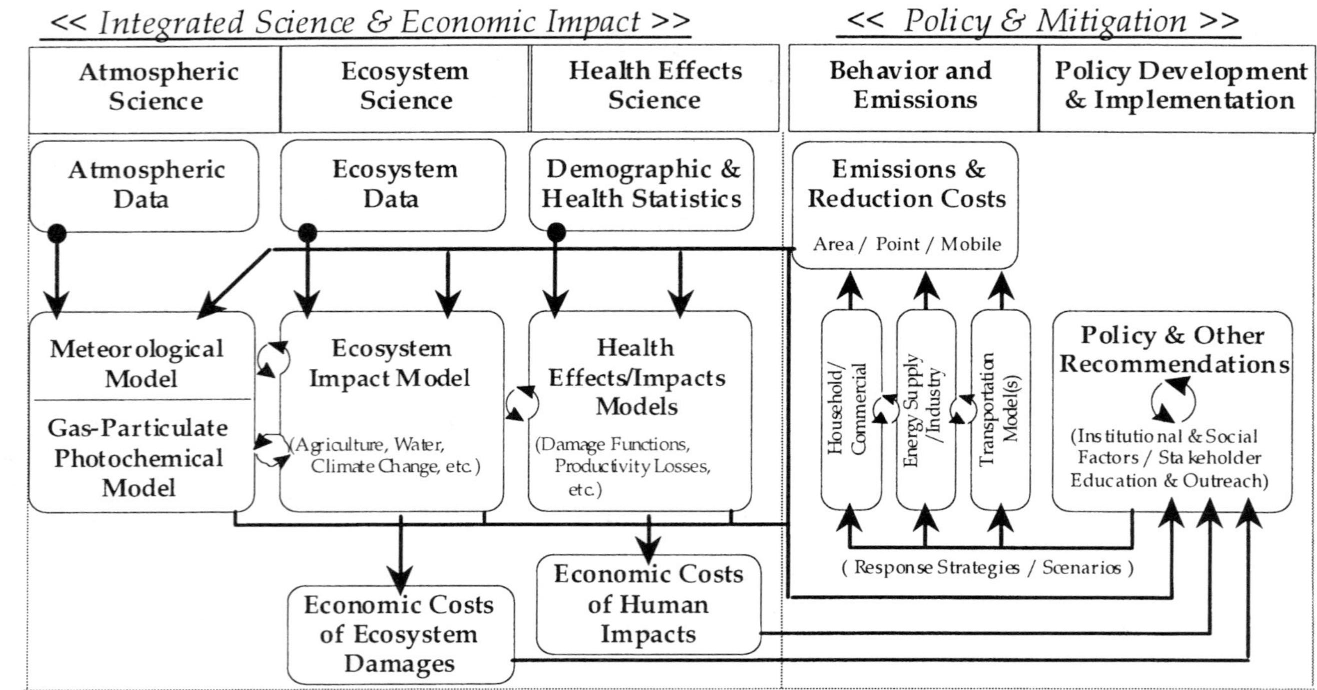

FIGURE 1. Framework for integrated assessment.

politan Area (MCMA). This case study of the Integrated Program on Urban, Regional and Global Air Pollution—a collaborative research and education program initiated at the Massachusetts Institute of Technology (MIT)—addresses in a coordinated and interdisciplinary manner the air pollution problems stemming from human activity in megacities. Moreover, the program involves active collaboration with Mexican government officials and decision makers. Although the original research was focused on the MCMA, the goal was to develop methods of integrated assessment applicable to other large cities throughout the world.

The MCMA epitomizes the types of environmental problems experienced by megacities around the world and the common obstacles to solving them. Although international attention has focused on global climate issues, most local decision makers do not take into account the relationships between urban, regional, and global pollution in addressing the common causes—scientific, economic, and social—that underlie these interrelated problems.

Through the integrated assessment approach, we have developed recommendations emphasizing the interaction between different disciplines. The approach required not just an understanding of air pollution science, but also how to balance economic, social, and technological factors, and how to make decisions in the presence of uncertainty and incomplete data. A schematic of the program's integrated assessment framework is illustrated in FIGURE 1.

During the initial phase of our program, we prepared a series of white papers for the Mexican Metropolitan Environmental Commission (Comisión Ambiental Metropolitana, or CAM, an interagency that consists of environmental authorities from the federal government, the State of Mexico, and the Federal District) that provided the foundation for its strategic planning for the new 10-year air quality management program.[3] These reports included an overview of the current situation and lessons learned from the air quality management programs to date, identified some of the near-term actions, and provided recommendations for research and institutional changes; some of the recommendations already have been adopted and implemented by the Mexican authorities. The first phase of our research also resulted in the publication of a book entitled *The Air Quality in the Mexico Megacity: An Integrated Assessment.*[4]

URBAN GROWTH IN THE MEXICO CITY METROPOLITAN AREA

The Mexico City Metropolitan Area (19°25′N latitude and 99°10′W longitude) lies in an elevated basin at an altitude of 2,240 m above mean sea level. The nearly flat floor of the basin covers ~5,000 km^2 of the Mexican Plateau and is confined on three sides (east, south, and west) by mountain ridges but

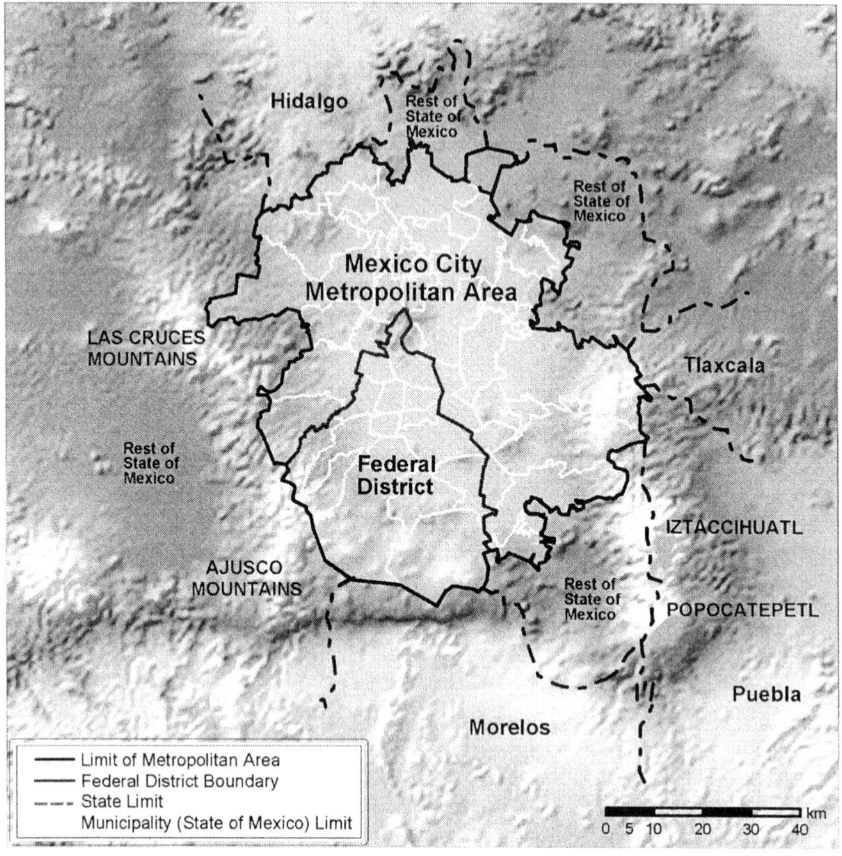

FIGURE 2. Topographical map of the Mexico City Metropolitan Area.

with a broad opening to the north and a narrower gap to the south-southwest. FIGURE 2 shows the topographical map of the MCMA.

Fifty years ago, Mexico City had fewer than 3 million inhabitants. In 2000, the population was six times higher, with more than 18 million people. Today, the MCMA is the second largest populated city in the world, exceeded only by the metropolitan area of Tokyo, which has 26 million inhabitants. As the site of the nation's capital, the MCMA is home to the national political institutions, the greatest concentration of economic investments, and most of the country's industrial and financial infrastructure.

During the 20th century, the MCMA has undergone a massive transformation in urban areas and demographics. It has attracted migrants from other parts of the country and stimulated economic growth as the nation began industrialization. The population grew rapidly and continually, occupying land further away from the historic center of the Federal District. In the last half century alone, the urbanized area of the region has increased more than 10 times, from just 120 km^2 in 1940 to 1,500 km^2 by 1995. The expansion pushed the city beyond the Federal District and into other municipalities of the State of Mexico and other neighboring states.

SOURCES AND TRENDS OF AIR POLLUTANTS IN THE MEXICO CITY METROPOLITAN AREA

The topography and meteorology of the MCMA contribute substantially to the problem of air pollution. The mountains, together with frequent thermal inversions, trap pollutants within the MCMA basin. The high elevation and

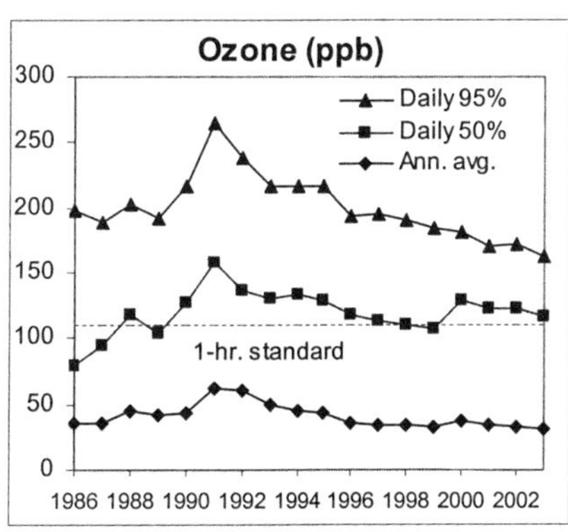

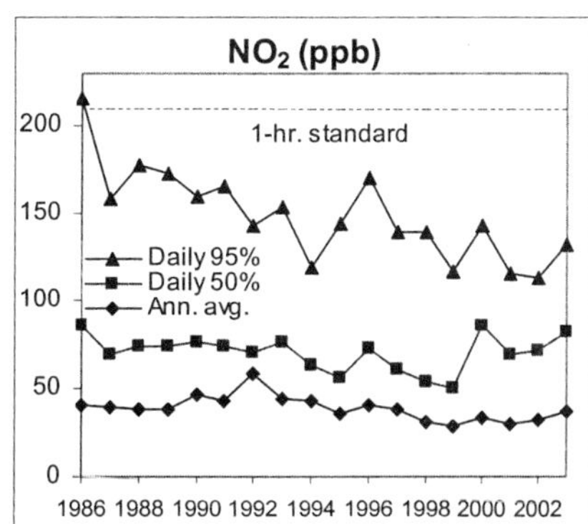

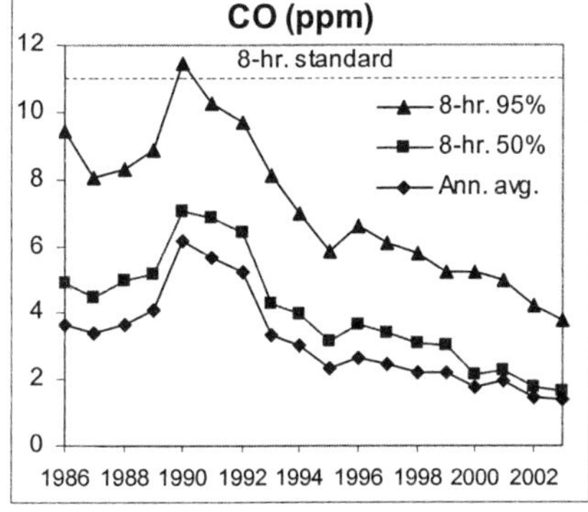

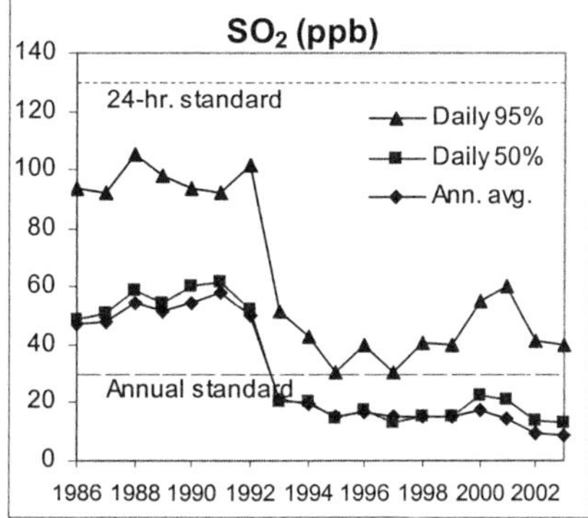

FIGURE 3. Trends in criteria pollutant concentrations for the MCMA showing the averages of data at 5 representative monitoring sites. Plots show the annual average concentrations from hourly data average, 50th, and 95th percentiles of the daily maximum 1-h concentrations for O_3 and NO_2; daily maximum 8-h moving averages for CO; daily maximum 24-h moving average for SO_2; annual average concentrations for PM_{10}, TSP, and lead; and 95th percentile of the daily maximum 24-h moving average for PM_{10} and TSP.

intense sunlight also contribute to photochemical processes that drive the formation of ozone. In this geographical setting, the metropolitan area's almost 20 million residents, 3.5 million vehicles, and 35,000 industries and services together consume more than 40 million liters of fuel per day, producing emissions of thousands of tons of pollutants, which can react in the atmosphere to generate other pollutants that can be more dangerous to health than the original pollutants. Air pollution is generally worst in the winter, when rain is less common and thermal inversions are more frequent.

Both the Mexican government and citizens have recognized air pollution as a major social concern since the mid-1980s. In the 1990s, there were successful reductions in the concentrations of some pollutants such as lead, carbon monoxide, and sulfur dioxide. Comprehensive air quality management programs were developed and carried out. The monitoring and evaluation of air pollution were improved. The government strengthened and began to enforce a vehicle inspection and maintenance program. Natural gas

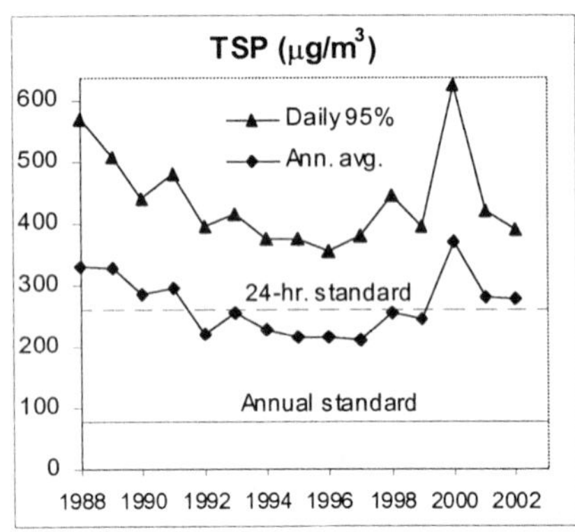

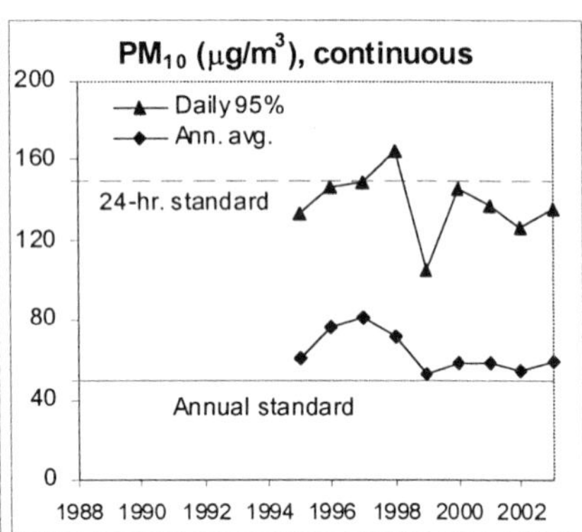

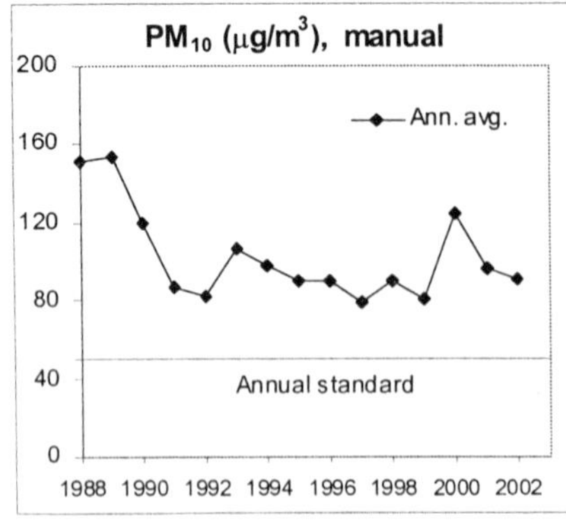

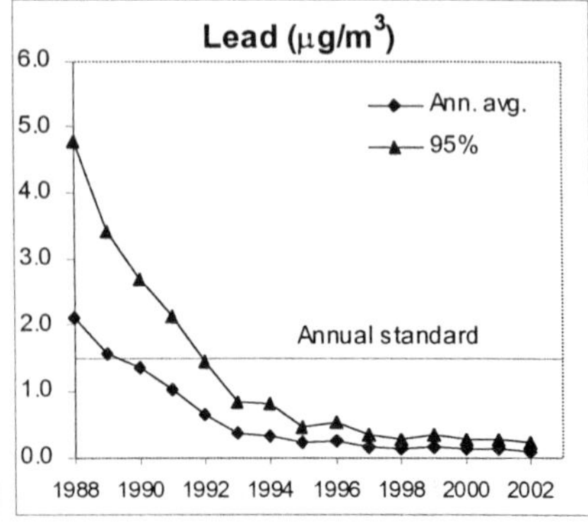

FIGURE 3. ***Continued.***

in industry and the power sector replaced fuel oil. Among other measures, specific actions reduced volatile emission from gasoline stations and storage tanks in industry, as well as removal of lead from gasoline and the implementation of catalytic converters in automobiles. In addition, programs such as "no- driving day" (*Hoy No Circula*) have been used as incentives to modernize the vehicle fleet and to help ensure the proper maintenance of vehicles.

As a result of the above control measures, important reductions in ambient concentrations of lead, sulfur dioxide, and carbon monoxide were achieved recently. However, serious air pollution problems still persist. Some measures have not fully been put into practice because of a lack of financial resources, lack of information, and inadequate follow-up. MCMA residents remain exposed to unhealthy concentrations of airborne pollutants, especially particulate matter and ozone, the two most important pollutants from the standpoint of public health.

Today, ozone and PM_{10} (airborne particulate matter with aerodynamic diameter of 10 μm) are the air quality standards most frequently violated, whereas other pollutants are usually below the air quality standard. In the case of ozone, the standard is violated on ~80% of days, and this has happened every year since 1988. The peak ozone concentrations, nearly 300 ppb, which occur a few times a year, are comparable to those in the city of Los Angeles in the 1970s and are higher than those observed in any city in the United States. For PM_{10}, the daily standard has been exceeded on more than 40% of the days in some years (although since 1999 the standard was exceeded on fewer than 10% of the days). On the other hand, the annual average concentrations have exceeded the maximum levels established by the air quality standard since 1995. FIGURE 3 shows the trends in criteria pollutant concentrations for the MCMA.

These problems will worsen, causing increasingly adverse health effects as the population continues to increase and development and fuel use also increase, unless intervention takes place. No single "silver bullet" will fix this tenacious problem. To have a substantial impact, an array of appropriate strategies must be identified and deployed to enhance air quality. The severe air pollution problem has spurred significant research and action in Mexico City, making it an ideal case study for learning about current challenges in air quality research, management, and policy.

INTEGRATED FRAMEWORK FOR AIR QUALITY MANAGEMENT PLANS

One of the primary challenges in the development of coordinated, robust, and cost-effective air quality management plans is to address all of the relevant scientific, technological, political, institutional, economic, and administrative aspects of a given problem. In evaluating the needs of the MCMA, it is essential to include not only all of these analytical approaches, but also the participation and the input of the most important stakeholders.

When considering various strategies to improve the environment, it is important to include in the analysis the possible impacts on economic development, among other indicators. For example, draconian measures to reduce air pollution by limiting the mobility of citizens in the MCMA may be beneficial environmentally; however, in the medium and long term, these strategies will have unsustainable impacts on economic growth and the quality of life. Robust technical solutions to the problem of air pollution must also be politically and socially viable.

In the following sections, we describe some of the recent activities of our Mexico City case study. We will use transport-related emissions as an example to illustrate the use of integrated assessment to develop recommendations that facilitate the interaction between areas as varied as health, atmospheric science, economics, technology, and policy. Throughout this process, the participation and input of the most important stakeholders has been a decisive factor. We also describe some of the actions taken by the Mexican government authorities recently to reduce transport-related emissions, the largest source of pollutants that are harmful to the health of the population.

HEALTH IMPACTS OF AIR POLLUTION

Human health is the major concern over air pollution and the major driver for policy actions in the MCMA. However, the Mexico City case study also considers the effects of air pollution on ecosystems, as well as the linkage with global warming. Mexico, like other countries in the world, contributes to global warming and is likely to be affected by it. In this article, we discuss only the impact on health.

Air pollution has a range of effects on health and imposes potentially substantial economic costs to society. Much of our knowledge of the effects of air pollution on health comes from studies of the daily fluctuations in deaths, hospital admissions, and respiratory symptoms in response to daily fluctuations in the levels of pollution in Mexico City and other cities throughout the world. These time-series (or "acute") mortality and morbidity studies have revealed the effects of various pollutants (generally PM_{10}, ozone, CO, NO_2, and SO_2).

A health effects subteam—led by the Harvard School of Public Health in collaboration with Mexican scientists from the Health Ministry and the Autonomous Metropolitan University—has assessed health risks posed by current and anticipated levels of air pollution in the MCMA. It has also estimated the economic implications of Mexico City's air quality. The study focused on exposure to the pollutants, mainly PM_{10} and ozone.[4]

The team found that in 1998 the average population exposure to PM_{10} was comparable to those in several of the largest cities in the world (~90 μg/m^3). Studies in various cities around the world, including Mexico City, show a correlation between daily fluctuations in deaths and daily fluctuations in air pollution levels. It is estimated that for each 10 μg/m^3 increase in daily levels of PM_{10}, an increase in daily mortality on the order of 1% may be expected. Most of these are cardiovascular deaths, perhaps of relatively elderly people already suffering from coronary heart disease. However, some recent evidence suggests that some of the premature deaths in the MCMA may be among infants. In a population as large as that of Mexico City (close to 20 million people), these health effects studies suggest that a 10% reduction in PM_{10} concentrations could reduce the number of premature deaths in the MCMA by approximately 1,000 per year. The effect could be several times larger if one considers longer-term responses to particulate-matter exposure.

PM_{10} concentrations also have been associated with nonfatal health outcomes, including increased cases of chronic bronchitis, hospital admissions for respiratory or cardiovascular cases, visits to the emergency room for respiratory or cardiovascular problems, asthma attacks, symptoms in the upper airways, and restricted-activity days.

Ozone levels have received much attention in Mexico City, because the 1-h air quality standard of 110 ppb is being exceeded on more than 300 days every year. Although the effect on mortality is not as striking as that of particulate matter, ozone has significant effects on respiratory function and on hospital admissions for respiratory conditions such as asthma.

The economic value of the health benefits expected from air pollution control is difficult to estimate because of the uncertainties in assigning monetary values to the reduction of health risks. Most estimates of the monetary value of reductions in mortality risks are derived by using estimates of society's willingness to pay to prevent an expected fatality within a time period, the so-called "value per statistical life." The first study of this kind in Mexico has been conducted as part of the Mexico City case study by surveying Mexico City residents to obtain a direct estimate of the values they placed on reduced health risks, which range from US\$150,000 to US\$500,000. Past estimates were extrapolated using values derived from studies conducted in the United States and other developed countries.

Recent research suggests that the most important factor for human health involves the presence of fine particles ($PM_{2.5}$). For this reason, measurements of the chemical composition of $PM_{2.5}$, the development of an emission inventory, and the design of control strategies aimed at reducing the levels of $PM_{2.5}$ are considered high-priority activities for the program. One of the recommendations coming out of our studies is to monitor $PM_{2.5}$ and to develop an emissions inventory for $PM_{2.5}$. In August 2003, the Mexico City government formally inaugurated the $PM_{2.5}$ network, which consists of eight automatic and six manual monitoring stations. The data obtained from this network will be very important in designing strategies for the abatement and control of this pollutant.

TRANSPORTATION SYSTEM: MOBILITY AND AIR POLLUTION

As cities grow in population, area, and wealth, their transportation systems inevitably become more complex, with more people and goods traveling greater distances to more dispersed origins and destinations. This complexity not only challenges the primary objectives of transportation—providing residents access to jobs, education, and other daily needs and wants and facilitating the exchange of goods and services—but also causes a host of environmental, financial, and social constraints which often inhibit transportation system development. Furthermore, as population swells and activities spread, additional problems arise stemming from the need for multi-institutional, multijurisdictional, and multigovernmental coordination for system planning, development, operations, and management. The case of the Mexico City Metropolitan Area offers an illuminating case study of these issues.

Transportation is a major source of air pollution in Mexico City, accounting for more than 99% of the carbon monoxide (CO), ~80% of nitrogen oxides (NO_X), 45% of the volatile organic compounds (VOCs), and 80% of the fine particulate matter. The growing problems of congestion, accidents, and lack of security also are very worrisome. Yet transportation is also a critical enabler of economic activity and beneficial social interaction. The challenge facing the MCMA is how to reduce the adverse environmental and other negative effects of transportation without giving up the benefits of mobility.

This dilemma becomes most pressing under conditions of rapid urban growth, which is likely to increase travel demand significantly. Given current trends, by 2020 the MCMA population will reach more than 25 million, with the largest growth in the State of Mexico rather than in the Federal District. Including the nearby cities of Puebla, Tlaxcala, Cuernavaca, Toluca, and Pachuca, the entire megalopolis will contain some 35 million people.

Although in some scenarios the projected rate of population increase may be reduced, even moderate population growth is likely to lead to substantial increases in both passenger and freight travel demand in the region. The increasing geographic dispersion of the metropolitan population is also likely to increase aggregate transportation demand, because the greater number of trips will also be longer and public transport will be less efficient and universal.

As the population has increased and the residential areas have decentralized, patterns of passenger trip mode choice in the MCMA also have shifted dramatically. The number of private automobiles has increased significantly, by most estimates at a rate of 6% annually in recent years. Moreover, for the following decade an average annual rate of economic growth of between 3 and 5% is expected. (However, very recent estimates are much more modest, with a projected growth rate of between 1 and 3% due to the downturn in the global economy.) This could mean a higher number of vehicles in circulation, a higher ratio of vehicles per inhabitant, and the possibility that the trips and the distances traveled will increase even more as a result of the escalation of economic and social activities.

Meanwhile, the percentage of total trips made by large, fixed-route buses has declined precipitously as a result of the emergence and growing predominance of other transport systems competing for patronage on the same routes, frequently under conditions of cutthroat competition and limited regulation. The percentage of total trips made on the Metro system has also declined, despite increases in system capacity and substantial government subsidies.

In contrast, the *colectivo* service (mainly minibuses)—making frequent stops to take on and drop off passengers—has increased dramatically, becoming the dominant mode of public transportation. Even at higher fares, these vehicles offer superior service and convenience, making them increasingly attractive compared with the Metro and relatively inflexible fixed-route buses. However, intense competition among thousands of proprietors/operators of minibuses generates chaos and accidents in the absence of an effective regulation. Frequent stopping and hazardous driving by *colectivos* contribute to congestion in Mexico City. An additional contribution to congestion comes from taxis that spend much of their driving time looking for passengers. Air quality is compromised by these high-use vehicles because emission control equipment on *colectivos* and taxis is not generally well maintained.

Overall, travelers are using high-occupancy modes of transport less frequently (e.g., buses and rail transit) and increasingly using low-occupancy public transport vehicles (particularly *colectivos*) and private autos. To a substantial degree, these changes have occurred because the existing transportation system has not adequately adapted to the changing population distribution, economic changes, and resulting new travel patterns. Because of weak development planning and land-use controls, low-income housing is constructed in locations that lack adequate road capacity and mass transportation options, and new commercial development occurs with inadequate roadway construction and transit access.

Freight transport has a special relevance because of its high polluting emissions, the excessive antiquity of the fleet, and the effect that it has on the traffic conditions in the MCMA. The concentration of economic activity in the MCMA makes it an important shipping destination. There is substantial intracity truck traffic; also, much intercity trucking travels through Mexico City on route to other destinations, lacking adequate circumferential routes.

Population and economic growth, increasing travel demand, metropolitan dispersion, and inadequate expansion of road and rail transit infrastructure in the areas of greatest growth have combined to produce increasingly severe traffic congestion throughout the MCMA; this results in inefficient vehicle operation and creates higher levels of pollution per kilometer traveled.

Our transportation team has provided recommendations in which the MCMA can work to create a sustainable transportation/mobility/environmental system.[4] In brief:

(a) *Fleet composition and operations:* Provide incentives to increase turnover rate for vehicle fleet and retrofitting of trucks with emission control devices; enforce existing regulations on maximum age of taxis and microbuses.

(b) *Public transportation:* Increase the use of public transport by improving service quality and personal security; facilitate intermodal transfers.

(c) *Fuels:* Establish new specifications with lower sulfur content in gasoline and diesel that enable the introduction of future cleaner vehicle technologies; develop natural gas as a potential fuel for public buses and trucks.

(d) *Infrastructure/technology:* Develop infrastructure to enable intercity truck traffic to bypass downtown core; evaluate the feasibility of implementing Intelligent Transportation System for traffic management.

(e) *Institutions:* Develop a regional planning architecture that more effectively links the transportation with environmental planning; strengthen the coordination among the local and federal institutions responsible for the transportation management in the MCMA; design an integrated policy for transport, land-use, and air quality at the metropolitan level; develop a regional database for the registration of vehicles and homogenize the Vehicle Verification Program of the Federal District and the State of Mexico.

As mentioned above, some of the recommendations have been incorporated in the Air Quality Management Plan.[3] Recently, the government authorities in the MCMA have taken major steps to implement some of the recommendations to reduce transport-related emissions and to enhance mobility. Most notably these recommendations include:

- The imposition of progressively tougher new car emission control standards.
- Improvement of fuel quality by reducing the sulfur content of both gasoline and diesel fuel so that new vehicle technologies can be introduced. The Mexican national oil company, PEMEX, plans to introduce two new types of gasoline in 2006: a 50-ppm sulfur content gasoline for the tier 2 vehicles and a 300-ppm sulfur gasoline for all other vehicles.

- Enforcement of an increasingly strict and technically sophisticated vehicle verification program for semiannual inspection of vehicle emission control systems. Currently, vehicles registered in the Federal District must be inspected in the centers located at the Federal District, the same with vehicles registered in the State of Mexico. Common procedures are in place for both Federal District and State of Mexico vehicle inspection centers.
- Increase in the use of high-capacity public transportation by extending the metro lines, introducing bus rapid transit, improving service quality and personal security and facilitating intermodal transfers.
- Provision of low-interest loans for vehicle substitution for taxis and *colectivos* older than 1992.
- Construction of roadway and other infrastructure.

Further

- The U.S. Environmental Protection Agency (EPA) is currently working with the Mexican authority to implement a diesel retrofit demonstration project designed to reduce pollution from a heavy-duty diesel bus fleet in Mexico City.
- The French Global Environmental Fund is planning to support the State of Mexico in the conversion of 3,000 public transport vehicles to natural gas starting in March 2004. A similar program was implemented in the Federal District in 2000, converting 990 vehicles to natural gas and liquefied petroleum gas (LPG).

MCMA-2003 FIELD MEASUREMENT CAMPAIGN

In the spring of 2003, an MIT-led multinational team of experts conducted an intensive, five-week field campaign in the Mexico City Metropolitan Area. The overall goal of this effort—funded by the Mexican government and other international agencies—is to contribute to the understanding of the air quality problem in megacities by conducting measurements and modeling studies of atmospheric pollutants in the MCMA. Such an understanding will help provide a scientific base for devising effective emission control strategies to reduce exposure to harmful pollutants in the MCMA and also provide insights to air pollution science in other megacities, including large urban centers in the United States.

The MCMA-2003 field measurement campaign was designed to cover the height of the annual photochemical season just before the onset of the rainy season. A mobile laboratory, equipped with a range of real-time trace gas and particle diagnostics, was deployed for mobile measurements at various locations in Mexico City. These included selected vehicle chase experiments to measure nitrogen oxides, formaldehyde, acetaldehyde, ammonia, and selected aromatic VOCs exhaust emission ratios from heavy-duty diesel trucks, diesel buses, *colectivos*, taxis, and other light-duty trucks and cars. The mobile lab also mapped background concentrations of these and other compounds in selected MCMA industrial, commercial, and residential districts. The 2003 campaign also involved a highly instrumented "supersite" located at the National Center for Environmental Research and Training of the National Institute of Ecology. The fixed "supersite" capability was enhanced with state-of-the-art instrumentation contributed by many U.S. and European teams. In addition, our collaborating Mexican research groups collected extensive meteorological data and a wide range of fixed site chemical data.

The results of the field measurements will be communicated to the scientific community and decision makers through publications and conferences. It is anticipated that the insight obtained through the field measurements and analysis of the data will be crucial for protecting human health and ecosystem viability in the Mexico City area.

METROPOLITAN COORDINATION AND CITIZENSHIP PARTICIPATION

One of the major obstacles to the implementation of antipollution measures in the MCMA is the lack of a powerful metropolitan institutional structure. The Metropolitan Environmental Commission (CAM) was created in 1996 to coordinate the policies and programs that are implemented in the metropolitan area. However, CAM does not have a specific budget for its own operation, nor does it have a defined operative organizational structure. Furthermore, the constant change of personnel according to political winds, its lack of independent budget, and its lack of power to enforce regulations have a negative influence on the functioning of this agency. To ensure continuity in the implementation of long-term action plans, we recommend that the CAM should be significantly restructured and should be empowered to conduct the planning, integration, and implementation of metropolitan environmental policies.

During the design of the new air quality management program, the CAM increased its efforts to encourage public participation and stakeholder input by forming working groups consisting of representatives from academia, nongovernmental organizations (NGOs), and industries.

EDUCATION AND CAPACITY BUILDING

One of the important components of our program is education and capacity building. The success and sustainability of environmental policies depend in great measure on a high level of citizen awareness and on the active and informed participation of stakeholders. Thus, it is necessary to develop and strengthen the environmental culture and to elevate the educational level to achieve a permanent change of attitude and behavior. Also, it is essential to improve the capacity of the human resources for the analysis, formulation, execution, and evaluation of the policies and programs aimed at improving the quality. The program has implemented several activities including workshops and symposia; exchange of faculty and scientists; air quality management workshop for professionals, policy makers, and environmental leaders from civil society, media, and industry; and stakeholder outreach.

The Mexico City case study has initiated and set up the Mexican Research and Development Network on Air Quality in Large Cities (*Red de Desarrollo e Investigación de la Calidad del Aire en Grandes Ciudades*). The network supports several research projects in Mexico that are complementary to those of the Integrated Program at MIT. In addition, the network organizes periodic meetings to promote collaboration and discussion on air pollution issues for the academic community and general public in Mexico. Although initially focused on the MCMA, the network will expand to include studies of other large cities in Mexico.

Note that during the field measurement campaign, more than three dozen postdoctoral associates, graduate students, and undergraduates from participating Mexican, U.S., and European institutions were involved in the measurement and data analysis. Thus, the MCMA-2003 campaign provides an excellent opportunity to build capacity for research, education, and policy in developing countries and contributes to international exchange.

ACKNOWLEDGMENTS

We acknowledge Fideicomiso Ambiental del Valle de México, MIT/AGS Program and the U.S. National Science Foundation for financial support for the Mexico City case study. We thank members of the Comisión Ambiental Metropolitana for their support, and Miguel Zavala, Agustín García, and Stephen Connors for preparing the figures.

REFERENCES

1. UNEP/WHO. 1992. Urban Air Pollution in Megacities of the World. Blackwell. Oxford.
2. NATIONAL RESEARCH COUNCIL, GLOBAL AIR QUALITY. 2001. An Imperative for Long-term Observational Strategies. National Academy Press. Washington, D.C.

3. CAM (Comisión Ambiental Metropolitana). 2002. Programa para Mejorar la Calidad del Aire de la Zona Rosa Metropolitana del Valle de México 2002–2010. Mexico.
4. MOLINA, L.T. & M.J. MOLINA, Eds. 2002. Air Quality in the Mexico Megacity: An Integrated Assessment. Kluwer. Dordrecht.

Health in the Urban Environment

Experience from Dar es Salaam/Tanzania

NICOLAUS LORENZ[a] AND DEO MTASIWA[b]

[a]*Swiss Tropical Institute, Basel, Switzerland*

[b]*Regional Medical Office of Health, Dar es Salaam, Tanzania*

ABSTRACT: Dar es Salaam is a typical example of the rapid urbanization process in sub-Saharan Africa. Health problems in the city are tremendous and reflect the epidemiologic transition, with the emergence of chronic diseases, as well as the prevailing problems related to infectious diseases. Not surprisingly, HIV/AIDS has become a major determinant of health. Public health services have been strengthened in the past 12 years through the support of a bilateral program called the Dar es Salaam Urban Health Project (DUHP). The program was jointly funded by the Government of Tanzania and the Swiss Agency for Development and Cooperation. The focus of the program shifted from the initial rehabilitation of the health infrastructure to a strengthening of the management capacities of the public health care delivery system. The basis for the collaboration and complementarity between public and private health care providers has been created. Partly thanks to the success of the DUHP, the health system has become the spearhead and testing ground for core health sector reforms and has had a substantial influence on the introduction of a donor-supported sectorwide approach in the health sector in Tanzania. Perhaps most importantly, the foundations have been laid for a more democratic health system in which both the staff and the population are involved.

KEYWORDS: **urban health; poverty; sectorwide approaches**

INTRODUCTION

Dar es Salaam, which means "the haven of peace" in Arabic, is a typical example of the rapid urbanization process that has been taking place in sub-Saharan Africa in recent decades. In the 1950s, Dar es Salaam had an estimated population of 150,000, while today the population is estimated to be at least 2,500,000, with an annual growth rate of ~5%.

Address for correspondence: Nicolaus Lorenz, Swiss Tropical Institute, P.O. Box 4002, Basel, Switzerland. Voice: +41-61-284-81-25; fax: +41-61-271-86-54.
nicolaus.lorenz@unibas.ch

**Ann. N.Y. Acad. Sci. 1023: 159–163 (2004). © 2004 New York Academy of Sciences.
doi: 10.1196/annals.1319.007**

The health problems of this population are tremendous and have not stopped increasing over the past years. As in many sub-Saharan African cities, HIV/AIDS has become the leading health problem in Dar es Salaam, accounting for almost half of all adult deaths. However, health problems related to the environment, such as malaria, are also important, and in recent years cholera has become endemic in the city.[1]

Epidemiological transition is also taking its toll, and, although not as visible as HIV/AIDS, rates for diabetes,[2] hypertension, and injuries[3] are increasing.[4] Violence-related health problems are not yet a major documented problem in Dar, but the example of nearby Nairobi and southern African cities of a comparable size are worrying.[5]

In the late 1980s, the public health care delivery system in Dar es Salaam was in bad shape to cope with these challenges. Its physical infrastructure was dilapidated, drugs were not available, and its overall performance had reached an unprecedented low level. All these factors triggered efforts to reverse this situation.

THE DAR ES SALAAM URBAN HEALTH PROJECT

On the basis of a bilateral agreement between the Government of Tanzania and the Swiss Agency for Development and Cooperation and a participative planning process, the Dar es Salaam Urban Health project was implemented in 1990 to improve the health status of the population of Dar es Salaam.

The project's focus evolved from the initial rehabilitation of the physical infrastructure of health services to the strengthening of management capacities at district/municipal and city level with strong aspects of community participation to the support of the ongoing health sector reform process in Tanzania and currently to a consolidation and experience capitalization effort.

The underlying assumption of the project was that before starting interventions that would address specific burden of disease or environmental health problems, a functional system would have to be put in place that would be able to handle the complex managerial tasks needed to effectively tackle these problems. Furthermore, it was also recognized that the nongovernmental sector and community involvement would have to receive particular attention if the system was to be sustainable.

After initial major investment in the rehabilitation of the physical infrastructure, the management capacities of the health administration were strengthened. A key element was the development of a Minimum Package of Health and Related Management Activities, a set of comprehensive task and job descriptions, covering all "roles of governmental urban health service tiers," its services (outputs), its needed resources (inputs), and its management and administration.

Health service providers now widely understand the potential role of the community and accept guidance from health boards. Equally important, health service providers also were provided with the necessary resources not only to plan, but also to implement these plans.

Today the project support has been replaced by resources coming from a donors' basket funding in the context of a sector-wide approach for the whole of Tanzania.

The creation of health boards at each health facility, in each municipality, and now as an association at the city level has strengthened the potential for effective community participation.

Parallel to the development of the governmental health care system, the private health sector, marginal in the late 1980s, has proliferated dramatically.

Over more than a decade, the Dar es Salaam Urban Health Project (DUHP) has achieved the followingresults:

- A rehabilitated system providing more and better-quality services to the population than before;
- An integrated health system, more efficiently organized, managed, and administered;
- A health system that is now decentralized under the regional and local government;
- A basis for collaboration and complementarity between public and private health care providers;
- A health system that has become the spearhead and testing ground for core health sector reforms; and
- A basis for a more democratic health system in which both the staff (through a complete set of health management teams) and the population (through its health boards per facility/district and the city) are involved.

The success of the DUHP also has to be seen against the background of a generally positive environment in Dar es Salaam, which facilitated some of the achievements. In the early 1990s, the government of Tanzania started with a comprehensive reform process in several sectors. The legal sector, public financial management reform, civil service reform, and particularly local government and health sector reform provided a favorable environment for the DUHP. For example, a review of health sector-wide approaches in Mozambique, Tanzania, Uganda, Cambodia, and Vietnam concluded that, of all the country case studies, Tanzania has the most advanced sector-wide approach even though it only began in 1999.[6]

However, there are still problem areas:

- The burden of disease is still overwhelming.

- The health sector reform process is not yet fully implemented.
- Coordination between the health administrations of the three municipalities needs attention.
- The rapidly evolving private health care delivery sector puts a strain on the health administrations, which have difficulties supervising their establishment and performance.
- Although the health sector reform has strengthened the system, community-based health initiatives are still comparatively weak.
- Although the financial basis of the public health system has improved, poverty is still a major factor limiting access to health services, because the financial burden of disease is largely on the side of the individual and his or her family.

CONCLUSIONS

Health in the urban environment is an important aspect for sustainable urban development. Poverty in Dar es Salaam has, as in other cities, a major negative impact on health. On the other hand, poor health in the city is also a major risk factor for poverty.[7] This highlights the importance of improving health in the cities.

Although health is influenced by numerous factors, the public health care delivery system has a role to play. To do this effectively, the system has to be enabled to implement health-specific interventions, such as those required to treat urban malaria. In Dar es Salaam, the public health care delivery system was strengthened in such a way that today it is in a position to efficiently address prevailing health problems.

As in many other cities, the liberalization process of the early 1980s has led to a rapid proliferation of private health care providers, which has improved coverage and quantity of treatments. However, monitoring the quality of care is important, and it needs to be continually supervised by the public health administration.

The urban environment can play an important role in testing and promoting reforms in other sectors. The positive DUHP experience of budget support supplied to the district/municipal level and the success in implementing district health plans has influenced external donors to Tanzania to embark on the sector-wide approach to health care in Tanzania. Thus, although it is difficult to determine a direct causal relationship, success stories in the city provide a basis for change in development-assistance approaches.

Finally, the DUHP has shown that there is still a long way to go to achieve health for all in an urban environment, because improvements on the health service delivery side alone cannot address all factors that influence health in the city.

REFERENCES

1. Majani, B.B. 1996. Coping with urban growth and development through environmental planning and management (EPM): the sustainable Dar es Salaam project. Urban Health Newsl. **28:** 26–31.
2. McLarty, D.G., N. Unwin, H.M. Kitange & K.G. Alberti. 1996. Diabetes mellitus as a cause of death in sub-Saharan Africa: results of a community-based study in Tanzania. The Adult Morbidity and Mortality Project. Diabet. Med. **13:** 990–994.
3. Nordberg, E. 2000. Injuries as a public health problem in sub-Saharan Africa: epidemiology and prospects for control. East Afr. Med. J. **77:** S1–S43 (Suppl. 12).
4. Bovet, P., G. Ross, J.P. Gervasoni, *et al.* 2002. Distribution of blood pressure, body mass index and smoking habits in the urban population of Dar es Salaam, Tanzania, and associations with socioeconomic status. Int. J. Epidemiol. **31:** 240–247.
5. Bradshaw, D., P. Groenewald, R. Laubscher, *et al.* 2003. Initial burden of disease estimates for South Africa, 2000. S. Afr. Med. J. **93:** 682–688.
6. Brown, A. 2000. Current issues in sector-wide approaches for health development: Tanzania case study. Strategies for cooperation and partnership/Global Programme on Evidence for Health Policy, WHO/GPE/00.6.
7. Wyss, K., P. Kilima & N. Lorenz. 2001. Costs of tuberculosis for households and health care providers in Dar es Salaam, Tanzania. Trop. Med. Int. Health **6:** 60.

Environmental Factors in HIV/AIDS Epidemic Development

New Perspectives for Gender Equity and Global Protection against HIV Transmission

ANNETTE ALFSEN

U.INSERM: Entrée muqueuse du VIH et Immunité muqueuse, 75014 Paris, France

ABSTRACT: The HIV/AIDS epidemic is increasingly regarded as a socioeconomic problem. Among factors causing poverty, cultural aspects, including religion and traditions, appear to play an essential role in the rapid and global development of AIDS epidemic. AIDS is a pathologic syndrome caused by the human immunodeficiency virus (HIV). Scientific knowledge is required to prevent and treat AIDS. Although considerable progress has been made in antiretroviral therapy, neither actual cure of HIV infection, nor an efficient protection method, nor a vaccine are currently globally accessible. Consequently, the funding of scientific research is of utmost importance. On the basis of recent scientific findings, new perspectives for global protection and gender equity against HIV transmission are emerging. Progress is being made in developing microbicides or virucides, anti-infective medication formulated for topical self-administration, to protect against HIV and other sexually transmitted pathogens. Such developments need to be supported by extensive education campaigns geared to women to give them the possibility of protecting themselves and their children from HIV transmission. The level of funding for microbicide and vaccine development needs to be greatly increased. New possibilities have emerged for an efficient vaccine which would engage the mucosal immune system, first involved in the sexual transmission of HIV-1. The idea of vaccine production in edible tissues of transgenic crop plants has also gained momentum. The use of minimally processed, low-cost, orally delivered immunogens is especially valuable when raising mucosal antibodies is the object and when frequent boosting is anticipated, as is the case for mucosal immunity.

KEYWORDS: HIV; AIDS epidemic; sexually transmitted infectious diseases; socioeconomic problems; women; children

Address for correspondence: Annette Alfsen, U.INSERM: Entrée muqueuse du VIH et Immunité muqueuse, Institut Cochin. Cnrs, Inserm, Université René Descartes, 22 rue Méchain, 75014 Paris, France.
alfsen@cochin.inserm.fr

**Ann. N.Y. Acad. Sci. 1023: 164–174 (2004). © 2004 New York Academy of Sciences.
doi: 10.1196/annals.1319.008**

INTRODUCTION

The AIDS epidemic is increasingly viewed as a socioeconomic problem. In some countries, it is considered more threatening to national security than war. As a result of this awareness, an important part of the funding to fight AIDS now goes to economists to demonstrate the links between the epidemic and poverty in poor countries and the consequence on the economy, wealth, and health of rich countries. Environmental factors contributing to the AIDS epidemic development certainly include poverty, overcrowding in inadequate housing, poor health conditions, high number of children per family, and nutritional problems. More importantly, the "cultural environment," including religion or traditions, appears to play an essential role in the rapid and global development of the sexually transmitted infectious diseases (STIDs). Within this context, the role of urban environments in the development and, possibly, treatment and prevention of HIV is particularly relevant. Although factors such as overcrowding, social dislocation, and poor health conditions may be particularly acute in poor cities, the density of urban networks also affords opportunities for efficient interventions.

However, to mount an effective campaign to fight the AIDS epidemic, it is important to remember that the AIDS syndrome is, first of all, a disease caused by a virus. Unlike wars, which are more often than not the consequence of socioeconomic factors, human pathology, to be prevented and treated, needs scientific knowledge resulting from scientific research. Although considerable progress has been made in antiretroviral therapy, thus extending the life of people with HIV and the reduction of maternal–fetal HIV transmission, neither actual cure of HIV infection nor efficient protection method or vaccine is now globally accessible. This is where financial resources are the most needed. It is essential to reach an understanding of the cause of the viral pathology and of the way viruses and, in this case, HIV is transmitted and infects human organism.

THE HIV-1/AIDS PANDEMIC IS A GLOBAL PUBLIC HEALTH CONCERN WITH FAR-REACHING SOCIETAL CONSEQUENCES, ESPECIALLY IN THE DEVELOPING WORLD

Year after year, since the discovery of the HIV and the first apparition of the AIDS syndrome, the same pessimistic forecasts have been made by organizations ranging from governments to the UN and nongovernmental organizations (NGOs). In September 2003, the Agènce Nationale pour la Recherche sur le SIDA (ANRS France) issued a declaration to the effect that "The HIV/AIDS epidemic is of unprecedented gravity and is spreading rapidly, notably in the disadvantaged regions of the world. The scale of the HIV/AIDS epidemic has exceeded the most pessimistic forecasts. Some 42 million people worldwide are currently estimated to be HIV-infected. Since the start of the epidemic, AIDS has caused over 25 million deaths. UNAIDS predicts that 70 million people could die of AIDS over the next 20 years in the 45 most-affected countries."[1]

CULTURAL ENVIRONMENT AND GENDER EQUITY

After being considered as "punishment by God" during the first period of the epidemic, when it mainly concerned homosexual transmission, AIDS is now recognized to be caused by the human immunodeficiency virus (HIV), a virus of different strains having an extensive global variability. The epidemic, which is now spreading among heterosexual partners, actually is associated with poverty in developing countries and is also recognized as a cause of desperate poverty, leading to economic disaster. Because of what could be called "cultural environment," it has been observed that unprotected sex remains widespread, even in the developed countries, as can be judged from the continuing growth of the global HIV epidemic. Ninety percent of the 4,932 women infected with HIV every day in the world are in developing countries, and 2.5 million children were at risk of HIV infection in 2001 through mother-to-child transmission. Even in developed countries such as the United States, 23% of all new AIDS cases are in women, 31% of new HIV infections among adolescents and adults occur in women, and 59% of new HIV cases among 14- to 19-year-olds occur in girls.[2]

These data clearly demonstrate that sexually transmissible infectious sickness (STI) is equally distributed among male and female individuals. It therefore would be appropriate to give men and women equal access to the capacity to protect themselves. It also would be essential to permit both men and women to participate in the decisions regarding protection and treatment of AIDS and other STIs. However, despite endless discussions and numerous "recommendations" to give the women the same rights as men, the UN Statistics Division[3,4] published the following numbers: of the 876 million analphabets in the world two of three are women; 113 million of children of primary school age do not go to school, and two of three of them are girls; and 14.2% of elected members of parliament in the world are women, including 16.8% in European countries and 4.6% in the Arab states.[5]

These numbers led Koichiro Matsuura, General Director of UNESCO, to recently declare:

> In all of the life domains and in the administration council, committies and commissions where essential orientation are decided, women are not able to reach the level where influence and authority are exercised .... Gender equity

> should not be considered as a problem restricted to women, but as a problem which raises fundamental questions on the nature of our social relations.[6]

It now clearly appears that poverty is increasing along with the epidemic. Women are the most affected by poverty. The rate of joblessness is the highest among women and young people. It is noteworthy in this context that population is increasing in the developed countries, but decreasing in developed countries.

All these factors are related to the status of women in the world and especially in countries where culture and religion maintain women in the position of sexual objects at the disposal of men. Note therefore that even in those societies in which the position of women is weakest, urban areas can provide more opportunities and access for women both to employment and education and to support networks as well.

In addition to the above-described parameters regarding the continuing extension of the AIDS epidemic, mother-to-child transmission is another problem, also related to the status of women, which contributes to the spread of AIDS. In the 21 years since the start of AIDS epidemic, 4.7 million children have died and 2.7 million children younger than 15 years are now living with HIV/AIDS. If HIV-infected mothers remain untreated, by the year 2010, the number of orphans will exceed 40 million.

In the developed world, therapeutic management of infected mothers has meant that very few children are now born seropositive. Treatment is both available and affordable. Urgent attention needs to be paid to prevent HIV transmission from mothers to child through education and delivery of low-cost drugs.

NEW PERSPECTIVES FOR GLOBAL PROTECTION AGAINST AIDS TRANSMISSION

According to many organizations, UNAIDS, NGOs, and scientists, an urgent and essential task is to develop the protection of women in the fight against the AIDS epidemic and to call for a mobilization against AIDS more specifically for women. The Rockefeller Foundation in Microbicide Initiative 2000,[7] using the above-cited statistics, emphasizes the importance of such a mobilization:

> The current HIV prevention strategies—monogamy, condom use, reduction in number of partners, and treatment of sexually transmitted infections—often are not feasible for them ... Women urgently need methods to protect themselves from infection with HIV and other STIs that are within their personal control. Although no product will address the underlying gender inequalities that constrain women's ability to protect themselves from infection, making such products available could save millions of lives.

That does not imply a choice between prevention and treatment because the approaches mutually reinforce one another. However, if the availability of highly active antiretroviral therapy (HAART) increases life expectancy of treated patients, its impact on HIV incidence will further depend on the extent to which risk behaviors are affected by such availability. In developed countries, reports have been made of a decreased awareness of HIV risks in the general population and of an increased incidence of STIs and high-risk behaviors, as HAART has become largely available.[8]

Therefore, the development of methods of protection, at low cost and controlled by women, against AIDS and other sexually transmitted pathogens as well as unwanted pregnancy, appears to be the most urgent aim in the fight against AIDS and has the highest global public health benefits.

HIV IS A SEXUALLY TRANSMITTED INFECTION

As stressed above, AIDS is a pathologic syndrome for which preventive methods, vaccines, protection, and treatment must be developed; the knowledge of viral pathology necessary would be achieved by fundamental research.

Mucosal surfaces, such as respiratory and digestive tracts, genital mucosa, or the lining of the gut, are the main point of entry for viruses into the body. Epithelial cells organized into complex structures cover these surfaces, and this epithelial organization often dictates the mechanism of viral entry and translocation. As such, almost all viruses interact with epithelial cells and make use, by "pathogenic trickery," of the host cell's normal epithelial signaling and trafficking pathways. However, viruses also have developed soluble virulence factors, which interact with epithelial cells independently of the virus and participate in the development of the virally induced pathology.

To understand the strategies that viruses have evolved to translocate across the epithelial barrier, according to the target cell structure and the nature of the virus, a description of the cell receptors that allow attachment and entry into the cell is required, as is knowledge of the viral proteins that interact with, and subvert, these receptors, allowing the virus to cross the cell membrane and act as a pathogen.[9]

Many viral receptors at the epithelial surface have been characterized. Viruses use host cell molecules referred to as "coreceptors" in addition to the "principal" receptor. An important class of coreceptor has emerged, namely, molecules from the extracellular matrix, such as proteoglycans, and from the cell membrane, such as glycolipids. Both these types of molecules are characterized by the presence of long chains of sugar, which have specific properties for the immunity. The virus acts as a lectin (a protein able to specifically bind sugars) by binding the carbohydrate as a coreceptor. Because of the nature of the lectin–sugar interaction, environmental factors characteristic of mucosal surfaces also must play an important role in viral entry.[10]

Considerable progress in experimental cellular models has been made recently, allowing experimental infection not only of epithelial cell lines but also of primary cells or epithelial tissue. This not only allows the polarized nature of the epithelium to be preserved, but also retains its interaction with submucosal cells. Consequently, studies have focused on the molecular mechanism of the pathology induced *in vivo* by a specific virus on its particular target cell (for a review, see Bomsel and Alfsen[9]).

MICROBICIDES OR VIRUCIDES

Using the current knowledge on the first target cells, that is, mucosal epithelial cells for the transmission and entry of HIV, the search was developed for products that, when used vaginally, or on other sexually exposed mucosa, would prevent the sexual transmission of the virus. Microbicides or virucides have been defined as anti-infective medication formulated for topical self-administration before intercourse to protect against HIV and other sexually transmitted pathogens.[11] The demonstration that products used to reduce risk of unwanted pregnancy not only attack sperm, but can also destroy HIV provided the initial stimulus to develop this field of research. Such products could be in the form of gels, creams, and foams. The chemical and physical actions of the product will protect the uninfected person from infectious agents that might be present in the genital secretions of the sexual partner. It can be used by the women without the need for the sexual-partner consent that is required for all previous protection methods. Unlike condoms, microbicides will not create a physical barrier to intimate contact and women would be able to apply them a long time before intercourse takes place. Moreover, the use of a microbicide needs not necessarily prevent conception, as the intention is to develop both contraceptive and noncontraceptive products. Several microbicides are scheduled to enter phase III clinical trials over the next year, including carragheenin, BufferGel, Pro 2000, and dextrin-2sulphate. The recent international consultation sponsored by the Rockefeller Foundation[7] concluded that at least one microbicide could be on the market as early as 2007. This first generation of microbicides might be no more than 6O% effective against AIDS transmission. By 2012, second-generation products could be on the market, being 70–90% effective against HIV with good activity against gonorrhea, chlamydia, genital herpes, and papilloma virus. By 2017, microbicides would be 85–97% effective against HIV (Rockefeller Foundation report).

However, how soon these benefits materialize will depend on how successful we are in tackling not only the scientific challenges, but also the societal issues. The development of the research for efficient product therefore should be one urgent aim of the global fight against AIDS. The level of funding for microbicide development needs to be greatly increased. Knowledge and expertise must be shared internationally. Such developments need to be accompanied by a large campaign for women's education, which can only give them the possibility to protect themselves and their children from the STIs.

The education program takes a specific importance in the domain of mother-to-child transmission of HIV. Despite the fact that such a transmission *in utero*, through the placenta, or during the birth of the child is still not very well understood, information to the seropositive mother during pregnancy is fundamental to give her the possibility to be treated to avoid the infection of her child. Such information should first allow any woman to be tested for a possible seropositivity and then give her accessibility to any drug able to prevent HIV transmission to the child. Also a possible transmission through colostrum during breast-feeding is to be documented.

NEW PERSPECTIVES FOR AN EFFICIENT VACCINE

Despite the success of extensive AIDS prevention programs and powerful antiretroviral drugs in limiting the spread of HIV-1 in high-income countries[12] it is generally agreed that, for the developing world, these efforts will have to be combined with effective vaccines. But two decades after the discovery of HIV, the need remains for improved vaccine designs that will deal with the genetic and the phenotypic variation of HIV and effectively prevent the establishment of lifelong infection. Design and testing of such vaccines have proved to be complex.[13,14] The "enterprise" of HIV vaccine development must be designed as a high-quality collaborative research system that goes well beyond the high-quality but separate research projects that we have today.[15] However, new vaccine candidates are on the way to be developed.

Because transmission of HIV-1 occurs most commonly through exposure of mucosal surfaces to virus, a vaccine that would engage the mucosal immune system against a broad range of HIV-1 subtypes and prevent the initial stage of infection is highly desirable. Protection of the genital or rectal regions through which HIV transmission most often occurs requires a vaccine, the reinforcement of specific mucosal immunity.[16,17]

Studies of HIV-1 transmission, infection, replication, and pathogenesis are providing several novel strategies for vaccine design. An HIV-1 vaccine of the future ultimately may be a multicomponent subunit vaccine designed to induce immune responses to block different steps in the viral life cycle. Because HIV-1 transmission occurs most commonly through exposure of mucosal surfaces to HIV-1–infected secretions—semen, cervicovaginal fluid, colostrum, and milk[18]—a possible component of such a vaccine should engage the mucosal immune system to interfere with the primary events associated with mucosal transmission of HIV-1.

The initial steps of HIV entry, as defined previously, lead to the transcytosis of the virus across the epithelial barrier and its trapping by submucosal dendritic cells (DCs), which disseminate it to their target CD4$^+$ monocytes, leading to fusion and spreading the infection.[19] The viral envelope proteins, gp120 and gp41, play a well-characterized role both in fusion of HIV-1 with target cells[20] and in viral transcytosis.[10,17,21,22] Among the regions of the envelope protein gp41 involved in the interaction with the host cell membrane, one domain, extending between the gp120 cap and the transmembrane domain,[23] spans several conserved neutralization epitopes recognized by antibodies, which are able to neutralize infection by most primary isolates.

Four lines of evidence suggest that these antibodies contribute to resistance to mucosal transmission of HIV-1. First, in the macaque model, immunization with inactivated simian immunodeficiency virus (SIV) targeted to mucosal or lymph node sites resulted in protection against both systemic and mucosal SIV challenge. Second, passive immunization of monkeys with monoclonal IgG antibodies protected macaques from a mucosal challenge.[24,25] Third, specific anti–HIV-1 antibodies have been detected at mucosal sites in **h**ighly **e**xposed **p**ersistently **s**eronegative (HEPS) individuals. Significantly, these antibodies are mostly directed against gp41.[26–28] The presence of these antibodies is one of but few indications of any contact with HIV-1 in HEPS individuals. More than a witness to viral exposure, these antibodies (together with mucosal cellular responses) are strongly suggestive of an efficient "natural" vaccination in these individuals and may prove to be one of the long-sought correlates of protection from HIV-1 infection. Fourth, *in vitro* experiments prove that anti–HIV-1 antibodies, isolated from mucosal secretions of HEPS individuals, block transcytosis of HIV across a tight epithelial cell barrier as well as a human intestinal biopsy and infection of CD4$^+$ monocytes.[17]

A NEEDLELESS VACCINE AGAINST HIV

In recent years, the idea of subunit vaccine production in edible tissues of transgenic crop plants has gained momentum with the successful outcome of several phase I/II clinical trials.[29–31] The attractive feature of transgenic plants is that they combine a cost-effective production system with a safe and efficacious delivery system that targets the gut-associated lymphoid tissue. The use of minimally processed, room temperature–resistant, orally delivered immunogens is especially valuable when elicitation of mucosal antibodies is the object and when frequent boosting is anticipated, as is the case for mucosal immunity. Several attempts in expression of HIV-1 antigens in plants have been reported.[32–34] Because of the complexity of HIV-1, it seems unlikely that a single form of vaccination would be effective in isolation.

However, a plant-based vaccine aimed at blocking HIV-1 transcytosis at the mucosal portals may be combined with other subunit vaccines in a multiformat, prime-boost approach to constitute an efficient and cost-effective vaccination strategy for the developing world.

In conclusion, the hope to win the fight against the AIDS epidemic lies first in scientific research on the viral pathology. However, in a sexually transmissible infectious disease, the fight for gender equity appears essential and can be won only through global women's education: the fight for human rights means a fight for gender equity. In all these battles, victory depends on human knowledge and human conscience. For, as said by the 16th century French writer François Rabelais, "Sapience n'entre point en âme malivole et Science sans conscience n'est que ruine de l'âme."

REFERENCES

1. Kazatchkine, M. 2003. ANRS Research on HIV Vaccine. ANRS Publications. Paris.
2. HIV/AIDS. 2001. AIDS Epidemic Update: December 2001. Joint United Nations Program and WHO. New York.
3. United Nations. 2000. The World's Women 2000: Trends and Statistics. Division des Statisitiques des Nations Unies. Paris.
4. OIT. 2001. ABC of Women Worker's Rights and Gender Equality. Organisation Internationale du Travail; p. 47–48. Geneva.
5. UNAIDS, 2003. Progress Report on the Global Response to HIV/AIDS Epidemic. Follow-up to the 2001 United Nations General Assembly session on HIV/AIDS. New York.
6. UNESCO, 2002. Le défi de l'equité entre les genres. Section pour les femmes et l'egalité des genres. Bureau de la planification stratégique. Paris.
7. Rockefeller Foundation. 2002. Mobilization for Microbicides: the Decisive Decade. Rockefeller Foundation. New York.
8. Moatti, J.P., I. N'Doye, S.M. Hammer *et al.* 2003. Antiretroviral treatment for retroviral infection in developing countries: an attainable new paradigm. Nat. Med. **9:** 1449–1452.
9. Bomsel, M. & A. Alfsen. 2003. Entry of viruses through the epithelial barrier. Nat. Rev. Mol. Cell. Biol. **4:** 57–68.
10. Alfsen, A. & M. Bomsel. 2002. HIV-1 envelope residues 650-685 exposed on native virus act as a lectin to bind epithelial cell galactosyl ceramide. J. Biol. Chem. **277:** 25649–25659.
11. Stone, A. 2002. Microbicides: a new approach to preventing HIV and other sexually transmissible infections. Nat. Rev. Drug Discov. **1:** 977–985.
12. Valdiserri, R.O., L.L. Ogden & E. McCaray. 2003. Accomplishments in HIV prevention science: implications for stemming the epidemic. Nat. Med. **9:** 881–886.

13. LETVIN, N.L., D.H. BAROUCH & D.C. MONTEFIORI. 2002. Prospects for vaccine protection against HIV-1 infection and AIDS. Annu. Rev. Immunol. **20:** 73–99.
14. MCMICHAEL, A.J. & T. HANKE. 2003. HIV vaccines 1983–2003. Nat. Med. **9:** 874–880.
15. KLAUSNER, R.D. 2003. The need for a global vaccine enterprise. Science **300:** 2036–2039.
16. DURRANI, Z., T.L. MCINERNEY, L. MCLAIN, *et al.* 1998. Intranasal immunization with a plant virus expressing a peptide from HIV-1 gp41 stimulates better mucosal and systemic HIV-1 specific IgA and IgG than oral immunization. J. Immunol. Methods **220:** 93–103.
17. ALFSEN, A., P. INIGUEZ, E. BOUGUYON & M. BOMSEL. 2001. Secretory IgA specific for a conserved epitope on gp41 envelope glycoprotein inhibits epithelial transcytosis of HIV-1. J. Immunol. **166:** 6257–6265.
18. POPE, M. & A.T. HAASE. 2003. Transmission, acute HIV-1 infection and the quest for strategies to prevent infection. Nat. Med. **9:** 847–852.
19. BOMSEL, M., M. HEYMAN, H. HOCINI, *et al.* 1998. Intracellular neutralization of HIV transcytosis across tight epithelial barriers by anti-HIV envelope protein dIgA or IgM. Immunity **9:** 277–287.
20. MOBLEY, P.W., R. PILPA, C. BROWN, *et al.* 2001. Membrane perturbing domains of HIV type 1 glycoprotein41. AIDS Res. Hum. Retrov. **17:** 311–327.
21. BOMSEL, M. 1997. Transcytosis of infectious human immunodeficiency virus across a tight human epithelial cell line barrier. Nat. Med. **3:** 42–47.
22. MENG, G., X. WEI, X. WU, *et al.* 2002. Primary intestinal epithelial cells selectively transfer R5 HIV-1 to CCR5 cells. Nat. Med. **8:** 150–156.
23. WYATT, R., P.D. KWONG, E. DESJARDINS, *et al.* 1998. The antigenic structure of the HIV gp120 envelope glycoprotein. Nature **393:** 705–711.
24. MASCOLA, J.R., G. STIEGLER, T.C. VANCOTT, *et al.* 2000. Protection of macaques against vaginal transmission of a pathogenic HIV-1/SIV chimeric virus by passive infusion of neutralizing antibodies. Nat. Med. **6:** 207–210.
25. BABA, T.W., V. LISKA, R. HOFMANN-LEHMANN, *et al.* 2000. Human neutralizing monoclonal antibodies of the IgG1 subtype protect against mucosal simian-human immunodeficiency virus infection. Nat. Med. **6:** 200–206.
26. DEVITO, C., K. BROLIDEN, R. KAUL, *et al.* 2000. Mucosal and plasma IgA from HIV-1 exposed uninfected individuals inhibit HIV-1 transcytosis across human epithelial cells. J. Immunol. **165:** 5170–5176.
27. DEVITO, C., J. HINKULA, R. KAUL, *et al.* 2000. Mucosal and plasma IgA from HIV-exposed seronegative individuals neutralize a primary HIV-1 isolate. AIDS **14:** 1917–1920.
28. MAZZOLI, S., L. LOPALCO, A. SALVI, *et al.* 1999. Human immunodeficiency virus –specific IgA and HIV neutralizing activity in the serum of exposed seronegative partners of HIV-seropositive persons. J. Infect. Dis. **180:** 871–875.
29. KOPROWSKI, H. & V. YUSIBOV. 2001. The green revolution: plants as heterologous expression vectors. Vaccine **19:** 2735–2741.
30. MASON, H.S., H. WARSECHA, T. MOR & C.J. ARNTZEN. 2002. Edible plant vaccines: applications for prophylactic and therapeutic molecular medicine. Trends Mol. Med. **8:** 324–329.
31. MOR, T.S. & H.S. MASON. 2003. Handbook of plant biotechnology. In press.

32. MARUSIC, C., P. RIZZA, L. LATTANZI, *et al.* 2001. Chimeric plant virus particles as immunogens for inducing murine and human immune responses against HIV-1. J. Virol. **75:** 8434–8439.
33. YU, J. & W.H. LANGRIDGE. 2001. A plant-based multicomponent vaccine protects mice from enteric diseases. Nat. Biotechnol. **19:** 548–552.
34. ZHANG, G.G., L. RODRIGUES, B. ROVINSKI & K.A. WHITE. 2002. Production of HIV-1 p24 protein in transgenic tobacco plants. Mol. Biotechnol. **20:** 131–136.

Inhabitants' Environmental Perceptions in the City of Rome within the Framework for Urban Biosphere Reserves of the UNESCO Programme on Man and Biosphere[a]

MIRILIA BONNES, GIUSEPPE CARRUS, MARINO BONAIUTO, FERDINANDO FORNARA, AND PAOLA PASSAFARO

Department of Social and Developmental Psychology, University of Rome "La Sapienza," Rome 00185, Italy

ABSTRACT: The article presents the main tenets of the UNESCO Programme on Man and Biosphere (MAB), launched by the United Nations at the beginning of the 1970s. The program aimed at supporting applied research and scientific knowledge for managing natural resources in a rational and sustainable way. The implication of the full ecological perspective, typical of the MAB, for promoting multidisciplinary and integrated approaches in the study of environmental issues is briefly outlined. In particular, we point out the role of the MAB, through the biosphere reserve concept, in supporting the collaboration between natural-biological and social-behavioral sciences when dealing with biodiversity conservation problems and with urban ecosystems. Then, the specific UNESCO-MAB Project on the city of Rome, launched at the end of the 1980s, is briefly presented, together with the recent project of the Department of the Environment of the Rome Municipality to propose Rome's urban and periurban green areas as a new UNESCO-MAB Biosphere Reserve. The results of the main research activities conducted therein are summarized. In particular, the specific research lines of the environmental psychology research group, involved in the MAB-Rome Project for approximately two decades, are presented. These research lines dealt with various aspects of residents' environmental perceptions and behaviors in the city of Rome. The practical implications of these results are also briefly discussed.

[a]The research lines presented in this article are part of a broader research project developed in collaboration with the Department of the Environment of the Rome Municipality and with the Department of Plant Biology of the University of Rome "La Sapienza."

Address for correspondence: Mirilia Bonnes, University of Rome "La Sapienza," Department of Social and Developmental Psychology, Via dei Marsi 78, 00185 Rome, Italy. Voice: +39-06-49917546; fax: +39-06-49917652.

mirilia.bonnes@uniroma1.it

Ann. N.Y. Acad. Sci. 1023: 175–186 (2004). © 2004 New York Academy of Sciences.
doi: 10.1196/annals.1319.009

Keywords: UNESCO-MAB Programme; ecosystem approach; urban biosphere reserves; biodiversity; sustainability; environmental psychology; environmental perception; environmental awareness; residential satisfaction; environmental evaluation; environmental concern; environmental education

THE ECOSYSTEM APPROACH OF THE UNESCO PROGRAMME ON MAN AND BIOSPHERE

The Man and Biosphere Programme (MAB) of the UNESCO Division of Ecological Science was launched by the United Nations in 1971 as "an international programme of applied research on the interactions between man and the environment," with the aim of providing "scientific knowledge and trained personnel to manage natural resources in a rational and sustained manner."[1] The main element characterizing the MAB is its *ecosystem approach* and its *full ecology* perspective,[2] aiming at integrating the understanding of both the natural and human/social processes of ecosystems and in particular their mutual interdependencies. This perspective should be distinguished from what can be defined as a *partial ecology* perspective, often characterizing natural and biological sciences, which tend to consider human processes and activities only as a disrupting factor of "Nature" and its processes. Conversely, in the full ecology perspective, humans are considered as either a possible threat to or source of nature conservation. In fact, the MAB Programme stressed the importance of the so-called "human dimension"—in a perceptual and behavioral sense—involved in environmental processes and changes, and thus in natural resource use, management, and conservation. With this aim, the concept of Human Use System (HUS) also was introduced as the main unit of analysis for the study of environmental phenomena, to complement the more general concept of ecosystem.[3] The HUS is considered as articulated into three main dimensions: (1) spatial, (2) temporal, and (3) perceptual. The spatial and temporal dimensions pertain to the physical-biological aspects of the environment, whereas the perceptual dimension pertains to its human components: that is, human beliefs, values, attitudes, and behaviors, which are typical objects of study of environmental, social, and behavioral sciences and, in particular, of current environmental psychology.[4–6]

The integrative approach of the MAB Programme also aimed at bringing together three different principal categories of *environmental actors* (i.e., environmental scientist/experts, environmental decision makers, environmental users) to (1) encourage scientists/technicians, working in the various environmental sciences, to develop knowledge and research methods as support for environmental decision making; (2) encourage environmental managers and decision makers to appreciate the advantages of this science-based approach in environmental decision making; (3) encourage the users of the considered environments to gain a greater environmental awareness of their own perceptions and actions and of the consequences of these upon ecosystems.

According to this full ecology perspective, the "Natural Sphere" and the "Human Sphere" are conceived as interdependent and not only as conflicting elements.[3] Therefore, continuity has to be seen between the more nature-dominated (e.g., wilderness areas) and the more human-dominated (e.g., urban settlements and cities) ecosystems. In line with this perspective, the MAB Programme initially focused its various thematic projects on different types of ecosystems, ranging from the more nature-dominated ones (e.g., Project 8 on biosphere reserves [BRs]) to the more human-dominated ones (e.g., Project 11 on Urban Systems).

In particular, thematic Project 11 dealt with "urban ecosystems."[1,7] This particular program aimed to apply the previously mentioned *ecosystem approach* to urban settlements and cities, starting from two major considerations. First, the limits of traditional approaches (often sectoral and fragmented) to urban planning for addressing the environmental problems of cities[1] were recognized. Second, it was assumed that problems related to cities and to human life in cities were, and will continue to in the following decades, gaining increased urgency all over the world. Thus, several MAB 11 projects developed during the 1970s and 1980s in various cities of the world (Hong Kong, Frankfurt, Mexico City, etc.) and also in the city of Rome.[8,9] At that time, the peculiarity of MAB Programme 11 was also stressed, observing how "perhaps surprisingly, the MAB Programme appears to be the first and only international initiative promoting ecological research on the places where an increasing proportion of the world's population live and work."[1] However, the interest for urban ecosystems within the MAB activities has decreased progressively over the last few decades, whereas other international bodies and intergovernmental agencies (e.g., HABITAT and the EU) have increased their programs on sustainability issues in urban settlements.

After the 1992 Convention on Biodiversity Conservation of the Rio Conference (UNCED), MAB activities have mainly focused on the projects originally designed with no. 8 on BRs to foster an active conservation of biodiversity. The main aim of the MAB Programme is now to implement and enlarge the world network of MAB-BRs for biodiversity conservation. These MAB-BRs are conceived as "field laboratories" for "sustainable development," according to three main local and global functions: (1) conservation, (2) development, and (3) logistic support (for research, monitoring, education, and training). Thus, the main characteristics of a MAB-BR are very different from traditional natural parks and protected areas. A MAB-BR is intended first of all as a tool for a *proactive* conservation of biodiversity and not as a tool for a simple *reactive* defense of the environment. According to the MAB perspective, a BR can, for example, include areas with a high biodiversity as well as damaged or degraded areas, where human activity is strongly present.[10]

According to the full ecology perspective of the MAB Programme, the BR concept clearly reflects a human-centered vision and stresses the importance of considering specific people–environment relationships when dealing with biodiversity conservation. The MAB Programme continuously affirmed this human-centered vision.[11–13] In particular, the 1995 Seville Conference on BRs launched the so-called MAB Seville Strategy for a more human-oriented management of BRs and of biodiversity conservation programs.[12]

THE URBAN BIOSPHERE RESERVE STRATEGY

The MAB Seville Strategy is now considered a fundamental step for the development of the BR concept and for the proactive conservation of biodiversity.[10] Furthermore, the BR concept, through this Seville Strategy, seems particularly suitable for its application also to highly populated contexts, such as urban settlements. The Seville Strategy specifically proposes differentiating the biodiversity concept according to its "natural" and "cultural" dimensions. Goal 1 of the Seville Strategy specifically recommends us to "use biosphere reserves to conserve natural and cultural diversity." This new way of considering biodiversity also was well outlined in the declaration of the attendees of the recent International Conference on Biodiversity and Society, jointly organized by UNESCO and by the Columbia University of New York in May 2001.[14]

Following this broad vision of biodiversity, programs for instituting MAB-BRs also in proximity of large cities thus have become more frequent in recent years. What can be defined as an "Urban Biosphere Reserve Strategy" is progressively taking shape within the MAB Programme.[7,15,16] In 2000, a MAB-Urban Group was specifically established during the 16th International Coordinating Council of the MAB Programme (MAB ICC) and then renewed in 2002 (at the 17th MAB ICC). This Group was specifically set up to explore and outline specific ways of applying the MAB-BR concept also to urban and periurban areas. The increased interest in linking the BR concept to urban issues, in connection with global trends of urbanization and associated sustainable development issues, was particularly stressed.

As a continuation of the MAB-Urban Group's activities, a specific workshop on "Urban Ecosystems and Biosphere Reserves" was held at the last 2002 EuroMAB Meeting in Rome. Its main aims were those of applying the full ecology paradigm to both BRs and urban areas, by (1) focusing on the continuity existing between nature and cities, and (2) outlining specific trends of scientific and policy actions to be undertaken in this direction.[17]

The interest in locating MAB-BRs inside or near urban areas also was discussed with the aim of further developing the above-mentioned "Urban

BR Strategy" as far as possible. This should help enhance urban dwellers' sense of "continuity," instead of opposition, between cities and their natural resources, and should help overcome the conceptual (and often physical) separation between cities and nature.[7]

THE ECOSYSTEM APPROACH TO URBAN SETTLEMENTS: THE MAB-ROME PROJECT AND THE PROPOSED MAB BIOSPHERE RESERVE ON THE GREEN AREAS OF ROME

A MAB Project 11 on the city of Rome was launched as a long-term research program by the plant ecologist Valerio Giacomini, of the University of Rome "La Sapienza," at the end of the 1970s, and it continued after his premature death in 1981.[9,18] In particular, the research activities in the MAB-Rome Project were organized around two main "urban subsystems" to promote a greater awareness of interdependence between them: on the one hand, the "bio-ecological subsystem," on the other, the "human socio-perceptive subsystem," the latter including a wide range of human produced features of the urban environment (e.g., architectural, technological, cultural, etc.). To achieve this "integrated approach" to the Rome urban system, various workgroups of different disciplinary backgrounds were invited to take part in the project from the very beginning. Each workgroup was formed on the basis of specific disciplinary or technical skills considered useful for understanding and managing the Rome urban system.

Over the years, the various workgroups have collected many interesting research findings on the city of Rome, considered as an "ecosystem." Some of these workgroups, in particular, the Social and Environmental Psychology group for the "human perception dimension" of the Project, and the Plant Ecology group, are still researching the city of Rome according to the philosophy started with the MAB-Rome Project. Most of the activities of these groups have been presented in numerous publications, ranging from scientific and intradisciplinary ones to interdisciplinary and popular ones. It is impossible to report on this huge corpus of results here. However, the most recent results were extensively presented at the previously mentioned workshop of the 2002 EuroMab Meeting in Rome.[17] In particular, we can mention some interesting results emerging from the various works conducted by the Plant Ecology Group of the University of Rome "La Sapienza" in their two decades of MAB-Rome studies.

Among the various aspects examined by the various bio-ecological studies, focusing on natural diversity in the urban environment, the extraordinary biodiversity richness, in qualitative and quantitative terms, of the plant and animal life in the Rome area has been pointed out.[19,20] Using an inventory grid of 190 squares (each one of 1.6 km^2), researchers counted ~1,300 species of flora (belonging to 591 genera and 131 families) within Rome's Great Ring Road. The overall results of this floristic inventory of the Rome area were also published in 1995 as an "Atlas of the Rome flora."[21] Interestingly, the richest areas are right in the center of the city, and they include, in particular, the archaeological area of the Roman Forum and the course of the River Tiber. These bio-ecological studies also showed how these natural aspects are organized around two important "Biological Corridors," which connect the outskirts of the city with the inner areas of the urban system.

On the other hand, the studies concerning the "human dimension" of the urban ecosystem have focused on various aspects regarding inhabitants' perceptions and behaviors of both the natural and the architectural features of the city, according to various research lines of environmental psychology.[18] At a theoretical level, these studied were based on the "place theory," originally outlined within environmental psychology by D. Canter[22] and further developed by other authors.[5,23,24]

Regarding the relation between people and the natural features of the urban environment, these studies dealt with the following four main topics:

(1) The perception of nature in the city among urban residents and their attitudes and behaviors toward urban green areas.[25–28]
(2) The role of urban green areas in affecting inhabitant's level of satisfaction/dissatisfaction and affective attachment toward the urban residential environment and the setting up of perceived residential environmental quality indicators.[29–32]
(3) The comparison of experts' and laypersons' evaluations of urban environmental quality.[33,34]
(4) The role of urban parks for the promotion of sustainable lifestyles among younger generations and the monitoring of environmental education programs conducted within urban natural protected areas.[35]

Studies on residents' perceptions and representations of Rome's green areas generally have shown the complexity and the multidimensional character of the inhabitants' relationship with nature in the city.[25,26] Inhabitants tend to take different "positions" of greater or lesser "integration/participation" or rather of "confinement/extraneousness" vis-à-vis the urban natural environment, depending on characteristics of age, sex, and educational level.[26] Inhabitants' use of green places appears to be driven by the need for psycho-physical "restoration," as well as by "social" motives. Green areas may, in fact, facilitate the interpersonal "urban sociability" that seems increasingly difficult to find in other open public spaces of the city.[27] Regarding residents' attitudes toward urban green spaces, recent research pointed to the emergence of two main opposite and independent attitude dimensions in the evaluation of urban green.[28] A first dimension can be defined as a people–nature "integration perspective" and groups together a set of positive beliefs about nature in the city. These positive beliefs regard, for example, the promotion of positive interpersonal interactions and the stress–recovery functions afforded by urban green spaces. Conversely, a second dimension, which can be defined as a people–nature "opposition perspective" groups together negative beliefs about nature in the city. These negative beliefs refer, for example, to the feelings of personal insecurity associated with urban green spaces, or to the right of humankind to rule over nature.

Regarding residential satisfaction, previous studies highlighted that inhabitants' satisfaction/dissatisfaction with the urban residential environment have a multidimensional nature.[29–31] On the one hand, this satisfaction/dissatisfaction relies on the evaluation of both spatial-physical and human social aspects and, on the other, it is based on three main modalities of person/place transactions," defined as "perceptual," "relational," and "action" modalities. Residents' satisfaction/dissatisfaction is affected not only by physical "molecular" characteristics of the places involved (e.g., the neighborhood), but also by characteristics of the "molar" context in which these spatial-physical peculiarities are experienced. For instance, inhabitants' socio-economic conditions are important factors in the perception/evaluation of the actual spatial-physical characteristics of the neighborhoods investigated.[29] Also, inhabitants' perceptions of the quality of the urban environment can be reliably and validly measured through standard psychometric tools, covering a broad range of features.[30] Within this general context, the natural environment seems to be an important factor affecting people's residential satisfaction and neighborhood attachment: in fact, the presence of green areas in the neighborhood is a significant positive predictor of neighborhood attachment.[30–32]

A third group of studies, aimed at investigating the relationship between experts' and laypersons' evaluations of the urban environment, was developed within a systematic collaboration with the other disciplinary groups involved in the MAB-Rome Project. These studies highlighted that the congruence between inhabitants' and experts' (architects, urban planners, and natural ecologists) evaluations of urban environmental "quality" is generally mild or weak.[33,34] In particular, a study by Bonnes and Bonaiuto[33] found the weakest congruence between inhabitants' and plant ecologists' evaluations of the quality of the city's green areas. What seems to be appreciated by inhabitants is not so much the "naturalness" of the urban green areas (which, on the contrary, is particularly valued by natural scientists) but rather its maintenance, stability, and duration in time, as well as its accessibility inside the urban area. Similar results were obtained in a further recent study, using a different research design.[34] In this case, attitudes toward, satisfaction for, and use frequency of urban green spaces were assessed among residents living in four different kinds of Rome neighborhoods, varying for the objectively rated quantity (high vs. low amount) and quality (high vs. low naturalness) of their green areas. In particular, objective quantity was operationalized as the amount of public green spaces *per capita* within the neighborhood considered, whereas objective quality was operationalized as the different location of the neighborhood considered for Rome's Biological Corridors (within vs. outside). The results indicate that subjective evaluations can be partly independent of the objective properties of urban green areas. In particular, the quantity of green areas per se or its interaction with quality may positively affect people's attitudes toward, satisfaction for, and use frequency of urban green areas. On the other hand, such a consistent pattern does not emerge for the quality of green areas.

A more recent research line, still in progress, is aimed at investigating the possible role of urban and periurban natural protected areas for the promotion of sustainable lifestyles and environmentally friendly worldviews, attitudes, and behaviors among the younger generation (8–12-year-old pupils). This research line has been developed, in particular, with the active support of the Regional Agency for Lazio's Parks. The specific purpose of these studies is that of assessing and monitoring the effects of innovative outdoor environmental education programs in schools, being conducted in many natural protected areas located in Rome and in the Lazio region, and coordinated by the Regional Agency for Parks. The preliminary results indicate that these programs positively affect children's general environmental concern.[35] Moreover, results indicate that the effects of the programs are more pronounced among pupils of schools located within the Rome area, compared with pupils of schools located in rural areas outside Rome. In other words, these results show how urban natural protected areas may have a crucial role for enhancing the efficacy of environmental education programs aimed at promoting environmental awareness and concern, specifically among the younger generations living within urban areas.

In line with the general aim of the MAB Programme, the MAB-Rome Project also was aimed at promoting stronger links among the various *environmental actors*, such as experts, public decision makers, and inhabitants. In fact, MAB-Rome activities received considerable support from local administrations, in particular, from the Department of the Environment of the Rome Municipality. The current and previous administrations of the Rome Municipality devoted considerable attention to the various indications and research results produced in these years, and frequently supported (both directly or in collaboration with the Italian MAB Committee) specific activities of the MAB-Rome Project, such as research projects and conferences and publications,[19–21] including a book for children.[36]

More recently, the specific activities of the MAB-Rome Project were concerned with the possibilities of setting up a new urban BR in the Rome area, along the current general orientation of the MAB Programme. As a first step in this sense, some years ago the University of Rome "La Sapienza," with the support of the Department of the Environment of the Rome Municipality, started a specific research project. It aimed to develop a scientific basis for setting up an "Observatory for Environmental Monitoring and Public Awareness," in view of establishing a new UNESCO-MAB BR in the city of Rome, as a further development of the long-term MAB-Rome Project. This project was set up in consideration of the "logistic support" function that, as previously mentioned, should characterize any MAB BR according to the Seville Strategy. The project outlined a new form of collaboration between the environmental psychology research group and the natural science research group (the latter composed of both plant and animal ecologists). The broader aim was to set up a system for monitoring the natural environment of the city of Rome and the related inhabitants' perceptions, attitudes, and behaviors in view of promoting inhabitants' awareness of and concern for nature in the city and urban biodiversity. There is now a growing concern of the Rome Municipality for the designation of the Rome urban and periurban green areas as a new MAB Urban BR. A new workgroup, coordinated by Professor C. Blasi of the Department of Plant Biology of the University of Rome "La Sapienza," and composed of scientists, technicians, and administrative staff from the Department of the Environment of the Rome Municipality, recently has been appointed by the Municipality to set up the specific Proposal of Designation to be submitted to UNESCO.

CONCLUDING REMARKS

By promoting an *ecosystem approach* in its *full ecology* perspective, thc UNESCO MAB Programme played a considerable role in encouraging the consideration of natural/biospheric and urban/societal processes as strongly interrelated and supported the importance, in general, of social and behavioral sciences to address environmental and biospheric issues. The MAB stressed the importance of considering both natural and human/societal processes also in urban areas, thus considering these as "urban ecosystems." In view of this aim, the MAB strongly recommended a multidisciplinary and interdisciplinary collaboration between natural and social/human sciences for understanding environmental processes and changes. Such a multidisciplinary approach was specifically followed and developed by the MAB Project on the city of Rome. Since its beginnings at the end of the 1970s, the research activity in the MAB-Rome Project has focused on two main "urban subsystems": the "bio-ecological subsystem" and the "human socio-perceptive subsystem."

The various environmental psychological research lines, conducted during the years within the MAB-Rome Project and described in the previous sections, are also in line with the more recent development of present-day environmental psychology, concerned with the issue of sustainability.[2,37] These studies first were concerned with how the apparent opposition between cities and nature may be differently articulated in the perceptions and behaviors of urban residents. On the one hand, the results of these researches have shown how, usually, the presence of green areas within urban settlements promotes people's satisfaction for, as well as people's positive emotional bonds with, their residential environment. On the other hand, they showed how the relationship between urban dwellers and the natural features of the city can range across different patterns of perception and evaluation (from active commitment and involvement in proenvironmental activities, to specific/general concern and awareness, to indifference or sometimes even hostility). Furthermore, there frequently can be a lack of correspondence between the "objective" assessments of urban environmental quality provided by experts and the "subjective" or "lay" perceptions of residents. Finally, these researches showed how the natural features of the urban environment and the presence of green spaces within the city might have a crucial role also for the promotion of sustainable lifestyles among the younger generations.

Also, the methodological aspects developed by these studies could provide specific tools to be used as support for urban decision makers and planners.[31,32] For example, the setting up and application of standard psychometric indicators for the measurement of inhabitants' environmental perceptions could be specifically useful for moving urban environmental planning in the direction of sustainability.[38]

A systematic study of the social psychological modalities (perceptions, attitudes, feelings, expectancies, behaviors, etc.) by which inhabitants relate to nature in the urban and periurban environment could be important for the development of more general programs on biodiversity and natural resources conservation both inside and outside urban areas. That is, promoting sustainable lifestyles among city dwellers may help in spreading "sustainability" not only in urban areas but outside cities as well.

REFERENCES

1. DI CASTRI, F. & M. HADLEY. 1984. Making land management more scientific: experimenting and evaluating approaches. *In* Ecology in Practice. F. di Castri, F.W.G. Baker & M. Hadley, Eds.: 1–22. Tycooly. Dublin.
2. BONNES, M. & M. BONAIUTO. 2002. Environmental psychology: from spatial-physical environment to sustainable development. *In* Handbook of Environmental Psychology. R. Bechtel & A. Churchman, Eds.: 28–54. Wiley. New York.
3. DI CASTRI, F., F.W.G. BAKER & M. HADLEY. 1984. Ecology in Practice. Tycooly. Dublin.
4. STOKOLS, D. & I. ALTMAN. 1987. Handbook of Environmental Psychology. Wiley. New York.
5. BONNES, M. & G. SECCHIAROLI. 1995. Environmental Psychology: A Psycho-social Introduction. Sage. London.

6. BECHTEL, R. & A. CHURCHMAN. 2002. Handbook of Environmental Psychology. Wiley. New York.
7. CELECIA, J. 2002. A synoptic overview of UNESCO's Man and the Biosphere (MAB) Programme and urban ecosystem research therein: the evolution and challenges of a three-decade international experience. Presented at the EuroMab/ESF/UK-Urgent/UK-Urban Forum Workshop. Birmingham, April 11–13.
8. GIACOMINI, V. 1981. Rome considered as an ecosystem. Nat. Resour. **17:** 13–19.
9. BONNES, M. 1984. Mobilizing scientists, planners, and local community in a large-scale urban situation: the Rome case study. *In* Ecology in Practice. F. di Castri, F.W.G. Baker & M. Hadley, Eds.: 52–67. Tycolly. Dublin.
10. BATISSE, M. 1997. Biosphere reserves: a challenge for biodiversity conservation and regional development. Environment **39:** 7–39.
11. KRUSE-GRAUMANN, L. 1995. Societal Dimensions of Biosphere Reserves—Biosphere Reserves for People. UNESCO-MAB Programme. Bonn.
12. UNESCO-MAB. 1995. The Seville Strategy. Biosphere reserves. Bull. Int. Netwk. **3:** 6–10.
13. EISTO, I. *et al.* 1999. Local involvement and economic dimensions in biosphere reserve activities. Edita Ltd. Helsinki.
14. ALFSEN-NORODOM, C. & B. LANE. 2002. Global knowledge networking for site specific strategies: The International Conference on Biodiversity and Society. Environ. Sci. Policy **5:** 3–8.
15. DOUGLAS, I. 1996. Cities and natural space. Nat. Resour. **32:** 14.
16. CELECIA, J. 2000. UNESCO's Man and the Biosphere (MAB) Programme and urban ecosystem research: a brief overview of the evolution and challenges of a three-decade international experience. Presented at the First Meeting of the Ad-hoc Working Group to Explore Applications of the Biosphere Reserve Concept to Urban Areas and Their Hinterlands–MAB Urban Group. Paris, November 9.
17. UNESCO AND ACCADEMIA NAZIONALE DELLE SCIENZE. 2003 (October). Proceedings of the EuroMAB 2002 Meeting. Accademia Nazionale delle Scienze. Rome.
18. BONNES, M. 2000. The "Ecosystem Approach" to Urban Settlements: 20 Years of the "MAB-Rome Project". Presented at the First Meeting of the Ad-hoc Working Group to Explore Applications of the Biosphere Reserve Concept to Urban Areas and Their Hinterlands–MAB Urban Group. Paris, November 9.
19. CIGNINI, B., G. MASSARI & S. PIGNATTI. 1995. L'Ecosistema Roma [The Ecosystem Rome]. Palombi. Rome.
20. ZAPPAROLI, M. 1997. Gli Insetti di Roma [The Insects of Rome]. Palombi. Rome.
21. CELESTI-GRAPOW, L. 1995. Atlante della Flora di Roma [Atlas of the Rome Flora]. Argos. Rome.
22. CANTER, D. 1977. The Psychology of Place. Architectural Press. London.
23. RUSSELL, J.A. & L.M. WARD. 1982. Environmental psychology. Annu. Rev. Psychol. **33:** 259–288.
24. BONAIUTO, M. & M. BONNES. 1996. Multiplace analysis of the urban environment: a comparison between a large and a small Italian city. Environ. Behav. **28:** 699–747.
25. ARDONE, R.G. & M. BONNES. 1991. The urban green spaces in the psychological construction of the residential place. *In* Urban Ecology Applied to the

City of Rome–MAB Italia Project 11, Progress Report no. 4. M. Bonnes, Ed.: 149–173. MAB-Italia and CNR. Rome.

26. Bonnes, M., A. Aiello & R.G. Ardone. 1995. Urban residents' representations of the natural features of the environment. *In* Societal Dimensions of Biosphere Reserves: Biosphere Reserves for People. L. Kruse-Graumann, Ed.: 13–24. UNESCO-MAB Programme. Bonn.
27. Bonnes, M., A. Aiello & M. Bonaiuto. 1999. Les espaces verts urbains dans les pratiques et les représentations des habitants. Villes en parallele **28/29:** 176–192.
28. Carrus, G., P. Passafaro & M. Bonnes. 2004. Ambientalismo, autoritarismo ed etnocentrismo: una scala di atteggiamento verso il verde urbano [Environmentalism, authoritarianism, and ethnocentrism: an attitude toward urban green scale]. Boll. Psicol. Appl. **242:** in press.
29. Bonnes, M., M. Bonaiuto & A.P. Ercolani. 1991. Crowding and residential satisfaction in the urban environment: a contextual approach. Environ. Behav. **23:** 531–552.
30. Bonaiuto, M. *et al.* 1999. Multidimensional perception of residential environment quality and neighborhood attachment in the urban environment. J. Environ. Psychol. **19:** 331–352.
31. Bonaiuto, M. & M. Bonnes. 2002. Residential satisfaction in the urban environment within the UNESCO-MAB Rome Project. *In* Residential Environments: Choice Satisfaction and Behavior. J. I. Aragones, G. Francescato & T. Gärling, Eds.: 101–133. Bergin & Garvey. Westport, CT.
32. Bonaiuto, M., F. Fornara & M. Bonnes. 2003. Indexes of perceived residential environment quality and neighborhood attachment in urban environments: a confirmation study on the city of Rome. Landsc. Urban Plan. **65:** 41–52.
33. Bonnes, M. & M. Bonaiuto. 1995. Expert and layperson Evaluation of Urban Environmental Quality: the "Natural" versus the "Built" Environment. *In* Values and the Environment. Y. Guerrier, N. Alexander, J. Chase & M. O'Brien, Eds.: 151–163. Wiley. New York.
34. Carrus, G. *et al.* 2004. More green or better green for sustainable cities? Quantity and quality of urban green areas and inhabitants' attitudes, satisfaction and uses. Manuscript submitted for publication.
35. Bonnes, M. *et al.* 2003. Le aree naturali protette per la promozione di consapevolezza, sensibilità e impegno ambientali [Natural protected areas for the promotion of environmental awareness and concern]. Research report. University of Rome "La Sapienza" and Regional Agency for Lazio Parks, Rome.
36. Cignini, B. *et al.* 1997. Animali a Roma [Animals in Rome]. Palombi. Rome.
37. Moser, G. *et al.* 2003. People, Places, and Sustainability. Hogrefe and Huber Publishers. Gottingen.
38. Vlek, C. 2000. Essential psychology for environmental policy making. Int. J. Psychol. **35:** 153–167.

The Application of the Biosphere Reserve Concept to Urban Areas

The Case of Green Rooftops for Habitat Network in Seoul

KWI-GON KIM

Department of Landscape Architecture, Seoul National University, Seoul 151-742, Korea

ABSTRACT: This article consists of two parts. The first shows how the principles of the ecosystem approach can be applied to green rooftops, and the second attempts to illustrate it through a case study. In particular, it suggests new approaches and techniques for creation of green rooftops in a perspective of urban habitat network and urban biosphere reserve. To endow urban rooftops with the roles and functions of urban habitat network and urban biosphere reserve, it is necessary to apply "an ecosystem approach to urban management." In this article, an ecosystem approach to urban management is illustrated with Seoul as an example. The Habitat Network in Seoul will be reviewed with a focus on the model suggested by MAB Urban Group. Then, the roles and functions of Myeongdong UNESCO Green Rooftop and its possible contribution to building the Seoul Urban Biosphere Network will be described. The UNESCO Green Rooftop is 628 m^2 and was created on the 12th floor rooftop of UNESCO Building in Myeongdong 2-ga, Jung-ku, Seoul. In the green rooftop, which was created with goals of securing green areas and biotopes in downtown, creating an urban econetwork, securing a base for urban ecosystem study and environment education, and disseminating an idea of coexistence between nature and humankind, wetland, meadow, scrub and woodland, wall revegetation, and a vegetable field are created. Also, rainwater recycling facilities and a solar energy water circulation system were set up. Rest facilities including observation and education facilities were built. Based on the Seoul example, as well as urban biosphere reserve models suggested by the MAB Urban Group, we suggest several principles to be applied for a green rooftops to qualify as a category of urban biosphere reserves.

KEYWORDS: green rooftop; ecosystem approach; urban habitat network; urban biosphere reserve

Address for correspondence: Kwi-Gon Kim, Department of Landscape Architecture, Seoul National University, Seoul 151-742, Korea. Voice: +82-2-880-4871; fax: +82-2-875-4818. kwigon@snu.ac.kr

Ann. N.Y. Acad. Sci. 1023: 187–214 (2004). © 2004 New York Academy of Sciences. doi: 10.1196/annals.1319.010

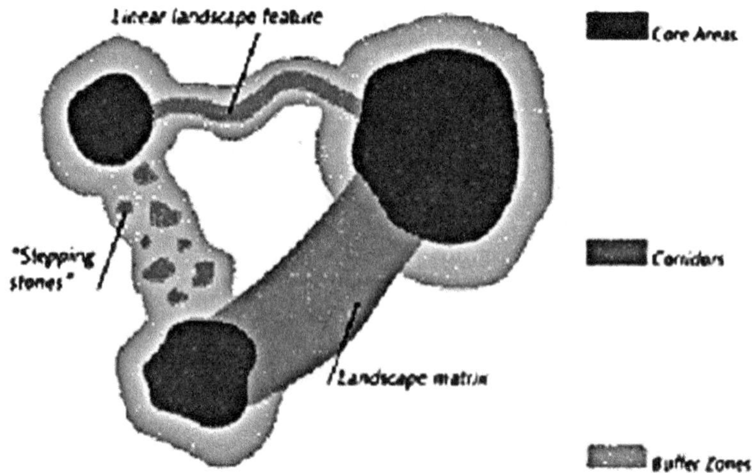

FIGURE 1. Schematic representation of an ecological network. Source: Council of Europe, the Pan-European Ecological Network, Questions and Answers, 1998, No. 4, p. 14.

INTRODUCTION

Recently, with cities continuing to grow in size and complexity, the search for potential green space has led people to look more closely at buildings themselves.[1] In the case of Seoul, 253.59 km^2 or 42% of the city is covered with buildings. A survey showed that among them, green rooftops could be created on more than 200 km^2, which is equivalent to 30% of Seoul area. This implies that green rooftops may contribute to solving a green area shortage issue that Seoul faces today and to creating the Integrated Habitat Network.

Well-created green rooftops can support animals and plants extensively and play an important role in conserving urban biodiversity. It is nearly impossible to link fragmented habitats continuously on ground and build a habitat network. Therefore, it is necessary to use green rooftops as "stepping-stones" in building a network (FIG. 1).

This article consists of two parts. The first shows how the principles of the ecosystem approach can be applied to green rooftops, whereas the second attempts to illustrate it through a case study. In particular, it suggests new approaches and techniques for creation of green rooftops in a perspective of urban habitat network and urban biosphere reserve. This article focuses on its value for biodiversity among the multiple functions of green rooftops.

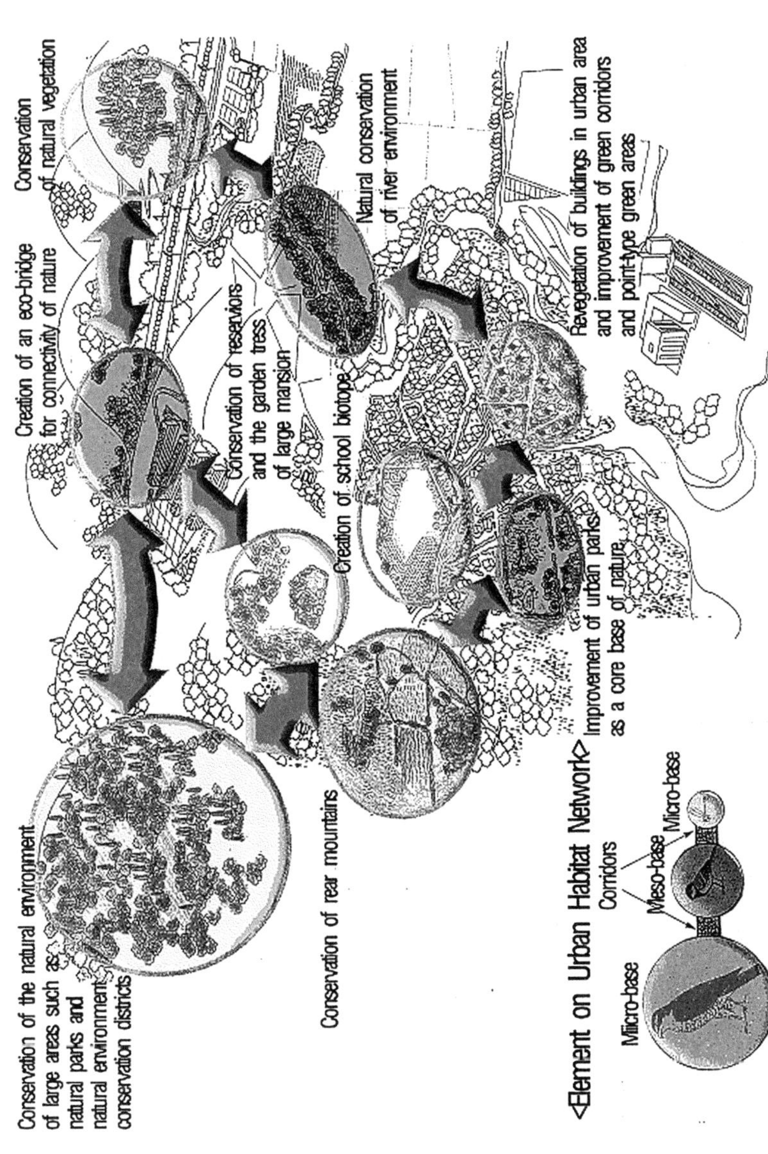

FIGURE 2. The elements and applied concept of the urban habitat network.

AN ECOSYSTEM APPROACH TO URBAN MANAGEMENT

An "ecosystem" approach to cities promises to provide a rich and dynamic conceptual framework for understanding cities holistically and comprehensively.[2] The ecosystem approach encourages analysts and planners to consider the "big picture" by emphasizing entire systems, their component parts, and the relationships between those parts. Here, note that there is a distinction between comprehensive and integrated approaches. By definition, comprehensive means all-inclusive. In contrast, an integrated approach retains most of the core ideas of being holistic but is more focused and therefore more practical.

The ecosystem approach has been adopted by the conference of the Parties of the Convention on Biological Diversity as the primary framework for action under the Convention.[3] Here, the ecosystem approach is defined as a strategy for the integrated management of land, water, and living resources that promotes conservation and sustainable use in an equitable way. The UNESCO/MAB booklet illustrates the application of 12 principles of the ecosystem approach in several biosphere reserves. The overall aim of the booklet is to contribute to the application of the ecosystem approach at the same time as promoting closer links between the work of the Convention on Biological Diversity and the World Network of Biosphere Reserves.

When considering a city as an ecosystem and building a habitat network, as shown in FIGURE 2, it can be categorized into macrobase, mesobase, and microbase. Green rooftops can play the role of microbases as a component forming the entire system.

At the 8th Meeting of UNESCO-MAB recently held in Mongolia, there were discussions that rehabilitation area can be designated as a biosphere reserve.[4] UNESCO-MAB states that "Can Gio Biosphere Reserve is the largest area of rehabilitated mangrove in Vietnam. Among the challenges of the biosphere reserve is to explore and demonstrate ways in which mangrove rehabilitation and conservation can be combined in a sustainable way."[5]

In case of green rooftops, if degraded areas are rehabilitated in sustainable ways and the principles of the ecosystem approach are observed, they may be seen as fulfilling the biosphere reserve concept. Summary Results of Application of the Principles of the Ecosystem Approach to the green rooftops are shown in TABLE 1.

GREEN ROOFTOPS FOR HABITAT NETWORK IN SEOUL

Policy Background

In Seoul, there are some public policies that relate directly to the ecosystem approach to urban management. According to the Green Seoul

TABLE 1. Summary of application of the principles of the ecosystem approach to the green rooftops

Selected Principles of the Ecosystem Approach	Application of the Principles to Biosphere Reserves	How green roofs could implement the principles	Application of the Principles to the Green Rooftop of UNESCO Building, Seoul
1. The objectives of management of land, water and living resources are a matter of societal choice.	■ To set up a management board for a biosphere reserve consisting of scientists, government administrations and representatives of local and private associations. ■ To apply biosphere reserve concept at the concrete field level, in a way that reflects the societal choices of the local population.	■ Green rooftops can be managed by a management board to reflect the societal choices of the local population.	■ Set up a Steering Committee consisting ecology experts, local elementary schools, parents, District Office, NGOs, and citizens.
2. Ecosystem managers should consider the effects (actual or potential) of their activities on adjacent and other ecosystems.	■ To relieve pressure on the biosphere reserve's core protected areas of forest, by improving the living conditions of the rural population and modifying existing resource use practices. ■ To make a real effort to consider adjacent land and marine ecosystems as an ensemble, with different areas, zoned for different functions and purposes and core protected areas identified in both terrestrial and marine ecosystems.	■ Green rooftops can relieve pressure on the other urban ecosystems, by improving ecological conditions of rooftops. ■ Green rooftops can function as stepping stones in creating urban ecological networks.	■ Influence on Seoul urban ecosystems is eased by improving the environmental conditions of rooftops. ■ Green areas and forests for outsourcing exist nearby and Myeongdong UNESCO green rooftop serves as a micro-base in building an eco-network with these green areas and forests.

TABLE 1. *Continued*

Selected Principles of the Ecosystem Approach	Application of the Principles to Biosphere Reserves	How green roofs could implement the principles	Application of the Principles to the Green Rooftop of UNESCO Building, Seoul
3. Recognizing potential gains from management, there is usually a need to understand and manage the ecosystem in an economic context. Any such ecosystem-management programme should :	■ To place a social and financial value on ecosystem services to justify conservation measures and a hollistic approach to environmental management.	■ Green rooftops can be popular environmentally sound tourist attraction.	■ Myeongdong UNESCO Green Rooftop has been visited by about 430 people since its opening on April 18.
(a) Reduce those market distortions that adversely affect biological diversity.	■ To increase economic importance of wildlife and nature tourism.		
(b) Align incentives to promote biodiversity conservation and sustainable use.			
(c) Internalize costs and benefits in the given ecosystem to the extent feasible.			

TABLE 1. ***Continued***

Selected Principles of the Ecosystem Approach	Application of the Principles to Biosphere Reserves	How green roofs could implement the principles	Application of the Principles to the Green Rooftop of UNESCO Building, Seoul
4. Conservation of ecosystem structure and function, in order to maintain ecosystem services, should be priority target of the ecosystem approach.	■ To bring degraded land and water areas back into 'productive' use. ■ To explore and demonstrate ways in which rehabilitation and conservation can be combined in a sustainable way. ■ To translate complicated concepts, jargon and knowledge on eco-system structure and functioning into understandable and practical guidance. ■ To encourage the involvement of local communities, school children and other stakeholders in education and training, and the production of visitors information about individual reserves and their importance for the conservation and sustainable use of biodiversity.	■ Green rooftops can be areas of rehabilitation which provides a basis for new ecological processes and bring new species back to the urban areas.	■ In Myeongdong UNESCO Building, a number of surveys and experiments are taking place to understand a dynamic relationship within species, among species and between species and their abiotic environment as well as the physical and chemical interactions within the environment. ■ The above surveys and experiments will be used for students and the public to understand green rooftop ecosystem structure and functioning through understandable and practical environmental interpretation programme. ■ A leaflet prepared for green rooftop of Myeongdong UNESCO Building provides a mini-guide for children to the plants and animals, the landscape and wetland of the green rooftop.

TABLE 1. ***Continued***

Selected Principles of the Ecosystem Approach	Application of the Principles to Biosphere Reserves	How green roofs could implement the principles	Application of the Principles to the Green Rooftop of UNESCO Building, Seoul
5. The ecosystem approach should be undertaken at the appropriate spatial and temporal scales.	■ To Promote connectivity between areas where necessary. ■ To be based upon the hierarchical nature of biological diversity characterized by the interaction and integration of genes, species and ecosystems.	■ Green rooftops can be 'biodiversity hotspots' in urban areas. ■ Green rooftops can provide dispersal linkages between protected areas and prevent isolation of protected areas within the city and facilitate management schemes of various kinds.	■ Myeongdong UNESCO green rooftop contributes greatly in improving the connectivity of Seoul Habitat Network ■ It is inhabited *by Rana amurensis coreana*; *Rana plancyi choseni* and *Kaloula borealis*, which are protected species, will be introduced for breeding; the place will serve as in situ conservation of protected species or a refugee.
6. Management must recognize the change is inevitable.	■ To utilize adaptive management in order to anticipate and cater for changes and events.	■ Green rooftops need to be maintained because they are under conditions of rapid environmental change. ■ Green rooftops can be long-term observation plots to provide baselines for studying ecosystem response to different patterns of disturbance in urban areas.	■ Myeongdong UNESCO Building has restored landscape features. Because of its location in downtown, various conditions and factors act as "deriving forces" for ecosystem changes. ■ Therefore, a number of management options were devised to address it.

TABLE 1. *Continued*

Selected Principles of the Ecosystem Approach	Application of the Principles to Biosphere Reserves	How green roofs could implement the principles	Application of the Principles to the Green Rooftop of UNESCO Building, Seoul
7. The ecosystem approach should consider all forms of relevant information, including scientific and indigenous and local knowledge, innovations and practices.	■ To make use of database developments, geographic information systems and networking technologies.	■ Green rooftops can be a good sites for organizing forums and other information exchange mechanisms for urban ecosystem managers.	■ According to "Green Rooftop Policy," Seoul city is initiating electric networking of information on Rooftop Project sites launched since 2002.
8. The ecosystem approach should involve all relevant sectors of society and scientific disciplines.	■ To bring together policy-maker, natural scientists and social scientists to generate specific strategies for restoring healthy ecosystems while also preserving the social and economic structure of local communities. ■ To represent biosphere reserves as a means for promoting management essentially as a pact between the local community and society as a whole.	■ A range of institutional links for green rooftops can be developed with national governmental departments, research and training institutions and non-government bodies, as well as with outside technical bodies and financial sources.	■ EEPL(Environmental Ecological Planning Laboratory) of SNU(Seoul National University), Eco-tech consulting firm, elementary schools, and Seoul city are involved in monitoring and research, but institutional links will be expanded, if required.

Agenda 21, several different types of biological corridors or habitat networks have been proposed. For building various biological corridors and habitat network to create an ecocity, The Seoul Agenda 21 proposes that ecological green area axes be connected, urban green areas be expanded, and rivers be revitalized as natural spaces.

Laws and regulations on rooftop greening are described in detail in landscape architecture criteria announced as Ministry of Construction and Transportation Notice (notice no. 2000-159) on June 20, 2000. Introduction of rooftop greening is proactively encouraged and promoted when developing a District Unit Plan under the Law on Comprehensively Revised National Land Plan and Use and when approving reconstruction, redevelopment, and new building construction. In addition, as for specific support plans, each local authority set up new regulations on supporting rooftop greening and is seeking ways to provide rooftop greening material and subsidies after receiving applications from citizens on rooftop greening. Seoul city has developed a matching fund rooftop greening support plan to promote private participation in building rooftop greening as a part of efforts to secure green area within downtown and supported 10 sites in addition to UNESCO Building in Jung-gu since 2002.

The greenbelt in Seoul is 166.64 km^2 or 27.5% of the entire size of Seoul administrative district. Large-scale destruction of natural areas is controlled for the land-use and conservation within the greenbelt. Seoul city set the following basic directions and goals to manage the greenbelt area:

(1) To restrict development activities to prevent reckless expansion of urban area

(2) To conserve quality natural environment in the greenbelt and to improve and restore degraded environment

(3) To improve the quality of life of residents and raise environment-friendly land-use in the greenbelt

(4) To realize the management of greenbelt area through a comprehensive and well-structured management plan on the greenbelt.

The capital region greenbelt area is 1,554.2 km^2, which is the largest area among metropolitan regions. The greenbelt area within the capital region sets a target for greenbelt adjustment range of each wide-area city region in a wide-area city plan to prevent excluding an area with high environmental conservation value from the greenbelt. To diffuse concentration to the capital region, criteria for setting adjustment available area are applied differently from provincial metropolitan cities. Even if the greenbelt restrictions are lifted, development density is kept lower than that of the existing urban area and natural green area in principle. Except for allowing some construction, structures, landform change, and land subdivision that do not affect the objectives of designating the greenbelt in the capital region, construction of buildings, installation of structures, landform change, land subdivision, and urban planning projects are prohibited.

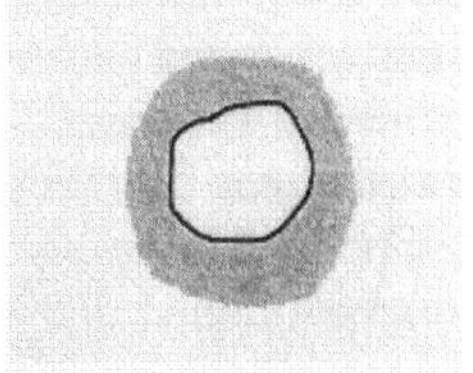 **Category 1. Urban Green Belt Biosphere Reserve** The city is surrounded by the Biosphere Reserve which helps protect the green areas from further urbanization and urban sprawl.	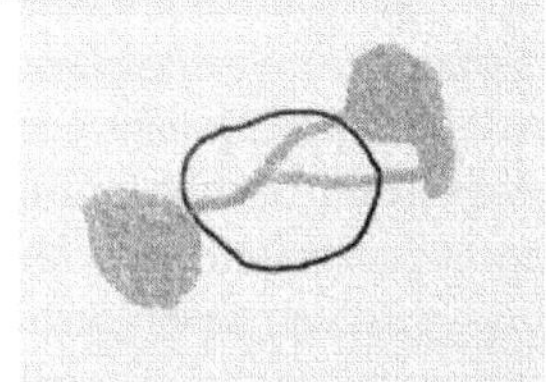 **Category 2. Urban Green Corridor Biosphere Reserve** Green corridors within the city help link-up green areas outside the city that otherwise risk being isolated.
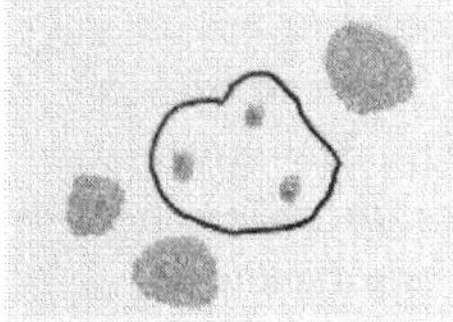 **Category 3. Urban Green Area Cluster Biosphere Reserve** Green parks and other valuable environments within and outside the city are combined into a cluster Biosphere Reserve	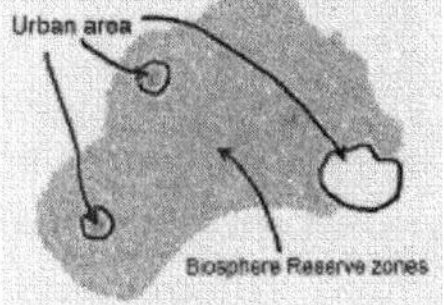 **Category 4. Urban Region Biosphere Reserve** An entire region, including towns and villages are zoned into the Biosphere Reserve

FIGURE 3. Examples of possible categories of urban biosphere reserves. Source: MAB Urban Group, Urban Biosphere Reserves in the Context of the Statutory Framework and the Seville.

Habitat Network and Potential for Urban Biosphere Reserves in Seoul

In this section, the Habitat Network in Seoul will be reviewed with a focus on the model of four possible categories of urban biosphere reserves (FIG. 3) suggested by MAB Urban Group.[a] Then, the roles and functions of Myeongdong UNESCO Green Rooftop will be described in a perspective of building the Seoul Urban Biosphere Network.

In the case of an Urban Greenbelt Biosphere Reserve (Category 1), the greenbelt, which is designated to prevent reckless expansion of Seoul and its nearby satellite cities and securing natural habitats, is designated primarily on the outskirts of 15–25 km from the central part of Seoul. The greenbelt area in the capital region including Seoul is approximately 1,554.2 km^2 (FIG. 4).

[a]MAB Urban Group, Urban Biosphere Reserves in the Context of the Statutory Framework and the Seville Strategy for the World Network of Biosphere Reserves, Draft June 2003.

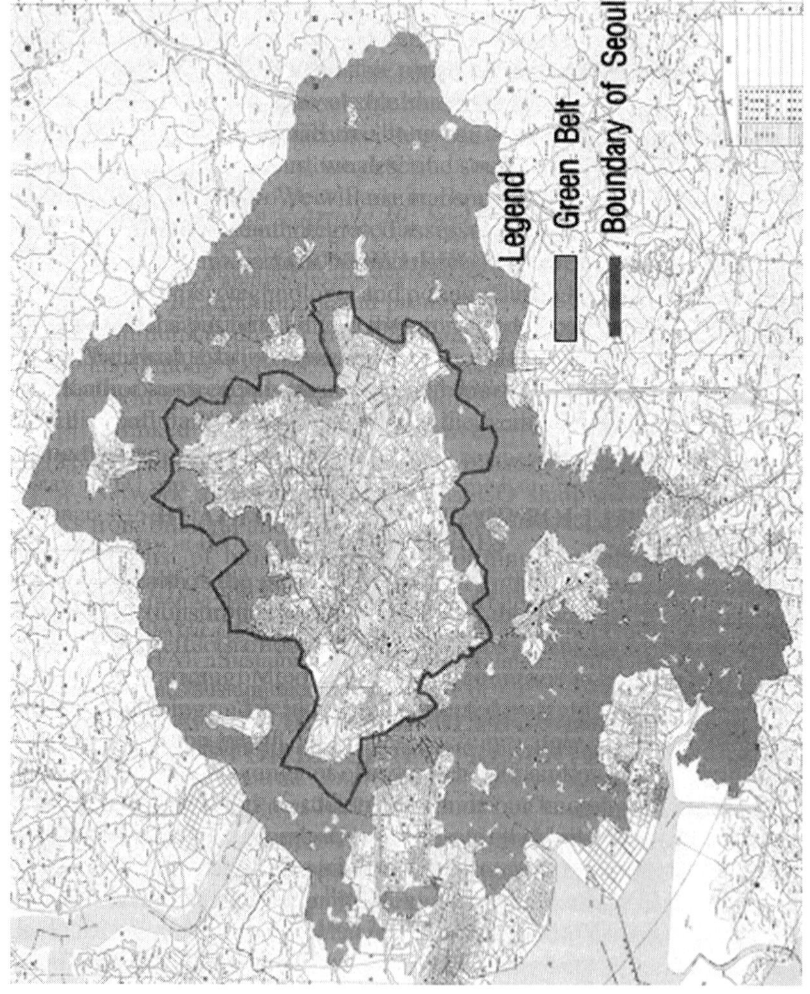

FIGURE 4. Potential for category 1: Urban Green Belt Biosphere Reserve in Seoul.

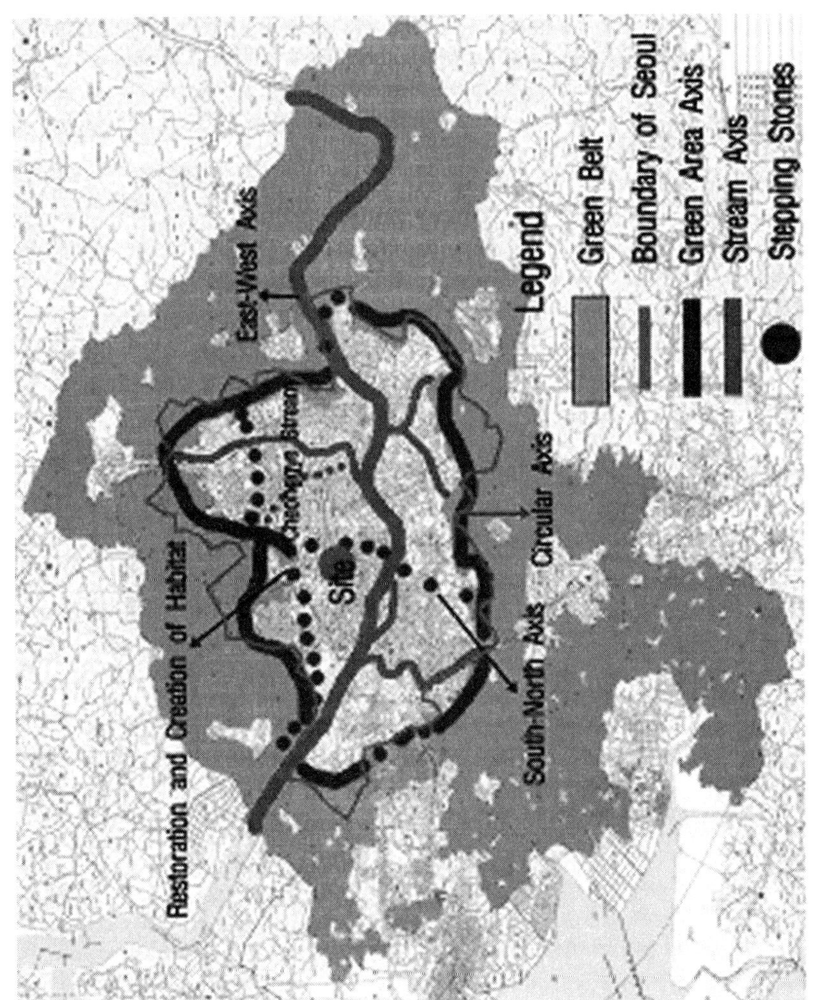

FIGURE 5. Potential for category 2: Urban Green Corridor Biosphere Reserve in Seoul.

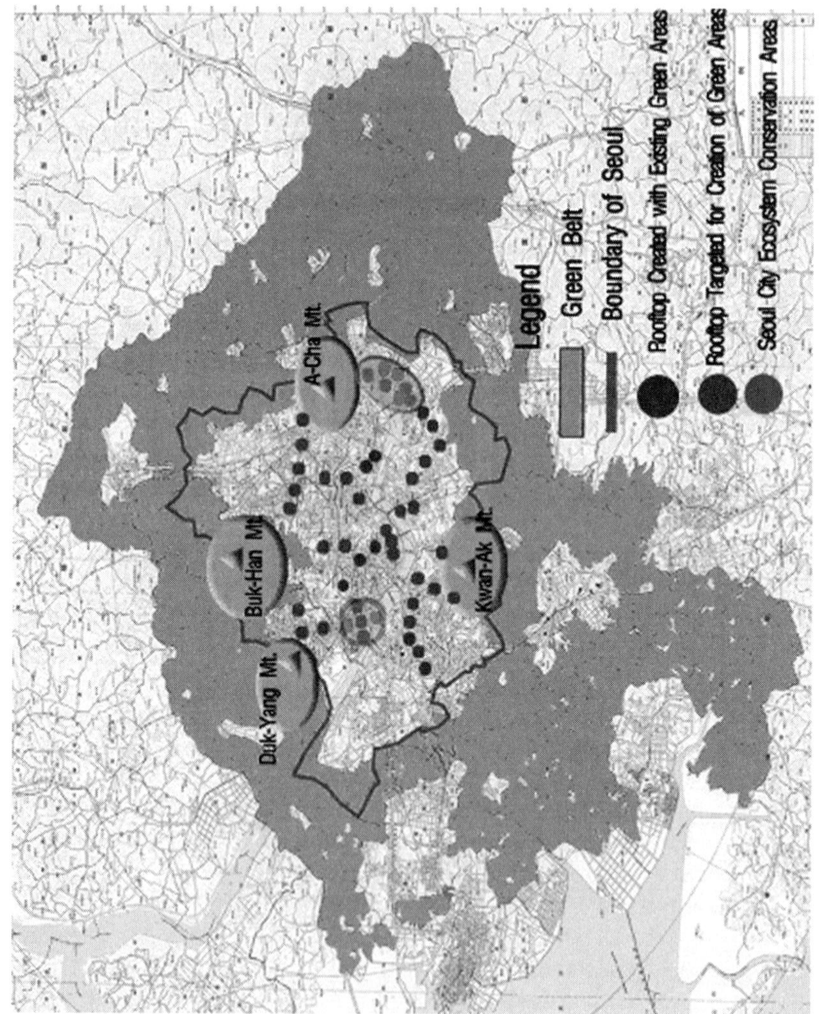

FIGURE 6. Potential for category 3: Urban Green Area Cluster Biosphere Reserve in Seoul.

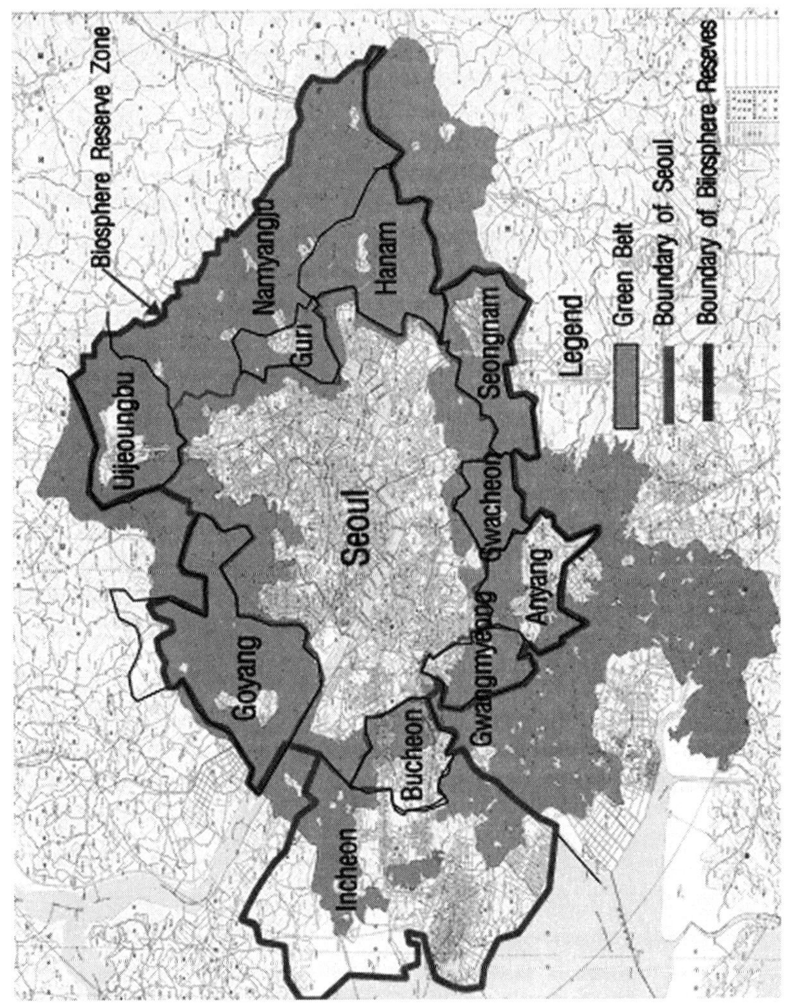

FIGURE 7. Potential for category 4: Urban Region Biosphere Reserve in Seoul.

The greenbelt begins near the boundary of Seoul administrative district and forms an approximately 10-km-wide circular green area. Such a greenbelt prevents further urbanization and urban sprawl of nearby satellite cities as well as Seoul and supports the habitats of various living organisms. Moreover, it also serves as the outsourcing of species in the bleak urban building environment of Seoul.

An Urban Green Corridor Biosphere Reserve (Category 2) would include diverse Urban Green Corridors including a circular axis connecting the outskirts of Seoul, a south–north axis linking Bukhan Mountain and Kwanak Mountain, and an east–west axis connecting the Han Riverside (FIG. 5).

According to "Vision Seoul 2006: Seoul Policy 4-year Plan (Seoul city, 2002)" presented by Seoul city, there are plans to create an ecocorridor between Chankyung Palace, which was destroyed during Japanese rule, and Jongmyo, as well as to restore the Cheonggye Stream and connect green area axes including Sewoon Shopping Center-Nam Mountain and Dongdaemun Stadium-Nam Mountain. In case of the Cheonggye Stream, dismantlement for restoration is already near completion. When such various restoration projects are completed, a much more diverse Urban Green Corridor Biosphere Reserve could be created.

An Urban Green Area Cluster Biosphere Reserve (Category 3) in Seoul could create and link large-scale green area clusters such as Bukhan Mountain, Kwanak Mountain, Dukyang Mountain, and Acha Mountain, which are major mountains on the outskirts of Seoul. In addition, small-scale green area clusters such as rooftop green areas in inner Seoul can be initiated. Seoul designated and is managing ecosystem reserves in six sites, which are inhabited by various species including birds. Therefore, if various types of habitats are restored or newly created on these sites, their potential as urban green area cluster biosphere reserves will be further enhanced (FIG. 6).

For an Urban Region Biosphere Reserve (Category 4), there exists the possibility of setting up and implementing a green area and biotope conservation strategy by defining Seoul and its nearby urban area as a Biosphere Reserve Zone (FIG. 7).[6]

The roles and functions of a green rooftop in contributing to an urban biosphere network may be summarized as follows:

- Application of the biotope concept can help overcome scale limitations in creating rich mosaics of ecological systems.
- The green rooftop can contribute to the welfare of inhabitants through food, climate regulation, water catchments, and recreation.
- Through appropriate zoning, space for each of the three major functions of a biosphere reserve can be provided.
- Green rooftops as "building-integrated habitats" require innovative and creative thinking on urban biosphere reserves as urban areas and their hinterlands.

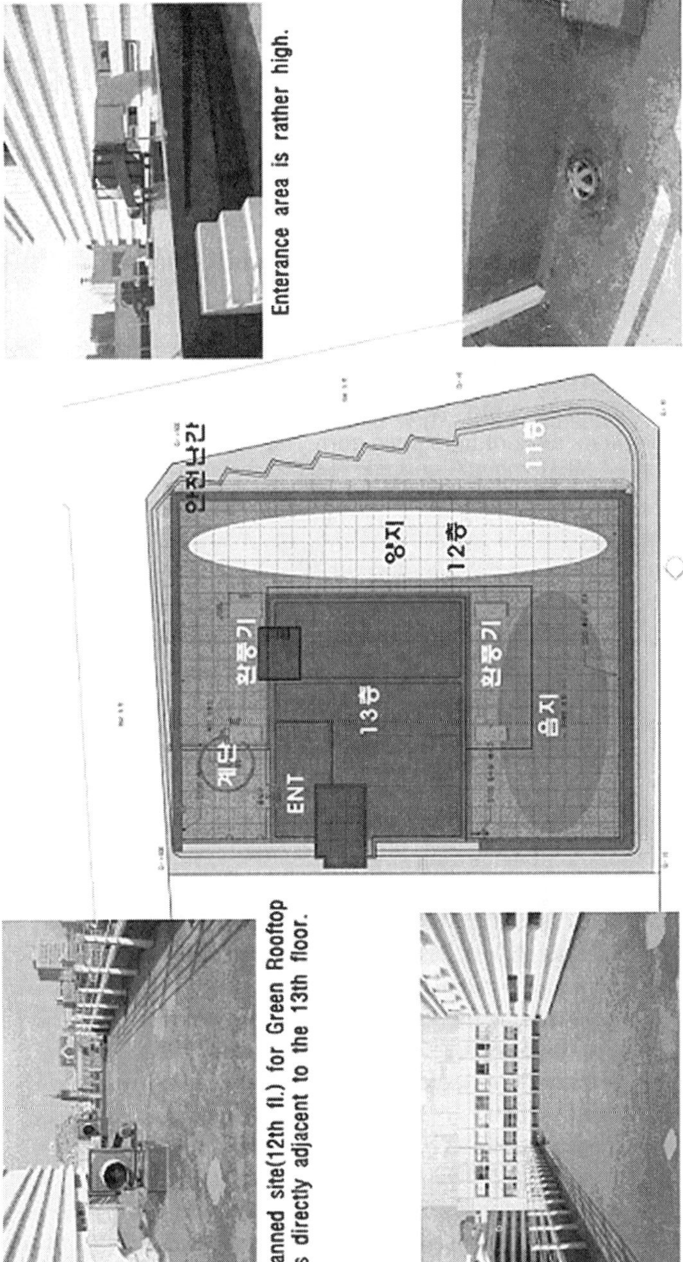

FIGURE 8. Inside of the site.

- Green rooftops have been created by several local authorities as pilot projects for the Local Agenda 21 or as Best Practices.
- Because a green rooftop contributes in connecting fragmented habitats, it can contribute in creating corridor biosphere reserves as well as cluster biosphere reserves by serving as a stepping-stone.

In understanding critical interactions between people and their environment, a green rooftop can contribute more than any other types of biosphere reserves. Therefore, as an important component in creating a sustainable city, green rooftop can be assessed to be compatible with "The Statutory Frame-

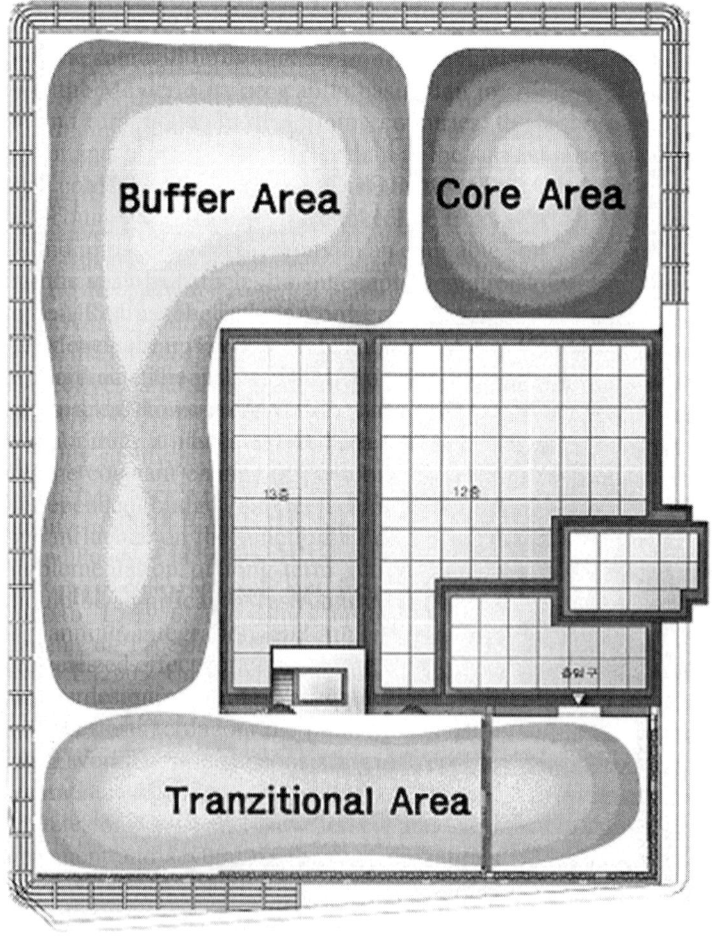

FIGURE 9. Application of biosphere reserve concept.

work and the Seville Strategy for the World Network of Biosphere Reserves" that cover general Biosphere Reserves.

Green Rooftop, UNESCO Building, Seoul

The UNESCO Green Rooftop is located in an area crowded by high-rise buildings and has high pedestrian traffic. It is a place where people from diverse socioeconomic groups gather. Green areas and spaces to create green areas are scarce because of dense buildings, as well as the proximity of the

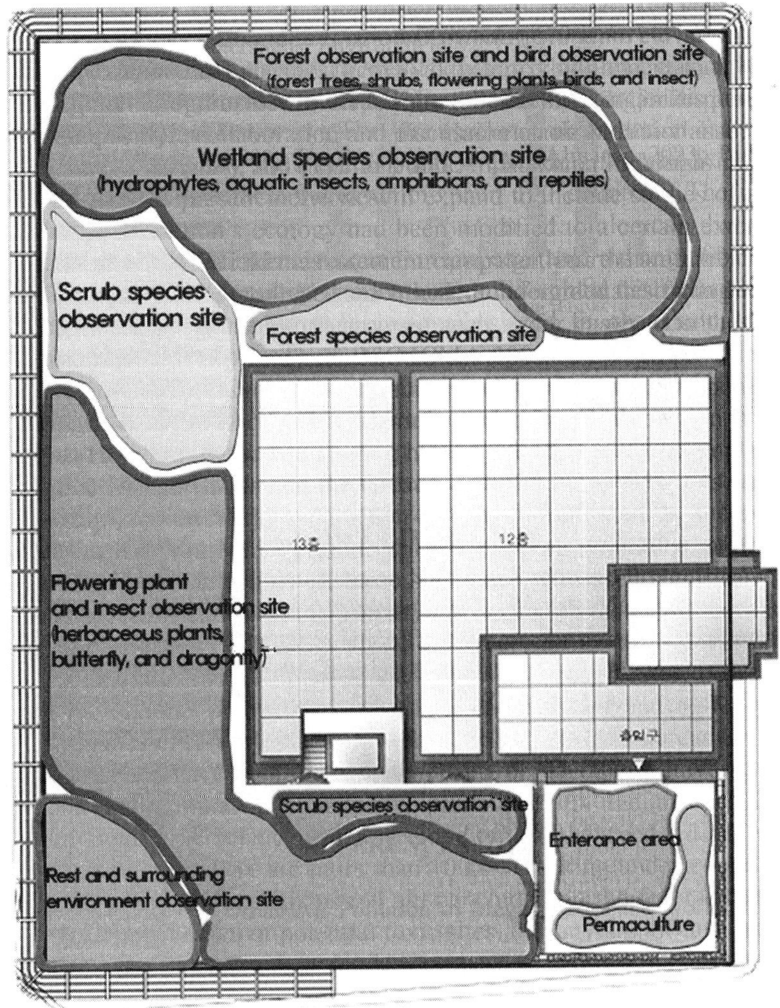

FIGURE 10. Basic concept map.

Chinese Embassy and of Myeongdong Cathedral. The site had restricted public access and was underused. The 12th floor rooftop, which is directly adjacent to the walls of 13th floor, is where ventilation facilities were located (FIG. 8).

In this study, the green rooftop was designed by applying the UNESCO's biosphere reserve concept. The concept was applied by separating the site largely into a core area, which is a strict conservation area, a buffer area, and a transitional area. The area zoning and area-specific features are shown in FIGURE 9.

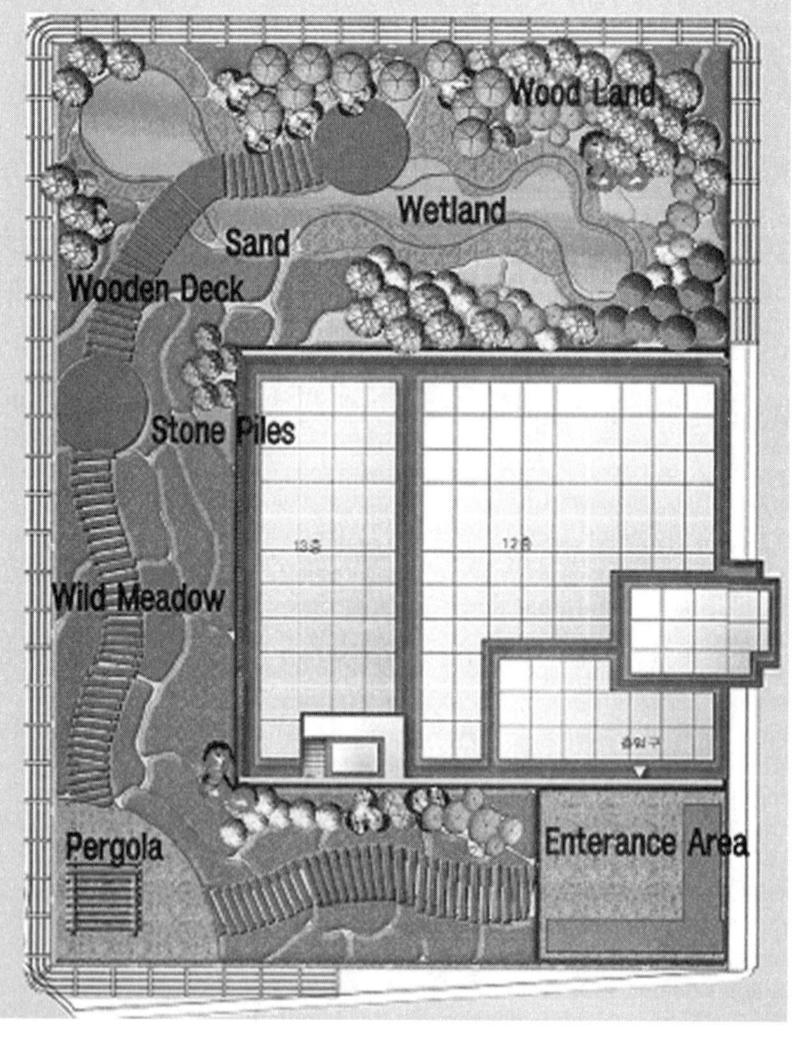

FIGURE 11. Master plan.

TABLE 2. Introduced space and facilities by progam

Goals and objectives	Programs	Introduced space	Introduced facilities (description)
Application of biosphere reserve concept	Urban biosphere reserve program	Core area	·Various wild animal habitats
		Buffer area	·Observation route and deck as facilities for environment education
		Transitional area	·Rest facilities, permaculture
Creation of wild life habitats	Plant habitat offering program	Wetland	·Hydrophytes community
		Meadow	·Meadow plant community
		Wild meadow	·Wild meadow plant community
		Scrub	·Wild shrub woods, thicket woods
		Wood land	·Forest trees
	Bird habitat offering program	Deep water	·Open water surface, rack
		Wetland	·Hydrophytes community
		Wild meadow	·Feed stand
		Scrub	·Shrub thicket woods (edible plants)
		Wood land	·Forest trees, dead trees
	Fishery habitat offering program	Deep water	·Fishery shelters (stone piles)
		Wetland	·Shelters using aquatic plant belts
	Amphibian & reptile habitat offering program	Wetland	·Shelters using aquatic plant belts
		Meadow	·Hygrophytes, stone piles for amphibians to rest
		Wild meadow	·Stone piles for amphibians to rest
	Insect habitat offering program	Deep water	·Rack
		Wetland	·Open water surface, emerged plants
		Meadow	·Flowering hygrophytes, dry meadow plants, dead trees
		Wild meadow	·Wild flowers, dead trees
		Scrub	· Wild shrub woods, thicket woods
		Wood land	·Forest trees, dead trees
Permaculture	Cultivation experience program	Vegetable garden	·Vegetable field, bulletin boards
Environment education	Environment education program	Observation area	·Observation route, deck, and environment bulletin boards
Emotion enhancement	Natural landscape appreciation program	Rest area	·Block pavement, pergola, observation deck

TABLE 3. Construction steps and their overview image

Step	Process	Overview image	Description
1	Pre-construction		- Before construction, the rooftop was a space where nothing was developed and access was controlled
2	Waterproof construction		- Conduct waterproof layer construction to prevent corrosion of the outer walls of the building and leakage from rainwater and moisture
3	Laying storage-drain boards		- In order to prevent dryness and over-dampness after plantation, water-holding and drain boards were laid on top of water-proof layer
4	Laying permeable sheets		- In order to prevent blockage of drainage due to soil loss and to control the rooting of plants, permeable sheets were laid
5	Paving lightweight soil		- Considering load, lightweight soil was paved to create a plantation base using pearlite, which is a lightweight soil
6	Facility construction: deck and safety fences		- Decks for observation and movement were built and fences for a safety purpose were installed in buffer area
7	Facility construction: pergola		- Pergolas to offer rest areas to visitors were built
8	Wetland construction		- Wetland construction in core area and transitional area
9	Plantation construction		- On top of ground base including mounding created using artificial soil, herbaceous plants, scrub, and woodland were planted; local residents were involved

Use of programs, introduced spaces, and facilities within the framework of the UNESCO Green Rooftop are described in TABLE 2. Space-specific introduced living organisms and facilities are shown in FIGURE 10. Based on the basic concept map, a master plan shown in FIGURE 11 was prepared.

To create the UNESCO Green Rooftop as a space maximizing the use of renewable resources and energy, rainwater is collected to be used in wetland, and solar energy concentrator collectors are installed to use energy for water circulation in the wetland.

A natural habitat model was applied to the UNESCO Green Rooftop. The planting design and habitat conditions were created considering soil and grading plans. A plan was developed to plant trees, herbaceous plants, and other species that can attract birds and insects. The planting base system introduced in the UNESCO Green Rooftop is a system in which a permeable sheet, a drainage layer, and a planting layer are set up on top of water-holding and drain boards. A drip irrigation system was built on the planting layer.

Based on the master plan, the UNESCO Green Rooftop was built over the course of several steps and processes. During construction, local residents and students were directly involved in several these, to create a green rooftop leveraging partnership (TABLE 3).

The site is evolving into a valuable ecosystem thanks to fast growth. The views of the site are provided in FIGURE 12. The overview of core area, buffer area, and transitional area in the site may be seen in FIGURE 13. Major habitats including wetlands are developing fast. Their current overview is shown in FIGURE 14.

On the UNESCO Green Rooftop, plants were selected and planted by considering the environmental features of each habitat. A total of 75 species were planted, including the typical species of each habitat. The results of monitoring that took place in August 2003, 5 months after the construction, showed that planted plants were mostly growing well. In addition to planted species, more than 40 species of plants had appeared spontaneously. In addition, diverse animal species had moved in, including birds such as *Pica pica serica* and *Passer montanus* and insect species including *Dolycoris baccarum*, *Gerris (aquarius) paludum insularis*, and *Orthetrum albistylum*.

Plant species have also become more diverse. To date, 39 species are estimated to have taken hold. Along with plants, wild animal species were able to adapt quickly to the site, because although the site is located at heart of downtown Seoul, Nam Mountain is close by and small green areas exist at the nearby Chinese Embassy and Myeongdong Cathedral.

The UNESCO Green Rooftop, created as a UNESCO Urban Biosphere Reserve area and an experimental site for urban ecosystem restoration, is continuously monitored for its ground environment and ecological environment today. Programs allowing students and local residents to participate in activities ranging from plantation to monitoring are offered. Also, utilization

FIGURE 12. Photographs of the site in five months after the construction.

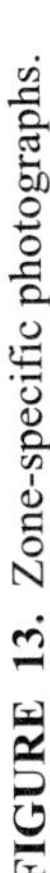
FIGURE 13. Zone-specific photographs.

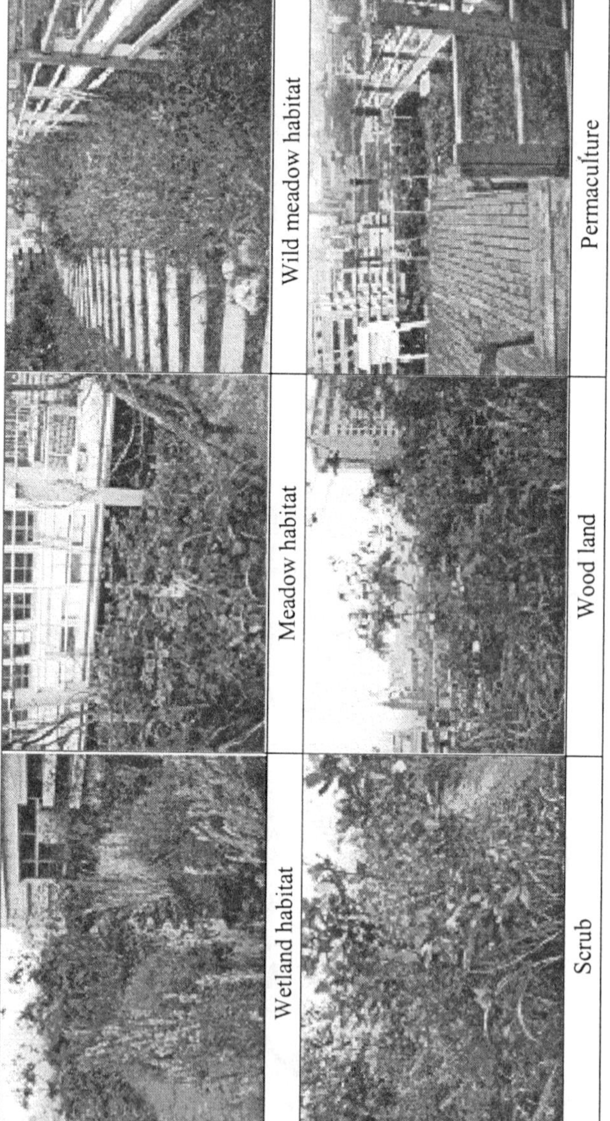

FIGURE 14. Photographs of the site at five months after construction.

and management plans are studied through expert advisory meetings held regularly.

To keep the UNESCO Green Rooftop functioning as an urban biosphere reserve and as a habitat-promoting biodiversity, certain management guidelines will need to be observed. The plantation should be controlled with regular monitoring and management. Spontaneous plants should be managed adequately because they may affect other plant species. The potential impacts of animals should be studied carefully, and their natural habitats should be identified to create environment where they can live. Rainwater should be used for irrigation and drainage system should be checked regularly. Regular checkups should take place to keep water depth, water temperature, and water quality suitable for wildlife.

CONCLUSIONS AND RECOMMENDATIONS

There is sufficient evidence to demonstrate that green rooftops can provide many environmental and associated aesthetic and health benefits, including reduction of urban ecological footprints. It is generally assumed that wildlife can benefit from green rooftops, and existing studies indicate that a wide range of plant, bird, and invertebrate species do occur on rooftops.[7] The Green Rooftop of Myeongdong UNESCO Building is functioning as a "building-integrated habitat specifically for biodiversity conservation." This green rooftop may well be in the vanguard of a movement to create similar features throughout the world's cities.

Although Seoul adopted and executes the green rooftop policy, it is regrettable that policies on urban planning, design, environment, drainage, ecology, and biodiversity do not proactively incorporate matters on green rooftops. Recognizing that Seoul has a huge potential for rooftop greening, the policies of the Seoul city government should be redefined. In addition, there should be efforts to raise the awareness of general public on the role of green rooftops in urban biodiversity conservation.

Meanwhile, based on the result of applying to Seoul the models put forward by MAB Urban Group, there seems sufficient ground to move forward in defining an urban biosphere reserve. In relation to this, the following is suggested. (1) An urban biosphere reserve centered on urban ecosystems should be conceived differently from those centered on natural ecosystems, such as coastal/marine biosphere reserves, grassland biosphere reserves, or forest biosphere reserves. (2) Similarly, in urban biosphere reserve, the zoning strategy for core areas, buffer zones, and transition areas should be applied differently than in traditional biosphere reserves.

Fundamental research and experimentation is still required. Hopefully, however, the UNESCO Green Rooftop can be included in the World Urban

Biosphere Reserve Network along with the Habitat Network in Seoul and contribute to the UNESCO MAB Project.

ACKNOWLEDGMENTS

This paper was presented at the "Urban Biosphere and Society Conference. Partnership of Cities Conference." 28–31 October 2003, organized by the Columbia University–UNESCO Joint Program on Biosphere and Society (CUBES) in cosponsorship with the New York Academy of Sciences, UN-Habitat, and the MAB Urban Group.

REFERENCES

1. EcoSchemes Limited in Association with Studio Engleback and Environmental Impacts Teams. 2003. English Nature, Green Roofs: their existing status and potential for conserving biodiversity in urban areas. Report no. 498, p. 9.
2. UNU Institute of Advanced Studies. 2002. Urban Ecosystems. UNU/IAS Report 2002. January–December 2001. p. 13.
3. UNESCO-MAB. 2000. Solving the Puzzle: The Ecosystem Approach and Biosphere Reserves. Paris. p. 2.
4. The 8th Meeting of UNESCO-MAB. 2003 (August 19–22). East Asian Biosphere Reserve Network, Hustai National Park, Mongolia.
5. UNESCO-MAB. 2000. Solving the Puzzle: The Ecosystem Approach and Biosphere Reserves. Paris. p. 17.
6. MAB Urban Group. 2003 (June). Urban Biosphere Reserves in the context of the Statutory Framework and the Seville Strategy for the World Network of Biosphere Reserves. Draft.
7. EcoSchemes Limited in Association with Studio Engleback and Environmental Impacts Teams, p. 40.

Chicago Wilderness

A New Force in Urban Conservation[a]

DEBRA K. MOSKOVITS,[b] CAROL FIALKOWSKI,[b] GREGORY M. MUELLER,[c] TIMOTHY A. SULLIVAN,[d] JOHN ROGNER,[e] AND ELIZABETH McCANCE[f]

[b]*Environmental and Conservation Programs, The Field Museum, Chicago, Illinois 60605-2496, USA*

[c]*Department of Botany, The Field Museum, Chicago, Illinois 60605-2496, USA*

[d]*Conservation Programs, Chicago Zoological Society, Brookfield Zoo, Brookfield, Illinois 60513, USA*

[e]*U.S. Fish and Wildlife Service, Barrington, Illinois 60010, USA*

[f]*Conservation Programs, Chicago Wilderness, Chicago, Illinois 60603, USA*

ABSTRACT: In 1996, a coalition of diverse and determined organizations launched a new initiative in the Chicago region. Our vision? Chicago Wilderness: a thriving mosaic of natural areas, connected by greenways and wildlife corridors, embedded in the nation's third largest metropolis. In this vision, the region's human communities reclaim a cultural tradition of protecting and restoring the globally outstanding natural communities that enrich our lives. Today, more than 170 organizations join forces to transform this vision into reality. A regional *biodiversity recovery plan*, the result of 3 years of assessment and planning by scientists, land managers, educators, and policy strategists, sets priorities and determines the lines of action for the coalition. This regional agenda stems from our vision and recovery goals for each ecological community; it encourages targeted research initiatives that focus on characterizing our native biological diversity and on analyzing elements critical to its recovery. Ultimately, though, the long-term survival of our natural wealth rests on the support from the public. Although the challenges to conservation educators and communicators are many, Chicago Wilderness allows us to work together in understanding our audiences, channeling our resources, and creating novel approaches to engage the widest public in our conservation efforts.

KEYWORDS: Chicago Wilderness; urban landscape; biodiversity; education; natural resources management; sustainability

[a]This paper is based on a previous paper of the same title published in 2002 in the *Annals of the Missouri Botanic Garden* **89:** 153–163.

Address for correspondence: Elizabeth McCance, Conservation Programs, Chicago Wilderness, 8 S. Michigan, Suite 900, Chicago, IL 60603. Voice: 312-580-2138; fax: 312-346-5606.
emccance@chicagowilderness.org

Ann. N.Y. Acad. Sci. 1023: 215–236 (2004). © 2004 New York Academy of Sciences.
doi: 10.1196/annals.1319.011

CHICAGO WILDERNESS: THE NATURAL CAPITAL

Chicago, the third largest metropolis in the United States, is anything but "untrammeled by man, where man is a visitor who does not remain" in the words of the Wilderness Act, which has shaped our modern concept of wilderness. And yet "Chicago Wilderness" is the emerging force in our urban landscape. Launched in 1996 by a coalition of 34 diverse and determined organizations, Chicago Wilderness joins forces to conserve the globally outstanding natural communities that survive in our metropolis.

The surprise to many is that the boundaries of Chicago Wilderness capture a spectacular array of rare ecosystems. These ecosystems include tallgrass prairies, oak woodlands, oak savannas, sedge meadows, marshes, bogs, fens, and other prairie wetlands. In fact, within Chicago Wilderness, which extends in a crescent around Lake Michigan from southeastern Wisconsin, through six Illinois counties, into northwestern Indiana, survive some of the best remnants of the prairie and oak-savanna communities of the Midwest (TABLE 1). These remnants shelter several species that are rare worldwide and that are listed as threatened or endangered in the states of Illinois, Indiana, and Wisconsin, species that once lived in the thriving grasslands and woodlands that have now become extensive monocultures of corn or soybean.

At the turn of the century, Chicago was blessed with far-sighted planners who created a system of forest preserves in and around the city. The wilderness in Chicago survives in parcels that range in size from half-acre remnants to the 19,000-acre Midewin National Tallgrass Prairie. Some of the natural remnants survive in old settler cemeteries or along railway rights-of-way. Most survive in the preserves that total over 250,000 acres (102,000 ha) of protected public lands and waters. All parcels exist within the much larger matrix of public and private, built, and natural lands that support the region's nine million residents.

Our natural communities suffer from several stressors, including habitat fragmentation, interruption of natural fire regimes, air and water pollution, and native and exotic invasive species. The long-term survival of these endangered plant and animal assemblages depends on the proper ecological management and aggressive restoration of degraded lands, even, or primarily, in the region's forest preserves and conservation districts. It is this need for co-

TABLE 1. Remaining high-quality natural areas in Illinois

Region	Original acreage	% Surviving
Galena	371,000	0.00005
Chicago	1,998,000	0.04
West Central	3,217,000	0.00006
Springfield	2,041,000	0.003

SOURCE: The Illinois Natural Area Inventory, Illinois Department of Conservation.

ordinated and rapid action that now brings together more than 172 institutions including landowners; local, state, and federal government agencies; education and research institutions; and conservation organizations to turn the vision of Chicago Wilderness into reality.

CHICAGO WILDERNESS: WHAT, WHERE, AND WHY

Chicago Wilderness is both the name of the coalition of organizations committed to protecting, restoring, and managing the natural communities in the Chicago region and the natural communities themselves, along with the plants and animals that depend on them for survival. Chicago Wilderness also is the people of the region, the human residents whose quality of life depends on a thriving regional nature reserve.

Urban living often results in an almost complete detachment of people from the land. An important goal of Chicago Wilderness is to reconnect a landless urban population with the pulse of nature. The name Chicago Wilderness is meant in part to emphasize the connections between wilderness in the conventional sense, in remote and inaccessible places, and wilderness in the places where people live and work.

But why strive for a regionwide coalition instead of working through more manageable, individual collaborations? The answer lies in the realities of the region: extreme fragmentation of the natural communities. The high-quality patches in the region are tiny. Nothing short of a massive, regionwide, coordinated effort will ensure the long-term survival of these natural communities, through the management of much larger lands that surround and connect the remnants. In the vision of Chicago Wilderness, we reconnect the 250,000 acres (102,000 ha) of fragmented natural areas through greenways and wildlife corridors. And in this vision, the human communities reclaim a cultural tradition of restoring, protecting, and managing our natural communities.

CHICAGO WILDERNESS: THE ORGANIZATION

Chicago Wilderness is a loosely structured organization, with an unconventional organizational chart (FIG. 1). In Chicago Wilderness, we are bound by our common goals and objectives and by our collaborative projects. We are in essence a volunteer-driven effort. Four teams focus on the central lines of action: science, natural resources management, sustainability, and education and communication. The teams attract participation of many nonmember institutions, which adds to the scope and strength of the coalition. Current and past chairs of the teams and staff from other member organizations form the nucleus of the coordinating group that develops central strategies, maintains

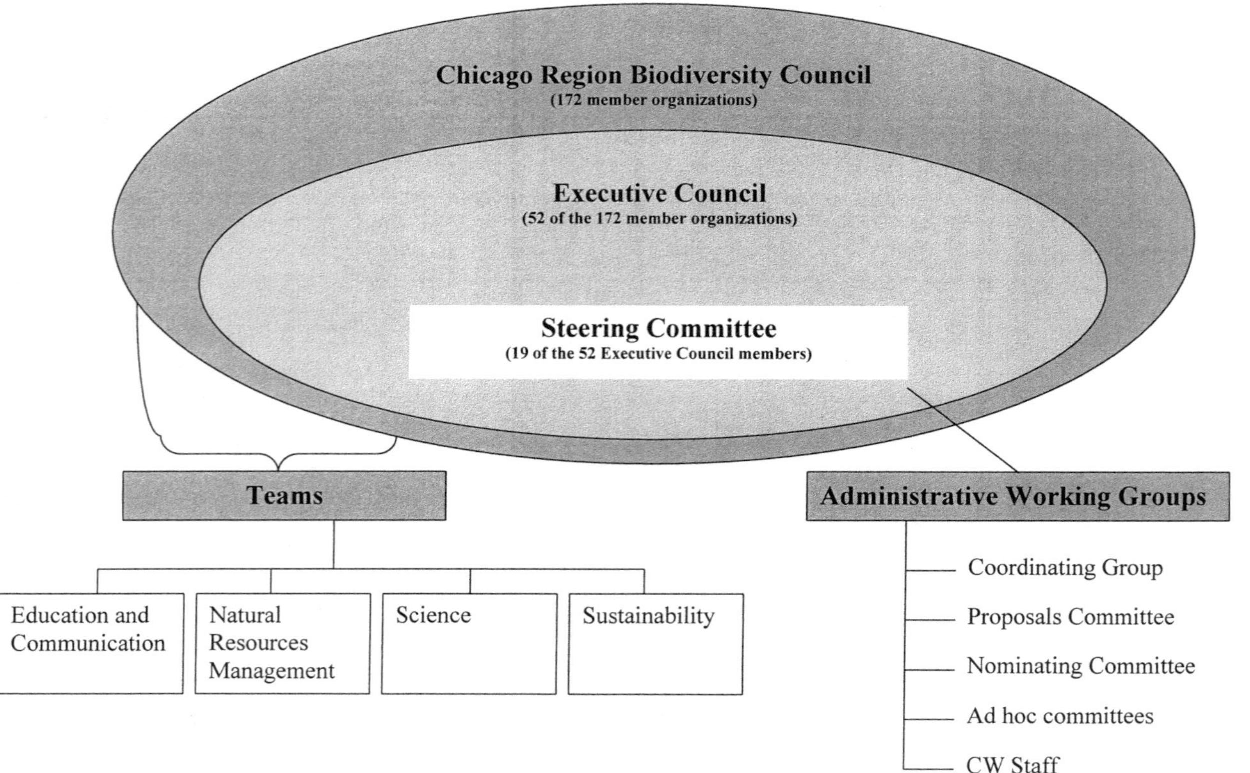

FIGURE 1. Chicago Wilderness Organizational Chart.

momentum, and resolves day-to-day problems. A steering committee of executives oversees the initiatives, including approval of budgets and projects, and the Chicago Region Biodiversity Council encompasses the chief executives of all member institutions. The Executive or voting members elect the steering committee. A proposals committee solicits and reviews proposals for priority conservation projects and recommends funding; the committee has one or two representatives from each of the four teams. And the Recovery Plan Task Force spearheaded the gigantic effort of developing, compiling, and writing the *biodiversity recovery plan* for the region (see below).

A few ingredients have been instrumental in allowing Chicago Wilderness to succeed as a massive coalition and indeed become greater than the sum of our parts rather than to collapse under our own weight. We briefly highlight these key ingredients below.

(1) A critical mass of people thoroughly—passionately—committed to seeing the work succeed and ready to put an inordinate amount of time and effort into making it happen. For us, this core energy came from the coordinating group.

(2) Early, visible, and popular successes. In Chicago Wilderness, these early successes came from some of our public awareness materials. The *Atlas of Biodiversity*[1] was the first publication of the Chicago Region Biodiversity Council. It characterizes the natural communities in the region, with their rich assemblages of plants and animals and helps bring these natural areas to the attention of a very broad audience, most of whom are unaware of the existence of such biological riches in our own backyard. The Atlas was one of the first concrete examples of how Chicago Wilderness could help individual members become more successful and effective in their work. The whole region needed a powerful, visual publication about our natural treasures. The *Atlas* is now in its fourth edition, with more than 50,000 copies already distributed.

(3) Mission-related benefits to individual members. For the coalition to thrive, individual members must become more successful in their individual endeavors because of their association with the coalition. Conversely, members must contribute in their own way and with their unique strengths to the coalition and to the pursuit of the collective mission. For example, one of the goals of The Field Museum is to direct its resources—scientific expertise, worldwide collections, innovative education programs—to the immediate needs of conservation at the regional and international levels and to create a link between academic institutions and the groups most closely tied to biological stewardship. Chicago Wilderness offers the museum a tremendous advantage in tapping into a wide, regional effort. In turn, with Chicago Wilderness, the Museum has directed much more of

its efforts in research, inventory, and tools for conservation to the Chicago region.

The potential for Chicago Wilderness to serve as a model for urban conservation attracted early attention of several federal agencies, including the USDA Forest Service, the US Fish and Wildlife Service, and the US Environmental Protection Agency, who have provided significant operating grants, bringing new conservation revenues to the region. Matching funds from members, and funds attracted by members for projects catalyzed by Chicago Wilderness, exceed 70% of the funds dedicated to this regional effort.

CHICAGO WILDERNESS: IMPACT ON SCIENTIFIC RESEARCH

Research focusing on local biodiversity and land-management issues in the region has been ongoing for more than 100 years. However, a recent resurgence of interest in local issues by the region's scientific community was coincidental with, and in large part a consequence of, the founding of Chicago Wilderness. This outcome can be attributed to several reasons, including that the consortium has been successful in bringing new resources to the area to support research. More importantly than the new funds, however, is that the partnerships and opportunities for collaboration fostered by Chicago Wilderness have created new research initiatives, identified important research questions, expanded interest in the resulting data, and created an enhanced atmosphere for the importance of biodiversity and ecological research focused on the region.

Several Federal and Illinois State agencies have provided grants to Chicago Wilderness to help enable the initiative to meet its goals. Chicago Wilderness makes requests for proposals each year to distribute these funds to outstanding projects. A proposals committee (see above) reviews submitted proposals and ranks them based first on merit and then on the relevance to the mission of Chicago Wilderness and on the degree to which the results will make unique contributions to the initiative; that is, it will serve as a model for other projects or will provide data that may serve as the underpinning for a series of other studies. The topics of funded research proposals fall into one of the following broad categories: Research/Inventory/Monitoring; Restoration; and Tools for Research—imaging projects, database projects, or other conservation tools.

The following exemplars of science projects funded through Chicago Wilderness provide an indication of the breath of the research undertaken by Chicago Wilderness member institutions. Although Chicago Wilderness funds only a small portion of the flourishing biodiversity research activity in the area, it has been greatly responsible for invigorating the interests of scientists in conducting research in the region.

Research/Inventory/Monitoring Projects

Projects within this category focus on increasing our understanding of the native biological diversity in Chicago Wilderness. Research projects concentrate on factors influencing that diversity and on the efficacy of current management practices to maintain and restore the region's native diversity. Funded projects have ranged from studying the effects of restoration efforts in oak woodland communities on a broad group of taxa (fungi, beetles, millipedes, amphibians, mosses, birds, and flowering plants), to documenting the diversity and distribution of the region's bats, to landscape level inventories of watersheds, to studying the role of arbuscular mycorrhizal fungi in prairie restoration.

Restoration Projects

The focus of projects in this category has been (1) to develop best practices transferable to other sites or (2) to restore specific sites of special significance. Funded projects have ranged from developing and testing methods for restoring specific threatened and endangered plants to restoring a degraded tallgrass prairie at Indiana Dunes National Lakeshore.

Tools

The goals of these projects are to develop useful tools that facilitate research and land-management activities in the region. These tools include imaging projects to develop multispectral vegetation maps using aerial fly-overs, to creating an integrated data management system for land owners, to using spectral data to track changes in land-use and land cover over the region. Funded database projects include compiling data from past breeding bird surveys into a user-friendly database and the development of a database of the current status and location of the region's threatened and endangered plant species. An example of another type of tool is the development of a user-friendly computer model to analyze strategies for deer removal in different land-management programs.

The continued growth and development of the Chicago Wilderness coalition, and the impact that the coalition is having throughout the area, has enhanced communication among scientific researchers, land managers, educators, and policy makers in the region. Such communication is critical for effective development of research programs that enhance the conservation of biodiversity. Through understanding the types of data most needed by the users of research results (i.e., land managers, conservation biologists, policy makers, educators), and how to present these data to the users, we have identified new research projects while enhancing the value of our research and expanding the audience for our results. In turn, the region has gained better recognition of the value of research and has increased opportunities for its continued funding. The positive cycle continues to foster further research activities in Chicago Wilderness.

OUR ROAD MAP: THE BIODIVERSITY RECOVERY PLAN

From the earliest days of the Chicago Wilderness coalition, member organizations recognized that to be effective, we needed a strong regional conservation agenda with clear priorities for action. The concept was to produce a biodiversity recovery plan, in some ways analogous to a single species recovery plan, which would provide an assessment of the current conditions along with a road map for how to reach desired vision and goals. An effective *recovery plan* would help shape decisions at both the policy and the land-management levels.

We completed the plan in late 1999, after almost 3 years of dedicated work by huge numbers of members and nonmembers, including the science, land management, education, and policy experts in the region. The *recovery plan* identifies the ecological communities of the greater Chicago region, assesses the overall condition of these communities and the threats facing each, lays out the vision and recovery goals for each species assemblage, and recommends actions to achieve our goals. The plan also lays out a process of conservation and information design that leads to coordinated research, inventory, and monitoring agendas to support these conservation goals and strategies and to anchor them on the best available science. And the plan calls for a massive communication effort to galvanize public support behind our conservation agenda.

The plan provides both an overarching vision for what Chicago Wilderness, the land and biodiversity, can become and a broad treatment of the details of how to get there. In developing the plan, we used a consensus-based approach, relying on the region's experts and the available data. The plan also provides the platform for organizing action at a further level of detail and it provides a strong foundation for communication about the challenges facing biodiversity conservation in the region.

The *recovery plan* process brought together expert actors from many backgrounds and disciplines to share their knowledge. The outcome is not only the region's state-of-the-art insights, but also a blending of our science, policy, and communications expertise. And the process resulted in heightened interest and commitment for collaboration in more detailed plans for conservation action within a regional context.

The plan contains 140 separate recommended actions that fall into the following six categories:

(1) Land management. Most natural areas in the region are not being managed in a manner that will sustain plant and animal diversity over time: more acres need to be under ecological management and the intensity of management must increase.
(2) Land protection. Additional land will need protection as the region's human population continues to grow. The primary concern in setting aside more land for conservation is to create larger, unfragmented protected areas, either from scratch or by enlarging existing ones. Because much of the land in natural conditions either is protected already or is in extremely small parcels, the *recovery plan* envisions the need for restoring to ecological health disturbed and converted areas, such as agricultural lands, as a strategy for creating larger units.
(3) Stream protection. We must protect remaining high-quality streams —where most of the remaining aquatic biodiversity resides—from additional degradation.
(4) Research and monitoring. Research needs relate primarily to understanding how best to address the threats to biodiversity posed by human development. For monitoring, the plan puts forward a system of adaptive management based on conservation planning (briefly discussed below).
(5) Education and communication. The plan recognizes that public understanding and support is a precondition to the success of a long-term, broad-based public undertaking such as biodiversity conservation. The plan lays out steps to achieve increased understanding of the importance of biodiversity and what it takes to conserve it on both short- and long-term scales (see further discussion, below).
(6) Local and regional development policies. The region is at a critical time for developing policies that will control anticipated growth in population and in urban space in the coming decades. The *recovery plan* stresses the impact of the region's management of growth on biodiversity and suggests steps to mitigate that impact.

THE PROCESS OF CREATING THE RECOVERY PLAN

The primary units of conservation in Chicago Wilderness are plant communities. Initial natural area inventories for the region, upon which most conservation strategies to date have been based, focused on remnant high-quality communities.[2] The *recovery plan* also adopts plant communities as its primary conservation targets, but it considers animal communities or assemblages, aquatic communities, and threatened species as well. A critical first step in the plan became to develop and adopt a plant community classification system that all Chicago Wilderness members could accept and upon which the region would base subsequent conservation and land-management decisions.

Most land-management agencies in the region traditionally have classified their holdings according to the community classification system used by the Illinois Natural Areas Inventory (INAI) in the 1970s.[2] Rather than adopt a completely new system for the recovery plan, Chicago Wilderness elected to develop a modified version of the INAI system. The modifications reflect a deeper current understanding of community gradients in fire-dependent forested lands in the region.[3] In addition, the new classification places more focus on degraded lands, recognizing those lands as the primary target of restoration efforts. Although the Chicago Wilderness classification system does not follow the emerging national standard for community classification, the *recovery plan* includes a crosswalk to these national standards.[4] The resultant community classification system includes 8 major community groups, 24 community types, and 55 subtypes distinguished primarily by soil moisture (TABLE 2).

Although the plan lays out actions covering all of the biodiversity of the region, not only what is unique or rare, it also incorporates a method to identify what is most important from a global perspective and what conservation targets need the most immediate attention. We undertook this evaluation primarily at the natural community level, but also included information from key groups of animal assemblages and of threatened species.

Regional experts first evaluated the status of animal groups or subsets of groups: reptiles and amphibians, breeding birds, mammals, and some terrestrial invertebrates. In workshops, the scientists grouped the species found in the region into broad assemblages associated with habitat types, for example, savanna birds or forest and woodland reptiles and amphibians. These assemblages are not mutually exclusive in that some species will fall into more than one grouping. The experts then assessed the significance of the Chicago Wilderness region to the global survival of each assemblage and its constituent species. The three ranks we used were Globally Critical, meaning that the Chicago Wilderness region is very important to the overall survival and well-being of the assemblage; Globally Important, meaning that the region contributes significantly to the overall well-being of the assemblage; and Locally Important, meaning that the assemblage is an important component of the region's biodiversity, but its status in the region will not have a substantial impact on the global well-being of the assemblage. Experts also assessed the condition of the assemblage in the region, ranking them as "of concern/declining" or "stable." Combining the rank in importance on the one hand, and the condition of the assemblage on the other, helped to identify the Chicago Wilderness habitats that need most immediate attention to stem declines or to

TABLE 2. Vegetation communities in Chicago wilderness

Community classes (8)	Communities (24)	Subcategories (55)
Forested communities	Upland forest	Dry mesic, mesic, wet mesic
	Floodplain forest	Wet mesic, wet
	Flatwoods	Northern, sand
	Woodland	Dry mesic, mesic, wet mesic
Savanna communities	Fine-textured-soil savanna	Dry mesic, mesic, wet mesic
	Sand savanna	Dry, dry mesic
Shrubland communities	Fine-textured-soil shrubland	Dry mesic, wet mesic
	Sand shrubland	Dry mesic, Wet mesic
Prairies	Fine-textured-soil prairie	Dry, mesic, wet
	Sand prairie	Dry, mesic, wet
	Gravel prairie	Dry, mesic
	Dolomite prairie	Dry, mesic, wet
Wetland communities	Marsh	Basin, streamside
	Bog	Graminoid, low shrub, forested
	Fen	Calcareous floating mat, graminoid, forested
	Sedge meadow	
	Panne	
	Seeps and springs	Neutral, calcareous, acid
Cliff communities	Cliff	Eroding bluff, dolomite cliff
Lakeshore communities	Lakeshore	Beach, foredune, high dune
Cultural (human-dominated) vegetation communities	Cropland	
	Unassociated growth	Grass, forb, shrub, tree
	Tree plantation	
	Developed land	

improve conditions. The exercise also helped us to determine the habitats in the region that are most significant in terms of global conservation. The moist grassland bird assemblage came out as both Globally Critical and in poor condition. Ten other assemblages in Chicago Wilderness are Globally Important and declining.

Before evaluating communities, planners also reviewed the threatened plant species in the region and placed them into six categories of priorities: from species that are globally rare to species that may be adequately protected or stable but are restricted to communities that are rare within Chicago Wilderness. Presence of threatened plant species was an element in evaluating priorities for conservation targets within biological communities.

To evaluate the relative need of different biological communities for additional conservation action, Chicago Wilderness members built on existing methods for ranking endangered ecosystems.[5,6] We modified these systems slightly, to include the key factor of condition (quality), which is one of the

TABLE 3. Conservation targets for recovery based on status, importance, and distribution

First (highest) tier
Woodland (all moisture classes)
Fine-textured-soil savanna (all moisture classes)
Mesic sand savanna
Sand prairie (all moisture gradients in dune and swale topography)
Dolomite prairie (all)
Panne
Graminoid fen
Fine-textured-soil prairie (all moisture classes)
Second tier
Dry sand savanna
Gravel prairie (all)
Basin marsh
Calcareous floating mat
Calcareous seep
Sand prairie (other than those in dune and swale topography)
Northern flatwood
Streamside marsh

most significant elements in the sustainability of biodiversity in this urban region. As with the animal assemblages, expert groups convened to assess available data and to rank natural community types against defined criteria. Four rankings—quantity, quality, biological importance, and contribution to global conservation—combined to make the final ranking.

- For quantity, experts considered (1) total amount (acres) remaining of the community, (2) amount lost since presettlement, and (3) number of patches large enough to sustain a relatively intact assemblage of constituent species over time.
- For quality, experts considered (1) remaining percentage in good quality, (2) degree of fragmentation and isolation, and (3) extent and effectiveness of current management efforts.
- For biological importance, experts considered (1) levels of species richness, (2) numbers of threatened species, and (3) key ecological processes.
- For contribution to global conservation, experts ranked communities as (1) endemic to the region, (2) at the center of the range, or (3) at the edge of the range. This assessment also considered the effectiveness of conservation efforts for the community type in other regions.

We combined the individual rankings to develop a tiered set of conservation targets, recognizing that all community types will require some degree of conservation effort to survive in the urban landscape. TABLE 3 shows the first two tiers of community targets. In all, Chicago Wilderness convened 13 daylong workshops for experts to rank community types and to discuss threats and conservation needs. Through a similar process, we evaluated the conservation needs of rivers, streams, and natural lakes in the region.

The ranking system to produce the conservation targets was not quantitative, but it represents a consensus of the experts in the region. The rankings—and the information behind them—are an important aspect of communication about biodiversity in the region and they provide a sound base for further planning. Key effort in the planning process went toward developing and adopting a process for further refining our conservation goals, developing strategies to obtain those goals, and setting up monitoring systems that enable information to feed back into refining management strategies toward these goals.

Once assembled, the draft of the *recovery plan* went through a formal, legal hearing process under the auspices of the Northeastern Illinois Planning Commission and the Northwestern Indiana Regional Planning Commission. Both Commissions and several municipal agencies adopted the plan. The value of the formal process was not only to gain feedback from a larger public, but also to seize on the opportunity to raise the issue of biodiversity in fora traditionally concerned primarily or exclusively with development and transportation issues. The final *recovery plan* is now on a level with other major plans that will guide the development of the region in the years to come. As a result, the issue of biodiversity will be discussed with business and civic leaders along with economic competitiveness, quality of life, and education.

CHICAGO WILDERNESS: IMPROVING LOCAL SUSTAINABILITY

Although the *biodiversity recovery plan* provides a general framework for our actions in the region, we have also developed several companion pieces for specific target audiences. *Protecting Nature in Your Community* is one of our tools that focuses on reaching public officials, policy makers, municipalities, zoning boards, and the more than 300 governing bodies that review and guide the design of hundreds of proposals for land development and redevelopment every week. The goal is to work with a variety of audiences to create healthy environments for both people and nature.

Although 250,0000 acres of natural areas are protected by various members of Chicago Wilderness, roughly 90% of the landscape is subject to the planning, development, and management decisions of local government. Building on the principles outlined in *Protecting Nature in Your Community*, Chicago Wilderness has been working both to educate and energize local officials regarding the significance and benefits of biodiversity protection in their communities and to identify techniques, mechanisms, and corresponding local examples through which local governments can collaborate with each other and other conservation organizations. This work has taken the form of several meetings and technical assistance to particular communities to explore ways to make development compatible with conservation. For example, after several presentations to the village board and planning and zoning commissions of Homer Glen, the village has begun to revise ordinances and guidelines for new development and now encourages conservation designs that protect its natural resources. Technical assistance to officials within the Boone Creek watershed led to revisions of local ordinances and guidelines for new development, which resulted in substantial changes to several development proposals to reduce their environmental impacts.

In addition, roundtable discussions were held with both local officials and local developers to discuss new design principles, model ordinances, and other innovative techniques to introduce conservation measures into planning and development. A group of Chicago Wilderness members proficient in sustainability also have conducted focus groups to learn explicitly how best to communicate these ideas to other developers and officials.

Addressing issues of sprawl and fragmentation requires work on multiple dimensions. Thus, in addition to working one-on-one with many local communities, Chicago Wilderness also works with a variety of regional planning initiatives. One of the largest regional planning initiatives, known as Metropolis 2020 was put together by The Commercial Club of Chicago. To promote the region's long-term health, the plan addresses a variety of areas including education, housing, crime, and transportation. Chicago Wilderness led workshops to discuss the future of natural areas and biodiversity in this visioning exercise. The workshops resulted in not only the inclusion of biodiversity considerations in the Metropolis 2020 plan, but also a detailed vision for green infrastructure for the Chicago Wilderness region.

Another example of working with larger regional planning efforts includes our work with the Chicago Area Transportation Authority, which puts together a plan for new transportation projects every 3 years. Chicago Wilderness became involved in the latest round of planning. As a result, the Chicago Area transportation plan specifically mentions biodiversity conservation as one of its goals, and we have developed a rigorous methodology for evaluating the impacts to biodiversity for each proposed project. This methodology provides citizens and planners another tool with which to evaluate the costs and benefits of potential projects.

OUR EDUCATION GOALS

Chicago Wilderness realizes that the future of our native landscapes depends on the support and involvement of our citizenry. On the encouraging side, Gallup surveys[7] and research by Belden and Russonello[8] report that most Americans consider environmental protection to be a priority. Concern about air and water pollution is widespread; citizens worry about destruction of tropical rain forests, toxic waste contamination, and habitat loss. But whereas concern about these issues is wide, it is not deep. Environmental issues often fade when economic matters compete. And biodiversity recovery faces additional challenges: public surveys report that only 20% of the population recognizes the term "biological diversity".[9]

Faced with these challenges, the Education and Communication Team of Chicago Wilderness has adopted (1) short-term communication strategies coupled with active public involvement projects, while (2) building and implementing longer-term educational strategies. To guide our actions, the more than 200 educators in Chicago Wilderness have embraced the internationally held definition of Environmental Education:

> Environmental Education is a learning process that increases people's *knowledge* and *awareness* about the environment and associated challenges, develops the necessary *skills* and expertise to address these challenges, and fosters *attitudes*, motivations, and commitments to make informed decisions and take *responsible action*" [10] [italics added].

The italicized words spell out thc five components essential for making a program in biodiversity education result in changed behavior and in informed decision making. Chicago Wilderness Educators have used these five components—awareness, knowledge, attitudes, skills, and participation—to develop a matrix that assesses our existing programs, from birth to death, against our targeted objectives.

TABLE 4 presents an abbreviated sample of this education matrix. An "X" indicates presence of the component in that program. For example, the BETA project incorporates all five essential components. Our compilation revealed that while our programs are strong in awareness and knowledge, they are weak or altogether lacking in attitude clarification, skill development, and active participation. To address these gaps and to reach the 80% who have never heard of biological diversity, while also ensuring that our education systems produce biologically literate graduates, we adopted program guidelines that (1) extend the scope of our existing, successful programs, to include attitude, skills, and action components; (2) develop new programs that specifically address the lacking components; (3) reach beyond our current circles by working with community-based organizations; (4) expand the distribution of our successful educational tools; and (5) ensure that students in the Chicago

TABLE 4. Sample matrix of existing programs in conservation education

Target audiences	Existing resources	Essential components of biodiversity education				
		Awareness	Knowledge	Attitude	Skills	Participation
Children (preschool–8th and teens)	An Atlas of Biodiversity	X	X			
	Chicago Tribune Biodiversity Supplement	X	X	X	X	
	Biodiversity Education through Action (BETA) Project	X	X	X	X	X
	Chicago Wilderness Communication Tools	X	X			
	Mighty Acorns Expansion Program	X	X	X	X	X
	IDNR Biodiversity of Illinois CD-ROM Series	X	X	X	X	
	EcoWatch	X	X	X	X	X
Adults	An Atlas of Biodiversity	X	X			
	Chicago Wilderness Magazine	X	X			
	Chicago Wilderness Communication Tools	X	X			
	EcoWatch	X	X	X	X	X
	It's Wild in Chicago	X	X	X		

Wilderness region—from elementary through university—are literate in biodiversity.

Promoting programs jointly, creating complementary (rather than competitive) projects, sharing teacher-education expertise, and submitting collaboratively developed proposals to schools are some of the new ways in which Chicago Wilderness reaches adults, children, and educators for greater impact. For example, Mighty Acorns is a stewardship program for 8- to 10-year-olds created by The Nature Conservancy. This highly successful program used to be limited to a few schools in one county. Today, through the leadership of Chicago Wilderness and two of its members, The Nature Conservancy and The Field Museum, the program has expanded to 21 Chicago Wilderness organizations in six counties in Illinois and one in Indiana, and it involves 80 schools, 325 teachers, and 8,000 students. Most of these 8,000 students come from underserved communities. These elementary students are engaged, actively, in learning about the region's plants and animals, experiencing nature, and practicing ecological stewardship—removing buckthorn and garlic mustard, collecting and planting seeds—to improve the health of our natural communities in the Chicago region.

Chicago Wilderness also has partnered with large distribution networks, such as the Chicago Tribune's NEWSPAPERS in the Classroom program, to develop and promote a curriculum and activity guide on the biodiversity of the region, using the Chicago Wilderness Atlas as the central teaching tool. Through its Web site, www.chicagowilderness.org, and a printed brochure, Chicago Wilderness provides to all in the region a full list of the local educational resources and how to obtain them.

PUBLIC INVOLVEMENT AND OUTREACH

To inform the public about pressing issues related to the protection of our natural communities and to engage a large constituency in the support and work of restoration, the *biodiversity recovery plan* outlines the following priorities:

- Increase the public's understanding of the role of ecological management
- Foster grassroots involvement in restoration and conservation activities
- Expand opportunities for "citizen science"
- Engage a wide public as volunteers.

Because environmental appreciation is garnered through experience of natural areas, Chicago Wilderness members have been working with several communities to find new ways of providing urban populations with opportunities to become aware of and explore the region's natural areas. Using the asset-based community development model, this work has help communities identify and promote their environmental assets. Other opportunities that foster wide public involvement include participation in Evanston, Illinois's Fourth of July parade and a biodiversity blitz. Last summer, 130 scientists and an unknown number of citizens donated their time to conduct an inventory of three sites in the Calumet region. Overall, the biodiversity blitz identified more than 2,250 species.

Our National Public Lands Day event, another effort fostered by Chicago Wilderness, enhances family involvement as volunteers and the engagement of a wide public in exploring the role of ecological management in the survival of our native communities. In 2003, more than 500 people participated in restoration activities at 18 Chicago Wilderness sites.

Through a program of the Illinois Department of Natural Resources, hundreds of citizens—adults and high-school students—gather data on the ecological condition of rivers, forests, wetlands, and prairies in Chicago

Wilderness. Several more hundred "citizen scientists" gather targeted data on birds and butterflies in the region. In many instances, the volunteers themselves enter the data online, to be analyzed by regional scientists and land managers, and by the state. Through our process of conservation design, we are now tying the data collection by citizens to the needs of land managers in monitoring and revising their management efforts.

As a result of Chicago Wilderness, Field Museum scientists and educators partnered with Illinois Department of Natural Resources to develop UrbanWatch with the following goals:

- Record the presence and distribution of groups of organisms—plants, animals, fungi—in an urban environment (we selected organisms that can be used to assess the condition of natural areas in urban centers)
- Examine environmental factors that influence the biodiversity in urban ecosystems
- Analyze and compile the information in a way that is readily usable by urban planners and park managers.

Focused on city parks, cemeteries, golf courses, corporate campuses, schoolyards, backyards, and tree-lined streets, UrbanWatch collects data to examine environmental factors that influence the native diversity in urban green space. Urban planners, park districts, site managers, and landowners will have access to these data and will apply them in the management of sites to improve or create urban spaces that are friendly to native communities and that address the needs of migrating birds and butterflies in our region.

OUR COMMUNICATION OPPORTUNITIES

Significant current challenges in ecological restoration require immediate strategies to increase public awareness and understanding. Chicago Wilderness has complemented its long-term approaches in public involvement with actions aimed at achieving the following short-term goals for communicating about biodiversity to the general public:

- Recognize biodiversity in everyday experiences
- Understand human impacts on biodiversity
- Recognize the connection between healthy nature and quality of life.

The Chicago Wilderness Communications Team has adopted the successful approach to crafting messages developed by the Biodiversity Project[9] in Madison, Wisconsin. The approach advocates having a clear goal and target audience, identifying core values of the target audience that the message embraces, and writing the message in short paragraphs. These paragraphs address (1) why the issue is important to the audience (leading with values), (2) what the threats are and who is responsible, and (3) what people can do to address the threats.

Through this method, the message directly incorporates the values of the audience. Equally important, each message ends with an action that the target audience can easily undertake.

We developed several attractive and highly effective communication tools using this method, including a video, tabletop display, and slide show. These tools are available to all Chicago Wilderness members, to deliver a consistent, compelling message. For the general public, the *Chicago Wilderness Magazine*, currently with over 9,000 subscribers, is sold at local bookstores, including Barnes & Noble and Borders, at gift shops of our member institutions, and at other outlets.

Although the challenges to conservation education and communication are many, the Chicago Wilderness coalition enables us to work together in understanding our audiences, challenging our resources, and creating novel approaches to engage the widest public in maintaining and restoring our local biodiversity.

Chicago Wilderness began with a larger-than-life goal: nothing less than rescuing vibrant natural areas by transforming the environmental culture of the people responsible for them. Through the partnerships formed and the collaborative work, Chicago Wilderness is proving itself equal to the task. From scientifically rigorous approaches in ecological inventory, restoration, and monitoring to creative advances in planning, policy, education, and outreach, the accomplishments of Chicago Wilderness are building a living legacy for the future.

THE URBAN CONSERVATION CULTURE

Conservation efforts in urban areas often are frustrated by the complexity of land-use issues, countless players, tangled politics, ecologically wrecked land, and a public dispossessed of nature. Yet it is crucial that we focus on urban areas because of the strong political forces concentrated in urban centers that need to be engaged in national conservation decision making, and because there is no other way to engage the great majority of people other than to take the messages to them. Moreover, urban residents are still plain members of Leopold's land community, regardless of how obscure the connections, and these connections are best illustrated in the places where they live. Fortunately, the Chicago region has an added bonus of harboring world-class biodiversity, which creates a local, immediately compelling reason for public involvement and action.

Some writers have argued that the American ideal of wilderness has tended to shape our dominant view of nature itself as a place that can be corrupted only by human influence. In urban areas, this has created an assumption that "real" nature cannot exist in these places, and it tends to absolve urban residents from local responsibility. Thus, it seems that Chicagoans are much more aware of the plight of Brazilian rain forests than they are of the plight of oak savannas, a globally rare community, in local forest preserves. In remote areas, the standard approach has been to specifically designate areas as wilderness and then maintain as complete a separation between people and these areas as possible. Chicago Wilderness proposes to redefine wilderness to include local plant and animal communities, which can be sustained only through direct, creative human intervention. A premise of the *recovery plan* is that if we do not adequately enlist people to directly or indirectly support management and restoration of our lands, they will not become or remain healthy.

It is appropriate to recognize that humans in the Midwest always *have* influenced landscapes, for better or worse, and that people can be a positive force in maintaining ecosystem health. It may be that by calling a 200-acre patch of prairie in a sea of development wilderness, and by involving people in its stewardship, we can promote a correct sense of unity between the places that we live and remote places we may never see except as pictures on calendars. Restoration and stewardship can be the antidote to dualistic thinking. Remote wilderness and Chicago Wilderness can perhaps then be seen as simply examples of nature, as part of a single system that includes people.

From a relatively straightforward beginning that focused on public land–management issues, this has become the broader goal of Chicago Wilderness—to reconnect people with nature and to make a societal commitment to sustain and nurture nature—for utility, for aesthetics, for spirituality, for all of the equally valid reasons for doing it—on all of our urban lands and in all of our land-use decisions. It begins with a process of educating the public about the natural wealth in the Chicago area, and hopefully ends sometime in the future with the development of an urban conservation culture of concern and personal responsibility for the health of all of our lands, both public and private.

CHICAGO WILDERNESS AS A BIOSPHERE RESERVE?

One tool that we are currently exploring as a means of reconnecting people with nature is the Man and the Biosphere program (MAB). According to UNESCO, "biosphere reserves are established to promote and demonstrate a balanced relationship between humans and the biosphere." A biosphere reserve designation has the potential to bring many exciting benefits to the Chicago Wilderness region.

First, a biosphere reserve designation would bring local, national, and international attention to the natural jewels that exist within the metropolitan Chicago region, many of global importance. It is a way of providing national and international prestige. Additionally, many Chicago Wilderness members, volunteers, and residents in this region have taken great strides to restore, protect, and preserve the region's rich biological diversity. Designation as a biosphere reserve would also bring attention to their efforts and potentially inspire other citizens to take action. We should think of a biosphere reserve designation as a seal of approval, which we hope will be a matter of civic pride.

According to its statutory framework, all biosphere reserves must fulfill three functions: conservation, development, and logistic support. Therefore, by its very definition of promoting both conservation ecosystems and fostering support of economic and human development, the designation would help advance a key objective of Chicago Wilderness, which is "to foster a sustainable relationship between society and nature in the region." The process to develop an application could lend support to existing efforts to integrate conservation of biodiversity into ongoing development and planning for land-use, transportation, and infrastructure. Although the designation carries no regulatory weight, it may motivate major land users to adopt practices that promote biodiversity and its sustainability.

Furthermore, the process of applying for biosphere reserve designation could trigger a healthy public debate about sustainability. Designation could draw new groups into efforts to evaluate the problem of urban sprawl. Likewise, by introducing fundamental questions about quality of life and racial equality into discussions about environmental matters in the region, a biosphere reserve designation could do much to enrich the quality of lives of the region's citizens.

Additionally, both the application process and official designation as a biosphere reserve could inspire greater participation in conservation by corporations and aid economic growth as the region further becomes and is recognized as an attractive place to live and work. It also may promote tourism to the region.

Also importantly, biosphere reserves are mechanisms for education programs and information sharing. If the greater Chicago region were to become a biosphere reserve, it would join a network of 425 biosphere reserves in 95 countries. As such, people and organizations working on improving sustainability and biodiversity conservation would have access to many others in the same line of work. The MAB program promotes the generation and sharing of new ideas, information, expertise, and personnel. The MAB program has produced several standardized databases containing information on flora and fauna. The people of Chicago would have access to this wealth of information and network of people to both learn from and to teach. This speaks to the type of collaboration that is at the heart of the Chicago Wilderness consortium and would further facilitate the spread of the urban conservation model and regional approach to ecosystem management.

ACKNOWLEDGMENTS

We thank the members of Chicago Wilderness and of its teams, along with the citizen scientists in the region. Collectively, they are the power behind this regional effort and the focus of this article.

REFERENCES

1. Sullivan, J. 1997. An Atlas of Biodiversity. Chicago Wilderness. Chicago, IL.
2. White, J. 1978. Illinois natural areas inventory technical report. Illinois Natural Areas Inventory. Urbana, IL.
3. Bowles, M.L. & J.L. McBride. 1996. Evaluation and classification of savanna, woodland, and barrens natural areas in northern Illinois. The Morton Arboretum. Lisle, IL.
4. Grossman, D.H., D. Faber-Langendoen, A.S. Weakly, *et al.* 1998. International Classification of Ecological Communities: Terrestrial Vegetation of the United States. Vol. I. The National Vegetation Classification System: Development, Status, and Applications. The Nature Conservancy. Arlington, VA.
5. Noss, R.F, E.T. LaRoe III & J.M. Scott. 1995. Endangered ecosystems of the United States: a preliminary assessment of loss and degradation. Biological Report 28. National Biological Service, US Department of the Interior. Washington, DC.
6. Noss, R.F. & R.L. Peters. 1995. Endangered ecosystems: a status report on Americans vanishing habitat and wildlife. Defenders of Wildlife. Washington, DC.
7. Gallup News Service, the Gallup Organization. 1999. US public worries about toxic waste, air and water pollution as key environmental threats. CNN/USA Today/Gallup Poll conducted March 12–14, 1999.
8. Belden and Russonello Research and Communications. 1996. Human Values and Nature's Future: Americans' Attitudes on Biological Diversity. Belden and Russonello Research and Communications. Washington, DC.
9. The Biodiversity Project. 1999. "Life. Nature. The Public. Making the Connection: A Biodiversity Communications Handbook." The Biodiversity Project. Madison, WI.
10. UNESCO. 1978. Final Report, Intergovernmental Conference on Environmental Education. Organized by UNESCO in cooperation with UNEP. Tbilisi, USSR. 14–26 October 1977. UNESCO ED/MD/49.

Application of the Biosphere Reserve Concept to Urban Areas

The Case of São Paulo City Green Belt Biosphere Reserve, Brazil—São Paulo Forest Institute: A Case Study for UNESCO

RODRIGO ANTONIO BRAGA MORAES VICTOR,[a]
JOAQUIM DE BRITTO COSTA NETO,[a] AZIZ NACIB AB'SÁBER,[b]
ONDALVA SERRANO,[a] MARISA DOMINGOS,[c]
BELY CLEMENTE CAMACHO PIRES,[a] MAURICIO AMAZONAS,[a]
AND MAURO ANTONIO MORAES VICTOR[a]

[a]*São Paulo Forest Institute, Department of the Environment, São Paulo, Brazil*

[b]*Department of Physical Geography, São Paulo University, São Paulo, Brazil*

[c]*Institute of Botany, Department of the Environment, São Paulo University, São Paulo, Brazil*

ABSTRACT: This report attempts to bring together contributions from technicians and scientists studying and dealing with the manifold aspects of the São Paulo City Green Belt Biosphere Reserve. It will highlight the understanding by UNESCO of the important role that biosphere reserves can play in the urban setting.

KEYWORDS: São Paulo City Green Belt Biosphere Reserve; São Paulo; Brazil; urban; environment; development; UNESCO

INTRODUCTION

Writing about the biosphere reserve is a daring task. Not because it is one of the most dynamic regions on the planet, with superlative population and a human history that dates back to before the discovery of Brazil, but above all because it is one of the greatest living laboratories ever known to humans,

This study was part of the Man and Biosphere (MAB) Program of UNESCO, São Paulo City Green Belt Biosphere Reserve (GBBR), Forest Institute State Department of the Environment, São Paulo, Brazil.

Address for correspondence: Rodrigo Antonio Braga Moraes Victor, São Paulo Forest Institute, Department of the Environment, São Paulo, Brazil.

Ann. N.Y. Acad. Sci. 1023: 237–281 (2004).
doi: 10.1196/annals.1319.012

involving a systemic structure characterized by essential relationships between a big city and its ecologically exuberant adjacencies.

The case study of the São Paulo City Green Belt Biosphere Reserve has planetary connotation. There is a clear worldwide trend, intensified during the 20th century, toward concentration of populations in and around urban areas, compounding any and all social and environmental problems that these zones have to face. This phenomenon has put into check the very conditions for life progress in the cities, especially big cities. Generation and disposal of waste, water and food supply, widespread pollution, and insalubrity of habitats seem to attract uncertainty rather than control.

Some findings have proved discouraging; we are destroying the urban and periurban environment we depend on before we even learn the basics of its functionality, and, worse, we are destroying its umbilical relationship with the city and its inhabitants. This scenario turns gloomy any prospects of habitability in the environment of big metropolises in the course of this century.

As to what should be done to counter this picture, we can say that every initiative is valuable. Research, implementation of rational public policies, socioenvironmental awareness, activism, planning, change of attitude, and great efforts to articulate people and institutions all are actions as efficient as they are enforceable.

The São Paulo City Green Belt Biosphere Reserve proposal has that in mind. In the absence of a jurisdiction in São Paulo's metropolitan region and adjacencies to act as a fomenter of policies and actions oriented to mitigate these issues, it is absolutely legitimate to assume that a biosphere reserve can make a contribution, especially if we understand that this is not a conventional and self-sufficient structure of environmental management.

On the contrary, the concept of a biosphere reserve in urban and periurban environments is increasingly being regarded by UNESCO as highly desirable, precisely because it addresses the socioenvironmental issue without competing with institutional prerogatives already undertaken by public and private organizations as well as civil corporations.

Indeed, the preparation of this document has a lot to do with this new understanding by UNESCO of the important role that biosphere reserves can play in the urban setting.

Launched in 2000, the Urban MAB program emerged from the verification that the urban and periurban environment is complex, packed with intricate cause-and-effect relations, retaining essential wealth for sustainable life in the cities.

At the worldwide level, it emerges as a forum suitable to combine existing efforts and promote initiatives for sustainable management of urban centers in years to come.

Bearing this in mind, we believe that biosphere reserves are suitable settings to implement strategic actions and, more specifically, that the São

Paulo City Green Belt Biosphere Reserve acts as a pilot project, very opportune in the urban MAB context.

A PANORAMA OF SÃO PAULO AND LARGE CITIES IN BRAZIL

São Paulo's metropolitan region occupies an area just under 0.1% of Brazil's surface and is home to more than 10% of its overall population, constituting today one of the planet's largest urban agglomerates. This concentration of population fits into a Latin American context characterized by intense increase in urban density during the 20th century.

In Brazil, the evolution of the urbanization process started to intensify in the early 20th century, being given a big boost as a result of industrialization during the second half of the century, according to TABLE 1.[1]

TABLE 1. Evolution of urban population in Brazil

Brazil	Approximate overall population	Population in cities
1940	70.0 million	26.3%: 18.8 million
1980	119.0 million	67.5%: 80.4 million
1990	146.8 million	75.5%: 110.9 million
2000	169.5 million	81.2%: 137.7 million

During this intense process, populations concentrated in large cities, with 13 metropolises boasting over one million inhabitants (São Paulo, Rio de Janeiro, Belo Horizonte, Porto Alegre, Recife, Salvador, Fortaleza, Brasília, Curitiba, Campinas, Belém, Goiânia, and Manaus). These cities are home to more than 30% of Brazil's overall population.[1]

City growth to assist some of the approximately 120 million inhabitants in the past 60 years, or 22 million inhabitants in the past decade alone, was governed by interests of the real estate market focused on urban areas with concentration of infrastructure, public services, and equipment and populated by high-income people, and by the continuous displacement of the poor to areas increasingly farther from consolidated urban areas.

The urban network expands through the sprawling of areas already urbanized and through "leap"[2] occupation, with new fronts being opened in faraway peripheries in the form of invasions and clandestine occupation, often installed in public areas, fountainhead areas under protection, and areas prone to flooding close to pollution sources that are at geological risk and environmentally vulnerable.

Urbanization advances centrifugally and predatorily over natural resources, thus creating (1) central areas of high density, resulting in serious environmental, health, and public safety problems; (2) peripheral areas with concentrated poverty, spatial segregation, pollution, violence and epidemics, to name a few; (3) intermediate areas with vast urban emptiness, oriented to real estate speculation and awaiting price increase as a result of public investments, which, in turn, originate in the struggle of the segregated portions of the population in faraway peripheries looking to create public services and equipment such as water and power supply, public roads, and transportation routes.

This process is compounded by the conurbation of several cities to form metropolises, where the central municipalities expand less than the peripheral districts, allowing peripheral areas to sprawl continuously and opening farther boundaries of environmental degradation, imposed on a variety of ecosystems, landscapes, and water resources.

True “illegal” cities are created by shantytowns and clandestine occupation, in several cases outstripping the regulated and legitimate cities in size.[1] Against this backdrop of social, economic, and environmental conflicts that these two city models reveal, the portion of the population unable to find alternatives to settle in the legitimate areas move on to swampland, mountain range slopes, islands, rivers, flooded bottomland, and areas at geotechnical risk.

To provide indicators for this current urban reality, we highlight the following excerpts from Maricato:[1]

> Concentration of income intensified in the eighties and nineties, (as TABLE 2[3] shows). This inequality not only resulted from reshuffling in production and retraction of social policies, as is the case of many central countries, it was also the aggravation of a society already unequal both historically and traditionally.
>
> One of the most expressive and conclusive indicators of deterioration in urban life conditions is the increase in violence to rates never experienced before in Brazilian metropolises. The national homicide rate (amount of homicides per 100 thousand inhabitants) in the late nineties was 24,10 […] 59 in São Paulo and 56 in Rio de Janeiro, in 1998 […]
>
> Taking 12 metropolitan regions, the central municipalities expanded by 3.1% in average between 1991 and 1996, whereas the peripheral municipalities expanded by 14.7%. Of these metropolises, the peripheries that expanded the most during this period were Belém (157.9%), Curitiba (28.2%), Belo Horizonte (20.9%), Salvador (18.1%), and São Paulo (16.3%).
>
> […] surveys carried out by the Department of Housing and Urban Development of São Paulo’s Municipal Government, classifying the situation and location of each shantytown base, revealed 763 bases in 1980 alone and 1592 bases in 1987.

TABLE 2. Income distribution: Brazil 1981 versus 1995

1981	1995
Poorer 50%: 14.5% of the income	Poorer 50%: 13.3% of the income
Richer 10%: 44.9% of the income	Richer 10%: 47.1% of the income
Richer 1%: 13.4% of the income	Richer 1%: 14.4% of the income

TABLE 3. Comparison of central area and periphery

	Central area	Periphery
Homicides per 100,000 inhabitants	14 on average	Up to 150
Total of unemployed (%)	5	18
Households equipped with sewer systems (%)	70	30
Households with piped water supply (%)	100, all official	70, mostly clandestine
Illiteracy rate (%)	3	20
Hospital beds per 100,000 inhabitants	530	180
Commuting time	40 min	2 h
Width of streets	6 m	2 m
Total no. of days/month with water shortage	0	7
Per capita annual income (in Brazilian reais)	15,300	2,600
Frequency of garbage collection	1 day	4 days

> The urbanization process comes as a machine producing shantytowns and threatening the environment.
>
> Expansion of the urban agglomerate in the period when the periphery produced around 180,000 ha of urbanized area, populated by 18 million inhabitants [...] The periphery is indeed a place where the poor live, it is socially segregated and land prices are low, and yet it is a mutating place, always reproduced in new stretches of land, whilst the old peripheries are gradually incorporated into the city, occupied by new residents and reorganized by capital [...].[4]

The above reality has been disseminated by the press. Take, for instance, thc cover story of *Veja* weekly magazine on January 24, 2001, entitled "Siege of the Periphery—middle-class districts compressed by a belt of poverty and criminality expanding six times as much as the central part of the metropolises." The same story shows contrasting findings[5] for central area as opposed to poorer areas, from estimates of eight Brazilian capital cities, including TABLE 3.

As far as Brazil is concerned, the São Paulo City Green Belt Biosphere Reserve (GBBR-SP) constitutes the greatest and best representing example of the conflicts arising from the industrialization and "metropolization" process, whether for the magnitude or the diversity of problems. The transformation of the landscape within the huge territory it occupies, comprising 73 municipalities, is characterized by opposition between massive predatory urban sprawl and conservation of the huge natural, cultural, and economical heritage represented by the large stretch of Atlantic Forest and associated ecosystems it comprises, as well as historical use of the land for horticulture and dairy farming to supply the metropolis, favored by proximity and ease of transport.

The operations to introduce the São Paulo City Green Belt Biosphere Reserve constitute important transformation vectors of this reality in the medium to long run. The continuous and progressive involvement of the communities occupying the Green Belt areas, who are subject to this immensely degrading pattern of growth, should definitely contribute to revert and invert this picture in the long run for reconstruction of the metropolitan environment on a sustainable basis, allowing the population to lead a healthy life while co-existing with a well-preserved natural heritage.

These actions will be reinforced by the advancing social fight for urban renovation and recovery of constructed urban environments, the fundamental principles of which being involvement and actual participation of the communities affected by the critical problems mentioned above, and the search for solutions for the city's entire territory rather than the territory occupied by the higher ranks of society only.

The Statute of the City, Federal Law 10257 dated October 7, 2001, is an example of this fight for new tools to secure community participation in the decision-making process concerning urban renovation.

There are two main movements potentially integrating with each other to render feasible the necessary transformation for a sustainable metropolis:

- The Green Belt Biosphere Reserve, with actions rooted in the peripheral communities and moving toward the urbanized central areas, affording maintenance of the benefits provided by large stretches of native forest remnants, water resource areas and other natural resources, and also by areas of food production, whether in the Green Belt or on the coast.
- Urban renovation, with actions rooted in the communities affected by critical urban problems, affording recovery of life conditions in the urban environment, reconstructing it with the help of optimized use of energy resources, land reshuffling, reduction and extinction of social/spatial segregation, recovery of water resources and areas with water infiltration in the soil, as well as implementation of public policies addressing public transport, housing, health, basic sanitation, environmental protection, and education to reach the population at large.

THE SÃO PAULO CITY GREEN BELT BIOSPHERE RESERVE

The São Paulo City Green Belt Biosphere Reserve was recognized by UNESCO on June 9, 1994 as an integral part of the Atlantic Forest Biosphere Reserve. It comprises an area of 1,540,032 ha, totaling 1,760,311 ha if we include the urban area. This area comprises 73 municipalities.

Forested Mountain Ranges Involving São Paulo Hills

The technical and scientific argumentation that afforded the creation of a biosphere reserve in the forested scarps of Serra do Mar and small mountain ranges discontinuously surrounding São Paulo Plateau involves a set of ecological and environmental facts. Serra do Mar is a unique instance of tropical scarps covered by biodiverse pluvial forests, important to the whole planet. Likewise, the forested mountain ranges surrounding São Paulo Plateau, with its metropolitan region boasting impressive dynamics of spatial growth, force environmentalists and ecologists to participate in a permanent campaign for integrated preservation, that is, preservation of the biodiverse ecosystems and ecological support to the entire forestal system, depressions, and watering places in them.

Spatial arrangement in the biosphere reserve extending from the Serra da Cantareira mountain range up to Serra do Mar mountain range and Baixada Santista lowland boasts a set of very differing strips and areas. In addition, the nucleus of the target area involves the metropolitan organism of one of the world's largest and most troubled cities. The existing contrasts within the biosphere reserve are so great and opposing that they call for customized characterization, from the coastal strip and lowland up to Serra do Mar and through the hills and small mountain ranges of São Paulo Plateau.

On the coastal strip of Santos-São Vicente, Guarujá, and Praia Grande, leisure-oriented urbanization was so intensive that it neutralized any action to protect this entire sector of the biosphere reserve. In the most intensive area of Baixada Santista-Vicentina, the mangrove ecosystems call for protection while they are still free from predatory anthropic actions (landfills, "edging" made by degrading barriers, especially in the internal borders of Canal de Bertioga and low valley of Itapanhaú river).

The few remnants of mangrove in the Santos estuary and interior lowland of São Vicente must be compulsorily preserved, regardless of any expectations from speculators and invaders. In sandy strips of the sandbank plains, overcrowded with beach and coastal urbanization, there is little we can do to protect whatever biodiversity there is left. With difficulty, we could find reasonable stretches of the Jundús ecosystem toward the interior sandbank plains of Bertioga, where there are still reasonable spaces to establish a "Jundú park," subject to dispossession and strong peripheral management.

Past the interior coastal lowlands comes a rich natural heritage consisting of the forested tropical scarps of Serra do Mar. Here, integrated protection has legal backing of a preservation order, to the extent that from the scarps' piedmont through the top (780–1,100 meters), the entire ecological/orographic space has to be compulsorily protected. The implementation of Cubatão's industrial complex in the 1960s created serious anomalies in the subarea of Paranapiacaba da Serra. The construction of Anchieta Highway, connecting coastline to plateau, caused the occupation of platforms and quotas on the relief along the middle and low part of the mountain range: this was initiated before the preservation order statute was promulgated. The most insidious thing, however, is the fact that the so-called "quota districts" continue to grow and become denser before the very eyes of compliant municipal and state authorities, who are culturally unprepared and incompetent to take into account negative physical, ecological, and social impacts.

The tragic events that took place in Serra do Mar's subarea Piassagüera-Cubatão fully illustrate the incomprehension and technical/scientific ignorance of some administrators only seeking reelection. Recently, some illegal and criminal attempts have been verified to set up real property developments in the mountain range's piedmont, starting a new chapter in the progress of guided predation.

Past the mountain range's top, with the differing physiographic components of São Paulo Plateau, verifying the preservation potential in the total area of the biosphere reserve becomes impossible. The hills, which serve as urban site for the metropolis, extend over 2,400 km^2 from Itapevi Barueri and beyond Mogi das Cruzes.

The furthermost peripheries expand toward the northwest between Serra da Cantareira and Jaraguá, over the hills and the once forested low elevations. Toward the north, they expand up to the foot of Cantareira. To the east, they expand to the hills, fluvial terraces, and lowland plains well placed in front of highways, roads, and central areas of old suburbs. Toward the south, they expand up to the undulated hills and mount platforms, streamlet margins, and fountainheads transposed by urban sprawl. Toward the south/southwest, they expand beyond Santo Amaro/Interlagos and reservoir margins. Toward the southwest, they expand to Taboão da Serra/Campo Limpo and Capão Redondo, always crossing extremely poor districts, and toward the west, beyond Cotia and Embu vicinities.

This urbanized complex of enormous size appears in recent satellite images (spectrum band 3-4-5) as a purplish shade, which documents the fantastic pollution dome above the local troposphere, observing that the green shade of the small mountain ranges is noticeable, while Cantareira woods come as an unclear green shade differing largely from the bright color of Morro Grande.

The set of parks scattered around the metropolis is absolutely insufficient in terms of biodiversity and open public space for permanent use. Some old subcentral parks of São Paulo, including Parque da Luz, Siqueira Campos, Buenos Aires, and Aclimação, remain with a degree of forestation that seems to have preserved biodiversity. Other parks, including Parque Dom Pedro and Anhangabaú, are deprived of their old arboreal biomass due to the interlacing of overpasses, underpasses, and open landscaping over large cemented plates. The most extraordinary and important metropolitan park in the City, Ibirapuera, was installed after a modern and creative landscaping project that forcefully had to discard biodiversity, even if relatively. However, all of them—whether boasting great arboreal diversity or extensive lawns, small lakes, or functional facilities—had to be surrounded by fences to close or partially close at nightfall, for reasons anyone can understand. The campus of São Paulo University and the Butantã Institute have managed to maintain an excellent degree of forestation with intervals of biodiversity. What is left in district parks and gardens is very reduced and insufficient considering the increased levels of density and verticalization within the confines of the expanded inner metropolis.

The most noteworthy remainder of biodiversity isolated in São Paulo's immense urban sprawl is Água Funda woods, a unique case of tropical plateau forest left in the middle of a metropolis and subject to the pressure of uncontrollable spatial constructivism. We note, however, that because of matters of comfort and abstention from land buying, administrative authorities of the past authorized some construction works for functionality in the periphery of this large network of biodiverse forests, showing lamentable ecological and environmental ignorance, irrespective of the fact that none of the institutions set up there are at fault, considering their cultural and administrative importance (Department of Agriculture, Geological Institute, etc.).

In great contrast with the scattered arboreal masses and open public spaces that surround São Paulo's inner metropolis, the situation of these immense spaces extending from the intermediary metropolis up to the poor peripheries of the outer metropolis reveal remarkable complexity and insufficiency. In the confines of the expanded inner metropolis lie small eucalyptus groves, unused tracts of land awaiting prices to go up and poorly kept little squares. We should point to some school patios built in former cultural times and deserving permanent care and protection against unqualified predation.

As we move away from the intermediary belt, the lack of forested open public spaces becomes dramatic owing to poverty, rusticity, and negligence. In these poor peripheries, competition for small leisurely space is commonplace. Children and adolescents use small earthen fields to play soccer on Saturdays, Sundays, and holidays. The areas used usually are owned by private people, companies, or local government. Often, however, the owners decide to build or subdivide the plots they own, thus barring any possibility of leisure in such tracts of land. In hilly areas boasting quieter streets, children and teenagers partially close the street by placing small portable bars to play.

History

Urban Sprawl in São Paulo's Metropolitan Region

In the early 19th century, the city occupied some valleys and lowland plains (prone to flooding), gradually expanding over the intermediary 740-meter platform embraced by the internal confluence angle of Tamanduateí and Anhangabaú rivers.

São Paulo's urban development and demographic growth may be understood to the extent that Brazil's economy evolves, taking as a reference the expansion of coffee plantations and, later in 1930, the beginning of the industrialization process in the southwest.

Urban sprawl is a spatial expression of the metropolization process, which resulted from demographic growth in São Paulo City from the late 19th century until World War II. From the 1940s onward, a process of metropolitan hypertrophy developed, leading to horizontal and vertical expansion.

From the late 19th century until early the next century, the growth of São Paulo was directly connected with European immigration and based on coffee plantations.

The advance of coffee plantations inland the state of São Paulo prompted the need to introduce the railroads that brought the benefits of the coffee economy to the capital, thus accelerating the urbanization process.

The city spread around its historical center where commercial and financial activities concentrated, while residential developments were distributed diffusely around the city center and often intertwined, and suburban districts and industrial plants concentrated alongside the railway lines.

Between 1930 and 1945, the coffee oligarchy gradually yielded its political power, with an ample industrialization policy following from World War II. The concentration of capital and labor in São Paulo reflected in the metropolization process and in the gradual occupation of land associated with economic interests. American attempts to open new markets in São Paulo caused the urbanization to be dependent on industrial and financial influences.

The metropolitan expansion started in 1950, with occupation of vast suburban areas, increased density in areas already urbanized and intense vertical growth. The urban sprawl started to incorporate Santo André, São Bernardo, São Caetano do Sul, Osasco, Santo Amaro, consubstantiating the first "conurbations" ever. In the 1950s, main public roads started to complement railroads, leading to expanded urbanization.

The services sector also expanded inordinately during that decade, with a fast-paced expansion of the city from 1930 through 1980.

With all this extraordinary development, São Paulo faced the first physical obstacles in the 1970s, expanding beyond the sedimentary basin to the pre-

Cambrian crystalline rocks. It extended to the mountains in the southeast, southwest, west, and northwest, and to the bodies of water in the south. Toward the northwest and west, the urban sprawl has more penetration in the direction of Campinas and Vale do Paraíba.

Despite all limitations to the growth of São Paulo, the expansion soon reached areas that ran serious risks of urbanization.

With an average annual increase of 5.5%, São Paulo's population was expected to reach 21 million in the 21st century. This has not happened because of a decrease in this rate. Still, it is expected to come to 21.2 million in 2015, according to UNO.

The fast-paced growth of São Paulo metropolis along with the expansion of industrialization originated a series of problems in the context of such gigantism, including infrastructure unsuitable for vertical growth, population driven to move horizontally, deficient means of mass transportation, basic sanitation, and lighting.

São Paulo's urban sprawl was processed through the occupation of land along the main means of penetration, connecting the industrial area to markets and sources of raw material. As this process gradually gathered momentum, the industry-based economy spread its new tentacles in all directions.

The expansion process extended south and southeast, advancing further to water reservoirs and finally reaching Itapecerica da Serra. Through the valley of Tamanduateí river it merged with São Caetano do Sul, Santo André, Mauá, São Bernardo do Campo, and Diadema. On the east–west axis, bordering Tietê river, the urbanization expanded to Mogi das Cruzes from Itapevi. On the right banks of the river, the built-up area spread from Pirituba in the west to Arujá in the northwest.

The industrial expansion marched along Via Anchieta, reaching Cubatão and Piaçaguera. Similarly, the industrial expansion in Baixada Santista advanced through the Alto Tietê valley, reaching Mogi das Cruzes toward Paraíba valley. Another expansion tentacle was noticed along Anhanguera Highway in the direction of Campinas.

Companies were trying to find low-priced land to set up, forcing factories out of the expensive areas and causing them to settle in the periphery of Greater São Paulo. The old industrial districts surrounding the urban network shifted to mixed districts and ended up as residential districts predominantly.

This process of horizontal expansion in the urbanization of Greater São Paulo has been a continuous process, especially in recent decades.

As industrial plants shift to the periphery, the proletariat too is compelled to follow suit, just as companies are relocated, land prices go up, and one- and two-story houses are pulled down to give way to apartment buildings for the middle class. Businesses too, bound to be near the city center, begin to occupy these areas, offering services such as medical and dental clinics, offices, and engineering companies.

TABLE 4. Vegetation covering in São Paulo's metropolitan region

Type of covering 1973: metropolitan area									
Woods[a]		Undergrowth[b] (capoeira)		Open country		Reforestation		Total	
Area/ha	%	Area/ha	%	Area/ha	%	Area/ha	%	Area/ha	%
126,160	15.67	137,910	17.13	2,420	0.03	58,370	7.25	324,860	40.35

[a]Primitive woods.
[b]Degraded primitive woods.

A City That Devours the Periurban Green Belt

In this continuous expansion of the city toward the periphery, the city devours its natural resources, green tissue, soil, water, air, and signs of the primitive site. At the start of the century, the old São Paulo province had 250,000 inhabitants only and the urbanized area between Tietê and Pinheiros rivers was under 4,000 ha, wrapped by a vigorous green belt, according to Usteri, who conducted the survey by unresourceful means (on mule's back). In 1973, an aerophotogrammetric survey revealed an anarchic, growing metropolis in the middle of a conurbation process, with no respect for life scale and surrounded by a relatively preserved green belt. In 1995, the fast-paced metastatic process advanced to critical and sensitive areas of the Green Belt, unable to hold back at natural obstacles and features such as the water catchment areas in the southeast supplying the city, the crystalline abrupt slopes of Serra da Cantareira in the north, and Serra de Itapeti massif to the west. Today, the dynamic of urban sprawl escapes official control, though its area definitely exceeds 300,000 ha and is home to 16,800,000 inhabitants.

The aerophotographic survey of 1973 characterized the Green Belt as shown in TABLE 4, defining the periurban areas of São Paulo's metropolitan region:

Based on authorizations for tree cutting granted by the State Department of the Environment, it is possible to estimate the destruction of the Atlantic Forest between 1973 and 1989, when Landsat-5 satellite picture was taken.

This destruction is estimated at 6,000,000 m^2/year, equivalent to two soccer fields a day, and from there we can calculate the fall in the Green Area Index per inhabitant. Although in 1973 the forestal area per 9,000,000 inhabitants was 324,440 ha, in 1989 it shifted to 294,315 ha per 16,800,000 inhabitants, indicating that said index decreased from 0.036 ha/inhabitant to 0.017 ha/inhabitant, which means less than half in metropolitan terms, a critical index. The concern of this study is precisely to know what the index will be in the 21st century to reverse this destructive trend.

From 1989 to 1990, there are no elements to measure deterioration in the Green Belt and metropolitan region of São Paulo, though we know empirically that the destruction continues at alarming rates. The municipality of São Paulo is a good indicator, and to a certain degree it can be extrapolated to neighboring districts. In 13 years, it lost 30% of its green tissue (from 1986 to 1999), the worst affected areas being water catchment areas (Billings and Guarapiranga) and ascents of Serra da Cantareira, with 142 examples of invasion and clandestine land occupation.

Genesis of the Biosphere Reserve

The creation of the Green Belt Biosphere Reserve is mapped by important facts: militant citizens from historical NGOs, such as OIKOS União dos Defensores da Terra (OIKOS Earth Defenders Union), SOS Mata Atlântica (SOS Atlantic Forest), etc., were disillusioned and frustrated by failed attempts to fight for the environmental cause, and, despite the profuse and prolix internal legislation, the environmental battle often ended in failure. This was a period of agitation just before Rio-92, with a widespread idea that with the internationalization of economy and information in the modern world, the environment too should be internationalized.

Brazil was emerging from the heavy days of military regime, where the whole environmental issue had gathered strength as the only form of critical reflection allowed.

Likewise, a sense of citizenship involving different levels of awareness and perception was building up, there being a considerable faction of environmental militants and activists identifying with the principles defended by Thoreau, the father of American civil disobedience, true opposer of the single-minded view of a mighty establishment and no control over the citizens' conscience.

Multilateral development agencies such as IDB and IBRD often have lent substantial sums for antisocial and antidemocratic projects in the Third World involving environmental degradation. These views and behavior began to be strongly opposed to in foreign countries, with American environmentalist Bruce Rich of the Environmental Defense Fund in Washington being one of note for his critical and consistent action against this state of affairs.

Next, the community developed a conviction that alliances and international partnerships should be created to deter these exogenous predatory forces. At first glance, the north zone community surrounding Serra da Cantareira was highly successful in suspending the IDB funding that was about to destroy the districts along Tremembé streamlet and expose the abrupt slopes of Cantareira, ultimately leading to uncontrolled invasion.

The proposal of President Collor de Mello (1989) concretely opened an outlet in federal legislation for the desired international articulation:

> The National Department of the Environment in cooperation with the Ministry of Foreign Affairs and support from research agencies and environmental bod-

> ies shall promote the studies and actions necessary for the remnants of Atlantic Forest to be declared a Biosphere Reserve by UNESCO.

These were the main elements that resulted in the GBBR declaration detailed below.

This scenario would be incomplete without the enormous receptivity of the São Paulo Forest Institute regarding this conservationist and sustainable proposal, because it has been for a century the precursor of actions and concepts involving the protection of Brazil's environmental and human heritage.

Citizenship Action and Resistance

In a country where the collective memory has been neglected, if not deliberately erased, it is critical to understand the efforts of a collectivity to protect their common heritage.

The history of protection to the city's green belt emerges as one of the most beautiful pages of Brazilian environmentalism and deserves to be rescued through some most outstanding facts.

Suspension of IDB Funding (Interamerican Development Bank)

In 1986, the municipal administration of Jânio Quadros, once the president of Brazil, obtained external loans from IDB for its program to canalize valley-bottom streamlets and construct express highways. This program included Tremembé streamlet, which grows from the foot of Serra da Cantareira, in its south side. The community realized that these works would be exposing the Cantareira massif to voracious real estate speculation and uncontrollable clandestine invasions. All administrative and legal jurisdictions in the country were contacted in vain. As far as the establishment was concerned, "the decision to get on with the construction works was final, even more so because foreign money was already on its way." Then a fierce battle began, nationwide and worldwide, to try and revert the situation. The community wrote a well-justified study of environmental, social, and cultural impacts involved, and IDB inspectors were asked to assess the situation in person. At the same time, an arch of alliances between NGOs in Brazil and abroad was articulated. In Brazil, they involved organizations such as OIKOS União dos Defensores da Terra, Pantanal Alerta Brasil, and Conselho Comunitário Santana-Tucuruvi, initial nucleus of the Friends of the São Paulo City Green Belt Biosphere Reserve Association, backed by the Church through charismatic cardinal Dom Paulo Evaristo Arns, a leader in the defense of human rights. Abroad, 17 international NGOs were mobilized under the coordination of the Environmental Defense Fund headquartered in Washington. That way, IDB officers were directly informed of the truth of facts and the American Senate itself, through its external loans committee, also demanded from IDB faithful compliance with the loan's contractual provisions, which were being continuously violated. Finally, on December 3, 1989, a commission of six IDB experts from Washington met with the community in the auditorium of Jornal da Tarde, in O Estado de São Paulo newspaper building, for one of the most outstanding democratic episodes that Brazil had ever witnessed, a country only just emerging from the military regime: a true public hearing between financing source and affected community. Once violation of Brazil's environmental legislation and violence against the affected population had been verified, the decision was fulminant: the loans to build the highway attempting against population rights were blocked. As for the Rodoanel works under way, Brazilian NGOs already have warned the IDB about the studies' inconsistency as well as the environmental crimes.

Suspension of IBRD Funding–The World Bank

In June 1989, the state government body launched the Metropolitan Perimetral Road project (VPM), known today as the Rodoanel. The project directly affected the heart of Cantareira massif, colliding with important water resources supplying the city, with thousands of residents being affected throughout. Again the government tried to get international loans, this time urging the World Bank to act. The widely known RIMA factories produced a technical study to justify the works and the government repeatedly opened public bidding for contractors to execute the job.

Once again the community proved resistant, prompting practically the same arch of alliances as above.

Several envoys were sent to the World Bank denouncing the irregularity of the process, ultimately leading this multilateral development agency to step back.

Without external funding, the initiative gradually lost momentum and political timeliness, causing entrepreneurs to retreat for good.

The Biosphere Reserve Campaign

In reality, the popular campaign against the Rodoanel developed in two dimensions strategically integrated: on one side the suspension of funding, on the other side, widespread national and international mobilization pleaded with UNESCO for the creation of the São Paulo Green Belt Biosphere Reserve. For 2 years, 150,000 signatures were collected for creation of the Reserve and suspension of the Rodoanel works. The petition reads:

> We, undersigned, manifest our opposition to São Paulo's Metropolitan Perimetral Road Project due to the impact it will have on the city's human and environmental heritage. We plead for the remainder of Atlantic Forest in the metropolitan area to be declared humankind heritage and a Biosphere Reserve, assuming that this action must begin with Serra da Cantareira, today more than ever under threat.

The campaign for the region to be declared a Reserve was one of São Paulo's most expressive civil movements, with the population being mobilized in the face of constant threats to its natural heritage, especially regarding the Metropolitan Perimetral Road works, known today as Rodoanel. Through the Forest Institute, the Department of the Environment undertook the plea and submitted the petition to UNESCO, finally including the São Paulo Green Belt Biosphere Reserve in the Worldwide Network of Biosphere Reserves.

A Perfectly Legal Act

While certain sectors try to disqualify the image of the biosphere reserve by way of casuist reasoning and argumentation, note that its creation is a perfectly legal act, having fully complied with the formalities necessary for the granting of the International Diploma. The basic study was formulated by widely renowned scientists of the Forest Institute and São Paulo Department of the Environment, headed by a UNO consultant charged with the formulation of Agenda 21. It was endorsed by well-respected NGO leaderships working in the environmental area and backed by 150,000 citizens as explained before, also underwritten by São Paulo's local government, being submitted to the Brazilian Committee for the Man and Biosphere Program[6] (COBRAMaB) in Brasília, a jurisprudence of the federal government. Once at COBRAMaB, the plea was analyzed for several months by Brazil's Planning Ministry, Itamarati, Ministry of Foreign Affairs, IBAMA, Environment Ministry, Ministry of Science and Technology, CNPq1, and the National Academy of Sciences. After being unanimously approved, it was also submitted to MaB-UNESCO, where, after strict analysis by competent bodies in Paris, it was awarded the diploma in June 1994, being automatically enforced thereon by international treaties and agreements, of which Brazil is a subscriber.

São Paulo's Forest Institute took the initiative to produce the technical studies that were to support the society's claims. It therefore is very clear that the biosphere reserve resulted from a legitimate, genuine, and deeply popular movement rather than from mere academic enterprise.

The Atlantic Forest and Its Associated Ecosystems: Importance of the Atlantic Forest Worldwide

The Hotspot–Atlantic Forest[7]

The "hotspot" concept was created in 1988 by Dr. Norman Myers, establishing 10 critical areas of conservation worldwide. This strategy was adopted by Conservation International to set priorities for its preservation programs, and by the John D. and Catherine T. MacArthur Foundation. In 1996, a new study led by Conservation International's president Dr. Russell A. Mittermeier improved Myers' initial theory, identifying 17 hotspots.

TABLE 5. Atlantic Forest diversity and endemism

Diversity of species		Diversity		Endemism		
Group	Planet's total	Total of species	Diversity (ranking)	Endemic species	Ranking and % of endemic species	Ratio (nonendemic/ endemic)
Mammals	4,809	261	7th	160	2nd (61.3%)	0.6/1
Birds	9,881	620	10th	73	12th (11.8%)	7.5/1
Reptiles	7,828	200	10th	60	13th (30.0%)	2.3/1
Amphibians	4,780	280	4th	253	3rd (90.4%)	0.1/1
Total	27,298	1,361	7th	546	6th (40.1%)	1.49/1
Plants	300,000	20,000	5th	6,000	7th (30.0%)	2.3/1

Recent studies conducted with the help of more than 100 specialists have amplified and updated this approach. After 4 years of analysis, the group of scientists established 25 current hotspots.

The Atlantic Forest ranks among the top five in the hotspots list. The mammals, birds, reptiles, and amphibians found there total 1,361 species, 567 of which are endemic, representing 2% of all species on the planet, only for these groups of vertebrates (TABLES 5 and 6).

The Implacable Devastation of the Biome in the Past 500 Years[8]

> The Atlantic Forest once occupied 1,290,000 km^2 of Brazilian territory. The impacts of different cycles of exploitation as well as concentration of large cities and industrial complexes caused the natural vegetation to be drastically reduced.

Brazil's occupation process caused this biome to have its original vegetation covering drastically reduced, scattered nowadays along the Brazilian coastline and inland the southern regions of Goiás and Mato Grosso do Sul states as well as inland the states of the Northeast.

Declared by UNESCO Humankind Heritage due to its natural importance, the remnants of Brazilian Atlantic Forest are part of the Earth's Biosphere Reserves (MAB Program).

Strategic Importance of the Green Belt Biosphere Reserve

Designed to ensure a sustainable city, the Green Belt Biosphere Reserve has a critical role, whether by its geopolitical position or its mission/view that implies profound changes in the way the community thinks and acts, to the

TABLE 6. Atlantic Forest ranking among 25 planet hotspots

Hotspots: richest and most endangered regions on the planet	Vascular plant diversity	Vascular plant endemism
1. Tropical Andes	45,000	20,000
2. Sundaland (Indonesia)	26,000	15,000
3. Mediterranean	25,000	13,000
4. Madagascar and Indian Ocean Islands	12,000	9,704
5. Atlantic Forest	20,000	8,000
6. Indo-Burma Area	13,500	7,000
7. Caribbean	12,000	7,000
8. Philippines	7,620	5,832
9. Cape Floristic Province	8,200	5,682
10. Mesoamerica	24,000	5,000
11. Savannah	10,000	4,400
12. Australia Southeast	5,469	4,331
13. China Center–South Mountains	12,000	3,500
14. Polynesia and Micronesia Islands	6,557	3,334
15. New Caledonia	3,332	2,551
16. Choco-Darien/Western Equator	9,000	2,250
17. Guinea Forests/Western Africa	9,000	2,250
18. Western Ghats (India) and Sri Lanka	4,780	2,180
19. California Floristic Province	4,426	2,125
20. Karoo Region of Succulent Plants	4,849	1,940
21. New Zealand	2,300	1,825
22. Central Chile	3,429	1,605
23. Caucasus	6,300	1,600
24. Wallacea (Indonesia)	10,000	1,500
25. Eastern Arch Mountains	4,000	1,500
Endemism total		133,499
Global diversity percentage (300,000 vascular plants)		44.5%

extent that it will inevitably bring about changes in development patterns and in people's lifestyle. Within this context, the network of conservation units owned by the Forest Institute, under special ruling and fully backed by the state, will be the centralizers and irradiators of this transformation.

As regards participative management, note that the Green Belt Biosphere Reserve came to life already under this influence, with the plea of over 100,000 citizens to be institutionalized. Along the same lines and in partnership with the Forest Institute, UNESCO sponsored Green Belt Biosphere Reserve Management Seminar I, held at the Biosphere Reserves' headquarters in 1994, convening various and multiple agents interacting in the process, who reached a clear consensus over the systems and methods of management of the Green Belt Biosphere Reserve. A Biosphere Reserve Transient Committee was elected democratically during this meeting for the chief purpose of proposing a management model. This transient committee discharged from its mission satisfactorily, delivering a body of very articulate rules and concepts that were submitted to São Paulo's Executive for analysis and edition of the relevant deeds in 1995.

Because of bureaucratic and political problems, the subject did not get ahead, though with new management at the State Section of the Environment Ministry, promises are that our plea will definitely be formalized.

BENEFITS AND THREATS TO THE GREEN BELT

Importance and Identity of the São Paulo City Green Belt

Most biosphere reserves around the globe consist of worldwide important ecosystems, integrated with equally significant human and cultural contexts. In Brazil, COBRAMAB adopted and implemented a policy to establish one large biosphere reserve as per biome, in such a way that every major formation and vegetation province in the country could be integrated with the World Network of Biosphere Reserves. The criterion to establish the GBBR did not exactly follow this guideline. Although its area is entirely composed of ecosystems of the so-called "Atlantic Forest Domain" and although the Green Belt itself is an integral part of the Atlantic Forest Biosphere Reserve, its conception was based on a specific thematic feature (it surrounds a metropolis) rather than on a biome per se.

Thus, the Green Belt's greatest asset resides in the environmental goods and services of its ecosystems. Ultimately, these goods and services can turn life in the metropolis feasible or unfeasible and determine the degree of quality of life of the populations involved (TABLE 7).

Threats to the Green Belt According to New Observations, Scientific Advances, and Current Relevance of Topics Considering the Current World Crises

To provide a counterpoint to the aforesaid benefits, the threats to the GB are enormous and, to a large extent, very particular. The most important are (1) urban growth and real estate speculation, (2) infrastructure works, (3) air

TABLE 7. Synthesis of main environmental goods and services associated with the Green Belt

Name of environmental goods/services	Description/importance of environmental goods/services
Water availability and maintenance	The resources within the GB supply water to 19 million people. If they are endangered, the entire supply can collapse.
Climate regulation	The GB is directly related to climate mitigation in the region, having implications for the comfort of the population, energy matrix, rain, etc.
Stabilization of hillsides and other sensitive areas	Fight against soil erosion, minimization of floods, and public calamities
CO_2 sequestration and pollutant buffering	The GB has 311,407 ha of capoeira, a growing vegetation that plays an important part in sequestration of CO_2 generated by the metropolis. In addition, the forests are an important physical barrier against the advance of pollutants. All this has global and local impacts, including public health.
Biodiversity	The Atlantic Forest is one of the Planet's most biodiverse biomes, so maintaining its biological abundance is an ethical duty of the population and, in many ways, a protection to the very biological safety of human beings.
Potential scientific discoveries	The Atlantic Forest is a source of discoveries to man's advantage, including production of medicines and economically valuable substances.
Food safety	Today, 10% of the world's food is produced in backyards and small land tracts (Ian Douglas, University of Manchester, 2002, personal communication). The GB has this tradition and today is one of the country's top organic produce regions (sustainability). Besides, the choice of agriculture in periurban areas is regarded as an alternative to the sprawl of big cities.
Social use	Metropolises such as São Paulo and Santos lack green areas. The GB is often the only choice people have to be in contact with the natural environment. This is crucial for humanization as well as for the physical and psychological health of the population.
A safe haven for history and cultural heritage	The GB witnessed important passages of Brazil's history before and after the discovery, retaining vestiges of this popular memory and immortalizing it.
Opportunities to generate income and fight extreme poverty	Finally, the GB is one of the last intact places capable of generating a sustainable and quality economy. Practices such as organic food produce, eco-tourism, and sustainable management could be essential alternatives for a recessive economy, helping to fight extreme poverty in several communities.

pollution, (4) clearance of the ground by fire and extraction of forest goods, (5) deficient public and private administration, (6) land regulation, (7) insufficient environmental awareness, (8) urban waste, (9) mining, and (10) industrial deconcentration.

Destruction of the Green Belt and Decline in the Quality of Life

From 1986 to 1999, São Paulo destroyed 30% of its green tissue according to a survey by the Department of the Environment (FAPESP–Research, Dec. 2000, No. 60). The number of green areas per inhabitant is internationally regarded as a quality of life index. In our case, the increase in heat islands, decrease in urban thermal comfort, increase in floods as a result of lessened absorption of rainwater and sedimentation of the drainage network, and alteration in the recharge of underground aquifers and consequently in the useful life of water catchment areas supplying the city all are indicators. Removing nature and replacing it with a "second nature" intensely degraded and altered affects the citizens' physical and mental health. The role of green areas in air decontamination is critical.

The Green Belt and the Heat Islands. It has been scientifically proved that the Green Belt surrounding the metropolis is a powerful climate stabilizer because it prevents heat islands from advancing toward the periphery. This implies complex synergy between the city's living organism and its green belt, affecting several natural mechanisms that involve thermal, water, and energy balance, with strong implications for the economy and public health.

Technicians from INMET (National Meteorology Institute) and Climatempo affirmed that there is strong scientific evidence that the heat islands of the overheated metropolis are accountable for the high precipitation in the city center because of localized factors such as low pressure and convective drafts. This means that the metropolis attracts excessive and widespread precipitation, generating increasingly more and far-reaching floods. As a counterpoint, in the Green Belt, where temperatures are pleasant, there is less precipitation, precisely where fountainheads and water catchment areas are. Unbalance becomes evident.

Destruction of the Green Belt Biosphere Reserve and the Flood Phenomenon. The flood phenomenon in São Paulo's metropolitan region has a well-known genesis: removal of primitive vegetation covering (happening fast, according to official sources); soil impermeability; increased amounts of rain in the city; change in rain patterns leading to magnetic storms with lightning, electric sparks, and hail, in other words, more water in less time; less transit of water in the soil, now impermeable; water seeks drainage network with more speed. This is how the flood phenomenon is potentiated, because some rivers have suffered deep disturbances and changes after classic rectification, channeling and very often "burial" (complete immurement). The mud resulting from exposed soil obstructs channeling. The classic technology they sell to us, whether curative or palliative, is also very well known: regulating barriers upstream; deepening riverbeds, which for Tietê river alone already cost more than US$500 million and is still unfinished; removal of 300 trucks of sediment a day from the bed of these rivers at a cost of US$6.3 million/year; construction of large water outlet pools at a cost of US$5 million each. We estimate that, to attenuate floods, more than a hundred large outlet pools are required in São Paulo.

Official surveys estimate that to keep floods under control in the city will cost US$3.3 billion.

There is a direct relation between removal of green, impermeable drainage network, and blockage or obstruction of water infiltration. In other words, less green, more outlet pools. A classic example is the basin of Aricanduva streamlet, a tributary of Tietê river, 30 km long, located in the east zone of the capital. In 1955, technical agencies of the municipal government identified 12 million square meters of green areas or free areas under the influence of this basin and suggested five large outlet pools to withhold a million cubic meters of water.

In 1999, these green and free areas were reduced to half, that is, 6 million square meters. The result is another eight large pools for Aricanduva basin, totaling 13 similar works in the region, according to a Macrodrainage Master Plan for Alto Tietê Hydrographic Basin devised by the government of the state.[9]

We must agree that destruction of the GBBR will encourage urban sprawl, inducing overheat and more anomalous rain, overload of the already oversaturated power matrix, soil impermeability, disturbance in natural hydrologic mechanisms, rupture of delicate flows and natural synergies, potentiating the aforesaid flood phenomenon.

Environmental Health and Human Health

"*A Sick City Generates Sick Children.*" A recent trial sponsored by UNESCO MaB Program (Man and Biosphere) in partnership with the Forest Institute/GBBR has put this delicate issue into perspective. Public health specialists warn that pollution is highly incident as the cause of death of a substantial portion of São Paulo's population, especially people suffering from respiratory and cardiovascular disease: in the city, vehicles rank as the number one polluting source. Controlled statistical data reveal an increase of approximately 25% in hospital admissions after each acute outburst of atmospheric pollution (which, in turn, interacts with thermal inversion, heat islands, and the Green Belt), being related to lung neoplasia and skin cancer, to name a few.

If we add to this number deaths from cardiovascular disease and cardiopathies, the life expectancy of people living in critically polluted areas is likely to be reduced by 4 years, as specialists warn in the trial cosponsored by UNESCO.

The same trial cosponsored by UNESCO has revealed that the most frequent causes of death related to environmental issues are neurosis (stress), systemic arterial hypertension, coronary disease, respiratory disease, dermatitis, skin cancer, and parasitical infection.

A recent seminar conducted by USP's INCOR (Heart Institute) has revealed some amazing findings: a study based on over 90,000 deaths in São Paulo's metropolitan region revealed a high rate of mortality in patients suffering from cardiovascular deficiencies resulting from pollutants such as carbon monoxide, sulfur, and nitrogen components, all present in the atmosphere of the areas under analysis.

It is vital to investigate further this correlation, especially considering that all the parameters regarding air quality and pollutant emission prevailing in our environment are copied and adapted from first world cities, thus not necessarily sensitive and accurate enough to represent the tropical and subtropical environment, where biogeochemical relations are magnified and sui generis, according to data from health sources.

Food Safety

The São Paulo City Green Belt Biosphere Reserve physically covers 73 municipalities, with Serra da Cantareira to the north and Serra do Mar to the south, being crisscrossed on the east–west axis by the Rio Tietê basin that travels across the São Paulo plateau and across extensive water catchment areas originating in the slopes of Cantareira, Japi and Serra do Mar mountain ranges. This extensive area holds in its interior important fragments of the old Atlantic Forest's ecosystem, renowned for its very rich biodiversity.

Each terrestrial ecosystem is a generator of biodiversity, with numerous species genetically programmed, each with their own potential to be, exist, and develop according to their DNA and to fulfill such potential throughout their existence through their organic and functional structures. With their own genetic potential to exist, species each have their own specific needs to be fulfilled by the environment that generates them. Therefore, terrestrial ecosystems not only are genetic banks of every species of microlife they generate, whether plants, animals, or human beings, they also maintain a complex system of natural mechanisms and laws of interrelation and interdependence that involve all components of this synergic living plexus.

Air, water, soil, radiation, biodiversity, climate, and landscape, all in constant interaction and transformation fulfill the evolutional program of a vast universe ranging from microscopic subatomic structures to macroscopic structures such as the billions of galaxies that compose this universe.

Historically, the purpose of the extensive São Paulo City Green Belt area was to provide the metropolis with horticultural products. The growth and sprawl of the urban network with intensive industrialization of the city generated the Greater Metropolitan Region, with around 20 million inhabitants. Consequently, the agricultural borders of São Paulo gradually got pushed away, creating a type of belt, still green, containing reserves of Atlantic Forest permeated by horticultural cultures and cattle raising to supply the metropolis.

During this expansion process, the local ecosystems suffered unbalance and destruction due to (1) deforestation, with loss of biodiversity; (2) creation of a radial road system flowing toward the city center from the periphery and causing complete chaos in urban transport; (3) heat islands caused by intensive soil isolation due to asphalt, cement, and concrete impermeability, which changes the climate by overheat and generates heavy rain in the city center, leading to floods and collapse of constructions in densely populated slopes; (4) concentration of supplying storehouses in São Paulo's city center, increasing the flow of trucks in and out of the city center with irrational movement of horticultural products from inland São Paulo to CEAGESP storehouses, only to be resold to inland retailers, who take them back to where they came from in order to distribute them; (5) concentration of population, polluting the air and water catchment areas; and (6) loss of fertility as the land is covered by sprawling urban works, in turn, resulting from the adopted industrial model.

It is in this historical context of life in terrestrial ecosystems and the saga of modern civilization in its quest for development at the expense of material growth and concentration of wealth that the São Paulo City Green Belt Biosphere Reserve comes as an important corrective strategy to fight the environmental mistakes made in the course of human history, as well as an opportunity to rescue lost qualities.

The São Paulo City Green Belt is the place where rural property owners, agricultural engineers, farmers and other professionals concerned with quality of life integrate, get organized, and embark on the process of consolidation and expansion of the region's organic food and medicine production.

Associations have been formed between organic producers, wholefood retailers, and quality assurance certifying companies. The natural development of this process has been producers and agronomists investing in research, thus generating production technologies not only for input and products but also for the procedures that ultimately revert in higher quality standards and reduced costs in the medium run. Partnerships, contracts, and agreements for trade and planned production all lead to better levels of expertise in the sector and turn the several regions of the Green Belt into setting of reinvigorated horticultural farming associated with preservation of remainders of local ecosystems.

Today, in view of the new methods to find alternatives for economic and ecological sustainability, the number of rural property owners interested in converting their properties into inns or camping sites or embarking on rural tourism by opening routes of visitation and allowing hands-on experience in production processes and rural lifestyle is on the increase. These regions where natural organic farming is installed also foster agriecological tourism, with routes of visitation integrating tourism, consumption, and trade. Whereas the southwest, west, northwest, and northeast regions of the Green Belt concentrate on agriecology and rural tourism, the south, southeast, and north embrace other categories of tourist routes with other use and occupation methods, because they boast mountain ranges and water catchment areas.

The rich biodiversity still present there leads us to believe (1) that our knowledge about these species and their role and importance to life and health is still limited; (2) that there are more things and processes to learn besides what we already know; (3) that besides being a seed and matrix bank regarding the local vegetal and animal biodiversity, it is a true database with possible answers to issues involving the recovery of health and quality of life of local populations.

It is not limited to regulating climate conditions and preserving beautiful landscapes and environmental and cultural heritage. It is also a valuable component regarding food safety for present and future generations as well as human health in the region, because it reminds us of the close relationship between the digestive and metabolic operation of the organic structure in human beings and the food and medicines that the ecosystems supply to their inhabitants.

Air Pollution

Effects of Air Pollution on Forests—Brazilian Scenario

Urban forests, as addressed in the previous chapter, provide local inhabitants with welfare, comfort, and health, among other things. Besides its esthetic and landscaping role, the urban forest reduces noise, blocks atmospheric pollutants and acts on big cities' biodiversity. It provides shade and reduces the amount of energy absorbed, thus modifying the local microclimate and reducing the 'heat island' effect. The changes in airflow generated by urban forests also affect the transfer and diffusion of energy and water vapor.[10]

On the other hand, population growth and the ever-increasing expansion of urban and industrial agglomerates, are gradually occupying the areas once covered by vegetation. Without the areas under preservation and the parks, the green areas and forested areas would have already disappeared. Even the remnants of forest protected by legislation are gradually disappearing, whether due to illegal occupation or man's polluting action.[11]

Chief pollutants in the urban and industrial atmosphere resulting from man's polluting action include particulates, sulfur (SO_x) and nitrogen (NO_x) oxides, organic compounds and components of photochemical smog, including ozone (O_3) and peroxi-acetyl nitrate (PAN). They are all harmful to biological systems, including humans and many vegetal groups.

The effects of pollutant deposition on vegetal formations, besides coming from different emitting sources, involve the emission, transfer, transformation, deposition, and reception phenomena of such pollutants. The consequences for terrestrial ecosystems are induced by the pollutants that reach receptors, a phenomenon many authors refer to as "imission" (Dässler & Börtitz,[12] for instance), not necessarily equaling what was emitted in the first place.

The existing genetic variability between different vegetal species, or even between varieties and individuals of the same forest species, is known to lead to different responses to stress caused by pollution. Thus, plants naturally living around polluting sources or introduced in such places integrate with the stressing environment as they grow, being able to present a normal appearance or survive such conditions, yet presenting chlorosis and necrosis of the leaves, undergrowth, fewer blossoms, fruits. and seeds or, in extreme cases, not tolerating the environmental conditions and dying.[13]

Plants are affected, to a greater or lesser degree and in different levels of biological organization, from cell to organism as a whole, by changes that ultimately reflect on the whole ecosystem. However, the origin of all these effects reside in changes at molecular level, which is where the reactions with pollutants occur.[14] Soil type, topography, meteorological conditions, nutritional condition of the plants, and competition among species affect the way in which a plant responds to a specific concentration or dose of pollutant or pollutant mixture.[12,13]

Pollutant emission in the atmosphere was found to cause the so-called forest decline syndrome, observed a long time ago in many temperate countries, characterized by progressive and generally fast deterioration in the vigor of one or several arboreal species, resulting in synchronic mass death that affects large or small portions of the forest.[15]

As regards tropical and subtropical regions, however, increased imission of air pollutants has been noticed only in recent decades, primarily as a result of fast economic growth, industrialization, and urbanization as well as increased energy demand. A lot of attention has been paid to the impact of emissions on human health, though little is known about pollutant concentration and the exposure patterns of the local vegetation to these pollutants.[16] The susceptibility of Brazilian native vegetation or vegetal species to air pollutants in particular is also little known.[17]

In Brazil, air pollution levels differ significantly from place to place, mainly because of its large territory and heterogeneous economic development. Therefore, pollutant concentration is higher in the south and southeast, in association with the presence of large industrial areas such as Cubatão's industrial complex in Santos lowland and megacities such as São Paulo. Inadequate planning of the structure of such industrial complexes plus disorderly urban sprawl can be an obstacle to pollutant dispersion, contributing even more to increase pollution levels in such areas.[18]

Recent research studies in São Paulo's metropolitan region by researchers from the Institute of Astronomy, Geophysics and Atmospheric Sciences of São Paulo University have revealed that sea breeze, mild air draft originating in the ocean, carries to São Paulo Plateau the pollutants discharged by Cubatão's plants, contributing even more to worsen air quality in the region. According to researchers, the metropolitan region of São Paulo, which includes the capital city and 38 adjoining municipalities, is also an exporter of pollutants, especially in the winter, being able to reach cities up to 100 km away from the capital, though in lower concentrations than the areas surrounding the roads or industrial complexes that generate them. If caught by strong winds, the city's polluted air can travel as far as 400 km, according to the report "Estufa que exporta poluição" ["*a greenhouse that exports pollution*"], published in FAPESP magazine, issue 71, January 2002 <www.revistapesquisa.fapesp.br>.

It is precisely in this scenario of air contamination that the São Paulo City Green Belt Biosphere Reserve (GBBR) is inserted. Its forest remainders, from Baixada Santista to São Paulo Plateau, whether in São Paulo city or in the periphery, are under serious threat because of close proximity to air pollutants of industrial and urban origin.

However, knowledge about the extent of damage pollution causes to these forests is still restricted to some regions. Therefore, it is not possible to delimit at a global level whether the Green Belt surrounding São Paulo is faced with the danger of disappearing as a function of pollution activity.

Case Studies in the GBBR

The best-known example of forest decline in the GBBR is around Cubatão's industrial complex. Studies conducted by researchers of the Botany Institute and CETESB (agencies of the São Paulo State Department of the Environment) since the early 1980s have revealed that large portions of Atlantic Forest covering the hillsides of Serra do Mar most exposed to pollutants are seriously affected.[17,18] Indications of the risk imposed by air pollution to a fragment of forest nestled in Fontes do Ipiranga State Park, south zone of São Paulo city, also have been presented by the same group of researchers.[11] The results of these studies, whose synthesis can be found in Klumpp *et al.*[17] and Domingos *et al.*[18] are briefly reported below.

Atlantic Forest Decline in Cubatão Region. The impacts of air pollution on the Atlantic Forest covering Serra do Mar, in Cubatão region, were first noticed on the landscape and physiognomy of the forest. From 1960 to 1985, time when emissions reached peak levels, decline of the forest's portions most exposed to pollutants was very noticeable, covering approximately 60 km^2, from sea level to over 800-m altitude. During that period, the forest's upper arboreal stratum was very damaged with many dead trees, resulting in sudden decrease in biodiversity and instability in Serra do Mar's hillside. Many landslides were registered during that time, placing both local people and industrial facilities at risk.

From 1985, after a series of governmental measures and the launch of a control program over pollutant emission, the quality of the environment improved significantly, resulting in gradual recovery of the forest, especially the areas farther away from the polluting sources. Nevertheless, phytosociological studies after 1985 revealed that the remaining vegetation near chemical plants and steelworks installed in the valley of Mogi river was still strongly affected, consisting of a thick herbaceous stratum and few arboreal species. High arboreal mortality and great heterogeneity in the crown canopy also was observed at the time in the portions close to petrochemical plants at the foot of old roadway Caminho do Mar, which connected São Paulo Plateau to Baixada Santista lowland.

Recent research throughout the past decade has revealed that current local levels of pollution continue to damage the forest. The studies are based on biomonitoring principles, a powerful tool to evaluate environmental health. Biomonitoring consists of techniques to evaluate the changes to the environment caused by anthropic activity, whereby specific reactions from certain living beings, the so-called bioindicators, are followed. This approach has been largely used in Europe to evaluate the risks imposed on forests by deterioration in air quality around urbanized and/or industrialized areas. In the Cubatão region, many plants are being used as bioindicators, including local native species. The analysis of vegetal reactions range from quantification of visible damage to the leaves to chemical, physiological, biochemical, and structural analysis of the leaves, branches, and roots.

The results of such studies indicate that, despite control measures and subsequently reduced emissions, the complex blend of pollutants in Cubatão's air may still cause damage to the Atlantic Forest. Fluorides, sulfur, and nitrogen compounds and particulates are causing disturbance to the forest portion on the hillsides of Serra do Mar facing onto the valley of Mogi river. Sulfur compounds and secondary pollutants are probably the main cause of damage to the forest around Caminho do Mar.

Young plants of native arboreal species (e.g., mountain manaca raintree *Tibouchina pulchra* and tropical American shrubs *Psidium cattleyanum*), if exposed to these polluted places, present metabolic changes indicating stress induced by oxidizing pollutants, changes to photosynthetic processes, reduced growth, and structural changes, among other aspects, which may be ascribed to airborne pollutants. Based on these results, it is applicable to say that at least these native species and other species equally sensitive to pollutants continue to be under threat in Cubatão region.

Decline of a Fragment of Atlantic Forest inside Fontes do Ipiranga State Park. Besides the effects of fragmentation and as they are inserted in a highly urbanized area in São Paulo's south zone, the portions of Atlantic Forest inside Fontes do Ipiranga State Park are affected by air pollutants emitted by industrial plants and the many vehicles circulating in the region. Because of close proximity to Serra do Mar's top, they are also affected by the pollution emitted by Cubatão's industrial complex.

In the early 1980s, some studies revealed that the large amount of pollutants emitted by a steelwork plant installed next to that fragment of the forest could be the cause of its strong degradation. A high rate of arboreal death and fast development of climbing plants on the forest's canopy was observed at the time, causing the vegetation to lose its physiognomy. Concentrations of sulfur, iron, zinc, chrome, lead, and nickel were extremely high in samples of soil, leaves, and burlap removed from the portion closer to the steelworks, with levels gradually going down as samples were taken farther away from the polluting source. Tree death could be associated with inlet and circulation of these toxic elements in the forest.

In the early 1990s, research studies were conducted in Fontes do Ipiranga State Park at a place adjacent to one of its forest portions, employing biomonitoring techniques and the same species of bioindicators as used in Cubatão.

The results revealed that the stretch of forest inside Fontes do Ipiranga State Park was exposed to phytotoxic levels of photochemical smog components, especially ozone and PAN. Considering the high oxidizing potential of these pollutants, during the research period and at least with regard to more susceptible native species, one could expect metabolic and physiologic disturbances possibly resulting in death of cells, tissues, and even whole organisms. In extreme cases, these changes would result in some species disappearing on the one hand, and other species considered more tolerant and opportunistic multiplying on the other hand.

However, these indications of threat to the forest inside Fontes do Ipiranga State Park should be regarded with moderation, because the relevant results originated from bioindicator exposure to one portion of the park only. Thus, result interpretations must be very cautious.

Future Prospects

Studies using biomonitoring techniques have opened a wide field of research in Brazil, proving a powerful tool to outline the impacts on the environment induced by human's polluting action.

If these studies expand to the entire area comprised by the GBBR and its surrounding areas, they will be highly valued, not only for spatial and temporal mapping of the risks imposed by pollution on its forest fragments but also to ensure suitable management and preservation of this important UNESCO's Biosphere Reserve.

PROPOSAL AND ACTION OF THE SÃO PAULO CITY GREEN BELT BIOSPHERE RESERVE REGARDING THE WHOLE ISSUE

GBBR Management

There is a worldwide shortage of management models for environmentally sensitive areas under strong human influence, as is the case of the São Paulo City Green Belt. This finding leads to two relevant reflections: (1) because of the aforesaid shortage of international references addressing the issue, the mission of the GBBR to a large degree is to construct a management model grounded on its own experience; (2) as a consequence to the previous item, there is a keen national and international interest as to how the GBBR has approached and will approach the solutions to this issue, which makes it already an interesting laboratory of actions and proposals within the World Network of Biosphere Reserves.

The GBBR's management system consists of two chief components:

- A Coordinating Board: it acts as an executive bureau to the reserve and is in charge of the Forest Institute of São Paulo Department of the Environment. Its role is (1) to propose and conduct programs and projects for the São Paulo City Green Belt Biosphere Reserve; and (2) to assist the GBBR's Management Council and implement its policies.
- A Management Council: created by government decree in year 2002, its mission is (1) to propose and assist closely the management of the reserve, through policies and strategies capable of implementing concrete actions for environmental conservation, sustainable development, and quality of life for the populations involved; and (2) to become a forum able to incorporate the longings and proposals of various segments of society, promoting participative management as set forth by UNESCO's MaB Program.

Scope of Action of the GBBR's Coordinating Board

The bond between the GBBR and the Forest Institute owes to two main reasons: (1) most core zones in the reserve are conservation units under integral protection administered by the institute; this allows better integration between direct management actions in the core zones and complementary actions in the buffer and transition zones within the scope of action of the biosphere reserve; (2) inversely, the GBBR's Coordinating Board acts mostly as an arm to the institute when it comes to preservation actions based on involvement of the community and dissemination of sustainable practices compatible with the conservation of a rich biological heritage in its conservation units.

As far as programs, projects, and proposals are concerned, the main actions of the GBBR's Coordinating Board are Youth Program (YP), Green Belt Research Program (GBRP), and Sustainable Tourism in the GBBR.

The Youth Program

Urban and periurban areas like those comprised by the Green Belt Biosphere Reserve are subject to all sorts of impacts, many of which very specific to the reality of the metropolis, as can be noticed in other texts of this document. The shortage of public policies regulating environmental issues, in counterpoint to the broad scope of the environmental legislation, only compounds the economic crisis installed globally and in São Paulo's metropolitan region for that matter. Increasing automation of the production means in substitution for human labor, along with a policy that concentrates efforts on the financial system to the detriment of developmental actions, both have generated a picture of social exclusion that has affected the population of São Paulo dramatically, according to data from the project Social Dynamic, Environmental Quality and Intra-Urban Spaces in São Paulo: A Sociospatial Analysis, developed by FAPESP's Public Policies Research Program. The analysis is based, among other parameters, on the Human Development Index (HDI). The survey reveals that of over 10 million inhabitants in the capital city, approximately 8.9 million live below what is considered suitable life standards. Exclusion grows toward the city's periphery, where the best preserved areas of the GBBR are. This characterizes an explosive situation as dispossessed human contingents are placed in direct contact with areas of extreme 123 vulnerability such as the Green Belt. According to project coordinator Aldaíza Sposati, "The worst evil is that these areas of water catchment and environmental preservation have "frozen" (…) both as regards investment and as regards betterment."[19] According to Aldaíza's analysis, this leads to devaluation of such areas and consequently to their occupation and degradation, placing at risk the conditions in the city afforded by the Green Belt. The coordinator concludes that there is no such policy combining environmental policy and human protection.

Against a backdrop of unemployment and no prospects, the Brazilian population resorts to "informal economy," illegal activities and violence, to secure survival. The exclusion process aggravated in the 1990s, victimizing young people in particular.[20] As regards violence,[21] a study by UNESCO[21] revealed that youths between 15 and 24 years old and living in São Paulo City are about twice as likely to die as the rest of the population, especially from homicide, and this accounts for 61.9% of the deaths in this age group. In the year 2000, it corresponded to 39.2%. These numbers make Brazil rank third among 60 other countries regarding youth deaths. According to UNESCO's Brazil representative Jorge Werthein, the worst of this picture is not homicide alone but the increase in homicide rate among youths: in the 1990s alone the rate went up by 9% per year on average.[21]

Likewise, suicide rates involving youths aged between 15 and 24 years increased by 42.8% in Brazil during a 20-year time span, according to a study by CLAVES (Latin-American Violence and Health Center).[22] Possible causes include depression, psychiatric diseases, hereditary disposition, family conflicts, relationship difficulties, drug or alcohol use, and social exclusion. We should note the argument of psychologist and CLAVES director Edinilsa Ramos de Souza, who maintains that "Mostly, they are people with poor education and a history of hardship, who often have to quit school and find work, earning little or nothing at all. Youths who, at the peak of their age, are subject to unbearable pressure."[22] In the 60-country ranking, Brazil occupies 51st position in youth suicide deaths. Although it is not as bad as the homicide rate, the fast-paced growth in suicide rate involving this age group is nonetheless worrying, as Fiocruz specialists explain.[22]

As has been pointed out, the lack of prospects only adds to this grim picture. A monthly employment survey conducted by IBGE (Brazilian Institute of Geography and Statistics) shows that unemployment involving the 15–17-year-old age group shifted from 11.7% in 1991 to 13.4% in 2001. With the 18–24-year-old age group, the rate shifted from 9.2% to 12.5% in the same period.[20]

According to Márcio Pochmann, the number of vacancies not requiring high qualification increased in the 1990s, implying more pressure for an academic degree. Likewise, lack of qualification leads youths to enter informal economy, which, in turn, provides no stability or registered employment, Christmas bonus, or vacation salary.[23] This situation is compounded by the inclination of students in the public system, typically low-income youths, to avoid the college entrance examination to join public universities such as USP, UNICAMP, and UNESP. According to data from the Ministry of Education, of 430,000 students who graduated from São Paulo's public education system, only 11.9% sign up for the college entrance examination.[24] To former State Secretary of Education Rose Neubauer, this is partly because students' low self-esteem and negative image revolving around the public education system. Specialist educators termed this phenomenon "self-exclusion," characterized by avoiding the college entrance examination. The students' degree of knowledge indeed has been below standards. The average mark in ENEM's examination (national secondary school examination) was 34.13 points in a 0–100 scale. Whereas students in the public network scored 30.39 points, students in the private network scored 47.22 points. Specifically with students whose parents are illiterate or who earn up to one minimum wage a month, the average score was 26 points approximately.[25] Although students in the public network have good performance in entrance examination for less popular careers, their performance is substandard for careers demanding better preparation.[25] This leads students in the public network to try private colleges, often unable to offer as good qualifications as those offered by public universities.

With no prospects for better qualification, professional growth, or stability, low-income youths become a prey to illegal activities, as was revealed by a study conducted by the Sciences Department of Fiocruz's Public Health School, involving 88 adolescents aged between 14 and 19 who live in Rio de Janeiro. The findings reveal that youths living in Rio de Janeiro's shanty-towns and working for local drug dealers are paid between US$33 and US$1,000 a week, in a structure that affords career climbing and payment increase.[26] According to the study, the money earned is used on expensive clothes, cars, visits to famous hangouts, and success with women, signaling complete lack of prospects regarding career and life growth. The study confirms this observation by revealing that these adolescents have no major ambition in life because of their social condition and poor education, thus rounding up the cycle of poor education, unemployment, and violence. Another sad finding is drug abuse by 52.3% of these youths, who use them two to six times a day and consequently become indebted to drug dealers, which ultimately leads to a no-way-out situation in case they wish to quit the business altogether. Although this information refers to Rio de Janeiro alone, the context of social exclusion and increase in drug dealing in urban environments is supposedly similar in São Paulo, thus an ideal setting for this type of event.

In dissonance with this terrifying picture, the public policies focusing on metropolitan and periurban environments strongly lack coordinated and guided initiatives able to integrate environmental conservation and recovery with programs and actions to fight poverty and ensure the needy population welfare, a major challenge in this millennium.

This context of social exclusion involving young urban people, in addition to the picture of degradation in the urban setting, is a dangerous recipe for bad quality of life, or life risk even, in the metropolitan region. For this reason, the São Paulo City Green Belt Biosphere Reserve's Youth Program defends a broad socioenvironmental proposal, with actions focused on youth education, qualification, and career training, all to ensure preservation and sustainable use of São Paulo state's natural resources as well as prepare them for citizenship.

Inspired by United Nations' FAO and sponsored by UNESCO, which adopted it for its socioenvironmental sphere of action, the Youth Program is an innovating proposal of socioenvironmental intervention, based on the verification that public policies in favor of the environment should necessarily involve society, whether through education and information or through the understanding that the environment can generate income for the community without implying degradation. It is coordinated by the Forest Institute, within the scope of the São Paulo City Green Belt Biosphere Reserve, and developed by a system of partnerships, with special emphasis on AHPCE (Núcleo da Terra Holistic Association for Ecological Community Participation), local government bodies fostering the Program, volunteers, private initiative, universities, etc.

Created by way of the "Agriforest Practices and Juvenile Participation in Periurban Zones–The São Paulo Case" program, through Decree 36861 dated 5/6/93 from São Paulo State Government, it is focused on:

- Conservation and recovery of the São Paulo City Green Belt
- Dissemination of awareness regarding environment and citizenship
- Technical qualification of youths in agriforest practices and other "eco-market" categories such as recycling, ecological tourism, and environmental monitoring
- Generation of income and new employment possibilities by promoting the "eco-job market"
- Generation and dissemination of new technologies applicable to the concept of "sustainable development"

History

The Youth Program was structured by a set of legal instruments and a pilot project in São Roque.

On June 5, 1993, Government Decree 36861 created the Youth Program of the São Paulo City Green Belt Biosphere Reserve (GBBR-SP) and Resolution SMA-15, dated 16/06/93, appointed a follow-up committee and a work group for the Program. Resolution SMA-23, dated 19/08/94, set up the first Program center in a public area of the state, municipality of São Roque, whereas conjoined Resolution SMA-SAA-03, dated 21/09/94, resolved that IAC Agronomy Experimental Station in São Roque should be the seat of the first center.

In 1996, UNESCO released US$72,000.00 to launch and conduct a pilot project in São Roque, designed to create a methodological proposal of youth training focused on the eco-job market, within the scope of the São Paulo City Green Belt Biosphere Reserve (GBBR-SP). In 1996, UNESCO hired Ondalva Serrano, PhD, to implement and conduct the pilot project from July that year through December 1997, when public network students received eco-job training along with a team of independent professionals and volunteers. In an attempt to sponsor, render feasible, and consolidate the program in the municipality, the AHPCE (Núcleo da Terra Holistic Association for Ecological Community Participation) was created in January 5, 1997, consisting of a technical team, Program students, their family and volunteers. During 15 months, the AHPCE coordinated the experimental phase of application of the methodological proposal, as well as a feasibility study in the local context, expanding the age scope of students, using funds from the Environment Ministry and Forest Institute of the Department of the Environment through UNESCO's branch in Brazil. In 1997, the activities in São Roque came to a halt because of insufficient outside funds and absence of a diversified system of partnership with the local municipality. The process was resumed in April 1999 with the launch of Santos Center, followed by Itapecerica da Serra in March 2000, São Bernardo do Campo and Santo André in April 2000, Guarulhos in September 2000, São Roque in April 2001, and finally Cotia in September 2002.

Pedagogical Proposal

The main purpose of the Program's pedagogical proposal is to

- Contribute to full development of human beings through alternation and transit in all areas of human knowledge, by practicing ethics, in-depth ecology and human values as well as fulfilling their essential needs.
- Create opportunities to construct an eco-job training profile, through reflexive training in practical workshops that, by awakening vocations, will help match them with potential market needs, that way allowing insertion and sustainability of eco-professionals in the economic community.
- Develop a teamwork and cooperation spirit for collective construction of knowledge, research, work, organization, trade, planning, and dissemination of information as well as technologies useful and suitable for life in the community.
- Develop an ability to read, interpret, and search for suitable solutions in a complex reality through transdisciplinary attitude and methodology, namely, language precision; clearness of principles, concepts and values; use of ethical principles; openness to new things–the unknown; tolerance for diversity; acceptance of things different; acknowledgment that reality is complex; and perception of different levels of reality.
- Search for a synthesis and complementarity of conflicting opposites at a higher level of reality through ternary dialogics and conflict transcendence.
- Provide tools by way of concepts, methodologies, technologies and suitable low-impact practices to enable production, transformation, and exchange of goods and services useful and necessary to the community,

saving energy by sustainable use of natural resources, affording dignified and safe working conditions and preserving life and its diversity.

- Prepare for local and global citizenship by developing human, social, and environmental awareness, by practicing a systemic, dynamic, dialectic, integrated, and interdependent outlook and experience of collective life in a complex reality, and by organizing civil society so as to meet its basic needs, having people participate in the definition of socioenvironmental public policies, participative and budgetary planning, and management systems.
- Develop diagnostic studies in the local job market to identify economic activities, conducting them suitably, with quality, safety, and sustainability as far as the concept of eco-job market is concerned, helping eco-professionals find work and assisting with adjustments of socio-environmental conduct, and conduct projects that motivate and move people to remedy inadequate actions as well as invest and help consolidate the network of program centers.
- Organize and conduct a system of partnerships between entities in the primary, secondary, and tertiary sectors to render possible the introduction, running and participative strategic management of the Youth Program network's local centers.
- Contribute for construction of a healthy, safe, unique, sympathetic, and sustainable community, holding the remainder of natural ecosystems on the planet as a model and source of reference to organize, operate, and manage biodiversity on Planet Earth.

Network Structure

Program Management. This is a very innovative and important aspect of the proposal and precisely what allows it to be financially sustainable. It is the job of the Green Belt Biosphere Reserve's coordinating board to maintain the structure of the program network, disseminating it, helping the municipalities create their centers, and allowing their actions to be visible and disseminated, offering nonstop technical, pedagogical, and marketing advice to all projects and, whenever possible, offering financial and material resources to the entire network. The municipalities are responsible for the centers locally, offering facilities and structures plus permanent technical and support teams. Articulating local partners on behalf of the project is also a job of each municipality.

To allow program maintenance, in addition to financial balancing, the Biosphere Reserve's coordinating board adopts some strategies for cohesion and increase in quality and motivation for the entire process. In short, these strategies translate into several actions seeking synergy between the seven Eco-job Training Centers.

Perspectives

In this continuous process of network growth and construction of new scenarios, the Youth Program foresees some new and important achievements.

In addition to the prospects of new Eco-job Training Centers, great efforts are being put forth to institutionalize the Youth Program through the creation of CERBIO, the country's first Eco-job Training Center of the São Paulo City Green Belt Biosphere Reserve, with a network format similar to the current structure of the Youth Program. The proposal foresees headquarters in an area owned by the Forest Institute, which would make its highly qualified technicians available for environment-related issues, with four other decentralized units in the municipalities of São Bernardo do Campo, Guarulhos, Itapecerica da Serra and Santos, the latter possibly entering a partnership with the Department of Education of São Paulo State. The idea is to allow continuous expansion of these decentralized units, that way assisting the Green Belt region. The proposal was initially submitted to the Ministry of Education and Culture's PROEP (Job Training Extension Program). The courses include basic and technical programs in: Agriculture and Cattle Raising, Tourism and Hospitality, Industry, Environment, Leisure and Social Development, hopefully assisting at least 1,500 students a year, observing and adopting Youth Program philosophy.

Another action under way is the structuring of Eco-business Incubators intended for those program students with an enterprising profile and for the community of municipalities with Eco-job Training Centers, looking to assist other people with this profile who may include the students in their staff list. Eco-business Incubators are a stage ahead of what we term "Eco-business Sower," where students experience eco-job training under guidance of center technicians until they reach the full legal age necessary to take on civil responsibilities, for example, starting a business or associating to cooperatives and other associations. The Incubator process is currently under discussion in São Bernardo do Campo Center, with support of local government through the Department of Economic Development and Tourism, SEBRAE, and (still in negotiation) local colleges and universities, possibly lending their laboratories and faculty to assist upcoming incubated businesses.

The Santos Center also has considered using the newly introduced incubator structure to include eco-business proposals, with the same supporting network: local government, SEBRAE, local colleges, and universities and FIESP.

We believe that within the next few years some eco-businesses (one in São Bernardo do Campo and one in Santos) should be ready for the incubators.

Initially tried in the municipality of São Roque, this proposal was submitted to USP by UNESCO through CETRANS (Transdisciplinary Education Center), and installed in the Escola do Futuro [School of the Future] as an applied project of transdisciplinary experience, becoming one of CETRANS' 40 pilot projects addressing transdisciplinarity.

Integration of the GBBR-SP's Youth Program and CETRANS/USP's Project for Transdisciplinary Development in Education: Contributing to Sustainable Development of Society and Humankind

The GBBR-SP's Youth Program was launched by UNESCO, in its 96/97 pilot project stage, proposing to formulate a participative and interactive methodology of collective construction contextualized in the human, social, and environmental reality of each scope area. To achieve that, it concentrated efforts on the training of teenagers attending public secondary school, through reflective workshops that would train them for future insertion into the eco-job market, thus generating means of sustainability for students in association with environmental recovery and sustainable use of biodiversity and natural resources.

The outcome of the first 3 years of activities at CETRANS/USP was very profitable and rewarding for everyone, as it supplied professionals with subsidies to face serious challenges regarding interpersonal and interinstitutional relations as well as regarding practical contextualization of the new epistemological paradigms. At the same time, participants had the opportunity to feel like human beings in search of their own integrity as whole creatures and perceive themselves as agents and objects of an interactive process of collective construction, somehow foreign to present-day academia. The large majority of these professionals should integrate in 2002 the body of mediators for CETRANS courses "on transdisciplinary thought for a fresh group of 30 professionals interested in the methodology."

In 2002, after phase I is complete regarding the training of CETRANS' Pilot Projects Coordinators, the "Transdisciplinary Development in Education" project should be offering courses in different levels, looking to expand the transdisciplinary training of instructors. This chance to include new professionals in USP's transdisciplinary experimentation meets Youth Program needs because, during the new course on transdisciplinary thought, it could have several technicians integrate the new 30-student group of CETRANS. The mediators in charge of teaching the new professionals are CETRANS' pilot project coordinators, qualified during the triennial 99/01 phase I of the Project. The objectives of the 2002 course on transdisciplinary thought are to:

- Provide participants with notions of transdisciplinary epistemology and methodology
- Pass on principles of transdisciplinary thought
- Start theoretical and applied transdisciplinary research

- Foment a reform in education based on a change of thought
- Boost the training of transdisciplinary instructors
- Test the process of procedural assessment regarding transdisciplinary training.

The Green Belt Research Program (GBRP)

(1) Knowledge and information constitute critical elements of environmental management. Thus, the environmental management and research that generates knowledge and information must be strictly connected. This is precisely why one of the roles of the biosphere reserve is to promote research.

(2) Bearing this in mind, the Green Belt Research Program (GBRP) proposal was formulated. Its main purpose is to develop systemically articulated studies and research about the Green Belt Biosphere Reserve as a concept, object, and space.

(3) The Program has the following premises. (i) The connection between the environmental conditions and dynamic of a mega-metropolis like São Paulo constitute a widely complex fabric. (ii) Considering this complex context, the environmental management of the GBBR requires that the existing and forthcoming knowledge of these connections be developed by articulating its components from a systemic and organic approach. (iii) Much information and knowledge have been generated with underexplored potential, and, if they are duly integrated and made available, they have great synergetic potential to turn actions operational and generate new knowledge.

(4) Therefore, the specific purposes of the Program are as follows: (i) generate knowledge and information about the City of São Paulo and its environmental conditions and connections, with the Green Belt in particular, according to several thematic areas; (ii) promote interdisciplinary integration between various areas of knowledge around a common thematic field; (iii) make available existing and forthcoming knowledge and information; (iv) turn knowledge and information operational for the purpose of environmental management and formulation of public policies; (v) promote integration between different society sectors: government agencies, academic and scientific institutions, nongovernmental organizations and private initiative; (vi) foment and stimulate research.

The implementation strategies include the following. (1) Define, with the help of specialists, the main related topics, with the relevant issues and problems involving each case. (2) Define, with the help of specialists, the main interactions and interfaces between different topics. (3) Survey and inventory the information and the state of the art of research in different topics. (4) Create a "portal" and database for surveyed knowledge AND information about to be incorporated. (5) Develop indicators, statistics, and other tools for environmental management deriving from the elements available. (6) Based on the events and portal, sponsor a network of researchers and specialists focused on the connections between São Paulo City and the Environment (GBRP Network). (7) With the help of the aforesaid researchers and specialists, promote discussions about topics considered critical and consequently define strategic priorities in regard to research techniques and projects to be fomented. (8) Define and develop new research projects integrated with different institutions. (9) Seek financing channels.

SCENARIOS

Scenario I—Nonsustainable Perspective

(1) Existing values prevail: the State is absent in strategic territorial planning; inconsistent public policies; inefficient legislation and judiciary; debilitated sectorial government apparatus; exacerbated consumerism; absolute prodevelopment doctrine with no regard for the environment; citizenship with no effective channels of participation; antidemocratic practices in space management; worldwide omission from preservation of common heritage.

(2) In 2015, São Paulo is expected to have 21.2 million inhabitants, according to UNO. It will be the largest human agglomerate in the American continent; migratory flow from rural to urban areas and vegetative population growth will exceed the desirable levels. The population will concentrate on sensitive areas of the Green Belt.

(3) Emphasis on "sustainable growth' alone to the detriment of "sustainable development." We understand sustainable growth as being the sensible use of natural resources today so that future generations will not lack them, although it only incorporates man's physical dimension; therefore it is finite. Sustainable development in its turn incorporates cultural and spiritual dimensions; therefore, it is infinite. Absence of "biosphere ethics."

(4) The organic/institutional design deliberately allows dilution of responsibilities, command duplicity, and omission from protectionist actions. Emphasis on Government's "cartorial" action.

(5) Negligence in regulation and control over the land network obstructs consolidation of the biosphere reserve's core and buffer zones and

favors assignment of large sums of public money to indirect indemnity actions promoted by the environmental indemnity industry.

(6) Degradation of the São Paulo City Green Belt continues at the same levels as observed from 1990 to 2000. Once the Belt's transition and buffer zones have been destroyed, the core zones will be invaded next. The "Maginot line" breaks, conurbation advances.

(7) Deterioration in quality of life is noticeable; concentration of income increases and so does social exclusion; the human development index (HDI) drops. Quality of life deteriorates in 76 of São Paulo City's 96 districts in a time span of 10 years. These districts are situated in periurban areas near the Green Belt.

(8) Nonsustainability leads to diseconomy in the urban agglomerate. According to the Kumazaki index, the direct and indirect costs resulting from the destruction of the green tissue rise to US$100 billion from 1990 to 2000.

(9) Extravagant cosmetic works (highly energy demanding) of a clearly political nature are favored, in the hope of getting votes, to the detriment of basic sanitation.

(10) Linear exploration of natural resources, with little emphasis on the cyclic exploration of such resources (recycling). The Green Belt continues to be a dump for contaminating industrial residue and the so-called sanitary landfills of domestic and hospital waste.

(11) The heat island expands from center to the periphery. This century the city will experience top temperatures of 40°C. The energy matrix's surplus will force the installation of thermoelectric plants or "mini breeders" to afford thermal comfort and living conditions in the urban agglomerate, with costs estimated to exceed US$10 billion.

(12) Floods will progress at a catastrophic pace. To keep them under control today, US$3 billion worth of investments is required; with degradation of the Green Belt, this sum increases.

(13) All the city's existing resources of drinking water will be lost; São Paulo will be forced to collect water 100 km away in Eldorado Basin, involving high costs.

(14) Air contamination will increase in the urban agglomerate; disturbances in gas exchange in the atmosphere; the Green Belt loses its ability to sequestrate carbonic gas from the atmosphere, estimated today as 50% of the aggregate produced by human activity in the urban sprawl. Levels of pollutant emission in SP's metropolitan region increase. The mechanical effect of aerosol and particulate filtering drops, vital for air regeneration, with Cantareira being an example.

(15) Chemical death or endangerment of the phytosanitary condition of primary woods or climaxes progresses, and so does the loss of bio-

diversity because of pollutant bombarding, following the example of Cubatão and recently Cantareira and other urban sites.

(16) The road network expands to allow circulation of 10 million private motorized vehicles to the detriment of public transport, increasing the outgrowth of these roads into green belt tissue. The Rodoanel project progresses a new vector of penetration and destruction of the Green Belt at an estimated cost of US$ 2.7 billion.

(17) Environmental health worsens just as human health does—a sick city generates sick children. Currently, average citizens' life expectancy has shortened by 3 years. This rate will increase, resulting in unbearable costs for social security, public health, and decrease in the human workforce.

(18) The city loses its natural ability to fight bacteriological threat (green areas are powerful biological decontaminants); the mitigation or buffering effect against propagation of thermonuclear waves is also at stake.

(19) Food safety is at stake. Food production units are removed from the Green Belt; the ability to generate jobs in the eco-job market gradually lessens. The public policy to introduce capital-intensive technologies to the detriment of labor-intensive technologies continues.

(20) The loss of urban memory progresses; alien nonsustainable patterns of culture and behavior prevail.

(21) Erosive phenomena increase; today the urban sprawl is subject to fast-paced erosion of 10 million m^3/year of fertile land; the city's dryness index increases and the drainage network and valley bottoms become impermeable.

(22) The contamination index of superficial and underground bodies of water increases; inland and ocean waters deteriorate and predatory fishing advances; today fish reserves are being explored to exhaustion, with three marine species nearing extinction; fishing becomes harder with implications for the population's diet. Sardine fishing specifically, the staple diet of ordinary people, dropped from 200,000 tons in 1980 to 20,000 tons in 2000.

(23) With the destruction of their natural habitat, the bird fauna and entire wild fauna diminishes both in quantity and diversity. Cantareira, currently boasting around 200 bird species, indicative of a profuse local wildlife, has this index drastically reduced because of the destruction of the forestal "continuum" and absence of natural corridors.

(24) There are more of the so-called "natural" disasters such as landslides, floods, electric sparks, etc, although, in fact, they have an environmental cause.

(25) Violence soars beyond control. Competition for vital space increases, including land, water, air and food. The current stage of socioenvironmental tension turns into socioenvironmental conflict.

Scenario II—Sustainable Perspective

(1) The prevailing values and behavior begin to reverse. Stronger presence of the State in planning; consistent public policies to protect diffuse interests; stronger sectorial government apparatus, efficient legislation and judiciary; sustainable lifestyles; conscious and participative citizenship regarding the use of vital space; new international order committed to the preservation of common heritage.
(2) Population explosion is controlled within the urban space.
(3) Emphasis is on sustainable development.
(4) The institutional/organic design is in tune with protectionist actions, having well-defined commands and responsibilities.
(5) Priority is given to regulation and control over the land network, especially in core zones of the GBBR, which should lawfully constitute public domain.
(6) Degradation of the Green Belt stagnates and reinvigoration begins.
(7) Quality of life improves, income is better distributed and the human development index rises. Spacewise the configuration of the human agglomerate is more equitable, with marginal elements disappearing.
(8) The public policies start to privilege urban space as a social asset rather than a market reserve. The goods and services offered by environmental resources are valued.
(9) The public works begin to favor basic sanitation.
(10) Recycling is emphasized and the Green Belt stops being a dump for the megalopolis.
(11) The heat island effect recedes; the energy matrix is compatible with the rhythm of human activity; reversion of the "city as an entropy island" concept.
(12) Floods are under control, with preservation of the natural mechanisms responsible for water stability in the human agglomerate; more vegetated open spaces allowing recharge of aquifers and less areas of water accumulation.
(13) The existing water catchment areas are recovered, in agreement with a policy of conservation of water resources, and end of the "planned obsolescence" concept.
(14) Air contamination levels are effectively controlled in the urban agglomerate. With its reinvigoration, the Green Belt is better equipped to sequestrate atmospheric carbon.
(15) The phytosanitary condition of green belt's woods improves.
(16) The road network respects sensitive areas of the Green Belt; radical inversion in transportation policies, now focused on public transport, and decline of the prohighway era.
(17) Environmental health is restored in synergy with human health, with prevalence of preventive medicine.

(18) The preserved city has a natural ability for defense; buffering against the propagation of thermonuclear waves.
(19) Food safety is secured, with food production units expanding, especially whole food as it does not contaminate agriecosystems; more eco-job offers; emphasis on intensive-labor policies.
(20) The urban memory is recovered and authentic patterns of culture and behavior are valued.
(21) Control is exercised over erosive phenomena.
(22) Bodies of water are recovered; inland and oceanic waters start to be restored, with the resulting orderly exploration of aquatic organisms, important to our nutritional diet.
(23) The bird fauna stabilizes and so does the entire wild fauna whose natural habitat is the Green Belt.
(24) Control is managed over natural disasters.
(25) Violence is kept under control; the degree of socioenvironmental tension decreases.

NOTES AND REFERENCES

1. Marcianto, E. 2000/2001. Brasil, cicades: alternativas para a crise urana [Brazil, citties: alternatives for the urban crisis]. Petrópolis, R.J. Brazil. Editora Vozes, 2001 and IBGE census 2000.
2. As quoted by Prof. Dr. Aziz Nicib Ab'Sáber. Geographer and Geomorphologist with the Advanced Matters Institute of São Paulo University IE/USP during interview for TV Cultura on June 1, 2002.
3. Source: Dieese quoted by Maricato (2001).
4. Mautner, Y. 1999. A periferia como fronteira de expansão do capital [Periphery as a boundary for expansion of capital]. In O processo de urbanização no Brasil [The urbanization process in Brazil]–Csaba Deák & Sueli Ramos Schiffer (orgs.)–São Paulo. Editora Universidade de São Paulo.
5. Source: *Veja* magazine, issue 24/01/2001.
6. Current Brazilian Commission for the MAN AND BIOSPHERE Program–COBRAMaB.
7. Excerpt from publications: Hotspots, Earth's Biologically Richest and Most Endangered Terrestrial Ecoregions, by Russel A. Mittermeier, Norman Myers, Cristina G. Mittermeier, and Patrício R. Gil, published by CEMEX and edited by Agrupación Sierra Madre. 2000. Publication produced by Conservation International do Brasil, sponsored by Hotéis Transamérica and Grupo Agropalma, information based on aforesaid book.
8. Source: SOS MATA ATLÂNTICA/IMPE/ISA–Atlas da Evolução dos Remanescentes Florestais e Ecossistemas Associados no Domínio da Mata Atlântica [Atlas of the evolution of forest remainders and associated ecosystems within Atlantic Forest domain] 1998.
9. O Estado de São Paulo newspaper January 25, 2001.

10. SHAW, D.C. & K. BIBLE. 1996. An overview of forest canopy ecosystem functions with reference to urban and riparian systems. Northwest Sci. **70:** 16.
11. DOMINGOS, M., C. BOUROTTE, A. KLUMPP, *et al.* 2002. Impactos de poluição atmosférica sobre remanescentes florestais [Impacts of atmospheric pollution on forest remainders]. *In* Parque Estadual das Fontes do Ipiranga (PEFI): unidade de conservação ameaçada pela urbanização de São Paulo [Fontes do Ipiranga State Park: conservation unit threatened by the urbanization of São Paulo]. D.C. Bicudo, M.C. Forti & C.E.M. Bicudo, Organizers. State Department of the Environment Press, São Paulo. In press.
12. DÄSSLER, H.G. & S. BÖRTITZ. 1988. Air Pollution and Its Influence on Vegetation. Dr. W. Jung Publishers. Dordrecht.
13. MANNING W.J. & W.A. FEDER. 1980. Biomonitoring Air Pollutants with Plants. Applied Science Publishers. London.
14. POSTHUMUS, A.C. 1991. Effects of air pollution on plants and vegetation. *In* Ecological Responses to Environmental Stresses. J. Rozema & J.C. Verkleij, Eds.: 191–198. Kluwer Academic Publishers. London.
15. FREEDMAN, B. 1995. Environmental Ecology: The Ecological Effects of Pollution, Disturbance, and Other Stresses. 2nd edition. Academic Press. San Diego.
16. EMBERSON, L.D., M.R. ASHMORE, F. MURRAY, F., *et al.* 2001. Impacts of air pollutants on vegetation in developing countries. Water, Air Soil Pollut. **130:** 107–118.
17. KLUMPP A., M. DOMINGOS & M.L. PIGNATA. 2000. Air pollution and vegetation damage in South America—state of knowledge and perspectives. *In* Environmental Pollution and Plant Responses. S.B. Agrawal & M. Agrawal, Eds.: 111–136. Lewis Publishers. Boca Raton, FL.
18. DOMINGOS, M., A. KLUMPP & G. KLUMPP. 2002. Disturbances to the Atlantic Rain Forest in Southeast Brazil. *In* Air Pollution Impacts on Vegetation in Developing Countries. M. Ashmore *et al.*, Eds. Imperial College Press, London. In press.
19. IZIQUE, C. O Mapa da Exclusão [The Exclusion Map]–FAPESP Research 83–January 2003, p.17.
20. POCHMANN, M. Inclusão Juvenil como Estratégia Pública [Juvenile inclusion as a public strategy]–Folha de São Paulo newspaper–"Brasil" Section–23/04/2002, p. A3.
21. O ESTADO DE SÃO PAULO [newspaper]"Cidades" Section–04/05/2002, p. C1 and C4.
22. FOLHA DE SÃO PAULO [newspaper]"Cotidiano" Section–27/10/2002, p. C4.
23. FOLHA DE SÃO PAULO [newspaper]"Folhateen" Section–29/04/2002, p. 7.
24. FOLHA DE SÃO PAULO [newspaper]"Cotidiano" Section–18/08/2002, p. C7.
25. FOLHA DE SÃO PAULO [newspaper]"Cotidiano" Section–13/11/2002, p. C1.
26. FOLHA DE SÃO PAULO [newspaper]"Cotidiano" Section–14/01/2003, p. C7.

Written in Stone

Memory and Reconciliation Intersecting the Urban Biosphere

MARTHA KOHEN

School of Architecture, University of Florida, Gainesville, Florida 32611-5702, USA

ABSTRACT: The article describes the process of planning the Memorial of Disappeared Detained Citizens in the City of Montevideo, Uruguay, the construction of which was completed in January 2003. It explores the role that memory, planning, and reconciliation carried out in the public realm can play in the context of an urban environment. It describes the procedures and involvement of different social agents in the achievement of a significant landmark where social healing is promoted in parallel to the materialization of the construction of the Memorial, the necessary interaction between the natural and the human dimensions, and how these relate to the city as a biosphere.

KEYWORDS: Memorial of Disappeared Detained Citizens; Montevideo, Uruguay; biosphere

Between 1998 and 2003, a process that led to the construction of a Memorial in remembrance of Disappeared Detained Citizens took place, intersecting an ongoing social healing process with a material intervention crossing the realms of nature and the city.

During the military governments of the 1970s and 1980s in the Southern Cone of Latin America, the unacceptable practice by the authorities in power of the forced systematic "disappearance" of persons became a widespread though undisclosed practice. More than two decades had to pass before the issue could find a healing path that included memorials in the three countries, Uruguay, Argentina, and Chile. In parallel to the investigation of the events, the search for a significant measure of justice and compensation procedures, civil societies, and the democratically elected governments at the local levels initiated a process of reconciliation with the difficult facts of the recent past.

Address for correspondence: Martha Kohen, School of Architecture, University of Florida, 231 Architecture Building, P.O. Box 115702, Gainesville, FL 32611-5702.
mkohen@ufl.edu

Ann. N.Y. Acad. Sci. 1023: 282–288 (2004).
doi: 10.1196/annals.1319.013

FIGURE 1. Relatives visiting the memorial during the daytime.

The proposals for memorials brought a focus for these activities. The Municipal Government of the City of Montevideo was a leader in these initiatives and the memorial in Montevideo was the first one to be completed in the region, in 2003 (see FIGS. 1–4).

Constructed memorials have been emblematic and important as metaphors since the beginning of recorded human life. They are sometimes the only physical remnants of the thoughts, practices, and culture of a civilization, such as the Indian mounds of Florida, built by the Timucuan, who disappeared without written records.[1] In Uruguay, unlike in the Andean nations that still harbor their native populations, the Stone Age original inhabitants long gone also left earth mounds and stone objects of their material life, which I profess to collect, and that constitute a testimony to their use of the territory and natural resources in a definitely sustainable mode.[2] Their numbers balanced their ecological footprint in the vast pastures overlooking the ocean. Their legendary spirit still guides our national soul as a metaphor of strength and perseverance, especially in the professional reporting of our sports accomplishments.[3]

Stone, written in stone, the least perishable of materials, to be found sometimes only by arduous digging, was the strongest and most significant material for the making of our design for the Memorial in Remembrance of Disappeared Detained Citizens.[a] Reference to the natural realm is one of the deepest appeals to the human soul.[4] It is associated with primeval times, as a symbol of the equilibrium of people's inner being and their surrounding

FIGURE 2. Juxtaposition of the natural and man-made materials.

environment.[5] Bringing nature into a memorial has the aim of transporting the spectators' minds to a realm beyond the particular conflicts portrayed and projects them to a reflection of events that transcends personal lives. In Uruguay, the construction of the Memorial was a keystone event in the public awareness about the need to clarify the destiny of the disappeared citizens. The commanding organization was integrated by notable persons from the church, culture, academia, sports, and political milieus.

The project is located in the outskirts of the city, in a traditionally working-class neighborhood, thus bringing the benefits of a monument of national significance to a peripheral location. This was an instance of the municipal strategy of dispersing public funding in the less privileged areas of the city.[6] It is located in a 50-year-old municipal park, on the Cerro de Montevideo, a 500-foot-high hill whose colonial fortress overlooks the historic Bay and Old Town. These urban landmarks date from the 18th century founding of the city.[7] The park views also encompass the River Plate, the 120-mile-wide estuary that separates Uruguay from neighboring Argentina, the river of main access to the central lowlands of the subcontinent, through the Uruguay, Paraguay, and Parana Rivers. It was to the waters of the River

[a]Authors: Architects Martha Kohen, Ruben Otero; Artist Mario Sagradini; Landscape engineer Rafael Dodera; extensive team and additional color pictures can be seen at <www.summamas.com/ summa 62/>.

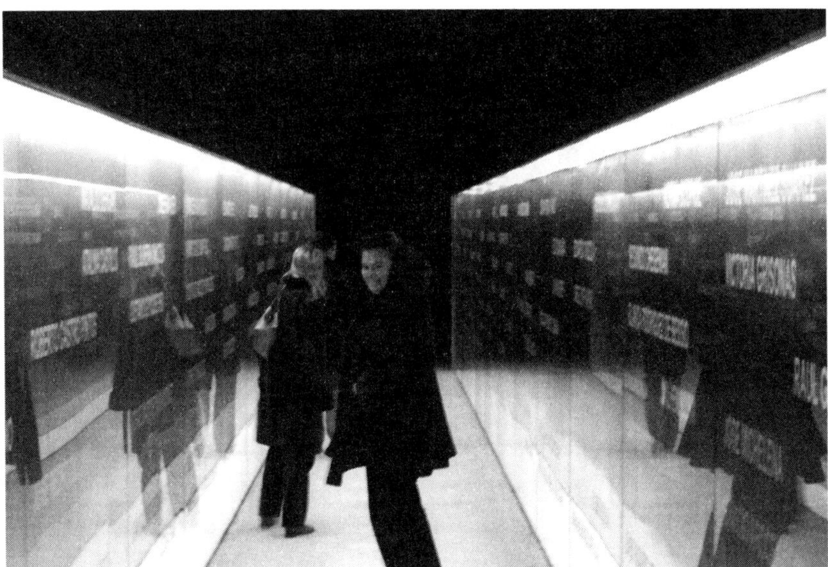

FIGURE 3. The double glass open corridor with the sandblasted engraved names.

Plate that many of the bodies were dropped (and "disappeared"), thrown out from military airplanes.

Instead of selecting a clearly visible and very public location for the Memorial, our project team selected a clearance in the dense woods, suggesting mystery and travail. A path was designed to climb uphill for 300 yards to the clearance, not disturbing a single existing tree. The underlying reason for the clearance was the close proximity of the stone substratum, that we discovered under the barely disturbed surface. The main idea for the Memorial arises from the exposure of the natural underlying stone bed to the sunlight as a symbol of truth revealed: the real nature of the hill and its rocky underground being the symbol of the most permanent values that are there. We took away the "skin and flesh" —the grass and earth—of the mound and exposed its "bones" (its rock), as the most permanent value. Not meant to be a burial ground, it evokes the image of death in all its strength, hardness, and eternity as an underlying thought. The cleared surface was bordered by a meditation bench that wraps the area and allows the visitor to contemplate the Memorial from a variety of points of view, always in close contact with nature, the trees, the natural vibrant life of birds that populate the park, from white doves and seagulls in the daytime to owls at night, butterflies in spring, and fireflies on the summer nights.

In the barren stone, little weeds make their way back to heal the rock wound; and children play thoughtfully with pebbles, unable to use traditional play or sport equipment.

FIGURE 4. Exterior perspective of the glass corridor showing the 174 names.

The central component of the Memorial is a double-glass open corridor, that traverses over the stones, but that does not take the visitor anywhere. The corridor only allows the transit of a limited group of persons. In the glass walls, the names of the 174 missing persons are inscribed, legible only from the interior of the corridor. The transparency of the superposed glass surfaces keeps the names floating in the landscape, integrated with the trees and the River Plate.

The Memorial's use of the environment exemplifies how we can intersect the natural and man-made realms into a powerful parable of past/present, a metaphor of life/death and a calm, secluded celebration of the significance of those few names. A collective memory comes into play, and a place for sharing stories, remembrances, and healing becomes part of the urban network. The time span between historical events and their related memorial reveals the acceptance of reconciliation or of continuing grief about the past. In a contemporary world of immediate communication and visual sharing of world events, time—psychosocial time—built into the conscious healing process can be brought about by the inevitably long timetables of the physical construction of the landmarks. The Montevideo Memorial took 5 years of dedicated work, from the conception of the idea, the integration of the multisectoral group of citizens that led the process, the public discussion of the selection of sites in the city, the national project competition, the fund-raising campaign, to the actual construction effort, which drew energies of different kinds into the Memorial and also became an integral part of the healing pro-

FIGURE 5. Evening general view.

cess. A parliamentary commission that worked in parallel to this process since has clarified the final destiny of about one fifth of the 174 names. The process involved the city and the people of the country and its realization, to a large extent, brought a measure of closure and finality. It is interesting to note that the emigrated, displaced, Uruguayan diaspora, living in Europe, Australia, and America, as well as the support of academic institutions abroad[b] were major contributors and supporters of the idea. Their input has greatly enriched and sustained the efforts of the local leaders, bringing a global perspective into the discussion.

The resonance of this project has been widely recognized internationally, as it has been distinguished in Latin America and in North America through awards and prizes.[c] These surely were assigned not only because of its architectural merits but also because of the recognition of its human and environmental values. The Memorial attempts to recognize ourselves in nature and, at the same time, to search in nature for the timelessness that we sometimes require and demand. It brings together our need to demand from nature the tools to help our urban souls nest in the larger realm of global nature and a timeless geological link that transcends our perceived biological urban life spans.

[b]New York University, 2000.

[c]Awards obtained: First prize (shared)/Landscape Architecture/Quito 8th International Bienal Ecuador 2002; First Prize/Architecture/5th International Architecture Bienal of Sao Paulo Brazil 2003; Silver Medal/Landscape Architecture/2nd International Architecture Bienal/Miami Beach USA 2003.

REFERENCES

1. Gordon, E. 2002. Florida's Colonial Architectural Heritage. University Press of Florida. Gainesville, FL.
2. Sala de Touron, L. 1968. Evolucion Economica de la Banda Oriental. Ediciones Pueblos Unidos. Montevideo, Uruguay.
3. Anton, D. 1996. Uruguaypiri. Rosebud ediciones. Montevideo, Uruguay.
4. Leakey, R. 1977. Origins. Macdonald and Jane's. London.
5. Pinkola Estes, C. 1992. Women Who Run with the Wolves. Ballantine Books. New York.
6. Plan de Ordenamiento Territorial de Montevideo. 1998. Intendencia Municipal de Montevideo. Montevideo, Uruguay.
7. P.R.O.UR. 1986. Taller de investigaciones urbanas. *In* Propuestas a la Ciudad. Montevideo, Uruguay.

Sustainability, Survivability, and the Paradox of New Orleans

RICHARD CAMPANELLA, DANIEL ETHERIDGE, AND DOUGLAS J. MEFFERT

Center for Bioenvironmental Research at Tulane and Xavier Universities, New Orleans, Louisiana 70112, USA

ABSTRACT: Some precepts of the urban sustainability movement derive from the premise that economic expansion, population growth, and physical sprawl lead to a decline in quality of life, ecological damage, and eventual unsustainability. But what about cities that are failing—losing population, losing investment, losing infrastructure, even losing land? This article challenges conventional sustainability concepts, usually derived from the experiences of ascending cities, with the notion of survivability that confronts declining cities. Should troubled cities, such as New Orleans, located on the eroding Gulf of Mexico coastal region of the state of Louisiana, be held to different sustainability standards? Could urban expansion, in some cases, actually stem environmental degradation and enhance survivability?

KEYWORDS: urban sustainability; urban sprawl; coastal erosion; New Orleans; Louisiana; Mississippi River; deltaic environments; wetlands restoration; declining cities

THE PARADOX OF NEW ORLEANS

Founded to exploit a dynamic natural phenomenon (the Mississippi River) and situated on a highly active geological base (the lower Mississippi River deltaic plain), the historic port city of New Orleans, Louisiana, USA, embodies paradoxes that challenge efforts toward urban sustainability. At various times in the early 19th century, New Orleans ranked as one of the largest, fastest growing, and wealthiest cities in the nation. A multitude of factors have since diminished New Orleans' population from a high of 627,525 in 1960 to 469,032 in 2003. Social and economic factors explain much of this decline, but impending environmental problems loom large in

Address for correspondence: Douglas J. Meffert, D. Env., MBA , Center for Bioenvironmental Research at Tulane and Xavier Universities, 1430 Tulane Avenue SL-3, New Orleans, LA 70112. Voice: 504-988-4618; fax: 504-585-6428.
dmeffert@tulane.edu

**Ann. N.Y. Acad. Sci. 1023: 289–299 (2004). © 2004 New York Academy of Sciences.
doi: 10.1196/annals.1319.014**

the near future. It is only recently in its nearly 300-year history that the "Crescent City" has addressed these troubles, which threaten its very existence within the lifetime of children born today. Cataloging these problems, and the current efforts to resolve them, offers a perspective on urban sustainability relevant not just to the famously unique city of New Orleans, but to numerous other historic cities situated in fragile deltaic or coastal environments. A recent U.S. Census Bureau study found that the old Southern port cities of New Orleans, Mobile, Alabama, and Savannah, Georgia, were among the fastest shrinking cities in the United States, despite their location in the otherwise booming "Sun Belt" along the southern tier of the United States. New Orleans lost 15,642 residents, or 3.2% of its population, between 2000 and 2003, the fifth-fastest loss pace among large American cities.[1]

Underlying New Orleans' dilemma is the paradox of its location. At the time of its founding, the geographical *situation* offered by the union of the Mississippi River and the Gulf of Mexico seemed optimal for the French colonial control of its vast Mississippi Basin claim. But seizing this situation meant founding a city in a particular geographical *site*, for which the lower Mississippi deltaic plain offered the worst possible options: thin, hydric soils and mosquito-infested swamps at or below sea level, surrounded by water and vulnerable to hurricanes and severe floods.[2,3,a] New Orleans prospered magnificently from its strategic geographical situation, particularly during the early 19th century, when, as a major center for shipping and finance, the "Queen of the South" ranked as the fastest growing and third- to fifth-largest city in the nation. But its problematic site has forced engineers to solve the crisis of the moment in a manner that often spawned greater problems in the future.[4] Following is a synopsis of some of these "urban paradoxes." (See FIGS. 1–4.)

Flood Control → Land Loss

Natural levees form along rivers in alluvial valleys and deltaic plains by seasonal overbank flooding and deposition of sediment, freshwater, and organic matter. Artificial levees—earthen dykes built upon the crest of the natural levee—were first erected in New Orleans starting in 1719 to prevent the deleterious effects of seasonal inundations, but these flood-control structures had the unintended consequence of depleting the surrounding wetlands of the riverborne depositions, which, under natural conditions, build up local land elevation and counterbalance natural subsidence. In large part because of flood control measures, southern Louisiana has lost a land area almost the size of the state of Delaware (4,860 km^2 from the 1930s to the 1990s) in the past century.[5] The loss of every 4.5 linear kilometers of wetland buffer

[a]See page 27 of Peirce Lewis' classic monograph for a "Catalogue of Difficulties" of New Orleans' site.

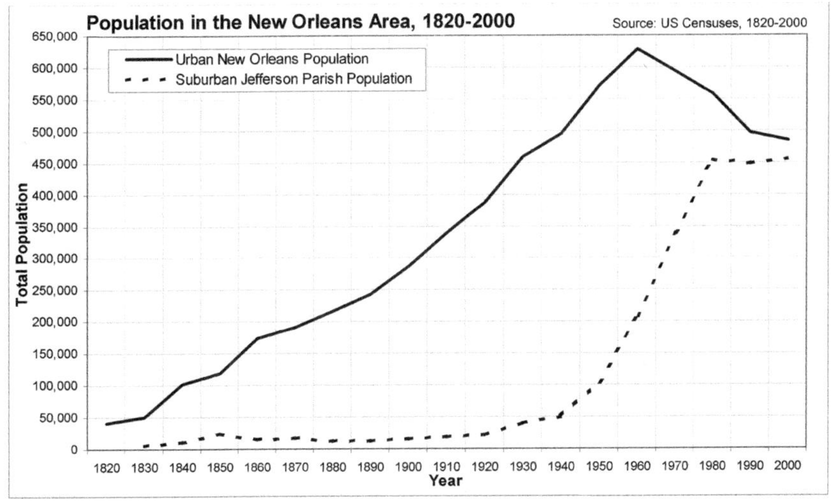

FIGURE 1. See text.

equates to roughly 30 extra centimeters of hurricane-induced storm surge upon New Orleans.

Drainage → Subsidence

The levees designed to keep floodwaters out of New Orleans unintentionally trapped rainwater within the bowl-shaped metropolis. Specially engineered pumps installed around 1900 drained the city's backswamp and allowed the city to expand toward Lake Pontchartrain, but the removal of the water mass allowed the hydric, highly organic soils to compact and shrink. Resultant high levels of subsidence have damaged homes and infrastructure. Beyond the city limits, subsidence now occurs without the counterbalancing annual deposition of riverborne sediments, leading to even more coastal erosion. Subsidence in the city and in the Louisiana deltaic plain, which naturally subsides but for the replenishment for riverborne sediment and water, is exceedingly difficult to measure. Studies have shown subsidence rates ~1 cm per year at some metropolitan sites, to roughly 30 cm per century in the rural deltaic plain, but measurements are extremely variable and subject to numerous factors.[6]

Navigation → Erosion

The obligation of New Orleans to keep its strategic situation competitive for shipping forced it to excavate canals to shorten the distance between port facilities and the Gulf of Mexico. However, this navigation advantage caused

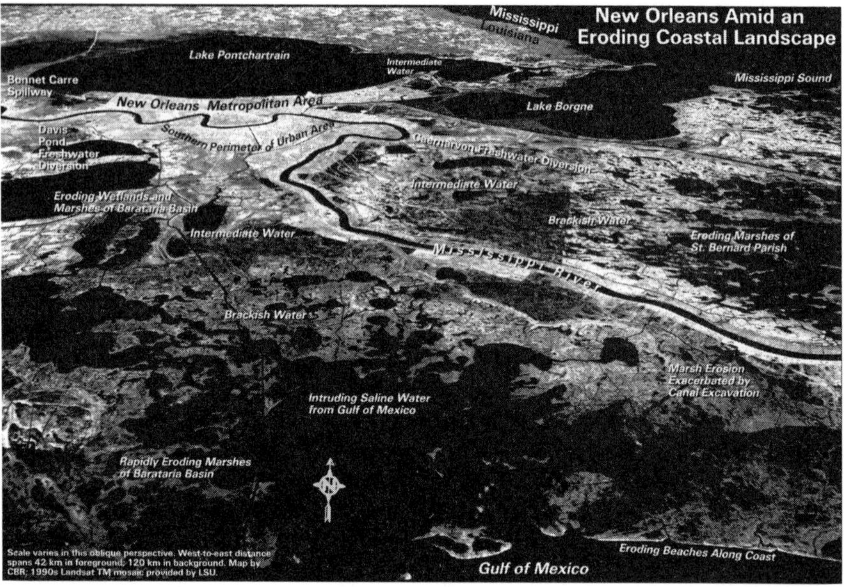

FIGURE 2. See text.

severe erosion by subsequent wave energies and saltwater intrusion in fragile interior marsh. The Mississippi River–Gulf Outlet (MR-GO) Canal, excavated in the 1950s and 1960s to streamline port access, has eroded to a width of 600 meters in places, destroying thousands of acres of wetlands, allowing saltwater and storm surges to intrude toward urban areas, and itself silting up and requiring more dredging at a cost of $16 million a year.[7]

Oil and Gas Activity → Erosion

Likewise, oil and gas exploration and extraction, which became the city's biggest economic sector during 1960s to 1980s, involved the excavation of canal networks in the coastal region. Recent research indicates that roughly 10% of erosion in southeastern Louisiana is attributable to canal excavation.[8] These waterways also contributed to coastal erosion by wave action and saltwater intrusion. In addition, petroleum extraction increases subsidence through the removal of subsurface deposits and the subsequent collapse of overlaying surface materials.

Shipping → Invasive Species

The optimal geographical situation that New Orleans exploits as the nation's busiest regional port also exposes the city to biological invasion from shipping sources throughout the world. Formosan termites, accidentally introduced from East Asia in the 1940s, cause $300 million of structural damage to New Orleans annually. The South American rodent nutria, intentionally introduced as fur bearers in the 1930s, hasten coastal erosion by eating marsh grasses and exposing thin soils to wave and wind erosion.[9]

Sediment

Damming of the upper Mississippi River and its western tributaries has reduced the quantity of riverborne sediments reaching the delta by approximately one-third since the mid-20th century. These sediments, critical to the rebuilding of wetlands by means of river diversion into the backswamp, currently are accumulating uselessly along the riverbed, in the outlets of the birdfoot delta (where they must be dredged for navigation), and near the continental shelf. Worse yet, the best land-building sediments—coarse sand particles, rather than finer silt and clay—are also the most likely to be trapped upstream and removed from the sediment mix delivered to the delta region, where it could have been tapped for coastal restoration.[10]

These various factors combine to eliminate 65–90 km^2 of land from southern Louisiana annually. If current trends continue, New Orleans (currently 152 km from the mouth of the Mississippi) will be a Gulf Coast city in little more than a lifetime. Coupled with the realities that New Orleans has lost over a quarter of its population since the 1960s, relies too heavily on tourism for its economy, and has declined from the South's premier city to one of the nation's poorest, the threat of coastal erosion and the associated vulnerability to hurricanes make many question the very survivability of the "Venice of America."

BACKGROUND: COASTAL EROSION IN LOUISIANA

The vast wetlands and marshes that comprise most of southeastern Louisiana were developed by the delta-building processes of the Mississippi River over the last 7,000 years, when sea level conditions were relatively stable.[11–13] The establishment of permanent settlements in the region during the 18th century exploited the strategic location of the Mississippi River/Gulf of Mexico interface. This dynamic natural setting on which New Orleans was founded proved a constant challenge, mostly in terms of seasonal river flooding—the initial impetus for human modification of this natural system. Modification meant levee construction, and whereas artificial levees reduced overbank flooding, they also caused—unbeknownst or ignored at the time—coastal erosion. Not until the 20th century did scientists address the alarming loss of land in this region.

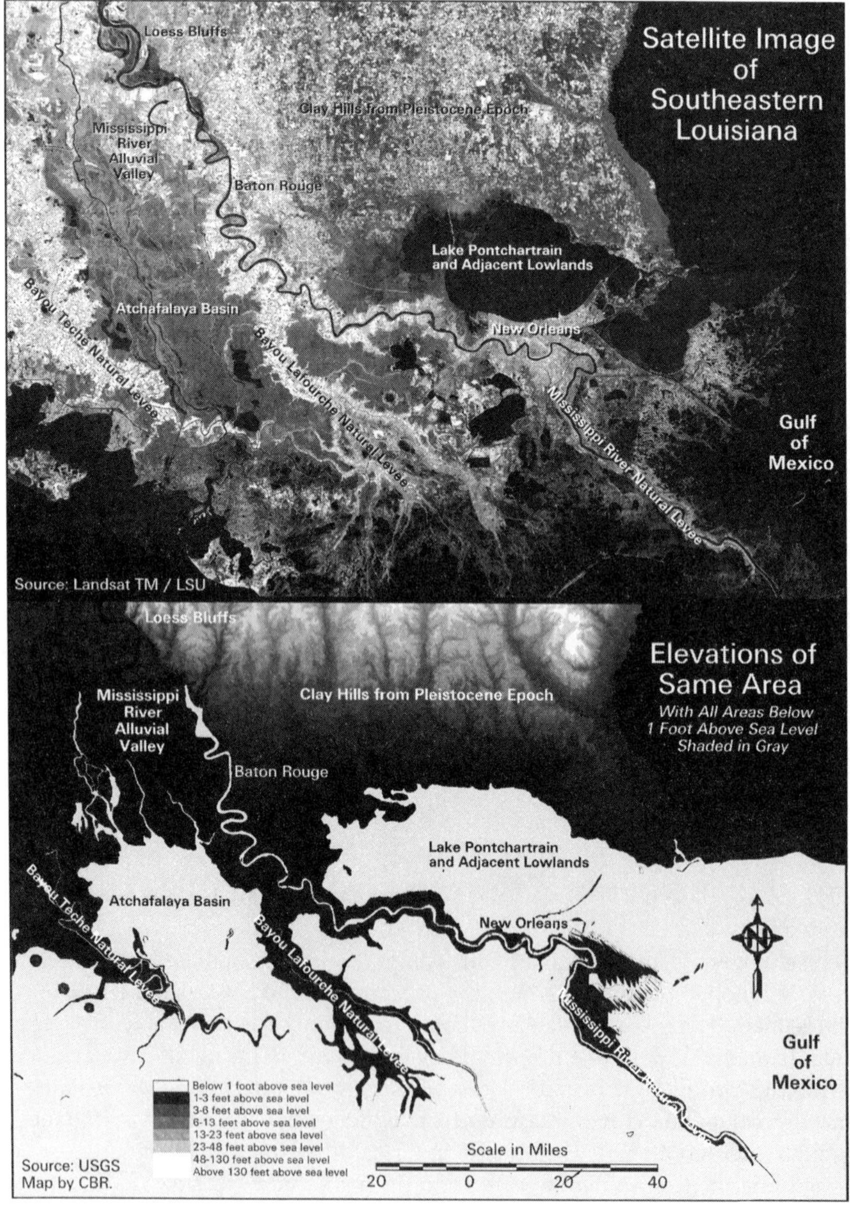

FIGURE 3. See text.

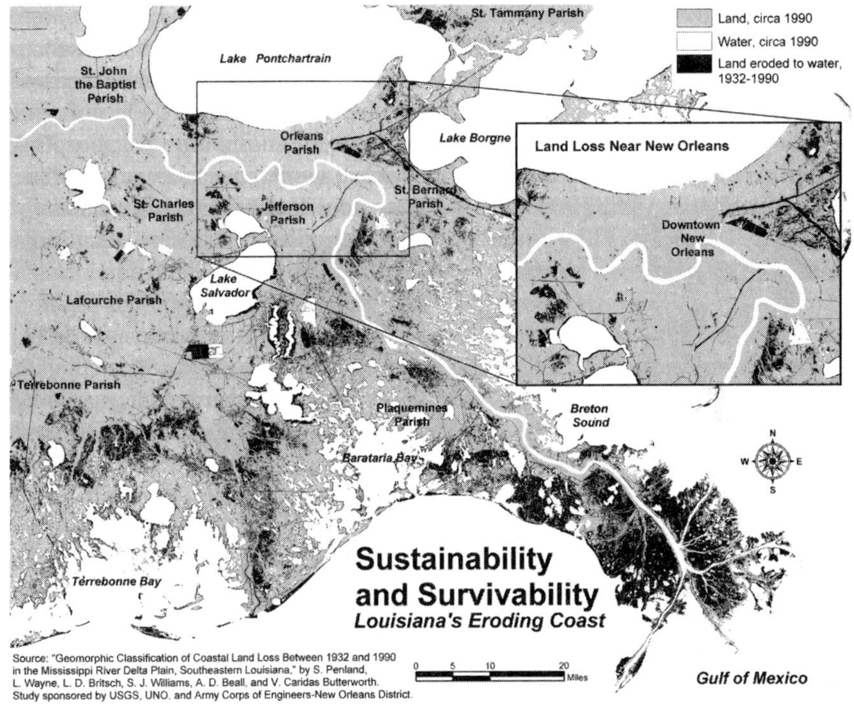

FIGURE 4. See text.

During the 1970s, as a result of comprehensive coastal mapping, scientists first quantified the magnitude of coastal land loss in Louisiana.[14] Massive erosion, which became apparent in the late 19th century and peaked in the mid-20th century, had converted almost 5,000 square kilometers of wetlands, marshes, ridges, and barrier islands in Louisiana's coastal region (roughly 20% of its historical land base) to open water. The deltaic plain system continues to lose its subsystem components and is approaching a condition of system collapse.[15] Main factors controlling Louisiana's wetland sustainability include local and global sea level increase, subsidence, sediment deprivation and compaction, hydrological modification, sinking of fault-bounded rocks, dredge and fill activities, herbivory, and large-scale storm events. The modes of interaction of these processes are myriad and complex; despite extensive research in recent decades, much remains to be learned about the exact nature of such interactions.

Legislation

Louisiana first responded to the land-loss crisis in the mid-1980s. The Louisiana Department of Natural Resources, financed by a state trust fund established through a constitutional amendment, initiated several coastal restoration projects in 1986. Three years later, the state legislature passed an act establishing a statewide coastal wetlands restoration program. A major legislative breakthrough occurred in 1990, when U.S. Senators John Breaux and J. Bennett Johnston introduced the Coastal Wetlands Planning and Protection Act. CWPPRA ("the Breaux Act") created a partnership between the State of Louisiana and five federal agencies: the Army Corps of Engineers, Department of Agriculture–Natural Resources Conservation Service, Department of Commerce–National Marine Fisheries Service, Department of the Interior-Fish and Wildlife Service, and the Environmental Protection Agency. CWPPRA availed approximately $45 million per year in federal funds for wetland restoration projects in Louisiana, matched on a 3-to-1 basis with Louisiana monies derived from its Wetland Trust Fund. The act also required the state to develop, by task force, a "comprehensive approach to restore and prevent the loss of wetlands in Louisiana." Additional federal support came in 1996 with the passing of the Water Resources Development Act, which reduced state cost-sharing responsibilities on certain projects to 10%. The task force in 1998 completed its coastal restoration plan, entitled *Coast 2050: Toward a Sustainable Coastal Louisiana*, with a goal "to sustain a coastal ecosystem that supports and protects the environment, economy, and culture of Southern Louisiana, and that contributes greatly to the economy and well-being of the nation." The plan's proposed regional ecosystem strategies were seen as a "blueprint for restoration," and the contents of the lengthy document were seen as the response to the CWPPRA bill's mandate for a comprehensive statewide plan.[16] Since CWPPRA was signed into law by President George Bush on November 1990, 143 projects have been authorized by the task force, of which 62 were completed through November 2003. These restoration projects target specific sites in the Louisiana coastal region, rather than extensive ecosystems.[15]

The Louisiana Coastal Area Comprehensive Coastwide Study (LCA) is the next step in the effort to adopt a strategic unified plan to address coastal erosion in Louisiana. The LCA approach differs from CWPPRA not only in terms of funding requirements but also in its approach to restoration. Whereas CWPPRA funded projects to improve specific sites and basins, LCA aims to restore and/or mimic ecosystem functions on expansive areas spanning multiple basins. LCA cost estimates range from $4.3 billion to $14.7 billion over an ~30-year period.[17]

Engineering

Restoration techniques funded by the aforementioned legislation include freshwater and sediment diversions, levee openings (crevasses), piping of dredged materials, hydrologic restoration, control of canal-bank and shoreline erosion, sediment capture, wave dampening, vegetative plantings, and marsh creation.[15] The Caernarvon freshwater diversion, the first large-scale restoration project in the region, was designed to divert up to 225 cubic meters of water per second from the main Mississippi River channel into the upper end of the Breton Sound Estuary, mimicking the flooding cycles of the river under historic conditions. Opened in 1991 ~48 river kilometers below New Orleans, Caernarvon has successfully pushed back encroaching salt-water, diminished erosion rates, and built some new land. Recent monitoring data have shown a sevenfold increase in freshwater marsh, whereas brackish marsh content has doubled. Caernarvon was followed by the much larger Davis Pond freshwater diversion, located 35 river kilometers above New Orleans and designed to divert up to 300 cubic meters per second into the rapidly eroding Barataria Basin. Construction phase of Davis Pond was recently completed and operational trials are in progress.

Louisiana and the nation are now addressing the environmental survival of the state's coastal wetlands, and its premier city located thereon, by moving from problem identification to legislation to engineering solutions. However, engineering solutions depend on funding, and funding—at the levels needed for these Herculean projects—depends on state and federal legislation, which, in turn, depends on the citizenry and their political representatives who advocate them. Fewer citizens in the rural coastal region, a declining population in urban New Orleans, an exodus of skilled workers, a departure of educated young people from Louisiana society, and the general economic divestment in the coastal region all translate to a smaller constituency, less political clout, and a diminished voice to be heard in a nation with countless other priorities in places with much larger and wealthier populations. Unlike many other environmentally sensitive areas, a case can be made that population decline in coastal Louisiana *exacerbates*, rather than ameliorates, its environmental problems.

SUSTAINABILITY AND SURVIVABILITY

When survivability is at stake, new notions of urban sustainability emerge. The urban sprawl that may constitute an unmitigated environmental disaster for American cities such as Atlanta, Denver, and Phoenix may, in fact, actually help promote New Orleans' sustainability. A new housing development along the southern fringes of the New Orleans metropolitan area may be viewed as an investment of property-owning citizens in the literal front lines of coastal erosion. Such citizens may help ensure the continued federal and state interest and investment to restore the coast (through costly engineering projects such as the Caernarvon and Davis Pond diversions) until a new equilibrium is reached. Urban growth upon a deltaic plain unquestionably comes with concerns, such as clearing of wetlands and federal bailouts of flood and hurricane victims. But even with these drawbacks, it may be argued that population growth and urban development in this eroding coastal region offer, paradoxically, a viable defense against the grave environmental problem of massive coastal erosion. Population loss, cultural decline, business relocation, withdrawal of insurance coverage, and decreases in real estate prices—all of which are already occurring in coastal Louisiana—conspire to hasten coastal erosion, in that they eliminate the most powerful factor in environmental protection: humans with something to lose.

Although some urban sustainability advocates may dispute this notion, most would probably agree that the prescriptions for urban sustainability should be gauged to locally relevant conditions. Poor, troubled cities such as New Orleans should not be held to the same sustainability strategies that make sense for prosperous cities, whose survival into the next century is unquestioned.

REFERENCES

1. U.S. CENSUS BUREAU. July 2003. As cited by Sealey, Geraldine, "Incredible Shrinking Cities: Perennial Census Losers Try to Stem Population Loss." ABC News, August 19, 2003.
2. JORDAN, T.G. & L. ROWNTREE. 1990. The Human Mosaic: A Thematic Introduction to Cultural Geography. Harper & Row. New York.
3. LEWIS, P.F. 1976. New Orleans: The Making of an Urban Landscape. Ballinger Pub. Cambridge, MA.
4. CAMPANELLA, R. 2002. Time and Place in New Orleans: Past Geographies in the Present Day. Pelican Pub. Gretna, LA.
5. PENLAND, S., L. WAYNE, L.D. BRITSCH, *et al.* Geomorphic Classification of Coastal Land Loss Between 1932 and 1990 in the Mississippi River Delta Plain, Southeastern Louisiana. Poster map funded by Argonne National Laboratory, Gas Research Institute, U.S. Army Corps of Engineers, and the U.S. Geological Survey.
6. HART, D. & D. ZILKOSKI. 1994. Mapping a Moving Target: The Use of GIS to Support Development of a Subsidence Model in the New Orleans Region. Urban and Regional Information Association (URISA) Proceedings.
7. TURNI, K. November 3, 1997. "Corps Battles Erosion in Gulf Outlet," The Times-Picayune.
8. DAY, J.W. JR., L.D. BRITSCH, S.R. HAWES, *et al.* 2000. Pattern and process of land loss in the Mississippi Delta: a spatial and temporal analysis of wetland habitat change. Estuaries **23:** 425–438.
9. CENTER FOR BIOENVIRONMENTAL RESEARCH. 2002. Portals and Pathways: The Geography of Invasive Species in Louisiana. Poster map funded by the Coypu Foundation.
10. MEADE, R.H., editor. Contaminants in the Mississippi River, 1987–1992. U.S. Geological Survey Circular 1133, Denver, CO.
11. FISK, H.N. 1944. Geological investigation of the alluvial valley of the lower Mississippi River. U.S. Army Corp of Engineers, Mississippi River Commission, Vicksburg, MS.

12. FRAZIER, D.E. 1967. Recent deltaic deposits of the Mississippi River: their development and chronology. Trans. Gulf Assoc. Geol. Soc. **17:** 287–315.
13. KOLB, C.R. & J.R. VAN LOPIK. 1958. Geology of the Mississippi River Deltaic Plain, Southeastern Louisiana. Technical Reports 3-483 and 3-484. U.S. Army Engineer Waterways Experiment Station. Vicksburg, MS.
14. GAGLIANO, S.M. & J.L. VAN BEEK. 1970. Geological and geomorphic aspects of deltaic processes, Mississippi Delta System. Hydrologic and Geologic Studies of Coastal Louisiana, Report 1, Coastal Resources Unit, Center for Wetland Resources, Louisiana State University, Baton Rouge, LA.
15. LOUISIANA COASTAL WETLANDS CONSERVATION AND RESTORATION TASK FORCE AND THE WETLANDS CONSERVATION AND RESTORATION AUTHORITY. 1998. "Coast 2050: Toward a Sustainable Coastal Louisiana." Louisiana Department of Natural Resources.
16. MEFFERT, D.J., S. UNDERWOOD, B. GOOD, *et al.* 1997. The 1997 Evaluation Report to the U.S. Congress on the Effectiveness of Louisiana Coastal Wetland Restoration Projects in accordance with the Coastal Wetlands Planning, Protection, and Restoration Act Public Law 101-646, Title III or "Breaux Act." Sponsored by Louisiana Coastal Wetlands Conservation and Restoration Task Force, Baton Rouge, LA.
17. AMERICA'S WETLAND. Campaign to Save Coastal Louisiana. www.americaswetland.com.

Governance Challenges and Coalition Building among Urban Environmental Stakeholders in Dar es Salaam, Tanzania

ANNA MTANI

Safer Cities Dar es Salaam, Dar es Salaam, Tanzania

ABSTRACT: Rapid urbanization is arguably one of the most complex and important socioeconomic phenomena of the new millennium. It represents major and irreversible changes in production and consumption patterns and the way people interact with nature. The impact of urbanization will continue to bring about major changes especially in many countries in the developing world that are experiencing rapid urbanization. The serious environmental and development challenges facing Dar es Salaam, the largest commercial center of Tanzania, are highlighted in this report.

KEYWORDS: Dar es Salaam; urbanization; resources;

Rapid urbanization is arguably one of the most complex and important socioeconomic phenomena of the new millennium. It represents major and irreversible changes in production and consumption patterns and the way people interact with nature. The impact of urbanization will continue to bring about major changes especially in many countries in the developing world that are experiencing rapid urbanization. Global transformation will witness unprecedented growth in the number of mega cities of more than 10 million, most of which will be in the developing world. According to UN-Habitat estimates, 60% of the world's population will be living in urban areas by 2015, most of them in the unplanned (spontaneous) settlements without access to basic services. Although cities in developing countries may continue to depend on agriculture, forestry, or mining as their primary means of economic livelihood, cities in the developing countries will continue to grow in terms of political and cultural influence and increase their role as centers of economic power, production, and consumption and as engines of economic growth. Despite the differences in these trends, urbanization is nevertheless an irreversible trend.[1]

Address for correspondence: Anna Mtani, Safer Cities Dar es Salaam, P.O. Box 9084, Dar es Salaam, Tanzania. Voice: 255 (22) 2130959; fax: 255 (22) 2130961.
saferdsm@raha.com

Ann. N.Y. Acad. Sci. 1023: 300–307 (2004). © 2004 New York Academy of Sciences.
doi: 10.1196/annals.1319.015

Because of high pollution and high consumption of resources, urban centers tend to have far-reaching and negative impacts on the environment. The negative effects are felt most in cities of the developing world that lack the capacity and resources to minimize them. Pollution of coastal waters, for example, in coastal cities and towns in Tanzania negatively affects marine ecosystems and consequently the communities living in the coastal areas.

Dar es Salaam, the largest commercial center of Tanzania, is located along the eastern shores of the Indian Ocean, covering an area of 1,800 km^2 with a population of 2.5 million and an estimated growth rate of 4.3% (Census 2002). It bears its name from when an Arab Sultan Seyyid Majid of Zanzibar shifted his residence to Dar es Salaam approximately 140 years ago, because of its cooler climate and peaceful nature of the sheltered waters. He named the surrounding harbor "Haven of Peace" meaning "Bandari Salama" in Kiswahili. Like all other urban areas in Tanzania, the "Haven of Peace" has experienced fast and uncontrolled growth, resulting in an increase of unplanned and unserviced settlements (FIGS. 1 and 2).

Efforts to plan the development of Dar es Salaam started in 1948 when a master plan was prepared by a foreign firm of consultants. Despite efforts to review the master plan to keep it in pace with the growth of the city, more than 60% of the population of Dar es Salaam live in unplanned settlements with minimum services. It is now recognized that this situation is a result of the inflexible nature of master plans and lack of strategic focus for development infrastructure services, as well as its control-oriented nature, with a rigid, sectoral implementation and inadequacy of planning for resources. Lack of adequate institutional capacity greatly contributed to the unpreparedness of the growing city to receive and provide services and shelter to the newcomers.

Administratively, Dar es Salaam was centrally administered until 2000 with one elected mayor and 52 elected councilors. Administrative and management problems manifested by poor service delivery, deteriorating revenue base and collection, and widespread abuse of authority-poor governance forced the central government to decide to dissolve the city local authority management and replaced them in 1996 with professional commissioners with different capabilities and experiences in administration. An appointed chairman led the team.

As a result, by the beginning of 1990, Dar es Salaam found itself faced with serious environmental and development issues. The following conditions stood out and became a threat to the residents of the city:

- The growth and densification of spontaneous settlements, with more and more people crowded in the unplanned areas of the city, constructing and occupying structures which were not suitable for human occupation (FIGS. 1 and 2).
- Invasion of ecologically and environmentally fragile land (hill slopes, floodplains/valleys and beaches).

FIGURE 1. Aerial view of unplanned settlement Hannah Nassif.

- Deterioration of the available infrastructure due to pressures as more and more people continued to use them. (This was worse in the informal settlements, where the only services were provided at very low standards and were grossly inadequate.)
- Inability of the city management to extend services to newly planned/designed areas such as Tabata, Mbezi Beach, Mbagala, and Tegeta.

To address the situation, the government called for yet another review of the master plan in 1990. The government invited the United Nations Human

FIGURE 2. Hannah Nassif settlement.

Settlements Programme (UN-HABITAT), the former United Nations Center for Human Settlements, to advise on the best way to try to reverse the downward trend of the major and thriving commercial capital. UN-HABITAT at the time was in the process of examining different approachcs to urban management and development and formalizing the establishment of the Sustainable Cities Programme. The Sustainable Cities program argued that sustainability of cities depended very much on the planning approach and was seeking ways of ensuring that the citizens of the city owned the process. The search had identified environment as the entry point and was developing conceptual principles on environmental planning and management (EPM). UN-HABITAT response to the government's request to review the Dar es Salaam City Master Plan was that the problem did not lie in the master plan, but in the way it is prepared. UN-Habitat proposed a process which would (1) ensure the effective participation of all key stakeholders in defining where the city development will go; (2) ensure cross-sectoral consideration; (3) be comprehensive and taking all the conditions into account before coming up with a fixed position; and (4) address itself to the issue of resource mobilization.

With UN-Habitat support, the City of Dar es Salaam embarked on a search for a solution to the deteriorated environmental conditions. Local experts prepared an environmental profile to record the situation and through an interactive process sensitize the citizens on the conditions in the city. In 1992, stakeholders from all over the city, representing various interests came together for 5 days in a city consultation workshop chaired by the then prime

FIGURE 3. Uncollected waste in the city center 1990.

minister, to discuss the findings of the consultative process using the environmental profile as the background. Guided by several proposition papers, the 350 stakeholders prioritized nine environmental issues to be addressed immediately. These included management of solid waste (FIG. 3), upgrading of unserviced settlements, servicing city expansion, management of open spaces, recreational areas, urban agriculture potentials and hazard lands, managing the economy and integrating petty trading, air-quality management and urban transportation, managing surfacewater and liquid waste, managing coastal resources, and coordinating city center renewal.

The consultation marked the beginning of a long journey toward rebuilding of the city, which by then had virtually collapsed. A new paradigm was ushered into the management and development of Dar es Salaam. City residents, for the first time, could walk freely into City Hall as partners, to share with the city "fathers" their time, knowledge, and resources. The city consultation formally launched the Sustainable Dar es Salaam Project (SDP) and endorsed the application of the EPM process. The SDP set out to (1) strengthen the capacity of the city council to better plan and manage the growth and development of the city in partnership with other stakeholders (public, private, and popular sector), and (2) prepare a long-term dynamic and strategic urban development plan and investment strategy in which partners in urban development can cooperate in a synergistic manner.

The process that followed with technical support of UN-HABITAT and funding from the UNDP was guided by the following principles:

(1) The first principle was cross-sectoral and institutional engagement ensuring that all interests and concerns were taken into account. Particularly, this meant that the public sector, the private sector, and the popular sector were for the first time working together and for a common purpose to achieve an environmentally sustainable condition of the city.
(2) The second principle was to address the prioritized issues through a careful process of analyzing each one of them and all the time identifying priority actions.
(3) The third principle was action-oriented engagement through working groups which were established and supported by resource persons to prepare pragmatic physical, financial, and institutional action plans to address the priority issues.

Following the above principles, strategies and action plans were prepared for the priority areas identified during the consultation. These include:

- Upgrading of roads and drainage system in Hanna Nassif unplanned settlement.
- Establishment of a community infrastructure project implementing the infrastructure projects for Tabata and Kijitonyama in partnership with the respective communities and other development partners.
- Introduction of one-way road system in the CBD.
- Privatization of solid waste collection system in the city (FIG. 4).
- Privatization of parking facilities within the city center.
- Pit-emptying demonstration and private sector involvement in Sinza "B".
- Community mobilization in managing city open spaces in Mwananyamala.
- Rehabilitation of city horticulture gardens with support of STOAS International (NGO).
- Utilization of household open spaces for food security by encouraging home gardening (fruits and vegetables) in the inner city and periurban agriculture for food security, nutrition, and income generation (Mbutu).
- Integration of petty traders into city economy through construction of Makumbusho and Temeke stereo market.
- Street sharing strategy for petty traders and pedestrians by use of display structures.
- Greening the city through planting of shade trees along street and road walkways.
- User fees to mineral extractors and transporters.

FIGURE 4. Private waste collection contractors at work.

- Relocation of scattered upcountry bus terminals from city center to a periphery "Ubungo Bus Terminal".

The emerging action plans were implemented gradually and with the involvement of all stakeholders (FIG. 4). The preparation of the action plans and their implementation through the involvement of stakeholders changed the way of doing business in the city. Note that before the adoption of the EPM process, the government and/or the city provided almost all the services for free and with no contribution or involvement of the citizens in terms of user fees or taxes.

The strategies formulated by the issue-specific working groups were integrated into a Strategic Urban Development Plan (SUDP) for Dar es Salaam. The SUDP is a major output of the EPM process. The SUDP fundamentally differed from the traditional master plan in that it evolved over time. It is not sectoral, and it is not geared to controlling development but rather directing through careful and negotiated management and coordination of interventions to achieve environmentally sustainable living conditions for all.

To arrive at the SUDP, considerable capacity building took place for all stakeholders. There was an important change in attitudes of political leaders and government officials toward participation of and contribution by citizens developed. Through their participation and contribution, citizens became protectors of the environment and resources. Citizens became owners of the achievements and continued to contribute in their maintenance and upkeep. As a result of this process, many of the professionals, practitioners, and academicians who participated have changed their thinking and approaches of planning and urban development.

The EPM process has influenced changes in the ongoing review of the Town and Country Planning Act (1956) CAP 378 to incorporate EPM as a key approach in preparation for strategic urban development plans. The new Environment Act under preparation also has adopted the EPM process as mechanism carry out a sustainable environmental management in Tanzania. Moreover, the University College for Lands and Architectural Studies has adapted the EPM process into its teaching curriculum in the Faculty of Urban and Country Planning.

After the successful implementation of EPM process in Dar es Salaam, other municipalities countrywide indicated their interest to join in the implementation, thereby seeking technical support from both Dar es Salaam and UN-Habitat. Through the alliance of mayors of regional municipalities in Tanzania, nine municipalities launched the SCP programs. The Ministry of Lands and Human Settlement Development is continuing the replication process in the small and medium towns in the country and is assisting them in the preparation of strategic development plans.

Through the implementation of the EPM approach in Dar es Salaam and in other cities and towns in Tanzania, a new perception of the role of stakeholders in urban development has been established, and sensitivity to biosphere has greatly changed. We can continue to exploit natural resources in a manner that will not endanger our lives and lives of others today and in the future.

REFERENCE

1. World Bank. 2000. Cities in Transition.

The Dynamics of Social-Ecological Systems in Urban Landscapes

Stockholm and the National Urban Park, Sweden

T. ELMQVIST,[a] J. COLDING,[b] S. BARTHEL,[a] S. BORGSTRÖM,[c] A. DUIT,[c] J. LUNDBERG,[a] E. ANDERSSON,[a] K. AHRNÉ,[d] H. ERNSTSON,[a] C. FOLKE,[a] AND J. BENGTSSON[d]

[a]*Department of Systems Ecology, Stockholm University, SE- 106 91 Stockholm, Sweden*

[b]*Beijer International Institute of Ecological Economics, Royal Swedish Academy of Sciences, Stockholm, Sweden*

[c]*CTM, Stockholm University, SE-106 91 Stockholm, Sweden*

[d]*Department of Ecology and Crop Production Science, SE-750 07 Uppsala, Sweden*

ABSTRACT: This study addresses social-ecological dynamics in the greater metropolitan area of Stockholm County, Sweden, with special focus on the National Urban Park (NUP). It is part of the Millennium Ecosystem Assessment (MA) and has the following specific objectives: (1) to provide scientific information on biodiversity patterns, ecosystem dynamics, and ecosystem services generated; (2) to map interplay between actors and institutions involved in management of ecosystem services; and (3) to identify strategies for strengthening social-ecological resilience. The green areas in Stockholm County deliver numerous ecosystem services, for example, air filtration, regulation of microclimate, noise reduction, surface water drainage, recreational and cultural values, nutrient retention, and pollination and seed dispersal. Recreation is among the most important services and NUP, for example, has more than 15 million visitors per year. More than 65 organizations representing 175,000 members are involved in management of ecosystem services. However, because of population increase and urban growth during the last three decades, the region displays a quite dramatic loss of green areas and biodiversity. An important future focus is how management may reduce increasing isolation of urban green areas and enhance connectivity. Comanagement should be considered where locally managed green space may function as buffer zones and for manage-

Address for correspondence: Thomas Elmqvist, Department of Systems Ecology, Stockholm University, SE- 106 91 Stockholm, Sweden. Voice: +46-8-161283.
thomase@ecology.su.se

**Ann. N.Y. Acad. Sci. 1023: 308–322 (2004). © 2004 New York Academy of Sciences.
doi: 10.1196/annals.1319.017**

ment of weak links that connect larger green areas; for example, there are three such areas around NUP identified. Preliminary results indicate that areas of informal management represent centers on which to base adaptive comanagement, with the potential to strengthen biodiversity management and resilience in the landscape.

KEYWORDS: **urban green spaces; National Urban Park (NUP); Stockholm County; green wedge**

INTRODUCTION

Urban green spaces are by their very nature highly patchy and also highly dynamic, influenced by both biophysical and ecological drivers on the one hand and social and economic drivers on the other.[1–3] Factors such as climate change, species extinction and invasion, constitute potential biophysical and ecological drivers, whereas human population change, urban sprawl, real estate, and banking practices act as primary social and economic drivers. Urban green areas produce several ecosystem services, providing recreational and educational values, as well as ecological processes such as pollination and seed dispersal and other services such as air filtration, microclimate regulation, noise reduction, rainwater drainage, and sewage treatment.[4] In the face of increasing and rapid environmental change in urban areas, a continuous generation of ecosystem services cannot be taken for granted, and a challenge is how to sustain the flow of services delivered in growing urban areas.

Focusing only on the production of ecosystem services does not, however, address the dynamic capacity of ecosystems to uphold the supply of these goods and services. The challenge is to sustain the capacity of ecosystems to generate services,[5] including appreciation of the social dimension that makes ecosystem management possible.[6] The role of functional biological diversity in urban areas has received surprisingly little attention despite that such diversity often is critical for a continuous generation of ecosystem services.[7]

Research on urban green areas reveal that their ability to support biodiversity over time depend on the degree of habitat connectivity and matrix permeability.[8–10] Drayton and Primack[11] showed that an isolated urban park, even though it was large, lost 25% of its plant diversity over a period of 100 years with a potential of severely influencing vital biological functions, for example, plant–pollinator interactions and plant–seed disperser interactions.[12,13]

Urban green areas also function as important communication points between urban residents and nature and meeting points for various social groups, elderly, immigrants, children, teenagers, thereby contributing to both cultural diversity and, paradoxically perhaps, social cohesion in the city. The importance of social functions of urban green spaces has been stressed in other studies.[14–17] Others have noted that nature helps to build and reinforce

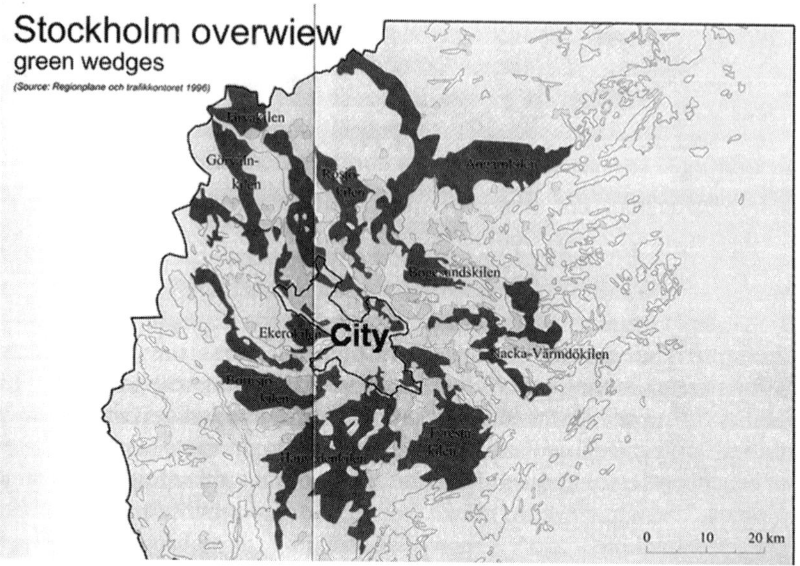

FIGURE 1. Overview of the Stockholm metropolitan areas with the location of green wedges. These form a star-formed pattern and represent important buffer zones with some restrictions in land-use and have a likely high importance for connecting urban green areas. (Source: Regionplane och traffikkontoret, 1996.)

cultural values and aesthetic appreciation of beauty.[18] It is surprising, then, that recreational values and other urban ecosystem services remain so poorly understood or investigated.

This case study focuses on the greater metropolitan area of Stockholm County (FIG. 1), with special attention paid to the National Urban Park (NUP) and its surrounding green areas, located adjacent to the inner city of Stockholm (FIG. 2). Green wedges extend from the rural parts of the county toward the central parts of Stockholm city (FIG. 1). The project is part of the UN-sponsored global program "The Millennium Ecosystem Assessment" (MA) (www.millenniumassessment.org) with the goal of providing scientific information on ecosystem change and addressing the options for responding to those changes.[19] The MA is a "multiscale" assessment and includes clusters of subglobal assessments at local, national, and regional levels. The Stockholm study is one of the few urban studies included in MA and has the following objectives: (1) provide scientific information on biodiversity patterns, ecosystem dynamics, and ecosystem services generated, (2) mapping institutional configurations, histories, and interplay between actors and institutions involved in management of ecosystem services, and (3) identify strategies for strengthening the social-ecological resilience of Stockholm Metropolitan Area.

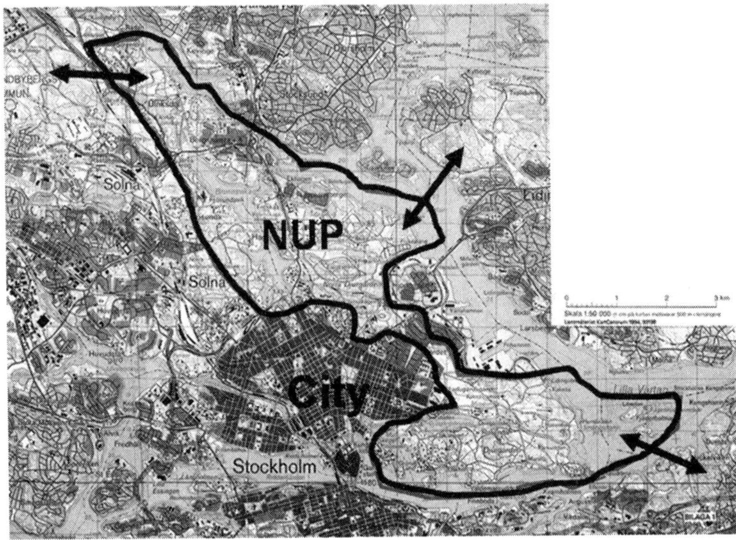

FIGURE 2. The National Urban Park (NUP) in central Stockholm. Arrows indicate areas of high importance for dispersal and migration of plants and animals in and out of the park.

Specific questions addressed in the study include: What are the main ecosystem services generated by urban green areas? What is the role of biodiversity in generation of services? What role does local ecological knowledge play in management of services and how is it related to scientific knowledge? How are the institutional and organizational structures linked? How may these cooperate to increase adaptive capacity to respond to uncertainty and crises?

STUDY AREA AND HISTORICAL BACKGROUND

Stockholm County consists of a total land and water area of 678,500 ha, representing ~2% of the total land area surface of Sweden and extending ~180 km from north to south. The county is one of the most densely populated areas of Sweden with 280 inhabitants/km^2 as compared with 21 inhabitants/km^2 for Sweden in total, and the population is expected to increase from 1.8 to 2.5 million in the next 30 years. The landscape in the region shows a large variation ranging from open agricultural areas to large forested areas and considerable areas of open water (e.g., Mälaren and Saltsjön) including many smaller lakes and riparian habitats.

The NUP constitutes a 2,700-ha area characterized by both broad-leaved and mixed forests and an open grass-dominated landscape. It stretches from Southern Djurgården in the middle of the city, via Northern Djurgården, Haga, and Brunnsviken to Ulriksdal and Sörentorp in the north (FIG. 2). The topography is typical for the region with remains from the latest ice age, for example, eskers, precipice, faults, and ice-grounded rocks. Because NUP is situated at the coast, some parts of the park are islands such as Fjäderholmarna and Skeppsholmen.

When humans first colonized this area some 6,000 years ago, most of the land was still submerged under water and only the highest peaks were exposed and used for settlements by hunters and fishermen. Land uplift processes have raised land continuously and have provided human settlers with increasing access to fertile fine-sediment soils suitable for agriculture and cattle herding. Humans have likely had a continuous strong impact on the area shaping the landscape and biodiversity during several thousands of years. In this open landscape, heliophilic species were favored. A relatively low nutritional status in the soil as a result of a long period of grazing have resulted in meadows with very high plant species richness.[20]

During the 12th to 14th centuries, large parts of the area that now constitute the NUP were owned by monasteries and the church, but in 1452 the southern part of Djurgården became royal property (TABLE 1).[21] This was the beginning of a royal management tradition that has continued up to today. In 1680, Djurgården was designated as a royal hunting park, and a royal management agency (KDF) was established to manage the forest and hunting grounds.[21] KDF is still in operation today and is managing the larger part of NUP. Large numbers of deer were enclosed behind a 20-km-long fence and deer grazing was the main ecological factor shaping the landscape for more than 100 years. In 1729, the numbers of deer were estimated to be more than 1,500.[21] The royal management deliberately favored stands of broad-leaved trees and particularly oak. During the mid- to late 1700s, there was an increased use of Djurgården for public recreation, and this expanded during the 19th century when many recreational institutions were created (e.g., an amusement park, a theatre, museums). In the early 1800s, up to 10,000 people a day could visit the area for recreational purposes.[22]

During the 19th and first half of the 20th century, the rapidly increasing population of Stockholm increased the demand for housing and this started an era of exploitation. The exploitation pressure was intense and led to several proposals in the Swedish Parliament to protect the area (e.g., 1809, 1913, and 1959). At the end of the 19th century, the industrialization strongly influenced the area through construction of new railways, a gas plant, and a harbor. The unexploited parts of the areas were continually diminishing, and, in 1963, 50% of the green parts from 1913 had disappeared in Djurgården, and core areas for biodiversity has decreased with 13% since 1947.[23] During the end of the 20th century, the exploitation pressure increased with plans to

TABLE 1. Historical overview of land-use and management of the area declared as National Urban Park in 1995

Land-use and management	National policy
Starting in the early 12th century, the church and monasteries were landowners. During the 14th century, grazing increased and negatively affected regeneration of broad-leaved trees.	In the years 1347 and 1442, laws were introduced that prohibited logging of oak.
In 1680, the Royal Hunting Park was established, enclosed by a 20-km-long fence. The royal management (KDF) was established to manage the area and the deer populations. Open areas were converted from agricultural fields to meadows for supplying the growing deer populations with fodder. Rapidly increasing grazing pressure. In 1729, the number of deer exceeded 1,500.	In 1647 and 1664, the king expropriated all oak forests.
During the 18th century, the hunting park was increasingly used for recreation and special areas designated for outdoor activities. Grazing intensity was extremely high and the area started to degrade and became in need of restoration.	At the end of the 18th century, the laws from 1647 and 1664 were abolished. This rapidly led to large-scale logging of oak forests around the country.
During the 19th century, the area was increasingly used for recreation and forestry. The deer population was permanently removed in 1809. Forest regeneration started and oaks planted.	In 1805, new regulations were introduced that prohibited logging of oak.
During the 20th century, the area was used for recreation. The last agricultural fields terminated in the 1950s. Forestry of less economic importance. Increased exploitation pressure from the growing city.	Proposals in the parliament 1913 and 1959 to reduce exploitation rates in Djurgården.
The first management plan for the whole area came in the mid-1980s.	
The 2,700-ha area was designated as National Urban Park having vital biological, cultural, and historical values. New management plans are under way.	A specific law passed in 1995 to protect the National Urban Park from exploitation.

NOTE: Modified from Herdin.[21]

build on the valuable land near the city core. However, this process was halted in1995, when the area became legally protected. The National Urban Park law (Naturresurslagen [NRL] 3 ch. 7 §, effective of January 1, 1995, is now part of the Environmental Code [MB] 4 ch. 7 §) states that construction in the park is allowed only if these do not damage the natural and cultural values in the historical landscape.

CHANGES IN BIODIVERSITY AND ECOSYSTEM DYNAMICS

The Stockholm Metropolitan Area

In a European perspective, the Stockholm region has a high coverage of urban green areas. Large green wedges extend from the rural parts of the county toward the central parts of Stockholm city (FIG. 1). These green wedges comprise both *core areas*, of social and ecological significance, and *green links* that bind together core areas in the wedges. Green wedges constitute the nucleus of the green area structure and are considered important in physical regional planning. Nonetheless, during the 1970s and 1980s, ~8% and 7% of green areas, respectively, were lost because of urban sprawl and this trend continues.[24] Within a distance of 30 km from the city's center, today there are 48 nature preserves and one national park with a total area of 19,000 ha or ~9% of the total area within the 30-km-radius circle. Several red-listed species have declined since the middle of the 1970s, with ~50% (223 species) disappearing from the most centrally located green areas.[25] Many groups of common species also show a sharp decrease in abundance, such as amphibians, reptiles, and some bird species. In metropolitan Stockholm, there are many exotic species (>100) recorded both in aquatic and terrestrial environments (e.g., gastropods such as *Arion lusitanicus*, *Potamopyrgus antipodarum*, *Dreissena polymorpha*, mammals such as *Mustela vision, Sus scrofa,* birds such as *Branta leucopsis*, and plants such as *Heracleum mantegazzianum*). Although there is a great deal of descriptive knowledge (e.g., Gothnier *et al.*[25]), specific knowledge about the role and function of exotic species in urban ecosystems is lacking (S. Östergård, Stockholms Miljöförvaltning, personal communications). An important question is what role introduced and exotic species may play in regeneration after disturbances and sustaining resilience and urban ecosystem services and what the management implications are.

The National Urban Park

The biodiversity that characterize the NUP today is a result of a long history of human interaction with the physical environment. There is no other area in Sweden of the same size, where similar high species richness has been described.[20] There are more than 1,000 species of butterflies alone recorded from the area and more than 1,200 species of beetles and 250 species of birds.

Within NUP, management policies over the years have intentionally favored oak dominated woodlands (*Quercus roburand Q. petrea*). Oaks are often viewed as major keystone species structuring communities in the ecosystem (cf. Herdin[21]). Within NUP, we find the largest population of giant oaks in all of Europe: more than 60 individual trees have a circumference larger than 5 m and many individual trees are older than 500 years.[24] The large number of giant oaks produce a unique set of niches for flora and fauna dependent on old hollow trees[26] hosting up to 1,500 other species of fungi, lichens, insects, birds, and bats.[27] There are more than 60 red-listed insect species of which 29 are threatened and 27 are vulnerable. Of all red-listed insects, 80% are linked to old growth oak trees and lime trees.[25] Among fungi, 32 species are red-listed and more than 20 species of red-listed vascular plants, mammals, amphibians, reptiles, and fish are found in the park.[20]

The oak woodlands in Mälardalen constitute one of the largest in the country and Sweden has an international responsibility for these areas.[28] The oak populations in metropolitan Stockholm have become of even more significant because oak forests have seriously declined because of epidemic oak disease over wide areas of Europe during the past two decades.[29] Natural regeneration rates of *Quercus* spp are often low, and several factors such as quantity and quality of acorn production, heavy predation and browsing on acorns and seedlings, and low growth rate of oak seedlings contribute to regeneration failures.[30] Natural regeneration of oak is dependent on animal dispersal of the acorns, particularly by the Eurasian Jay (*Garrulus glandarius).*[31] Long-term viability of Jay populations is crucial for natural regeneration of oaks and studies of Jay population dynamics and dispersal patterns of oak recently have been initiated.[32]

The long-term risk is that continued urbanization results in an increased isolation of NUP and that biodiversity over time will steadily decline.[23] Crucial areas for dispersal and migration of organisms in and out of the park are indicated with arrows in FIGURE 2. It is essential that these areas are managed for serving a role as dispersal corridors and facilitating migration movements.

ANALYSES OF INSTITUTIONS AND MANAGEMENT OF URBAN ECOSYSTEM SERVICES

Local ecosystem services generated in urban green areas include air filtration, regulation of microclimate, noise reduction, surface water drainage, recreational and cultural values, nutrient retention, seed dispersal, and pollination (e.g., Bolund and Hunhammar[33]). All of these identified ecosystem services have a substantial impact on quality of life in metropolitan Stockholm but usually are overlooked by urban planners and decision makers. For example, Jansson and Nohrstedt[34] found that ~40% of the CO_2 generated by traffic and ~17% of total anthropogenic CO_2 potentially can be accumulated by the green area structure in Stockholm County. Recreation is also a major service, and it is estimated that the NUP has 15 million visitors per year, many of which visit the park for recreation purposes. More than 90% of the urban population in Stockholm visit the city's green areas at least once a year, 45% visit every week, and 17% more than three times a week.[35]

The Royal Djurgården Administration (KDF) manages almost 80% of the NUP and has done so since 1809. Much of the early planning, from the beginning of the 19th century, concerns tree management trough pruning, thinning, and planting. In the current management plan, from 1992 to 1993, the main purpose of management was to secure the continuity in the natural and cultural environment and within these frames also satisfy the recreational needs of visitors. In different areas different values are prioritized, cultural, recreational, or natural, and therefore the management goals are diversified in NUP. A challenge is the balance between preservation and development. Focus has always been on the landscape perspective, but earlier management mainly concerned the cultural environment. Now focus is on preserving biological diversity with a high priority of conservation of endangered species. Old *Quercus robur* are identified as the most important contributor to biological diversity and another important factor is the mosaic of biotopes. The plan also reveals different demands of the flora and fauna to be preserved in viable populations. Prioritized measures are replanting and care of trees with the aim of age diversification and preservation of old trees. Clearing of bushes and introduction of grazing is done to overcome these problems. Another important measure is preservation of dead wood within Djurgården.

A new management plan is under development and will consist of long-term prioritized management goals, investigated development possibilities, and methods for evaluation.[20] Important outlines are the landscape perspective, scale connections, and the gap between common outlines to practical measures. The plan is made for the whole park, and eventually the other managers will find it useful. It is important that the plan is flexible and allows continual changes. An essential approach is the focus on evaluation of outcomes in management and also long-term monitoring to discover slow changes. Another important issue is to look beyond the borders of the park, to reveal interactions with neighboring green areas. Effective public communication is to be created by an informative Web site.

Within NUP, there are in addition 65 organizations involved in management of ecosystem services.[36] Twenty-two of these organizations have management rights (TABLE 2). Of them four are *claimants*; that is, they have bundles of rights that include the right to regulate internal uses of resources and transformations by making improvements. Eleven are *proprietors*; that is, they have the same rights as the claimants but with the additional right of exclusion; seven are owners. In addition there are 44 authorized users. Recreational values are the services that are associated with the highest number of management organizations, whereas others such as nutrient retention is associated with very few (TABLE 2).

Included in this inventory are locally evolved interest groups that participate in governing ecosystems in the NUP. Many are organized in the umbrella organization "Förbundet för Ekoparken," consisting of 48 voluntary associations with more than 175,000 members. It was founded in 1992 when

TABLE 2. Local urban ecosystem services connected to organizations active in the National Urban Park

Local urban ecosystem services	Connected to organization with management rights		
	Owners	Proprietors	Claimants
Recreation/cultural values	5	5	4
Seed dispersal	2	8	4
Pollination	1	9	2
Noise reduction	5	6	0
Insect pest regulation	1	7	1
Surface water drainage	3	2	1
Regulation of microclimate	4	1	0
Air filtration	5	0	0
Nutrient retention	0	2	1

NOTE: Modified from Barthel *et al.*[36]

exploitation plans in the park were made public. In 1995, the alliance held a key role in the process of securing legal protection for the park.[37] These actors are often forgotten when assessing natural resource management systems. The study by Barthel *et al.*[36] indicates that this group has substantial power and has to be incorporated in management of urban ecosystem goods and services.

ANALYSES OF SOCIAL-ECOLOGICAL INTERACTIONS

In comparison with certain criteria for ecosystem based management,[38,39] the current management of green areas has certain indications of an ecosystem approach, but also severe deficits.[40] A study of five different green areas in the Stockholm County revealed that managers are good at gathering and compiling knowledge and creating plans, but the implementation is limited and there is almost no monitoring and evaluation of practices.[40] A management without continual monitoring cannot be evaluated and has no chance of becoming adaptive. Proper indicators, which monitor management success, need to be developed and connected to management objectives and goals. The study also revealed that there is limited ecological modeling, an important link between complex knowledge and effective practice and serving an important role in adaptive management, by which managers can test management alternatives and try to predict the outcomes for deciding how to best achieve certain management goals.[40]

Most of the management organizations were found to recognize basic ecological functions, such as biological diversity, keystone species, dead wood, and nutrient cycling.

However, there is little understanding about the role of surrounding ecosystems to the one being managed. Management often appears to be conducted in isolation from other ecosystems being managed in the surroundings. This may be because of a lack of scientific knowledge about the relationship of isolation effects on biodiversity. Furthermore, the green structure in the study area is spread out over several municipalities and includes land, water, and parts of settlements. Because of the system of self-governing municipalities, actions taken by one municipality affects adjacent municipalities' use of the green structure. Thus, there is an expressed need for intermunicipal coordination to reach the goals of sustainable development for the region.[41]

In the summer of 2002, the Swedish government appointed the County Administrative Boards of Stockholm to develop a regional program for the protection of urban ecosystems in recognition of the increased fragmentation in these settings[41] including a program for the establishment of 73 new reserves in the Stockholm region. If the program is implemented in full, an additional 20,000 ha of lands will be protected in the region or ~17% of the land surface area. Hence, the program holds promising effects for mitigating the increasing loss of urban green areas and strengthens the ecosystem services generated by the NUP and other larger green areas. In this context, the research related to landscape connections might provide important information/incentives to local managers to consider larger scale issues of ecosystem management and to foster a closer collaboration among local managers in a particular area through adaptive comanagement designs.

In NUP, the County Administrative Board of Stockholm has the responsibility for the coordination of the stakeholders involved in the park in a comanagement group. Formal broad communication procedures are lacking, and there are numerous conflicting interests that create tensions due to different perceptions and perspectives on urban development.[36] Also, there is a limited dialog about practical management among the stakeholders. The lack of an actual comanagement process can be exemplified by the absence of important stakeholders for water management of NUP, although a main objective is to restore wetlands and to decrease polluted inflow from urban surroundings. The many watercourses, lakes, and rich wetlands are managed by Stockholm Water Inc. Although the lakes are ecologically connected to the rest of the landscape, Stockholm Water Inc. is not represented in the comanagement group.[36]

The users and the steward groups constitute a set of networks that exist throughout the metropolitan area. Where do these network members come from and what is the nature of their interactions? How does information and knowledge spread between different organizational levels of governance, including local resource users? How are these networks promoting social learning and what is the role of trust in this context.[42,43] There are some compelling indications that social networks embedded in different levels of governance enhance social-ecological resilience. The significance of such networks for social-ecological resilience building in the Stockholm urban landscape remains to be seen, because no previous empirical work has been performed on the topic. We intend to develop the social network approach further by identifying and characterizing these networks and assess how their interactions may contribute as agents for shaping values and choices for the future uses of urban green spaces.

CONCLUSIONS

In management of urban green areas, more efforts need to be put into monitoring and evaluation and developing models of both the social and ecological dimensions. To sustain ecosystems, spatial and temporal scales for important ecological processes need to be documented, and these scales have to be matched by appropriate spatial and temporal scales for management and communication. Preliminary results indicate that areas of informal management represent centers on which to base adaptive comanagement or polycentric networks, with the potential to strengthen biodiversity management and resilience in the landscape. The interplay between informally managed green areas and those formally protected and managed cause important landscape dynamic interactions that need to be recognized by physical planners and conservationists. The patches of informally managed landscapes may be crucial in times of unanticipated natural disturbance and hence contribute to spatial resilience in the landscape.

Recent results of international projects illustrate the great potential of management models of complex social-ecological systems where scientific knowledge is combined with practices and knowledge that are generated among resource users locally in adaptive comanagement processes.[6] Co-management already exists in some parts of the Stockholm County. For example, a wetland project known as "Tyreså-projektet" within a major system of lakes south of Stockholm aims to coordinate the lake management between six municipalities and to handle upstream/downstream problems related to eutrophication.[40]

A major future aim will be to evaluate the prospects of introducing arenas of adaptive comanagement to supplement the current management paradigm.[36,44] Such arenas may be especially useful to establish around unprotected green areas managed by local stakeholders that promote ecological support functions. Comanagement also may be useful in areas where protected areas exist and where locally managed green space may function as buffer zones and for management of weak links that connect larger green areas (e.g., see areas with arrows in FIG. 2). A challenge in this context is to analyze management practices and local ecological knowledge among the locally evolved interest groups to strengthen their role in adaptive comanagement processes and to engage them in monitoring and evaluation of outcomes from management projects.[36,44]

ACKNOWLEDGMENTS

This study is financed by Vetenskapsrådet and Formas. We thank Henrik Niklasson KDF for valuable support and members of Ekoparksförbundet for generously sharing information.

REFERENCES

1. COLLINS, J.P., A. KINZIG, N.B. GRIMM, *et al.* 2000. A new urban ecology—modeling human communities as integral parts of ecosystems poses special problems for the development and testing of ecological theory. Am. Sci. **88:** 416–425.
2. GRIMM, N.B., J.M. GROVE, S.T.A. PICKET & C.L. REDMAN. 2000. Integrated approaches to long-term studies of urban ecological systems. Bioscience **50:** 571–583.
3. PICKETT, S.T.A, M.L. CADENASSO, J.M. GROVE, *et al.* 2001. Urban ecological systems: linking terrestrial, ecological, physical and socioeconomic components of metropolitan areas. Annu. Rev. Ecol. Syst. **32:** 127–157.
4. DAILY, G., Ed. 1997. Nature services: societal dependence of natural ecosystems. Island Press. Washington, D.C.
5. FOLKE, C.S., B. CARPENTER, B. WALKER, *et al.* 2004. Regime shifts, resilience and biodiversity in ecosystem management. Ann. Rev. Ecol. Syst. **35:** in press.
6. BERKES, F., J. COLDING, C. FOLKE, Eds. 2003. Navigating social-ecological systems: building resilience for complexity and change. Cambridge University Press. Cambridge.
7. ELMQVIST, T., C. FOLKE, M. NYSTRÖM, *et al.* 2003. Response diversity, ecosystem change, and resilience. *In* Frontiers in Ecology and the Environment. Vol. 1, no. 9. p. 488–494.
8. NIEMELÄ, J. 1999. Ecology and urban planning. Biodivers. Conserv. **8:** 119–131.
9. HARRIS, R.J. & J.M. REED. 2002. Behavioural barriers to non-migratory movements of birds. Ann. Zool. Fenn. **39:** 275–290.
10. MELLES, S., S. GLENN & K. MARTIN. 2003. Urban bird diversity and landscape complexity: species–environment associations along a multiscale habitat gradient. Conserv. Ecol. **7:** [online].
11. DRAYTON, B. & R.B. PRIMACK. 1996. Plant species lost in an isolated conservation area in Metropolitan Boston from 1894 to 1993. Conserv. Biol. **10:** 30–39.
12. STEFFAN-DEWENTER, I. & T. TSCHARNTKE. 1999. Effects of habitat isolation on pollinator communities and seed set. Oecologia **121:** 432–440.

13. LUNDBERG, J. & F. MOBERG. 2003. Mobile link organisms and ecosystem functioning: implications for ecosystem resilience and management. Ecosystems **6:** 87–98.
14. SUTTLES, G.D. 1968. The social order of the slum: ethnicity and territory in the inner city. University of Chicago Press. Chicago.
15. BOURNE, L.S. *et al.*, Eds. 1989. The Changing Geography of Urban Systems. Servicio de Publicaciones de la Universidad de Pamplona. Pamplona, Spain.
16. BOURNE, L.S. & D.F. LEY, Eds. 1993. The Changing Social Geography of Canadian Cities. McGill-Queen's University Press. Montreal.
17. ALLEN, J., M. DORREN & M. PRYKE, Eds. 1999. Unsettling Cities: Movement/ Settlement. Routledge with the Open University. London.
18. ORR, D.W. 1994. Earth in Mind: On Education, Environment, and the Human Prospect. Island Press. Washington, D.C.
19. ALCAMO, J. *et al.* 2003. Ecosystems and Human Well Being. Millennium Ecosystem Assessment. Island Press, Washington, D.C.
20. BRÅVANDER, L.-G. & R. JAKOBSSON. 2003. Skötselplan–Nationalstadsparken remissversion. November 2003. KDF.
21. HERDIN, C. 2002. Nationalstadsparkens ekpopulationer-skötsel och förvaltning från 1600-talet till nutid. Examination paper 2002:12. Department of Systems Ecology, University of Stockholm.
22. LUNDEVALL, P. 1997. Djurgården Kungens och folkets park. Stadsbyggnads-kontoret. Västervik.
23. LÖVENHAFT, K. 2002. Spatial and temporal perspectives on biodiversity for physical planning—examples from Urban Stockholm, Sweden. Katarina Tryck, Stockholm, Sweden.
24. LÄNSTYRELSEN I STOCKHOLMS LÄN. 1999. Nationalstadsparken mål och riktlinjer för skötsel av park och natur. Miljö-och planeringsavdelningen nr 18.
25. GOTHNIER, M., G. HJORT & S. ÖSTERGÅRD. 1999. Rapport från ArtArken. Stockholms artdata-arkiv. Miljöförvaltningen, Stockholm.
26. RANIUS, T., K. ANTONSSON, N. JANSSON & J. JOHANNESON. 2001. Inventering och skötsel av gamla ekar i eklandskapet söder om Linköping. Fauna Flora **96:** 97–107.
27. HULTGREN, S., H. PEIJEL & M. HOLMER. 1997. Ekjättar. Stenungssund, Naturcentrum.
28. BARTHEL, S., J. COLDING, C. FOLKE & T. ELMQVIST. Stadsbyggnadskontoret, Strategiska avdelningen. 1997. Nationalstadsparkens ekologiska infrastruktur 36. Social-ecological interactions in the formation of an urban green area: The National Urban Park of Stockholm, Sweden. In progress.
29. FÜHRER, E. 1998. Oak decline in central Europe: a synopsis of hypotheses. *In* M.L. McManus and A.M. Liebhold, Eds. Proceedings: Population Dynamics, Impacts and Integrated Management of Forest Defoliating Insects. USDA For. Serv. Gen. Techn. Rep. NE-247.
30. LOF, M., P. GEMMEL, U. NILSSON & N.T. WELANDER. 1998. The influence of site preparation on growth in *Quercus robur* L. seedlings in a southern Sweden clear-cut and shelterwood. For. Ecol. Manage. **109:** 241–249.
31. FROST, I. 1997. Dispersal and establishment of *Quercus robur*. Importance of cotyledons, browsing and competition. Uppsala University, Uppsala.
32. LUNDBERG, J., E. ANDERSSON, G. CLEARY & T. ELMQVIST. 2004. Sustaining ecosystem capacity in urban landscapes: the functional role of mobile link species in oak forest regeneration. Ecol. Appl. Submitted.

33. BOLUND, P. & S. HUNHAMMAR. 1999. Ecosystem services in urban areas. Ecol. Econ. **29:** 293–302.
34. JANSSON, Å. & P. NOHRSTEDT. 2001. Carbon sinks and human freshwater dependence in Stockholm County. Ecol. Econ. **39:** 361–370.
35. WIRÉN, L. 2002. Dynamik i urbana nätverk-sociala och ekologiska perspektiv på förvaltningen av Nationalstadsparken i Stockholm. Examination paper 10. Department of Systems Ecology.
36. BARTHEL, S., J. COLDING, C. FOLKE & T. ELMQVIST. 2004. Social-ecological interactions in the formation of an urban green area: The National Urban Park of Stockholm, Sweden. In progress.
37. WALDENSTRÖM, H. 1995. Ekoparken blir nationalstadspark. Kampen om Ulirksdal-Haga-Brunnsviken-djurgården. *In* Sankt Eriks Årsbok 1995. Uppsala.
38. CHRISTENSEN, N.L., A.M. BARTUSKA, J.H. BROWN, *et al.* 1996. The report of the Ecological Society of America Committee on the Scientific Basis for Ecosystem Management. Ecol. Appl. **6:** 665–690.
39. DALE, V.H., S. BROWN, R.A. HAEUBER, *et al.* 2000. Ecological principles and guidelines for managing the use of land. Ecol. Appl. **10:** 639–670.
40. BORGSTRÖM, S. 2003. Management of urban green areas in the Stockholm County. Masters thesis 18. Department of Systems Ecology, University of Stockholm.
41. LÄNSSTYRELSEN I STOCKHOLMS LÄN. 2003. Aldrig långt till naturen. Skydd av tätortsnära natur i Stockholmsregionen. Remiss 2003. Länsstyrelsens Miljö- och Planeringsavdelning, Stockholm.
42. LEE, K.N. 1993. Compass and Gyroscope. Island Press. Washington, D.C.
43. SHANNON, M.A. & A.R. ANTYPAS. 1997. Open institutions: uncertainty and ambiguity in 21st-century forestry. *In* Creating a Forestry for the 21st Century: The Science of Ecosystem Management. K.A. Kohm & J.F. Franklin, Eds.: 437–446. Island Press. Washington, D.C.
44. COLDING, J., T. ELMQVIST, J. LUNDBERG, *et al.* 2003. The Stockholm Urban Assessment (SUA-Sweden). Beijer Discussion Paper Series No. 182. Beijer International Institute of Ecological Economics, The Royal Swedish Academy of Sciences. Stockholm, Sweden.

The Changing Perception of the Wetlands in and around Kristianstad, Sweden

From Waterlogged Areas toward a Future Water Kingdom, Kristianstads Vattenrike Biosphere Reserve

SVEN-ERIK MAGNUSSON

Ekomuseum Kristianstads Vattenrike, Biosphere Reserve Candidate Office, Kristianstads Kommun, 291 80 Kristianstad, Sweden

ABSTRACT: Kristianstads Vattenrike (The Rich Wetlands of Kristianstad/Water Kingdom) is a 35-km-long wetland area surrounded by cultivated landscape in the south of Sweden. The project area covers some more than 100,000 hectares and includes the lower catchment areas of River Helge å and the coastal areas of the bay Hanöbukten, a part of the Baltic Sea. The River Helge å flows from upstream forests through agricultural land, lowland lakes, and wetlands and passes straight through the town of Kristianstad, which is the regional capital. An MAB candidate office is now in the process of completing the application form to become a biosphere reserve according to the UNESCO-MAB concept, but in the past the wetlands often were seen as waterlogged areas, especially in the 19th century.

KEYWORDS: Kristianstads Vattenrike; River Helge å; changing perception; wetlands; waterlogged areas; ecomuseum; biosphere reserve

THE CHANGING PERCEPTION

There has been increasing pressure on the wetlands and the values they provide since Kristianstad (Christianstad) was established 1614, on a small island near the River Helge å. The Danish king Christian IV used the surrounding wetlands as a defense against the enemy, the Swedes.

Address for correspondence: Sven-Erik Magnusson, Biosphere Reserve Candidate Office, Kristianstads Kommun, 291 80 Kristianstad, Sweden. Voice: +46-0-44-13-64-80; fax: +46-0-44-13-64-84.

sven-erik.magnusson@kristianstad.se

**Ann. N.Y. Acad. Sci. 1023: 323–327 (2004). © 2004 New York Academy of Sciences.
doi: 10.1196/annals.1319.018**

Using wet grasslands for harvesting hay and grazing is an ancient tradition in Sweden described for the area by Carl von Linné in his journey through Scania in 1749.

The size of the lakes and the wetlands in the area of lower River Helge å has been considerably reduced over the last 400 years (FIG. 1).

In 1774, the farmers of Yngsjö village, near the Baltic coast, dug a ditch to the sea to prevent the annual high water from flooding their land. Unfortunately, the spring flood of 1775 was so severe that it transformed the ditch into a new channel for the River Helge å to reach the sea. This venture lowered the water level in the water system more than 35 km upstream. At Kristianstad, the water level was decreased 0.6 to 0.7 meters.

Building embankments and dredging to control the river have further decreased the size of the wetland area.

In the late 19th century, there was a large embankment project east of the town Kristianstad. The northern bay Nosabyviken, in the lake Hammarsjön, was embanked for agricultural purpose. Nowadays, some of the eastern parts of the town are situated on this embanked area, some areas even under the sea level.

A dredging project between 1940 and 1945 was conducted to speed the flow of water through the wetlands and prevent flooding.

During the 20th century, several other embankments have been made. The increasingly bad water quality in the early 1900s caused by untreated sewage water from industry and households was apparent by the many public complaints and the fact that the city of Kristianstad stopped taking its drinking water from the River Helge å in 1941.

In 1964, there was a massive incidence of fish mortality in the area, and it is believed that this event wiped out the population of the rare European catfish (*Silurus glanis*) in the river.

Because of the bad water quality, people did not find the river and the surroundings attractive. Some companies turned the backyards of their factories to the river, and at this time (1960s) the municipality, with support from the county administration board, established a garbage dump on the wet grasslands (Härlövs ängar) close to the west of the town, despite protests from local and national nongovernmental organization conservation interests.

The worthless swamps were described by the public health committee at the Municipality of Kristianstad in 1958 as "water infested" and "unhealthy swamp areas should immediately be cleaned up."

In 1967, there were plans to embank wet grasslands at the shore of Lake Hammarsjön (Håslövs ängar), south of the city, to permanent agricultural

---

FIGURE 1. Periurban wetlands at Kristianstad, Sweden. Two tributaries of the River Helge å join downstream of the medieval ruined castle "Lillö." In summer, the surrounding wet grasslands are used for grazing, and it becomes a continuous lake landscape when flooded in winter. Several of the rare plant species that Linné found here in 1749 still grow in the area. Photo: P. Olofsson/N.

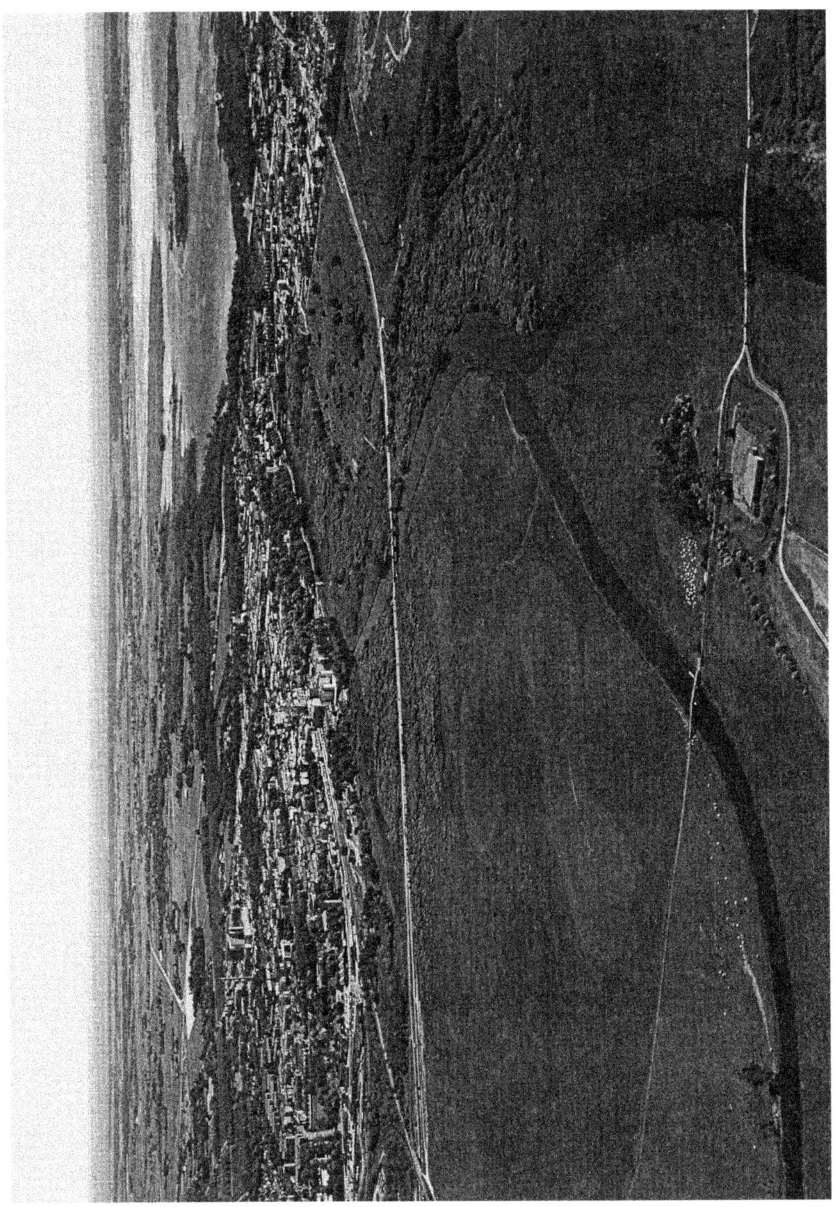

FIGURE 1. *See previous page for legend.*

land. Among conservation interests there were protests, and for the first time the county administrative board decided to protect cultivated wet grasslands in this region by establishing a nature reserve.

In 1971, there was a presentation of a plan for restoring Lake Araslövssjön and Lake Hammarsjön. This was to protect the lakes from becoming overgrown by reed and other macrophytes.

During the 1970s, inventories were made by the state, and some parts of the area were declared to be of international interest for nature conservation, cultural heritage, fishing, and recreation.

In 1975, a 35-km stretch of wetlands along the lower part of River Helge å was designated as having international importance by the Convention on Wetlands, known as the Ramsar Convention.

However, despite all the inventories, plans, policy documents, and protection efforts, several inventories and observation during the 1980s indicated that the values of the lower parts of the River Helge å and the Ramsar area continued to disappear. This was linked to the fact that the wet grasslands used for harvesting hay and grazing had decreased drastically.

In 1988–89, we started a discussion on how to manage the decreasing ornithological values in the wetlands. We found out that we had to widen the approach; otherwise, we would not get any support for our ideas. Very soon, we provided overall goals and vision in a holistic approach to wetland management.

The objective was "to preserve and develop the ecological values and cultural heritage of the area while at the same time making careful and judicious use of them."

The name Kristianstads Vattenrike (The Rich Wetlands of Kristianstad/ Water Kingdom) was coined. We linked people and ongoing projects connected to water in the area into a network dealing with nature conservation, environmental protection, tourism, education, and cultural heritage management. As a tool to explain and to be very concrete in our way of working, we started to build an ecomuseum with lots of different visitors' sites spread throughout the 35-km-long wetland area.

Our work is now an example of cooperation between local, national, and international authorities and organizations. The inhabitants in the area are of course key partners. The staff at the Ekomuseum Kristianstads Vattenrike coordinates many of the activities, and the ecomuseum office comes under the direct supervision of the chairman of the local municipal executive committee.

At the request of the municipal executive committee, we are now in the process of completing the application form to become a biosphere reserve according to the UNESCO-MAB concept. Therefore, we think that the old ideas of the wetlands as waterlogged areas have changed quite a bit.

REFERENCES

1. MAGNUSSON, S.-E. 1981. Helgeåns nedre sjösystem—något om människors ingrepp under närmare 400 år. [The lake system of the lower part of River Helge å: the impact of humans over the last 400 years.] Skånes Natur, Skånes Naturvårdsförbunds Årsskrift 68.
2. OLSSON, P., T. HAHN & C. FOLKE. 2003. Social-ecological transformations for ecosystem management. The development of adaptive co-management of a wetland landscape in Southern Sweden. Doctoral Dissertation 2003. Per Olsson. Building capacity for resilience in social-ecological systems. Department of Systems Ecology, Stockholm University, Sweden.

Sustainable Energy Planning with Efficient Office Buildings and Cogeneration Plants in Frankfurt am Main

WENDELIN FRIEDEL[a] AND WERNER NEUMANN[b]

[a]*Department of Education, Environment and Gender Affairs, City of Frankfurt am Main, DE-60311 Frankfurt am Main, Germany*

[b]*City of Frankfurt am Main – Energiereferat – Municipal Energy Agency, DE-60486 Frankfurt am Main, Germany*

ABSTRACT: Sustainable development of a city not only is determined through the amount of protected areas, but it is also an important task to integrate sustainable development in urban energy planning. In the last 10 years, many new areas for offices and residential buildings have been developed in Frankfurt am Main. In this context, the municipality has taken over a new role as organizer for the integrated energy planning. This article gives an overview of the achievements.

KEYWORDS: sustainable development; office buildings; urban energy planning

BACKGROUND

Frankfurt am Main is well known as the banking center of Germany, hosting the European Central Bank as well as many other German and international banks. Most people may know only Frankfurt Airport as a main hub of European and international aircraft companies, but, as an economic center in Germany, Frankfurt am Main is also dedicated to environmental issues.

The City of Frankfurt was one of the founding members of the "Climate Alliance" of European Cities, which now has more than 1,200 members in 14 European states. Frankfurt also has set up guidelines for a sustainable development in accordance with the "local agenda 21." Our aim is to integrate the

Address for correspondence: Wendelin Friedel, Department of Education, Environment and Gender Affairs, City of Frankfurt am Main, Braubachstraße 33 a, DE-60311 Frankfurt am Main, Germany. Voice: +49-69-21248610.
wendelin.friedel@stadt-frankfurt.de

**Ann. N.Y. Acad. Sci. 1023: 328–334 (2004). © 2004 New York Academy of Sciences.
doi: 10.1196/annals.1319.019**

three important "branches" of local agenda 21 toward sustainability, economic development, ecological aims, and social items.

It might not be known that Frankfurt also could contribute to the main subject of this conference—the protection of urban biosphere. The City of Frankfurt set up the "Green Belt Convention" in 1991. Because of this convention, a large green space surrounding the city including our city forest, one of the largest forests in Germany located in a city, was protected to prevent future construction in this area. The "Green Belt" covers 80 km^2 (8,000 ha), approximately one third of the city area. The "Frankfurt Green Belt" is not only a huge recreation area for the citizens but has become a major field for educational projects concerning protection of nature. The "Frankfurt Green Belt" was awarded at the United Nations HABITAT II conference in Istanbul in 1996 as a good example for a sustainable city development.[1]

However, the sustainable development of a city is determined not just by protected areas, but also it is necessary to integrate sustainable development into urban energy planning.

PLANNING AND BUILDING FOR SUSTAINABILITY: THE FRANKFURT EXPERIENCE

In the last 10 years, there have been many development areas in Frankfurt am Main for new office buildings and residential areas. Typically, there are many questions to solve concerning (1) the energy demand of the buildings and (2) the type of energy supply. There have been two major aims to reach: (1) to reduce the energy demand of buildings to low-energy buildings and (2) to provide an energy supply based on the principle of combined heat and power, thus saving at least 30% of CO_2 emissions and primary energy.

At first glance, because of national legislation, the city has only a small influence concerning the energy demand of buildings and the supply side. However, we have shown that it is possible to develop arrangements and planning processes in cooperation with development companies, architects, and investors to reach much better results than national legislations demand.[2] Energy planning thus is organized in a new form of public–private partnership with advantages for both sides.

In this context, the city, or better to say the municipality, has (or regained) a new role as organizer of the energy planning of new city districts. In the past, energy planning was the task of the municipality, but because of the liberalization of the energy market in Germany this task has vanished. Nevertheless, all institutions involved in urban energy planning have recognized that the role of the municipality cannot be denied. I will give three examples of how sustainable energy planning is organized in Frankfurt am Main.

ENERGY PLANNING OF DECENTRALIZED DISTRICT HEATING WITH COGENERATION

The city council decided in 1991 that all possibilities should be used to integrate combined heat and power production (CHP) and "on-site" electricity production in heating stations and new development areas. We therefore have set up a consultation service for all building owners to offer free information about what kind of cogeneration plant may be integrated in different buildings.[3,4] We organized information meetings and discussion groups for owners of CHP stations, where experience can be exchanged. We regularly set up a market survey on the German, and to some extent on the European market, for small and medium CHP installation.[5–7] As a result, up to now ~90 new CHP stations with a total electric power of ~22,000 kW_{el} have been constructed. The range of the electrical power is 5–3,000 kW_{el}.[8] As an example, the CHP stations can be found in office buildings, schools, kindergarten, fire brigade stations, hospitals, recreation centers, our botanical garden, some industrial sites, and many new local district-heating networks. The consumption of primary energy was reduced by ~30% and the CO_2 emissions have been reduced by more than 60,000 tons per year.[9] In addition, the on-site production of electricity also increases the security of electricity supply (FIG. 1).

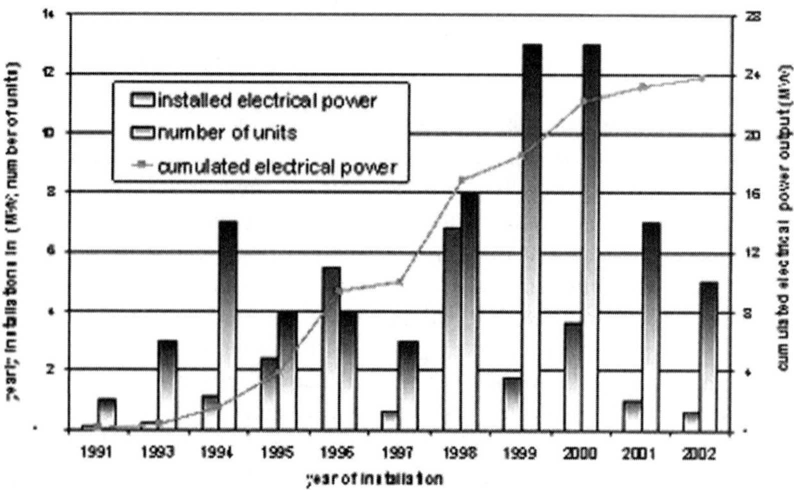

FIGURE 1. Development of decentralized cogeneration in Frankfurt am Main.

BENCHMARKING OF ENERGY DEMAND IN OFFICE BUILDINGS

The efficient way of energy conversion using cogeneration has to be combined with an efficient use of energy. In office buildings, the main part of energy consumed is electricity. However, in many cases, the owners and users do not know much about their consumption of electricity, although it is a main part of the total energy bill. In 1992, we started a working group with some of the major investors of high-rise buildings at that time to find out methodologies to construct "low-energy" high-rise buildings.

The "Commerzbank Tower," the highest building in Europe to date (300 m), was constructed in a way that the energy demand could be reduced by ~30% compared with the first planning designs.[10] At that time, it was an architectural revolution that in a high-rise building windows could be opened, and a large part of energy for air-conditioning and ventilation could be saved.

Meanwhile, many other new office buildings have been constructed, with even a much lower energy demand compared with the first "efficient office buildings." The new buildings of the Helvetia Insurance and the German Credits Bank for Reconstruction (KfW) have a primary energy demand of less than 150 kWh/m^2. (Note: the electricity demand has to be multiplied by three to get the primary energy demand!) Office buildings from the 1990s have primary energy demand of 300–500 kWh/m^2, some of the old office buildings up to 1,000 kWh/m^2 (Fig. 2).

High insulation standards of the outer façade, variable blinds, free cooling at night, highly efficient lighting systems with occupancy controls, and daylight controls are the main factors to reach low energy demand with even a higher comfort level. Those buildings are some of the most efficient office buildings in Germany and maybe the world.

One of the main false assumptions is that, in general, efficient office buildings will have higher investment costs. The examples in Frankfurt show that in many cases higher investment for lower energy demand is economical, and in some cases the investment costs for efficient buildings are even reduced. This opens the way to new cooperations with investment companies, architects, planning offices based on a public–private partnership toward low-energy office buildings.[11] The energy department of the municipality has organized "benchmarking workshops" to determine and to compare the energy demand of planned and existing office buildings. The buildings have to be treated according to their life cycle, and the City of Frankfurt has motivated investors to set up "facility management" systems in their buildings.[12]

Sustainability in this context means to construct and to use office buildings in such a way that they will provide the required comfort level with the lowest possible energy demand. It turns out that not only can ecological target (reducing CO_2 emissions) and social items (comfort level) be met, but these buildings are also economically optimized. Ecological aims as climate pro-

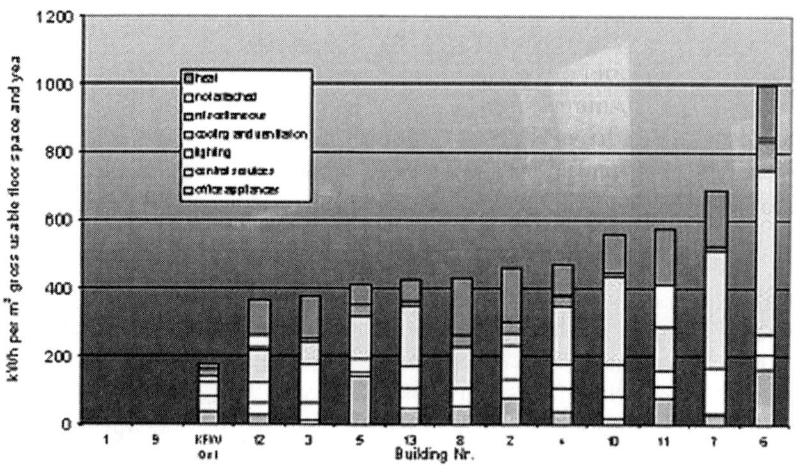

FIGURE 2. Primary energy demand of the analyzed buildings.

tection therefore are not a danger for economics; ecology may help to find the best economical solution and can help to set up new markets of ecological products as efficient lighting systems, energy management systems, and new constructional solutions for the façade of office buildings.

Actually, the City of Frankfurt leads a European project with seven European energy agencies to develop and to test a new methodology to analyze in detail the electricity demand of office buildings. This methodology will help to determine saving potentials, in the range of 20% or more, in lighting, ventilation and cooling devices, and office equipment.

INTEGRATED PLANNING OF ENERGY DEMAND OF BUILDINGS AND ENERGY SUPPLY

The next logical step is to integrate both the energy demand of a building and the energy supply system. In some cases, we have reached better energy supply, but the energy demand of the building was not optimized and vice versa. Nevertheless, integrating both components will open a potential for new synergies. As an example, in a residential area the insulation of the buildings has been improved up to the level we call "low-energy house," in which the energy demand for heating is reduced by more than 30% compared with the national legal level. If this design is combined with a cogeneration plant and in some cases with solar thermal plants for hot domestic water, another saving of 30% can be reached. Thus, the energy demand could be reduced by ~50% compared with typical reference values.

Integrating demand and supply is not always an easy task, because in some cases, there has to be a decision on the energy supply system (i.e., local district heating) before the new investors have made their decisions or they are not known at early stages of urban energy planning.

In Frankfurt am Main, there have been some ways to solve this problem. In one case, the city council decided that in one residential area only low-energy houses should be constructed; in two other residential areas, the city council has set up a local statute that only district heat with cogeneration can be used. In both cases, the politically compulsory acts have been made on the basis that the solutions are economical for the supplier, the investor, and the user. In another large development area for office buildings, it has been not the city at first, but the investor, who has asked to develop an integrated energy concept based on the know-how of the municipality in energy planning.

Totally Integrated Power (TIP) by Siemens started in 2000, with public and private stakeholders, a new initiative for innovative and integrated planning, and sustainable constructing to point out that sustainability, efficiency, cost saving, and private and public interests are not necessarily in contrast to each other.

The TIP Team of Siemens Frankfurt is the sponsor of the panel "TIP Dialog" initiated by IP-Building, in cooperation with the Municipal Energy Agency of Frankfurt am Main. The panel is a communication platform for different competencies in construction and urban development. Investors, architects, users, industry, public authorities, and universities present their success stories with focus on the interdependencies of their concepts and projects. More details of this project will be presented in another report.

SUMMARY

The city now has the role of a competent and independent agent for sustainable energy planning in Frankfurt am Main. The examples given in this article demonstrate that there is a possibility to combine public and private interest; that is, ecology and economy are not necessarily contradictory. The implementation of integrated energy planning into the city's planning process was possible only because of intense public–private cooperation. Information, motivation, demonstration—and not only legislation—were the keys to ensure success. We will continue on this way of public–private partnership for sustainable energy planning for integrating the demand and supply side based on energy efficiency, cogeneration, and the very important integration of renewable energy sources. This, together with our efforts to protect our urban biosphere, will lead us toward a sustainable urban development.

REFERENCES

1. UMWELTAMT STADT FRANKFURT AM MAIN. 1996. Protecting and Recovering Open and Green Areas—Green Belt Frankfurt am Main. At Habitat II Globale Best Practice—Initiative zur Verbesserung der Lebensumwelt Deutsch Breest Practices, Bundesministerium für Raumordnung, Bauwesen und Städtebau. Bonn, Germany.
2. FRIEDEL, W. 1998 (Nov.). Fighting to protect the climate—evaluating the experience. Salamanca Conference: Transport, Energy, and Telematics in Historical Cities. Salamanca, Spain.
3. FRIEDEL, W. & R. MAASS. 1995 (March). Erfahrungen mit flächendeckenden Untersuchungen zum Einsatz dezentraler Kraft-Wärme-Kopplungsanlagen. VDI-Conference. Essen, Germany.
4. FRIEDEL, W. 2000 (Oct.). Implementing decentralized co-generation—the Frankfurt case study. Cogen Europe, 7th Annual Meeting, Brussels, Belgium.
5. FAY, P. & W. FRIEDEL. 2000. Kraft- Wärme und Kraft-Wärme-Kälte-Kopplung. Energiever(sch)wendung, Handbuch zum rationellen Energieeinsatz elektrischer Energie. Klartext Verlag. Essen, Germany.
6. FAY, P. 2000. Heizkraftwerke mit Verbrennungsmotoren Teil 5.5.3 Richtpreisübersicht MHKW Anlagen. Praxis der Kraft-Wärme-Kopplung. Verlag C.F. Müller. Heidelberg, Germany.
7. FAY, P. 2001. BHKW Kenndaten 2001. ASUE; Arbeitsgemeinschaft für sparsamen und umweltfreundlichen Energieverbrauch e.V. Kaiserslautern, Germany.
8. FRIEDEL, W. 1999 (April). Co-generation units with capacities up to 1.500 kW. Presented at Workshop: La Petite Cogénération: Ca marche!, Rhônealpénergie-Environnement. Clermont-Ferrand, France.
9. NEUMANN, W. & W. FRIEDEL. 2002 (May). Systematic implementation of CHP-plants in Frankfurt am Main. Second International Conference on Energy Efficiency in Commercial Buildings. Nice, France.
10. NEUMANN, W. 2002 (May). Advanced Office Buildings in Frankfurt am Main. Second International Conference on Energy Efficiency in Commercial Buildings. Nice, France.
11. THERBURG, I. 2002 (May). Economical and Organisational Framework for a successful implemention of Energy Efficiency in Commercial Buildings. Second International Conference for Energy Efficiency in Commercial Buildings. Nice, France.
12. THERBURG, I. 2003 (Nov.). Energieeffizienz in komplexen Bürogebäuden—Auf dem Weg zu mehr Transparenz? Deutscher Fachkongress der kommunalen Energiebeauftragten. Bad Homburg, Germany.

Index of Contributors